PROCLAIMING LIBERTY

Also by Timothy Sandefur

The Right to Earn a Living: Economic Freedom and the Law (2010)

The Conscience of the Constitution: The Declaration of Independence and the Right to Liberty (2013)

The Permission Society: How the Ruling Class Turns Our Freedoms into Privileges and What We Can Do About It (2016)

Cornerstone of Liberty: Property Rights in 21st-Century America (with Christina Sandefur) (2016)

Frederick Douglass: Self-Made Man (2018)

The Ascent of Jacob Bronowski: The Life and Ideas of a Popular Science Icon (2019)

Some Notes on the Silence (2022)

Freedom's Furies: How Isabel Paterson, Rose Wilder Lane, and Ayn Rand Found Liberty in an Age of Darkness (2022)

You Don't Own Me: Individualism and the Culture of Liberty (2025)

PROCLAIMING LIBERTY

JOHN ADAMS, THOMAS JEFFERSON, AND THE DECLARATION OF INDEPENDENCE

TIMOTHY SANDEFUR

First published in hardback in the United States by the Cato Institute.

Cover design by Faceout Studio, Addie Lutzo.
Imagery from Getty Images and Shutterstock.

Hardcover ISBN: 978-1-969284-03-8
Ebook ISBN: 978-1-969284-04-5
Audiobook ISBN: 978-1-969284-05-2

Library of Congress Cataloging-in-Publication Data available.
Library of Congress Control Number: 2026932546.

Printed in Canada.

Cato Institute
1000 Massachusetts Ave. NW
Washington, DC 20001
www.cato.org

DEDICATION

For Harry V. Jaffa and Roger Pilon

τὸν κρατοῦντα μαλθακῶς θεὸς πρόσωθεν εὐμενῶς προσδέρκεται

CONTENTS

— PROLOGUE —

A letter from you . . . carries me back to the times when, beset with difficulties and dangers, we were fellow laborers in the same cause, struggling for what is most valuable to man.
—Thomas Jefferson to John Adams[1]

In the summer of 1826, with the United States approaching its 50th birthday, many Americans turned their thoughts to the nation's surviving revolutionaries. Thomas Jefferson and John Adams had once been comrades, then adversaries—even enemies—before reconciling in their retirement. Now, as private citizens at their famous homes in Virginia and Massachusetts, respectively, they were not just revered elders, but literal tourist attractions for countless visitors who wanted to meet the principal authors of the Declaration of American Independence.

Jefferson found it all rather amusing. When his grandson planned a trip north and asked for a letter of introduction to carry with him to visit Adams, Jefferson obliged with a sardonic note. The young man "wishes to be able," he said, "to recount to those around him what he has heard and learned of the heroic age preceding his birth, and which of the argonauts particularly he was in time to have seen."[2]

With the semicentennial on its way, many Americans asked those old argonauts for words of wisdom to accompany the festivities. One was a young Roxbury clergyman named George Whitney, who visited Adams that June. He was planning to attend an Independence Day banquet and wondered if the 90-year-old ex-president might compose a toast he could recite for the attendees. Adams agreed. "I will give you: '*Independence forever!*'"

John Adams in 1824 (top) and Thomas Jefferson in 1821 (bottom)

Whitney felt a little nonplussed. He had hoped for something more elaborate. Did Adams perhaps want to say anything else? No, the old rebel replied. "Not a word."[3]

Jefferson had also been invited to a celebration but was too frail to attend. However, he offered something more than Adams did. Declining an invitation to a Washington, DC, dinner, he wrote out a message to be read to the attendees in which he reflected on the "bold and doubtful election" that he, Adams, and other members of the Second Continental Congress had made in 1776 "between submission, or the sword." Much remained to be done, he said, but he was delighted with humanity's progress toward the principles enunciated in the Declaration. "All eyes are opened, or opening, to the rights of man." People around the world were awakening to "the palpable truth, that the mass of mankind has not been born with saddles on their backs, nor a favored few booted and spurred, ready to ride them legitimately, by the grace of god." Future generations, he hoped, would ensure that "the annual return of this day forever refresh[es] our recollections of [our] rights and an undiminished devotion to them."[4]

THE SPIRIT OF '76

They had been young back then. Adams was 41 and Jefferson 33 when they met in Philadelphia during the summer of independence. They were both lawyers and writers, scholars and farmers, fathers of young children (Adams had five, Jefferson two), and book lovers as familiar with the writings of ancient Roman senators and Elizabethan poets as they were with the politicians and scientists of their own day. Both had earned reputations for their radical writings—Adams for newspaper essays such as his "Novanglus" series, and Jefferson for his booklet *A Summary View of the Rights of British America*. Both were zealous for separation from England.

But there were differences, too. The short, pudgy Adams was militant, pushy, often sarcastic. He was also a dynamo, serving on scores of committees and speaking daily on the floor of the Congress. The tall and slender Jefferson, by contrast, was reserved, even shy; so averse to public speaking that he never participated in debates. Adams was an experienced trial lawyer, talkative and intense.

A lifelong diarist, his writings alternated between cynical observations about the weaknesses of others and self-deprecation, or even dark repentance. Jefferson, on the other hand, was a romantic at heart, but strove all his life to master his powerful emotions by the lights of ancient philosophy. Seeking above all to avoid candid displays of feelings, he kept no diary, but wrote streams of letters in a cultivated, elevated tone that many have likened to a mask. Adams secretly envied the Virginian's cool reserve. Jefferson, recognizing the Bostonian's greater age and experience, looked up to Adams as a leader.

Most members of the Continental Congress had been persuaded of the need for independence by early 1776. But powerful opposition remained, and progress had to be made slowly to ensure that the colonies presented a united front. In truth, they ultimately failed to accomplish even that. But by the time they signed their names to the Declaration, most Americans saw separation from Britain as overdue.

It had come after a century and a half of struggles to define the colonists' place in the empire's constitutional scheme. By 1700, they had settled into a stable, largely autonomous position; Parliament regulated the empire as a whole, but not local or "internal" affairs, which were governed by colonial legislatures. The colonies fell within the king's "dominion"—subject to his administration—but not within the "realm" of Parliament—and therefore, not subject to its legislation. The one exception was the control of commerce. There, Parliament was often intrusive, even unfair, and colonists groaned under its mercantilist economic policies, which imposed such severe strictures that many resorted to lawbreaking to make a living. A colonist could not even make a nail out of iron or a hat out of fur trapped on his land, and if he cut down a pine tree without a government permit, he could have his property confiscated.

Nevertheless, Americans regarded these burdens as exceptions. As a general rule, Britain's was the best political system in the world. That was because it largely satisfied the demands of justice and respected individual rights, principles they understood through what philosophers call natural law. Natural law refers to the rules of legality and order that depend for their validity on human nature, as opposed to social rules based on mere culture, habit, agreement, or command. In the century before independence, thinkers such as John Locke, Algernon Sidney, John Trenchard, and Thomas Gordon had asked, not what political institutions were good for some particular group of people, but what principles should guide the relationships between people *everywhere* and *always*—based on qualities common to all humanity. Legitimate political societies, they argued, were governed, not by the mere will of a king or legislature, but by rules that protect the people's ability to flourish, that is, to "pursue happiness." That goal was best achieved through constitutional devices such as the separation of powers and a mix of democratic and legal institutions that ensured the people's voices were heard and that the majority did not tyrannize over the individual.

To most colonists, the constitution that best met these standards was that of the British empire, which, whatever its imperfections, followed the English common law, with its guarantees of such rights as private property, freedom of speech, trial by jury, and the right not to be taxed or legislated for except by representatives of one's own choosing.[5] The constitutions of France or Russia—let alone those of Asia—were based on mere power: their kings, czars, and emperors claimed to rule by divine authority, and were the sole judges of every claim or purported right of the subject. To Britons, that looked more like a master–slave relationship than like the reciprocal bond that existed between ruler and ruled in a free nation. Nobody really *owned* anything in France, Russia, or China—not even their own words. Instead, everything was effectively the property of the state. Under Britain's unwritten constitution, by contrast, not everything the king said qualified as law, and subjects had rights that could not be revoked by the authorities' mere say-so. Probably the most cherished example of this principle was the "castle doctrine": the rule that even the king and his deputies had no lawful authority to enter someone's home without a warrant. "The house of everyone is to him as his castle," declared Sir Edward Coke, the nation's greatest legal thinker.[6] No other nation boasted such a principle.

Yet in the 1760s, under the reign of the new king, George III, Britain's government began taking a more aggressive posture toward the colonies. Starting with the Sugar Act of 1764 and the Stamp Act of 1765, Parliament began seeking to raise revenue by taxing the colonists directly. Dispensing with the old "requisition" system, whereby Parliament politely asked colonial legislatures to impose taxes and send over the revenues they considered sufficient, these new laws extracted funds from Americans directly.

The money was not the problem. "It is not the value of the tax," declared the citizens of Philadelphia, "but the *indefeasible right of giving and granting our own money* (A RIGHT FROM WHICH WE CAN NEVER RECEDE) that is the matter now in consideration."[7] For Parliament to directly tax colonists represented an innovation in constitutional thought. The Lords and Commons were claiming that they could unilaterally change the nature of the empire itself—that the constitution was whatever they said it was. Parliament, said judge William Blackstone, could do "everything that is not naturally impossible."[8] It could override even the most basic doctrines of Britain's legal order and legislate for the colonies *in all cases whatsoever*.

Beneath all the arguments over taxation, regulation, and legislation flowing from London, it was this idea of Parliamentary Supremacy that lit the fuse of the American Revolution.[9] Reluctant to break their ties with a constitutional scheme they considered precious, Americans longed for some answer short of separation. For a decade, lawyers like Adams and Jefferson devoted tremendous amounts of time to scholarship, debate, and sometimes delicate negotiations, searching for that solution. But none could be found. Instead, Parliament became increasingly high-handed, refusing to listen to the colonists' petitions; shuttering their legislatures; threatening to extradite them to London for trial when accused of crimes; forcing them to pay the salaries of customs inspectors, judges, and soldiers—for whom they were also required to provide housing. It sent an army to occupy Boston, closed that city's port to starve it into submission, then shut down trade in other colonies, too. When Americans again asked King George to listen to their complaints, he instead declared them the legal equivalents of foreign enemies. His troops burned American cities, conscripted American sailors into serving in the Royal Navy, and recruited Native American warriors to attack colonial settlements.

At last, on June 7, 1776, Virginia delegate Richard Henry Lee formally moved that Congress declare that "these united colonies are, and of right ought to be, free and independent states, that they are absolved from all allegiance to the British Crown, and that all political connection between them and the state of Great Britian is, and ought to be, totally dissolved."[10]

WHAT WOULD YOU SAY?

It has become common in modern times to deprecate the American Revolution as a cynical exercise in power politics, or a petty dispute over taxes that spiraled inexplicably out of control. Leftist political science professor Leland Stauber wrote in his book *The American Revolution: A Grand Mistake*, "If through more moderate actions on both sides . . . a relationship of underlying cooperation had been maintained, American colonial leaders might have sought the help of the British in nation-building," which could have brought about better outcomes, such as an earlier end to slavery and the implementation of socialism.[11] More recently, conservative author Conrad Black declared that the revolutionaries were "self-interested opportunists" who took advantage of discontent over taxes (taxes that were "not . . . unjust") and seized power by concealing their Machiavellianism under "a thick coat of conjured virtue."[12] He meant this as a compliment. Meanwhile, libertarian economist Bryan Caplan wrote in 2007, "It's hard to see why American independence was worth a war."[13] The distinguished historian Robert Middlekauff even felt it necessary to explain that he meant no irony when he titled his book about the revolution *The Glorious Cause*.[14]

The story of independence is far more profound, and far more dramatic, than those statements suggest. By 1776, Americans had endured generations of dominating, often arbitrary rule by kings and Parliaments who alternated between neglecting them and imposing policies on them that violated their fundamental rights, such as economic and religious liberty. Parliament even proclaimed that these rights were nothing more than privileges it gave to Americans and could revoke at pleasure. Colonists petitioned for redress time and again, only to be ignored, then cruelly punished, then violently repressed. British government in North America became one of domination, rather than equal participation—tyranny rather than willing allegiance. "Britain," wrote Thomas Paine, "has declared that she has a right (not only to TAX) but 'to BIND us in

ALL CASES WHATSOEVER,' and if being bound in that manner is not slavery, then is there not such a thing as slavery upon earth."[15] True, the oppressions of 18th-century colonial rule pale in comparison to 20th- and 21st-century totalitarianism. But in separating from Britain, the Americans were taking a pioneering step in defense of human rights—a step bold, wise, and just.

Reason alone did not always chart their course. The romantic Jefferson, a decade after the war, wrote that passion had guided them to some degree, and rightly so: "If our country, when pressed with wrongs at the point of the bayonet, had been governed by its heads instead of its hearts, where should we have been now? hanging on a gallows."[16] Adams offered an equally characteristic memory, recalling a conversation he heard in a tavern in 1774. "The people of Boston are distracted," said one customer (meaning hysterical). "What would you say," replied another, "if a fellow should come to your house and tell you that he was come to [make] a list of your cattle [so] that Parliament might tax you for them at so much a head? And how should you feel if he should go and break open your barn to take down your oxen, cows, horses, and sheep?"

"What would I *say*?" the first man answered. "I would knock him in the head."[17]

In other words, ordinary Americans understood—sooner and sometimes better than did the alleged "self-interested opportunists"—that the principle of Parliamentary Supremacy endangered their most essential rights, and that only revolution could secure them. That is why, in the first half of 1776, thousands of common citizens—from local town meetings to trade associations—wrote to the Continental Congress asking its members to declare independence.

That was a grave step, and everyone had known the colonies would have to act in unison. Lee's June 7 motion triggered weeks of complicated political maneuvering—and in the meantime, Congress asked a five-man committee to prepare the formal language of the independence resolution in case the motion was formally approved. That committee had delegated to Jefferson, its youngest member, the job of preparing the initial draft. He completed it in about two days. The others then edited it a little before submitting it to the Congress, which after more days of editing, finally approved it on July 4.

Written in the rush of a sometimes-desperate war, by busy revolutionaries who had a thousand other things to worry about, the Declaration was a masterpiece of concision. Little in it was original, but that was just the point: It was supposed to be a succinct statement of what everybody already agreed on. Its purpose, as Jefferson explained 50 years later, was "not to find out new principles, or new arguments," but "to place before mankind the common sense of the subject [in] terms so plain and firm, as to command their assent. . . . It was intended to be an expression of the American mind."[18] But crafting that consensus had been tedious work, and success only came after years of legal and philosophical controversy.

Now, in the summer of 1826, as Jefferson lay in the alcove bed he had designed in the private sanctuary of his mountaintop home Monticello, and John Adams sat in an overstuffed armchair in his Massachusetts farmhouse Peacefield, the two old argonauts could look back with awe and bewilderment at the changes in which they had participated. Romantic as he was, Jefferson wanted to see the dawn of the 50th Independence Day if he could. Suffering from pneumonia and drifting in and out of consciousness, he asked his doctor during one lucid moment in the night, "Is it the Fourth?" Reassured that it soon would be, he lapsed again into sleep, and he vanished peacefully that afternoon. Meanwhile, Adams had been thinking about all those people who had signed the Declaration and who had since passed away. He and Jefferson were the last ones, he thought. And as he slipped into oblivion, he simply said, "Thomas Jefferson still survives."[19]

THE AMERICAN MIND

This book examines the Declaration of Independence through the lives and ideas of these two extraordinary men. Idealistic lawyers and politicians, they found after the war that they had different visions of the country they had helped create. But in the summer of 1776, they shared the same "American mind"—and had a unique opportunity to express it. My goal here is to explore how and why they did so; to consider the arguments that led up to the Declaration, the personalities and ideas that went into its writing, and the influence it has had up to the present day—including the disturbing trend of modern intellectuals who dismiss it as either a ruse or as a merely rhetorical document, devoid of legal significance. I also explore the philosophical and legal foundations on which the Declaration rests.

Historians have long debated whether the American Revolution was motivated by the classical liberal ideology of individual rights and limited government most famously articulated by John Locke—and typically known today as "libertarianism"—or whether it was actually more "conservative," concerned with preserving the traditions of English legal and political culture. That debate sometimes takes on the color of caricature, as when conservative journalist Irving Kristol said it was "wise to ignore" the Declaration, or when Progressive historian Carl Becker claimed it was "essentially a meaningless question" to ask whether its propositions regarding equality and liberty are "true or false."[20] Some have gone so far as to minimize the relevance of Locke's ideas generally, and to argue that the revolution was really only a mundane legal dispute.[21] Historian Kevin Phillips shrugs off the arguments made by colonial lawyers and statesmen as "legal clip-and-paste jobs"—an incoherent rhetorical mashup of theoretical assertions designed to mask the fact that "might ultimately made right."[22]

But the opposite is true: The classical liberalism of the revolution was and remains a coherent, well-considered, and ultimately persuasive political philosophy. It was also ubiquitous in colonial America, pervading every aspect of public debate for years before the revolution.[23] The principles of natural law and natural rights, observes political scientist Michael Zuckert, "figure[d] decisively in shaping and validating the American vision of the imperial constitution"—and, of course, in forming the ground on which the colonists renounced that constitution.[24] The imperial crisis did start with legal and constitutional disputes, but it morphed over time into a broader, society-wide rejection of British rule, for reasons of justice and political legitimacy.

Philosopher Hannah Arendt, who was skeptical about the idea of universal human rights, once remarked that the problem with that idea is that one typically asserts these rights only after being stripped of more specific legal protections that should have provided security. They are only invoked "as a last resort by those who [have] lost their normal rights as citizens."[25] That was precisely the situation in which Americans found themselves in 1776. That was when they gave up legal and constitutional debates, ceased to assert the "traditional rights of Englishmen," and put forward their rights as human beings instead.

And that is what gives the American Revolution its lasting worldwide significance. Had the dispute with Britain been confined to the constitutional controversy that started with the Stamp Act, the ensuing fight would probably bear as little interest as, say, the Toledo War of 1835. The reason people worldwide are still fascinated by the events of 1776 is precisely because Adams, Jefferson, and their comrades took a step *beyond* English culture, and invoked the rights of all mankind. Abraham Lincoln made this point memorably when he prepared a toast for a banquet held on Jefferson's birthday. "All honor to Jefferson," he wrote (although his words apply equally to Adams),

> who, in the concrete pressure of a struggle for national independence by a single people, had the coolness, forecast, and capacity to introduce into a merely revolutionary document, an abstract truth, applicable to all men and all times, and so to embalm it there, that today, and in all coming days, it shall be a rebuke and a stumbling-block to the very harbingers of re-appearing tyranny and oppression.[26]

What makes the Declaration more than "*merely* revolutionary" is the electric spark animating its circuits: the idea that all men are created equal, with inalienable rights, which government must respect, and which people may justly vindicate by rebelling against tyranny.

***

It's an intimidating task to write about a subject that has already been the focus of so much attention by so many first-rate scholars. I am therefore grateful that in adding my two pence, I have had the assistance of skillful friends and colleagues. I thank Cato's Ivan Osorio and Eleanor O'Connor for inviting me to write this book; my colleagues at the Goldwater Institute for their "patient sufferance" as I completed it, particularly Timothy Minella and Jasmine Hinkey, who offered helpful suggestions; and my wife, Christina Sandefur, whose feedback was priceless as always. My mentor and former boss, Deborah J. La Fetra, who taught me many lessons in writing and has helped me with nearly all my books, offered vital suggestions this time, too. Through an unaccountable oversight, I failed to acknowledge her assistance with my previous book, *Freedom's Furies*, and I'm glad to have the chance to rectify that omission here. I also thank the editors of *The Dispatch* for permission to reprint the Afterword, which originally appeared as "The 1619 Project: An Autopsy."

The constitutional democracy Jefferson and Adams helped establish has grown beyond anything they could have imagined, and with that growth has come immense risks. One danger the Founders did foresee was complacency—that Americans would become so satisfied with their circumstances that they would lose interest in the values and virtues necessary to preserve their freedom. This book is written in the hopes that by recalling the lessons these men taught, Americans of the next 250 years can ensure that the blessings of liberty are not merely preserved, but expanded into dimensions yet unknown. It has been my ambition to express in some measure my love for this country, and my wish that she may yet rise up and live out the true meaning of her creed.

Author's Note: I have modernized (and Americanized) the spelling, capitalization, and punctuation of all quotations herein for the reasons Craig Nelson gives in his superb biography of Thomas Paine. Standardized orthography was in its infancy in the 18th century. John Adams, Thomas Jefferson, and their contemporaries were "forward-thinking *avant-garde*, [and] absolutely modern."[27] To parrot their sometimes-idiosyncratic writing styles can give a false impression of quaintness or even ignorance. At a minimum, I hope that modernizing their spelling will avoid diftraction.

— PART ONE —

THE SONS, NOT THE BASTARDS, OF ENGLAND

John Adams was a 31-year-old lawyer in 1766.

— CHAPTER 1 —

THE EDUCATION OF JOHN ADAMS

My enthusiasm for sports and inattention to books alarmed my father.
—John Adams[1]

John Adams was 14 when he decided to become a farmer. His father—known as Deacon John Adams because his years of diligent labor and community involvement had earned him a leading position in the church—wanted the boy to study hard and eventually go to college to become a minister or a physician. But the younger John found his "Latin school" boring. He preferred being outdoors, shooting, flying kites, and making boats to sail on ponds. A farmer obviously had no need for tedious lessons in ancient languages. So why not follow his father's career? He would till the soil, he announced. A farmer did not have to memorize Latin declensions.

Deacon Adams was not amused. "A farmer!" he cried. "Well, I will show you what it is to be a farmer!" The next day, he had the boy up before sunrise to gather thatch in the field outside Braintree, the town 15 miles south of Boston where the Adamses lived in a two-story clapboard house the deacon had built himself. There followed an exhausting day of physical labor that only ceased when the sun went down. As father and son returned home at dusk, the sore, exhausted young man was already convinced he had made a mistake.

But he was stubborn. When his father asked how he was feeling, John pretended he was just fine. So his father had him out in the fields again the next dawn with a shovel, digging ditches. When that

The Adams homestead in Braintree, Massachusetts. John Adams was born in the structure on the right; his father gave him the house on the left in 1761.

toilsome day finally ended, John must have been worn out. As the two straggled back to the house, his father once again asked him, perhaps a bit smugly, "Well, John, are you satisfied with being a farmer?" Yet the teenager still refused to admit his mistake. Mustering up all his strength, he answered, "I like it very well, sir."

His father was through with that game. "Aye, but I don't like it so well," he snapped. "You shall go to school today."[2]

A CLASSICAL EDUCATION

In truth, John did love farming. It was honest, productive, strenuous work, and a source of relaxation and meaning. Even as he pursued his legal and political careers, raising his own crops would always seem more real to him. His farm, he said, was "all the amusement that I ever had in life."[3] Tilling the soil was not just restorative, though. It represented his conception of the good life: independent domesticity, privacy, and a source of earned pride—everything he and his revolutionary colleagues would fight for in the revolution against Britain. Far as his travels would take him, the family homestead in Braintree was always home. When he and his wife built a new house for themselves in 1783, which he named Peacefield, it was only two miles from the house where he was born.

But Deacon Adams and his wife Susannah had already decided that their eldest son would be more than a farmer. He would get a good education and attend Harvard, then take up one of the learned professions. Accordingly, John Adams's schooling focused primarily on the classics of ancient Greece and Rome, as well as the basics of Christian literature, including the Bible and works associated with New England's Puritan heritage. Greek and Latin were crucial, not mere ornaments of learning, but keys to the great philosophical and scientific treasures of Western civilization. These had been effectively rediscovered during the Renaissance, four centuries earlier, but new rediscoveries were still taking place. Pompeii's sister city Herculaneum, for example, was only unearthed in 1738, and Aristotle's *Politics* was not translated into English until 1776.

The writings of the ancient Greeks and Romans were valuable not only for their philosophical insights, but also for the windows they opened on societies untouched by the mysticism and theocracy of the European Middle Ages. By reading such historians as the Greeks Herodotus and Thucydides, or the Romans Tacitus, Livy, and Polybius, one could, in a sense, step outside Christian society, to compare and contrast their cultures with one's own. The student could learn from such diverse personalities as Xenophon (the Greek philosopher and military leader who knew Socrates), Cicero (the Roman lawyer and statesman who lived four centuries later), Seneca (the Spanish-born philosopher and playwright who lived in Nero's Rome), or Justinian (the Byzantine emperor who oversaw an influential set of legal reforms in the 500s CE).

Nothing better suited the spirit of the 18th-century Enlightenment. Although often characterized today as an intellectual monolith dominated by white men, the reverse is actually true: The Enlightenment was an era of unprecedented intellectual diversity, and its participants aspired to a spirit of universalism in hopes of discovering moral principles and political institutions whose authority derived not from the accidents of history, the dictates of rulers, or the idiosyncrasies of culture, but from universal human nature. Enlightenment thinkers sought political and moral ideas that were *actually true*, not just "true for" one group of people or another. And the histories of Greece and Rome offered the most thoroughly studied examples available for any scholar seeking alternatives—or improvements—to existing European societies.

For the young John Adams, the foremost teacher of these lessons was Marcus Tullius Cicero, whose writings were first on the list that his Latin teacher assigned him when he returned to school from his brief stint digging ditches. A contemporary of Julius Caesar's—he was killed in the civil war that followed Caesar's assassination—Cicero became the single most influential ancient thinker for the American Founding Fathers generally, and for John Adams, specifically. As an admirer of the philosophy known as Stoicism, Cicero had believed that self-mastery, particularly emotional self-control, is the key to resolving the tensions and pains of daily life. Stoics sought the "good flow of life" (*euroia biou*), and they believed this could be accomplished by regulating one's passions and desires to attain a sense of detachment, or what would today be called emotional perspective. Cicero admitted that this perspective could come at the cost of realism. Some Stoics, for example, maintained that virtue is its own reward—indeed, so valuable that even a person who suffered every worldly evil could be contented if he still possessed virtue. Cicero, on the other hand, concluded that the real challenge is not merely to pursue virtue, but to find ways to bring it into actual practice and thereby attain the happiness that is the goal of life.

It was Cicero's political writings that Adams considered most valuable. In his book *De Re Publica*, Cicero argued—relying in part on the scholarship of Aristotle four centuries before—that the essential difference between legitimate political rulers on one hand and a gang of robbers or pirates on the other is that the former wield power for the public good, whereas the latter only seek to enrich themselves. Despotism is therefore not merely an unjust *type* of government; it is, strictly speaking, no *government* at all.[4] (Many political thinkers in Adams's day shared this view. "All governments," declared 18th-century writers John Trenchard and Thomas Gordon in their book *Cato's Letters*, "ought to be administered for the good of society; when they are otherwise administered, they cease to be government, and become usurpation."[5]) Thus, for Cicero—himself a lawyer—the highest political ideal was the rule of law. Life, liberty, and property can only survive, he thought, if human action is subordinated to the guidance of rules. "This is the bond of that dignity which we enjoy in the commonwealth," the Roman declared in 69 BCE, "this is the basis of our freedom, this is the source of justice; the heart and soul and policy and sentiments of the state are founded upon the laws. . . . In short, we are all subservient to the laws to this end, that we may be free."[6]

Government's main role was to protect ownership rights and ensure that people honored their contracts. "It is the peculiar function of the state . . . to guarantee to every man the free and undisturbed control of his own particular property," Cicero wrote. "They who pose as friends of the people and . . . propose that [property or wealth be redistributed by the government] are undermining the foundations of the commonwealth . . . [by] destroying harmony, which cannot exist where money is taken away from one party and bestowed on another."[7]

Cicero argued that these were not just cultural prejudices—not just "the Roman way"—but universal truths, because "right is based, not upon men's opinions, but upon nature."[8] Humanity is subject to a universal moral law because all people share in mankind's distinctive quality: reason. This is proved by the fact that everybody everywhere loves the same things ("courtesy, kindliness, gratitude, and remembrance of favors") and hates the same things ("the haughty, the wicked, the cruel, and the ungrateful").[9] Thus, the principles that serve as the foundations of law are valid everywhere. "All men have received reason; therefore all men have received justice."[10] This also meant that government does not *give* people rights, or *create* notions of right and wrong, as some philosophers argued. It merely clarifies those ideas through legislation and implements them to maintain order.

Because government is bound by these universal principles, rulers must respect the limits of justice, too. If a king—or, in a democracy, the majority—becomes so corrupt as to use power only for self-enrichment, he or they cross the line dividing true government from the arbitrary rule of a criminal gang. That sets the stage for civil war. The role of the statesman was to preserve the rule of law, thereby balancing the legitimate needs of the majority against protections for the rights of the minority—to "unite all on the basis of impartial justice"[11]—and to ensure that the wisest rulers can guide the state.

Along with other classical thinkers, Cicero established the framework in which the natural law philosophers of the Christian era, most notably John Locke, would do their pathbreaking work. Locke's argument that all men are born inherently free—meaning that political organization is not something inherent in the world, but is instead created by human beings, who may rightly change it—harmonized with the Christian principles of personal responsibility and self-reliance that were a mainstay of New England thought. Adams would have learned from Locke and his followers—especially Trenchard and Gordon in their *Cato's Letters*—that the inherent "equality" of all men means not that they are identical in talents or capacities, but that all people are inherently *individual* creatures, each responsible for his or her own personality and actions. With that responsibility comes a right to liberty. Because all mature adults are accountable for their own behavior, each has an obligation to exercise judgment—and exercising judgment requires the freedom to make operative choices. In short, to be self-responsible means to be free.

That self-responsibility, and the freedom intrinsically connected with it, can never be voluntarily surrendered. Just as it is impossible to give away one's tastes, fears, education, or appetites, so this innate quality of individual self-direction can never be abandoned. It is literally "inalienable." One can be *robbed* of it, by being subjected by compulsion, or being deluded or defrauded into living for the sake of another person—compelled to obey the commands of, and seek permissions from, a dictator, a priesthood, or a gang of political manipulators. But that was "slavery," a word that in Adams's day was routinely used to describe not just the chattel status of Africans and their descendants, but the situation of any person living under the domination of another instead of directing his own life. When Patriot leaders, in the years leading up to the American Revolution, accused imperial officials of seeking to enslave Americans, they meant that Parliament was trying to force them to labor for London's enrichment, to follow London's rules, and to ask London's leave for every step of their lives.

One contemporaneous thinker who brought these ideas home to the 14-year-old Adams was a Boston minister named Jonathan Mayhew. Mayhew's two sisters lived in Adams's neighborhood, and when Mayhew visited them, he would stay to preach at the local church. Officially a Congregationalist, he was so devoted to the classical liberal theories of thinkers such as Locke that he was considered a radical, even a subversive. In 1749, he preached a sermon on the centennial of the execution of King Charles I—a day Parliament had set aside as a patriotic commemoration of the monarchy. But instead of honoring the dead king, Mayhew took the opportunity to address the question of why Christians should obey political rulers at all, and when it was proper for them not to.[12] The young Adams was thrilled.

"The true ground and reason of our obligation to be subject to the *higher powers*," Mayhew argued, "is the usefulness of magistracy (when properly exercised) to human society, and its subserviency to the general welfare."[13] Government officials "have no authority from God to do mischief," and those who do so "forfeit the character of rulers."[14] It naturally follows that the people are justified in resisting and overthrowing such governments "to break the yoke of tyranny and free themselves and posterity from inglorious servitude and ruin." The English had done just that when they overthrew Charles—a rebellion "fruitful of happy consequences to Great Britain."[15] Anglican clergymen might praise that king as a "*great saint* and *martyr*," but in reality he was "black with guilt and *laden with iniquity*." He "lived a tyrant" and deserved his death.[16] Those who now praised his memory did so because they, too, were seeking to destroy freedom: "not because he bravely suffered death in the cause of truth and righteousness, but because he died an enemy to liberty and the rights of conscience."[17]

Mayhew's sermon touched off a furious debate in the Boston newspapers, as conservative ministers condemned him as a zealot. He cast no aspersions upon the present king, George II, under whose reign New Englanders were prospering, and whom Mayhew said was "satisfied with ruling according to law, as every other *good prince* will." But his condemnation of the Church of England, whose leaders he characterized as power hungry, and his appeal to the "legal rights of the people against the unnatural and illegal encroachments of arbitrary power," certainly seemed seditious.[18] The teenage Adams, however, relished his bold arguments. When Mayhew's sermon was published as a pamphlet, he read and reread it "till the substance of it was incorporated into my nature and indelibly engraved in my memory." In his retirement years, he sent a copy to Thomas Jefferson, remembering how it had been "a tolerable catechism for the education of a boy . . . who was destined in the future course of his life to dabble in so many revolutions."[19]

I READ FOREVER

When he read Mayhew's sermon, Adams was preparing for his Harvard entrance exam. Actually, he was petrified, not just about having to interview with the intimidating college president, Edward Holyoke, but also about his future in general. Much as he admired men like Mayhew, he was already doubtful that a career in the clergy would suit him. He was drawn more to law than religion. Yet several members of his family distrusted lawyers, seeing them as hired guns whose job it was to argue even for a wrongful position, if that was what a client needed. Was that not sinful? How to reconcile such a profession with the demands of morality would trouble Adams intensely in the years to come.

He passed Holyoke's entrance exam, and at Harvard, threw himself into science, philosophy, literature, and mathematics (which he particularly enjoyed), as well as the classics. Holyoke was a liberal-minded leader, and, like Mayhew, an adherent of Lockean political philosophy. He saw to it that students learned that government is not a means of glorifying the nation or enriching the rulers, but a kind of contract that exists for the citizens' benefit. "A public station is a place of trust," he said in a 1736 speech. Government officials "have a high trust committed to them; even our civil liberties and privileges, and the cause of religion, too."[20] But, he added, "I mean not . . . to recommend the senseless doctrine of passive obedience and non-resistance." The idea that a good Christian must always obey the government was "a doctrine calculated for none but a nation of slaves." Because "all forms of government originate from the people," it was both their right and their duty to obey only *just* commands.[21]

Holyoke's classical liberalism eventually brought him into conflict with prominent religious figures, including preacher George Whitefield, who accused him of allowing students to read "bad books."[22] But Harvard's faculty was undeterred, and Adams fell in love with scholarship at the liberal college. "A growing curiosity, a love of books and a fondness for study," he found, "dissipated all my inclination for sports, and even for the society of the ladies. I read forever."[23]

His philosophical turn of mind might have fit Adams for divinity school—he delighted in intellectual discourse and argument—but he was turned off by a seemingly pointless religious argument that broke out around that time in his hometown of Braintree. The controversy concerned pastor Lemuel Bryant, whom Adams described as "a jolly, jocular, and liberal scholar," but whose religious views led to disputes over his fitness to preach.[24] The quarrel appeared in the columns of local newspapers, and eventually Bryant was called to account by a group of ministers, who met at the Adams home. Young John read both sides' writings and attended the meeting. What he saw persuaded him that a religious career was not for him. "I saw such a spirit of dogmatism and bigotry in clergy and laity, that if I should be a priest I must take my side, and pronounce as positively as any of them, or never get a parish. . . . I perceived very clearly . . . that the study of theology and the pursuit of it as a profession would involve me in endless altercations and make my life miserable, without any prospect of doing any good to my fellow men."[25]

Yet even as it became more obvious that his true aptitude was for law, he continued to hesitate. Introspective and intensely self-critical, he confessed in his diary to a longing for respectability and greatness, which he considered blameworthy vanity. Such self-doubt was commonplace in the 18th century, when intellectuals used the term "ambition" as a pejorative but at the same time viewed the "love of fame" as (in Alexander Hamilton's words) "the ruling passion of the noblest minds."[26] Adams did have a powerful streak of narcissism in his character, which sometimes led him into pettiness and resentment. But in this case, his ambition was a healthy one, reflecting some of his best virtues: curiosity, a love for ideas, and a desire to make something meaningful of his life. After briefly considering medical studies, he instead decided to become a schoolteacher. It did not take long to realize that that was not for him. Managing a room full of "little runtlings" was "a school of affliction," he wrote, and it left him too tired even to read.[27] At last, he decided to return to his first choice and study the law.

The legal profession offered great prospects for a Massachusetts man. Along with New York and Philadelphia, Boston was one of the New World's commercial centers; a shipping hub where a steady flow of contracts, deeds, transactions, and legal disputes required the involvement of legal professionals. That also meant plentiful competition. To succeed would require much personal exertion, including constant travel to meet clients, examine documents, and attend court sessions. Also, there were no law schools in the colonies, which meant an aspiring attorney had to learn by "reading law," that is, apprenticing with a practicing lawyer, who would give the student room and board as well as instruction, for a fee. Once his master was satisfied that he had acquired sufficient learning, Adams could obtain a certificate to be presented to the bar. But reading law was a risky prospect; Thomas Jefferson—who also read law—later remarked that it was "rather a prejudice than a help," because working attorneys tended to treat students as hired labor, assigning them tasks that "encroach[ed] on that time which should be devoted to their studies."[28] In 1756, Adams signed on with a competent, if not top-notch, Worcester lawyer named James Putnam—and, it appears, suffered just that fate.

His studies involved no lectures, but instead the reading of textbooks and the memorization of arcane elements of the English legal system, known as the common law. The common law—then and now—relies on legal precedents to guide one's understanding of the principles of social order. These principles, along with statutes adopted by legislatures and approved by the monarch, were interpreted and applied by courts that operated primarily through writs and injunctions—judicial orders that commanded people to act or refrain from acting.

Studying law meant becoming familiar with the complex ways of obtaining these orders, which depended, in turn, on principles articulated both in precedential court decisions and in the works of august thinkers such as Cicero; the Byzantine legal reformer Justinian; scholars of international law such as Hugo Grotius; natural law theorists such as Samuel von Pufendorf; and, most of all, Sir Edward Coke, the lawyer, judge, and scholar whose four-volume *Institutes of the Laws of England* formed the indispensable basis for any 18th-century legal education.

Coke, who lived from 1552 to 1634, was an obsessive collector of legal precedents, and published a collection of judicial opinions known as *Coke's Reports* that helped cement the principle of stare decisis (rule by precedent). Still an important resource for lawyers today, his *Institutes* are extremely dense, written in a mix of Latin and Elizabethan English, with much of the text devoted to obscure, highly technical concepts.

Young Adams labored through it, as would Thomas Jefferson, who found it so grueling that he told a friend, "I do wish the devil had old Coke."[29] "The study of the law was a dreary ramble, in comparison of what it is at this day," Adams recalled in old age. Scholars such as William Blackstone later published textbooks that were much easier to read, and "smoothed the path [for] the student," but when Adams was studying, books were hard to get through—and hard to find. "I suffered very much for want of books," he recalled. "I know not whether a set of the *Statutes at Large* . . . was in the country."[30]

Adams felt that his studies under Putnam were haphazard, and probably resented the lawyer for using him as a gofer instead of focusing on his education. When the time came to seek admission to the bar, he did not even obtain a recommendation from Putnam, as was the norm. Instead, he decided to approach several Boston-area lawyers to ask them to sponsor his admission. That was an unusual step, but a characteristic example of Adams's personal initiative. "It is my destiny to dig treasures with my own fingers," he later told his diary. "Nobody will lend me or sell me a pickaxe."[31]

He first asked Jeremiah Gridley, who at 56 was already considered an eminent figure among Boston lawyers. Gridley reacted coolly. What, he asked, had Adams read while studying under Putnam? "I have read too fast," the young man confessed, "much faster than I understood [nor] remembered as I ought." But when Gridley quizzed him further, he found that Adams was more knowledgeable than he admitted, and was eager to learn more.

Had he read Coke's *Institutes*? Adams said he had tried. "You must conquer the *Institutes*," Gridley prodded. "He has conquered all the difficulties of this law, who is a master of the *Institutes*."[32] What about international law? "Have you read Grotius and Pufendorf?"

"I cannot say I have, sir," Adams answered, "but it was my intention to read them both as soon as possible."

Gridley urged him to do so. "A lawyer through his whole life ought to have some book on ethics or the law of nations always on his table. They are all treatises of individual or national morality and ought to be the study of our whole lives." He offered to lend Adams whatever books he might need. Then he pulled out his watch. "I must go to court," he said. "Attend in the morning, and I will present you to the court to be sworn."[33]

Adams also approached James Otis, Jr., a member of a prominent family, now in his 30s, who was on a path that would make him an esteemed pioneer in the cause of independence. Where Gridley was avuncular, Otis was to become "more like a brother" to the young Adams.[34] Unlike the retiring Gridley, Otis was an outspoken, eloquent courtroom lawyer who caught and held jurors' attention. In the years to come, Adams studied his style to develop the skills of persuasion and harangue that made him an effective advocate. Adams was well aware that the broader world looked upon the work of trial attorneys as slightly disreputable, and for the rest of his life he envied the way elegant men like Jefferson could gain the world's renown despite retiring within themselves, whereas those who descended into the cockpit like he did, and engaged their energies to win a point, were afterward viewed with vague suspicion as a result of their very success.

It was wise to join the bar in Braintree, within the Boston judicial district, where Adams would have access to the profitable and interesting legal work of the city. But over the next two years, he would face a considerable challenge building a reputation in a busy community where lawyers simultaneously helped each other—offering advice and lending books—and hazed each other through teasing and condescension. When one of his first cases ended badly due to a paperwork error he should have caught in time, Adams blushed to think that Robert Treat Paine, a fellow lawyer whom he admired but who often teased the young attorney, would "pick up this story to laugh at."[35] But he learned much from observing Otis, Gridley, and others in court, and they, in turn, came to respect him. He was overjoyed when Gridley at last invited him to join Sodalitas, an intellectual salon that gathered regularly to discuss legal subjects.

THE CHILD INDEPENDENCE WAS BORN

By 1761, Adams had gained enough respectability and income to consider marrying. He had met Abigail Smith briefly a few years earlier, but now she was 17, and she drew the 26-year-old John's attention with her good looks and sharp mind. Her father was a minister who had hired a tutor to give her an education far superior to what was common for the era. A serious student of literature, history, and politics, she was every bit John's intellectual equal. After three years of courtship visits and playful and charming letters, they married in her family's house in Weymouth, with her father presiding. For the next 54 years—much of which they spent separated due to John's political business—the Adamses would accompany each other through one of the most celebrated marriages in American history.

The couple looked forward to a comfortable life in their home colony, and with good reason. Its 200,000 inhabitants were farmers, mechanics, sailors, and fishermen, dignified and hardworking, proud that their ancestors had built a civilization on the margin of an immeasurable wilderness. Its people were also proud to be British;

James Otis was a brotherly figure to John Adams. Although a gifted lawyer, he suffered from a mental disorder that crippled him in later years.

members of a unique political society. "We have rights we justly claim our own," wrote an anonymous poet in 1741, in a pamphlet addressed to the Prince of Wales:

> Where LAWS to kings prerogatives assign,
> Those to known bounds the regal pow'r confine.
> Where LAWS to subjects PRIVILEGES give,
> They're independent of prerogative.
> Our kings have all a virtuous soul desires,
> And subjects all that LIBERTY inspires.
> This is the CONSTITUTION *BRITONS* boast.[36]

Massachusetts's own constitution was also unusual, particularly in its democratic elements. Although its governor was chosen in London, his power was constrained by the fact that he typically could not act without the concurrence of his council—and councilors were chosen not by the king or the governor, but by the elected House of Representatives. (The governor could reject the House's nominees but not name his own.) Consequently, if the House placed the right men on the council, Massachusetts voters could exercise a degree of veto power over royal government. In addition, colonial officers were paid not by London but by the House, which meant the people's representatives could punish governors or judges whose actions they disliked by refusing to pay. This arrangement operated as a kind of checks-and-balances system against royal power.

Of course, the governorship was still an important position. The representatives could not meet without his summoning them, and he could "prorogue" them (order them to take a recess) whenever he wanted, or even "dissolve" them—closing down their legislative business until he called for new elections. He could also veto their choice of Speaker of the House and could fire judges. But if he sought, for example, to put down a riot, he first needed the council's agreement to issue the required proclamations—and a council sympathetic to protestors might refuse, thereby depriving him of power to summon the militia.

The judicial system in which Adams practiced law was also special. Colonial juries were elected by the people. And in addition to settling ordinary disputes, these juries could also vindicate the rights of individuals against overbearing government. They had power to indict and convict officials for committing "trespasses" even if they were acting under orders, if the jury thought those orders unlawful.[37] That meant a customs inspector who searched a ship for contraband might be held financially liable or even sent to jail despite having a warrant, if the jury held the warrant to be invalid. Although its original Puritanism had faded, Massachusetts remained a deeply religious society, whose people took matters of principle seriously and had few compunctions about speaking their minds. "People here are loyal," the governor reported in 1762, "but jealous of their liberties (of which they form high and sometimes unconstitutional ideas) to a great degree."[38]

That jealousy was particularly evident in the colonists' resistance to the Navigation Acts. Adopted between 1651 and 1733, those acts curtailed the Americans' economic freedom in an effort to prevent them from competing against English industry. Among other things, they forbade colonists from selling certain products to any country except England (or sometimes even to other colonies). The list eventually included sugar, molasses, tobacco, tar, pitch, iron, lumber, potash, coffee, coconuts, hides, furs, silk, copper, hemp, rice, whale fins, whale oil, dyeing materials, and even pimentos.[39] All had to be sold to the mother country instead of the highest bidder.

Many Americans hated these laws and ignored them—and for more than a generation, London did little about that. The 1733 Molasses Act, for example, imposed a substantial tariff on sugar imported from the French West Indies to force Americans to buy sugar from British colonies, instead. The act contained severe punishments: Convicted smugglers forfeited their goods, one-third of which went to the treasury, one-third to the governor, and one-third to the informant.[40] Had it been rigidly implemented, this might have hampered New England's rum industry and seriously harmed its fishermen, whose product was often traded for West Indian sugar. But colonists often flouted the law, and the imperial government—through a combination of incompetence, inattention, and corruption—generally let violations slide.[41]

Actually, historians debate the extent to which Americans resorted to smuggling at this time. It was probably not as extensive as the British government thought it was.[42] And many colonial merchants benefited from the acts' protectionism. That makes it hard to calculate the financial burden these laws imposed—or the costs Americans would suffer from separating from Britain. Such questions loomed over many merchants' heads in the decade before independence.[43] But it is clear that the colonies managed to fashion a livable compromise with the mother country: Between about 1680 and 1760, London made a pretense of controlling intercolonial trade, but generally left the management of internal affairs to the colonists themselves. The Massachusetts in which young Adams set out to make his fortune was already largely independent—a community of farmers, merchants, and sailors who effectively governed themselves and liked it that way.

That all began to change in 1760. George II, the German-born king who had reigned since 1727, died that year and was succeeded by his 22-year-old grandson, George III. Shy, well-educated, and fond of science, art, and legal theory, the new king was proud that, unlike the first two Georges, he had been born in Britain.[44] He attentively studied British law and wrote private essays about the glories of the nation's constitution, praising its principles of free speech and private property, as well as the separation of powers.[45] Yet he was a firm believer in the constitutional doctrine that legal historians call Parliamentary Supremacy, which held that Parliament was not just the legislative branch of the government, but actually possessed absolute power over the state. As William Blackstone claimed in his *Commentaries on the Laws of England*—which George read soon after they were published in the 1760s—Parliament had "irresistible, absolute, uncontrolled authority," and could "change and create afresh even the constitution of the kingdom."[46] That conception stood in contrast to the older legal theory known as Prescriptive Right, which viewed Parliament's authority as circumscribed by the limits of custom, tradition, and morality. Throughout the crisis that was to come, George was to prove an unwavering champion of Parliamentary Supremacy, whereas American colonists adhered to the Prescriptive Right theory, insisting that neither Parliament nor any other legislature could have such total power.

Those disputes seemed purely academic when George III took the throne. His immediate concern was money. A worldwide war between Britain and France—known as the Seven Years' War or the French and Indian War—was then entering its fourth year, and the nation's debt was exploding. That presented a threat to national security, since it might make it impossible to borrow funds for military needs. In casting about for ways to increase revenue, British leaders saw one obvious answer: the New World colonies were rapidly growing in population and wealth. They could and should pay more.

The empire's first step, initiated by George II shortly before his death, was to ramp up enforcement of the Navigation Acts—which meant hunting smugglers and seizing their merchandise. That posed a challenge, given the scale of illicit trade, the labyrinthine geography of North America, and the fact that colonists, especially New Englanders, hardly considered tax evasion illicit to begin with. The government therefore relied on two vital tools: paid informants and documents called writs of assistance, which empowered customs inspectors to enlist local law enforcement officers to help them search buildings and confiscate smuggled imports. These writs were the equivalent of search warrants, but they specified no limit on the time or location for a search, and they could be issued without any particular suspicion of wrongdoing. Writs of assistance had been around for many years, but London's new enforcement policy meant they would be used far more aggressively—and the governor of Massachusetts, Francis Bernard, who took office in 1760, was prepared to do just that.

Use of the writs raised legal concerns, however. Six months before Bernard became governor, *London Magazine* reported that a bill for restricting the importation of wool had been introduced in the House of Commons, only to be protested by English merchants who complained that its enforcement provisions were excessive. In particular, the bill authorized search powers far beyond what was normally accepted under the common law. The anonymous *London Magazine* writer—evidently a competent lawyer—argued that warrants were supposed to be supported by specific, sworn statements testifying to some particular reason to suspect wrongdoing. They were not supposed to be blanket authorizations for officials to search however they pleased. The wool bill violated that rule by allowing "general" warrants, instead.

When the article was reprinted in Boston, attorneys like Adams took notice. The colony's merchants and shippers already resented writs of assistance. Now, they saw a way to challenge their constitutionality by filing a lawsuit. And the attorney they asked to make the argument was Adams's friend James Otis. The eloquent and passionate Otis was renowned for his legal talents, although he did have erratic traits, particularly flashes of temper and a tendency to ramble, which years later grew into a serious mental illness. But in 1761, he was at the height of his powers, and Adams idolized him.

The case Otis brought against the writs that February involved a customs official named Charles Paxton, whom one historian calls "an arch-practitioner of search and seizure on information received."[47] Relying on informants who were paid a portion of the goods he confiscated, Paxton was able to pursue suspected violators of the Navigation Acts with impunity—except that Boston merchants hated him for it. He used the writs to search their storehouses and even private homes for contraband, which was then deemed forfeit, and then he split the proceeds with his snitches. He even found a way to pay them out of the third that was supposed to go to the colonial treasury, which had the result of increasing his own share.

Paxton's accounting trick gave Otis an opening. He would demand an audit and use the resulting lawsuit to assail the writs' legality. On February 24, 1761, he rose in Boston's State House to speak, while Adams sat watching, scribbling notes, awed by his "rapid torrent of eloquence." Otis's argument was like "a flame of fire!" he later said.[48] Citing the slogan made famous by Sir Edward Coke—that a man's home is his castle—and the writings of Coke's contemporary, Sir Matthew Hale—who had declared that warrants must specify the particular place to be searched or specific persons to be arrested—Otis denounced the writs of assistance for intruding on long-standing rights and violating the common law.[49] According to Adams's notes, Otis said:

> Everyone with this writ may be a tyrant; if this commission be legal, a tyrant in a legal manner also may control, imprison, or murder anyone within the realm. . . . Every man may reign secure in his petty tyranny, and spread

> terror and desolation around him. . . . A person with this writ, *in the daytime*, may enter all houses, shops, etc., at will, and command all to assist him. . . . [E]ven *their menial servants, are allowed to lord it over us*. . . . Now one of the most essential branches of English liberty is the freedom of one's house. A man's house is his castle; and while he is quiet, he is as well guarded as a prince in his castle. This writ, if it should be declared legal, would totally annihilate this privilege.[50]

Adams later claimed that "the child Independence was born" at that instant.[51]

That was an exaggeration. For one thing, Otis may have been eloquent, but he failed to persuade the court. Chief Justice Thomas Hutchinson—a loyal servant of the Crown who hated Otis for "tend[ing] to raise heats and animosities, and to destroy the powers of government"—postponed his ruling to consult officials in London.[52] When the answer finally came, it confirmed the writs' legality, ending the case. Nevertheless, Otis had accomplished a larger purpose: the dispute served as an initial spark of resistance for the people of Massachusetts.[53] Already suspicious of royal government, the lawsuit helped transform their resentments into outright animosity.

THE SUGAR ACT

Around this time, Adams began to notice that colonial officials, notably Governor Bernard and Chief Justice Hutchinson, were taking on a more pompous and authoritarian tone, one more suited to despotic government than to the hardscrabble republicanism his home colony was used to. Hutchinson and the other justices began wearing elaborate robes and wigs in court, something Massachusetts judges had shunned before. And the courtroom in which Otis argued was now decorated with two gigantic portraits—not of King George or his grandfather, but of Charles II and James II, whose reigns had previously been regarded as a dark age of despotism. The former governor had refused to hang the paintings, Adams recalled.

"He was no admirer of Charles' or James' [so] they were stowed away in a garret among rubbish."[54] But Governor Bernard had ordered them taken out of storage and prominently displayed.

Adams's suspicions were confirmed when London unveiled the next step in its plan for making the colonists pay for imperial expansion. The war with France ended in 1763 with a clear British victory, and George III named a new prime minister, George Grenville, with a mandate to bring down the national debt, which had grown to a staggering £9 million. Grenville's plan was to magnify London's authority to tax the colonies and force America into the mercantilist economic system. Such a step would have much more than financial consequences, however. It represented a fundamental change in the imperial constitution, one that expanded London's control over British America in an unprecedented way.

Governor Bernard thought that change was long overdue. Months after Grenville took office, Bernard sent an extraordinary series of letters to London, urging the government to formulate what he called "a new regulation" of colonial America—that is, an overhaul of its entire political system.[55] In his eyes, the problem with the colonies was that they had no hereditary nobility, as England did. That made them excessively democratic, and therefore disobedient toward the mother country. "The government ought not to be dependent upon the people," he declared.[56] The best idea would be to create something like the House of Lords, to more rigidly stratify American society and subdue the populace.

Bernard admitted that the colonial charters issued a century earlier promised Americans a degree of autonomy, recognizing them as having the same rights as residents of England. But Parliament was not bound by those promises, he argued. Its power was "absolute, uncontrollable, and accountable to none," and that meant even the charters did not "preclude the Parliament of Great Britain from interfering . . . in such manner as [it] shall think fit." The idea that colonists had a right not to be taxed or regulated except by legislatures in which they had a voice, and that this bound Parliament—either as a matter of English law or because natural law requires one to honor one's promises—was nonsense. Such a principle "must be confined to the inhabitants of Great Britain only."[57]

Grenville paid no attention to Bernard's proposals.[58] His own plan was more incremental. His first step was the Sugar Act of 1764, formally known as the Revenue Act, which reduced the tariff on molasses that had first been imposed three decades earlier.[59] The new act kept restrictions on the importation of sugar in place, and it also forbade the importation of foreign rum and the direct export of lumber and other items to Europe—these had to go through England, first. But it also imposed new taxes on wine, coffee, and cloth, and, most strikingly, it created a powerful enforcement mechanism. Shipowners would have to swear that their cargoes were legal, post a bond before setting sail, and have their documents rechecked by customs officers at every port their vessels entered. And, as usual for customs laws, violations of the act were punishable by forfeiture of ship and cargo.

Parliament also created a new Court of Vice-Admiralty for All America, located in Halifax, Nova Scotia, whose judges would hear cases involving alleged violations of the Sugar Act "or any other act or acts of Parliament relating to the trade and revenue" of the colonies.[60] Vice-admiralty courts had been a feature of colonial law for many years, but their reach had been narrowly limited. Now, Grenville's new Halifax court would have jurisdiction over all British New World colonies, and over any alleged violation of tax laws and trade regulations. That had important consequences, because unlike common-law courts, vice-admiralty courts operated without juries and proceeded "in rem"—a technical term that means suspected contraband is *itself* treated as if it were the defendant. That legal fiction meant the traditional rules of criminal procedure would not apply: The property's owner was not entitled to counsel or to the presumption of innocence. (The same mechanism is used today in so-called civil asset forfeiture cases.)

Worse still, if a vice-admiralty judge declared a forfeiture, the property would be sold at auction, with part of the revenue going to the judge himself. This obviously compromised the judge's objectivity. Equally distressing was a provision of the act specifying that even if an owner managed to prevail, the judge could still declare that the initial seizure had been done with "probable cause"—which would immunize the officers involved from any lawsuit the owner might try to bring afterward. As a consequence, a merchant's goods might be seized by mercenary enforcers, compelling him to defend his property in a juryless court 400 miles from home, where he was allowed no attorney, where he bore the burden of proving his innocence, and where the judge kept part of his property if he lost. He would then be forced to pay the costs of the trial, and even if he prevailed, he could not sue those responsible.[61] Such an "acquittal" might easily bankrupt an innocent merchant.

All these risks were heightened when Parliament empowered Royal Navy vessels to capture suspected smugglers. It dispatched 44 ships to patrol the Atlantic coastline, and rewarded their crews with a percentage of confiscated cargoes.[62] They were "very active in their new employment," complained Benjamin Franklin to a friend in London. "Every boat [is] stopped and examined, and much incumbrance by that means brought upon all business." Franklin conceded that "illicit trade ought to be stopped," but the navy men were going too far. "A ship from Lisbon is seizable for [carrying] a chest of lemons. Methinks such trifles are not proper objects of laws. Lemons are no produce of Britain. In our hot summers they are necessary to our health. Why may we not be indulged with them? To carry them first to England and then bring them here is the way to have them spoiled."[63]

STRIKING AT OUR BRITISH PRIVILEGES

These new policies incensed James Otis. Soon after the Sugar Act was adopted, he published a pamphlet titled *The Rights of the Colonists Asserted and Proved*, railing against the fact that the "inestimable privilege of a jury" was being "taken away in all trials in the colonies, relating to the revenue, if the informers have a mind to go [to] the admiralty, as they ever have done, and ever will do, for very obvious reasons."

Supporters of the act claimed the vice-admiralty provisions were necessary because colonial courts were biased against the government. But Otis poured sarcasm on the idea that "judges of the admiralty, those *mirrors of justice*," who "have so much per cent on all they condemn, be it right or wrong," were more impartial. "Trade and traffic, says Lord Coke, 'is the livelihood of the merchant, the life of the commonwealth, wherein the king and every subject hath interest,'" yet by expanding the vice-admiralty court, Parliament was trampling on the rights of hardworking colonists. "Are not the merchants of British America entitled to a livelihood also?"[64]

Equally alarmed by the Sugar Act was John Adams's 42-year-old cousin Samuel. Suspicious for years of British treatment of the colonists, Samuel Adams immediately denounced the Sugar Act for violating basic constitutional rules: "The most essential rights of British subjects are those of being represented in the same body which exercises the power of levying taxes upon them, and of having their property tried by juries. These are the very pillars of the British Constitution, founded in the common rights of mankind."[65] The act not only violated those rules; it also threatened to establish a precedent that, if not immediately checked, would make colonists into servants of the home country, instead of equal partners. It "annihilates our charter right to govern and tax ourselves," he wrote. "It strikes at our British privileges, which as we have never forfeited them, we hold in common with our fellow subjects who are natives of Britian."[66]

Some Americans responded to the act with outright defiance. In July 1764, when a Royal Navy vessel, the HMS *St. John*, halted a suspected smuggler, the merchant crew violently resisted, throwing several navy men into the water. The *St. John*'s crew eventually overcame the colonists, but when the two ships reached the Newport docks, the captain sought to "impress"—that is, conscript—several of the American sailors into the navy. That sparked a riot, and when the *St. John*'s crew tried to flee, the Rhode Islanders fired on the ship with cannons.[67]

Months later, when a ship called the *Polly* was found smuggling near Newport, locals prevented customs officials from taking control of it, and the county sheriff sided with them.[68] In Boston, some merchants organized a boycott of British goods. New York, Rhode Island, and Virginia petitioned the government in London, decrying Parliament's decision to "impose taxes upon the subjects *here* by laws to be passed *there*" and to disregard "the wisdom of our ancestors in contriving trials by juries."[69] But the House of Commons refused to accept the petitions, citing what it claimed was a long-standing rule against receiving any messages disputing its constitutional authority.

The Sugar Act, however, ultimately failed of its own accord: It generated less than one-tenth of the revenue Parliament had expected. Prime Minister Grenville and his allies therefore decided to take the next step in their plan. In the same speech in which he had first proposed the act, Grenville had also announced that Parliament was considering imposing another tax on the colonies, one that would focus on written documents—everything from playing cards and newspapers to government licenses and property deeds. All would have to be printed on paper featuring a seal, and the seal would only be provided to those who paid the tax.

Aware of colonial objections to parliamentary taxation, Grenville offered to postpone implementation of this stamp tax to allow the colonists time to propose some alternative. Yet this seeming magnanimity was a ruse; Grenville never communicated it to the colonial legislatures, and when Massachusetts representatives approached Governor Bernard about crafting some other option, he said no, because he had received no instructions on what terms Grenville would consider acceptable. Meanwhile, colonial agents in London, including Benjamin Franklin, met with the prime minister to ask what he had in mind. They found that he was not actually interested in their ideas; instead, he was hoping they would offer some pretext whereby he could claim that they had agreed to parliamentary taxation. He was "besotted with his stamp scheme," Franklin remarked.[70]

What Grenville was really attempting was not a fiscal change but a constitutional change. He was seeking to establish as a matter of principle that Parliament had authority to levy taxes on the colonies directly instead of requesting funds from the colonial legislatures as had always been done before. His treasury secretary, Thomas Whately, observed that the stamp tax proposal was the most important part of Grenville's plans, "on account of the important point it establishes, the right of Parliament to lay an internal tax upon the colonies."[71] That, however, was precisely the point Americans were determined to refuse. And their reasons reached back over a century to a time when England and its infant colonies had been wracked by revolution and civil war.[72]

— CHAPTER 2 —

THE REVOLUTIONS BEFORE THE REVOLUTION

The people of England, and the cause of liberty, truth, virtue, and humanity, gained infinite advantages by that resistance [to Charles I]. . . . England has been a principal bulwark, from that period to this, of civil liberty.
—John Adams[1]

Britain's decision to tax the colonies reopened an old wound in America. Virtually from the moment England's first colony was founded in Jamestown, Virginia, in 1607, Americans had struggled to define their relationship with the mother country. By 1700, a relative calm had descended, as London more or less left the colonists alone. But that peace had only come after long and painful conflict. Now, Prime Minister Grenville's new policy would upset that hard-earned balance—indeed, it would entirely transform the Anglo-American relationship.

Actually, the word "policy" is misleading. London was almost always too preoccupied with matters closer to home—civil wars and military confrontations with European enemies—to focus on America, let alone to formulate a coherent "policy." The religious dissenters who founded Massachusetts and Maryland had been troublemakers England was glad to get rid of, and colonies like Virginia, although intended as profit-making ventures, often proved more of a hassle to England than they were worth. That made it easy to forget about the colonists. Moreover, instability was the norm in London. In the two decades before 1776, Britain went through seven prime ministers. And during that period, it fought

Sir Edmund Andros served as dictator of the Dominion of New England for three years before being overthrown by outraged colonists in 1689.

the Seven Years' War—a sworldwide conflict in which England barely held off a French invasion of the homeland—as well as three wars in India, all while narrowly avoiding combat with Spain and Russia.

Defeating France in 1763 did not improve things much. Britain remained isolated, with no European allies who could provide supplies in the event of future conflict. All those resources would have to come from overseas colonies instead. Yet the colonies were not governed by an efficient, professional civil service, but by a network of corrupt, lazy, incompetent officers, chosen not for their expertise, but through nepotism or the desire to ship a bankrupt nobleman abroad. Britain's "policy" toward America therefore ended up being a patchwork of measures, often ill-considered, sometimes expressed in bold language, but carelessly enforced or completely ignored.

Another reason the word "policy" can mislead is that the crisis sparked by Grenville's American plan concerned not a *policy* disagreement but a *constitutional* dispute. To appreciate it, one must first grasp how British and American lawyers thought about constitutional law. Today's American law evolved from the centuries-old English common-law system, which means the debates of the revolutionary era resemble the way modern attorneys address constitutional disputes. Yet there are also crucial differences. The most significant is that the English constitution was (and is) unwritten, which meant that defining its terms depended less on linguistic analysis or inquiries into the motives of a group of "founders" than on questions of custom, tradition, and precedent—not just written precedents from courts, but the practical precedents of history.

Eighteenth-century constitutionalism was based largely on "usage" or "prescription," meaning that institutions and practices could *acquire* legitimacy due to longevity and popular acceptance. Just as a person today can obtain property by "adverse possession," so the government could acquire power—and individuals could acquire rights—merely by acting in a certain way for long enough. "Whatever is consented to by a civil society becomes a law of such society," wrote legal scholar Thomas Rutherforth in 1756. "Any rules which arise out of such usage, [and have] continued for time immemorial without being interrupted by any act of the public, become laws to all."[2] Thus, if the king or a community took an action, public acquiescence could later be considered proof of that act's constitutionality.[3]

This kind of constitutionalism anathematized the *new*. To call a practice an "innovation" was effectively to condemn it as unconstitutional. Not everything old was *necessarily* legitimate—there were ways to remedy old practices if they contradicted important moral principles or had clearly outlived their usefulness—but generally speaking, the older something was, the more legal it was. When colonists argued over whether Parliament could tax the colonies or regulate their trade, each side tended to support its claims less by citation to judicial decisions—although these mattered—than by arguing over whether things had "always been done this way."

Because constitutional interpretation depended heavily on the lessons of the past, lawyers strove to uncover historical examples that supported their positions, and to avoid establishing new precedents or even using language that might be construed as lending credence to their opponents. As a result, constitutional debates of the era often sound to us more like diplomacy, or even what we would today call passive aggressiveness. When, for example, John Adams proposed that the First Continental Congress declare its willingness to "cheerfully consent" to Parliament's regulation of colonial trade, it sparked a lengthy debate, because using the word "consent" subtly implied that the colonies could *withhold* their consent—something imperialists denied.

Although the arguments leading to independence were often legalistic and technical, they were also grounded in deeper principles of morality and justice derived from the ideas of ancient philosophers. Unlike many attorneys today, lawyers of Jefferson and Adams's era did not view law as a mere expression of power. Nor did they consider philosophical questions beyond the lawyer's purview. Instead, they thought natural law—rules of ethics and prudence discovered over the centuries by observing human nature and needs—formed the basis of all legitimate legal rules. In their eyes, might without right was simply not law at all.

As one modern scholar defines it, natural law is concerned with "those binding norms which are valid for the whole of mankind on the basis of nature itself and not just in consequence of the authoritative expression of some will or other."[4] Virtually all attorneys of the revolutionary era viewed law this way—as a philosophical enterprise, dealing with objective truths of social organization, in the same way that physicians deal with the objective laws of nutrition and medicine. "The common law," wrote Sir Edward Coke, "is nothing but reason," meaning not just one person's reason, but the "artificial perfection of reason, gotten by long study, observation, and experience."[5] Through that study, observation, and experience, one could come to understand the moral and practical grounding of man-made laws. "The law of nature is part of the law of England," Coke declared, and we comprehend natural law through the "artificial reason" of legal analysis. Eventually, we develop a well-considered, rationally defensible conception of justice—a conception rooted not in the dictate of any authority figure, but in the facts of human existence.[6]

Today's lawyers often dismiss natural law as an esoteric or even mystical way of thinking. But the revolutionary generation saw nothing obscure about it. To take a simple example, a statute that both requires and prohibits the same act would be void, not because some government official declares it so, but because the rules of logic render it incoherent. In the same way, natural law reasoning holds that the statutes adopted by legislatures or precedents issued by courts are limited by—and are built on top of—principles that derive their binding force not from government but from reality. Alexander Hamilton, for example, was employing natural law reasoning when he argued in *The Federalist* that certain legal principles are "not derived from any positive law, but from the nature and reason of the thing."[7] When combined with a robust understanding of human nature, this legal perspective offers a powerful tool for ensuring that government exercises authority, rather than mere power—that it is based on justice instead of (in Hamilton's words) "accident and force."[8] Natural law can both explain and justify a constitution—helping lawyers and judges make it the best it can be.

PRESCRIPTIVE RIGHT VERSUS PARLIAMENTARY SUPREMACY

Yet the imperial crisis that led to American independence did not start with arguments about natural law. Instead, it concerned a disagreement over Parliament's constitutional authority. Those who eventually became known as Patriots embraced the theory of Prescriptive Right, which viewed the constitution as a matter of historical usage—of long-standing principles and practices, discovered and developed over the centuries. According to this theory, something only qualifies as law if it combines power with right—and right is determined by both abstract principles and practical experience. Unchecked or unjustified power—or the exercise of power by political leaders to enrich themselves rather than serving the public good—is not actually *law* at all, but mere force or compulsion. It is "arbitrary," and every individual has the moral and legal right to resist arbitrary force.

One of the most important limits on Parliament's authority was the principle that taxes and legislation were only legitimate if consented to by the people or their chosen representatives. The logic behind this principle was that property means ownership—the right to possess one's belongings and to decide how to dispose of them—which means the individual must have the right to decide whether to turn it over to governing authorities in the form of taxes. That was why English tax laws traditionally used the phrase "give and grant": The king was not *seizing* the people's wealth; the people were choosing to "give and grant" it to him. To modern eyes, this looks like a legal fiction, and even Benjamin Franklin admitted it was something of a pretense.[9] But it manifested a crucial norm: Governing officials are the people's employees, not their bosses. The distinguishing trait of English law, as opposed to, say, the rule of the Russian czar, was that the king did *not* own all property in the realm; he could not simply take whatever he wanted, but had to request it from the people, as represented in Parliament.[10] But by the same principle, Parliament could not give consent on behalf of Americans because they were not represented in Parliament and, due to their distance from England, could not be. Instead, they had their own miniature parliaments—their provincial legislatures—which alone could give consent to taxation.

On the opposite end from Prescriptive Right theory was the constitutional theory of Parliamentary Supremacy. This theory held that the Lords and Commons possessed absolute power—that their authority over the empire was, in the words of Britain's chief justice, Lord Mansfield, "complete, entire, and unconditional."[11]

This theory held that every political society contains a spark of irresistible power—of total right to command. This power can never be divided or extinguished, and it takes precedence over every tradition or formality. In England, this sovereignty was held not by the king but by Parliament, which after a century of civil war had emerged triumphant even over the claims of monarchical power. Parliament itself had actually created the modern monarchy, by declaring William and Mary king and queen of England in 1689. If it could do that, it could do anything.

To suggest that Parliament's power was limited was to question the legitimacy of the state itself. Advocates of the Prescriptive Right theory might point to traditions, customs, or written charters to support their arguments, but these were all irrelevant. If, as William Blackstone wrote, the Lords and Commons could "change and create afresh even the constitution of the kingdom," they certainly could set aside charters and traditions.[12] "An act of Parliament," declared philosopher William Paley in 1785, "can never be unconstitutional in the strict and proper acceptation of the term."[13]

Appreciating this clash between Prescriptive Right and Parliamentary Supremacy is essential to understanding the constitutional and, ultimately, philosophical dispute that brought about American independence. Historians who overlook it are often misled into seeing the revolution as a petty fight over taxes that inexplicably spiraled out of control, or, more cynically, as a scheme by "the rich" to "take over land, profits, and political power" from Britain.[14] Such notions are nonsense—for one thing, wealthier colonists tended to resist independence, whereas ordinary Americans were often its most emphatic supporters. In any event, such a superficial description of the events that took place between 1763 and 1783 cannot account for the astonishing amount of legal and philosophical debate surrounding the revolution, much of it involving the greatest thinkers in American history.

Nevertheless, even reputable writers often fail to grasp the nature of the constitutional issues at stake, resulting in distorted scholarship. In his 2021 book *The Last King of America*, for example, historian Andrew Roberts sought to vindicate George III by insisting that the king acted out of a scrupulous adherence to British law. According to Roberts, it was unfair for John Adams, Thomas Jefferson, and their colleagues to accuse the king of "trying to subvert the

British constitution," when it was actually "his unshakeable respect for it that helped him lose America."[15] That assertion is question-begging, however, given that the entire dispute concerned whether the theory of Parliamentary Supremacy to which King George clung so unshakably was, in fact, the *genuine* British constitutional doctrine, or whether it represented an untenable, even immoral, view of the law. To praise the king for his unwavering support for the constitution without addressing whether his understanding of its meaning was the correct one is to miss the point entirely.

Adams put it well. Asked to admit that advocates of Parliamentary Supremacy held their views in good faith, he replied that he had once known a man who thought the end of the world was coming, and that this entitled him—as one of the blessed few who knew this mystical truth—to take whatever property he wanted from sinners who refused to repent. "Mankind pitied the poor man's infirmity," Adams concluded. "[They] thought it, however, their duty to confine him that he might steal no more."[16]

THEY MAY ENJOY THE SAME FREEDOM AND PRIVILEGES

The clash between the theories of Prescriptive Right and Parliamentary Supremacy had its roots in a century of bloody strife in England. Between 1600 and 1700, Parliament and the monarchy had argued, negotiated, and ultimately gone to war over the exact nature and scope of their powers. Although the colonies were usually ignored during those fights—out of sight, out of mind—to the extent that they had any say, they tried to retain ties with the mother country while keeping enough distance to preserve their autonomy. They inhabited a strange kind of constitutional limbo, interrupted at times by oppressive acts from London. When at last the 17th century ended, one thing seemed settled: The colonies were connected to Britain through the *king*, not *Parliament*. The monarch ruled over the whole empire, but American laws were made in American legislatures, which were the legal equivalents of the Lords and Commons in Westminster. And this arrangement seemed to Americans not just convenient but also consistent with natural law.

One could say that the trouble began when Queen Elizabeth I died in 1603, and her cousin, James I, succeeded to the throne,

Lawyer and judge Sir Edward Coke was a powerful opponent of absolute monarchy in England whose writings profoundly influenced the American revolutionary leaders.

inaugurating the Stuart dynasty. Elizabeth's reign had witnessed the maturing of English culture, the flourishing of Protestantism, and the formalization of the common law, thanks largely to the efforts of her attorney general, Sir Edward Coke. An ingenious legal scholar, who had almost single-handedly established the common-law principle of precedent, Coke viewed English law as a process of concentrated reasoning whereby one can discern the principles on which a proper social order is based. These principles—articulated in such documents as the Magna Carta, which he considered the basic source of English liberties—made England unique, because unlike in authoritarian countries such as France, the monarch's will was not automatically law. Instead, in England, the law *limited* the king's power, thus protecting the rights of Englishmen.

James took a different view. Born and raised in Scotland, where kings were far more powerful than in England, he believed that he ruled by divine right, and that the monarch stands above the law. "Kings [are] the authors and makers of the laws," he wrote, "and not the laws of the kings." To think otherwise was "seditious."[17] After all, the whole point of a monarch was that he imposes law on the people, who otherwise would live in violent anarchy. Surely the people could not impose law on *themselves*. That would be a self-contradiction, because they would inevitably be tempted to ignore the law or change it whenever it became inconvenient.

Yet by the time James was crowned, the English had come to view the king's power as circumscribed by Parliament. Englishmen thought lawmaking authority resided in the "King in Parliament"—a phrase never precisely defined, but which certainly meant the monarch could not govern autocratically.[18] Thus, James almost immediately found himself in conflict with the House of Commons. Only a year after taking the throne, when he refused to allow one member to take his seat on the grounds that the man was an outlaw, the Commons replied that he had no right to make such a decision—the House alone could decide whether to seat him.[19] When James remained obstinate, the House tried patiently explaining to the new king just how things were done in England: "Our privileges are our right and due inheritance, no less than our very lands," they declared. "They cannot be withheld from us, denied, or impaired, but with apparent wrong to the whole state of the realm."[20] Annoyed, James prorogued the House, calling the members "fools" and telling them to "make use of your liberty with more modesty."[21]

It was the first of what became a lifelong series of quarrels between James I and Parliament. A legendary spendthrift, the king squandered funds on luxuries and presents for supporters, and when lawmakers sought to curtail his wastefulness, their efforts just confirmed his belief that elected legislatures were a nuisance. When the Commons refused to approve new taxes, he devised various schemes to raise money on the side, such as imposing tariffs (or "impositions") without their consent. When Parliament insisted in 1610 that this was illegal, James dismissed them in a fury and ruled for the next four years without convening them again. When at last a shortage of funds forced him to summon them once more, they still refused him money, and he dismissed them yet again. "I am surprised that my ancestors should ever have allowed such an institution to come into existence," he fumed.[22]

James resorted to other devices, including establishing a lottery, selling government land, and trying to marry his son to the princess of Spain to secure a dowry. He pressured noblemen and wealthy commoners to lend him money, arresting those who refused and putting them on trial in a special court called Star Chamber that was not part of the common-law judicial system. Named for the decorations on its ceiling, this court operated without a jury and became a powerful tool for enforcing royal power. When one merchant refused James a loan, and said that "the merchants are in no part of the world so screwed and wrung as in England; in Turkey they have more encouragement," Star Chamber convicted him of sedition, fined him £2,000, and sentenced him to six years in prison.[23] Star Chamber frequently imposed excessive fines as a fundraising scheme, and inflicted cruel punishments to terrorize the populace—most infamously, cutting off people's ears. In 1637, Puritan lawyer William Prynne, whose ears had already been "docked" for publishing a book insulting the queen, was arrested for a second offense. Star Chamber ordered the remaining stumps of his ears cut off.[24]

These inroads on the legal protections provided by the normal common-law courts offended Sir Edward Coke. James I had been persuaded to promote Coke to the role of chief justice in 1606, despite the judge's opposition to his measures. He soon regretted that, for Coke was a formidable adversary. Their tension erupted two years later, when the king insisted that he had power to resolve a dispute over the jurisdiction of the courts, which Coke denied. When James told him that there was no need to fear royal power, because he would always "protect the common law," Coke corrected him. "The common law," he said, "protects the king."

James exploded. "A traitorous speech!" he yelled, shaking his fist. "The king protects the law, and not the law the king!" Coke immediately begged the king's pardon, and James did not send him to jail—but Coke remained unpersuaded.[25] Kings, he wrote in his notebooks, "should not be under man, but under God and the laws."[26] In the years that followed, he and James I continued to spar over the powers of the monarch and elected lawmakers.

The two also clashed over the sale of monopolies. As one means of raising funds without Parliament's involvement, James sold "patents"—licenses that entitled one person or company to engage in a business, while outlawing all competition. Previous monarchs had sold monopolies, too, but Coke declared them unconstitutional. In his view, the Magna Carta, which promised that the king would not deprive any "freeman" of "liberty" except by the "law of the land," prohibited monarchs from using their power to enrich themselves and their cronies.[27] Monopolies increased prices and worsened unemployment, and Coke denounced them as unjust and wasteful: "At the common law, no man could be prohibited from working in any lawful trade," he wrote in one 1615 decision, "for the law abhors idleness, the mother of all evil . . . and especially in young men, who ought in their youth (which is their seed time) to learn lawful sciences and trades, which are profitable to the commonwealth, and whereof they might reap the fruit in their old age."[28]

Only months after that ruling, James reached the end of his patience and removed Coke from his position as chief justice. The judge did not retire quietly, however. In 1620, when James found himself forced to convene Parliament yet again to request funding, Coke was elected to the House of Commons, where he helped lead opposition to the king's authoritarian rule—especially his sales of monopolies. This time, when Parliament agreed to impose taxes, it demanded in exchange that he approve a law Coke wrote called the

Statute of Monopolies, which prohibited the government from outlawing economic competition except in cases of temporary patents for new inventions. The Statute reaffirmed that all English subjects had the right to practice a trade without arbitrary government interference.[29]

In the meantime, the colonization of North America was getting underway. James I authorized the Virginia Company to operate a for-profit colony in the New World in 1606, and a dozen years later, that colony's governor called for the creation of an elected legislature. Virginia's House of Burgesses began meeting in July 1619.[30] A decade after that, the Crown agreed to a charter for Massachusetts Bay that empowered its people to "assemble and hold and keep a court or assembly of themselves . . . for the handling, ordering, and dispatching of all such businesses and occurrences as shall from time to time happen, touching or concerning the said company."[31] New England's colonies quickly became the most democratic communities in the English-speaking world. Voting rights were severely restricted by today's standards—only white male property owners could vote, and in Massachusetts, only members of the Congregational Church—but suffrage was still more liberal than in England, and voters had far greater control over their governments than the people of England had over theirs.

Americans soon thought of their colonies as partners in the imperial system: subject to the king, but with their own legislatures in the place of Parliament. And the Crown seemed to accept that view. When the Virginia Company went bankrupt in 1624 (due to an Indian attack that killed a quarter of the entire settler population), James assumed personal control, transforming it from a "charter" colony into a "royal" colony. Virginians, fearing he might shut down the House of Burgesses, wrote to request reassurance, and received what seemed like an affirmative answer. James's son, who succeeded to the throne that year and became King Charles I, replied that he considered Virginia, as well as New England, "a part of our royal empire. . . . The government of the colony of Virginia shall immediately depend upon our self."[32] In other words, Virginia was not governed by Parliament, but by the king directly. A decade later, the Privy Council reiterated that Charles "does not intend that the interest which men had settled when there was a corporation should be impeached, and . . . for the present they may enjoy their estates and trades with the same freedom and privileges as they did before the recalling of their patents."[33]

Interpreting that to mean their legislature would keep operating, the Burgesses continued to hold meetings. These were briefly interrupted in the 1630s, when Governor Sir John Harvey tried to rule the colony as a dictator—but even then, lawmakers defiantly met despite being told not to, and Harvey was eventually recalled to London because of the Virginians' complaints. His replacement, Sir Francis Wyatt, arrived in 1639 with instructions to convene the legislature "once a year or oftener if urgent occasion shall require." The king's ministers said the Burgesses "shall have power to make acts and laws . . . correspondent as near as may be to the laws of England."[34] The House was therefore made official.

Virginians, wrote lawyer Richard Bland more than a century later, reacted to this with an "affection for the royal government [that] grew almost to enthusiasm."[35] But people back in England were not so affectionate. For one thing, King Charles was married to a Catholic Frenchwoman, which created a potential constitutional crisis, given that the kingdom was officially Protestant. This was a serious concern at a time when the pope continued to command political as well as religious allegiance from Catholics, and deemed the English monarchy an apostate regime. Only 50 years earlier, Pope Pius V had issued the *Regnans in Excelsis* against Elizabeth I—essentially a fatwa calling for her assassination—and in 1610, a Catholic terrorist stabbed France's King Henry IV to death for granting toleration to his Protestant subjects. James I himself narrowly escaped assassination by the Catholic fanatic Guy Fawkes in the infamous Gunpowder Plot of 1605.

Another problem was that Charles shared his father's ideas of divine right and absolute monarchy. When Parliament granted him only one year's worth of funds, and then sought to impeach one of his deputies for malfeasance, Charles sent the members home. A year later, he convened another Parliament, but again the lawmakers demanded impeachment and refused to provide funding, so Charles again dismissed them and resorted to the same forced-loans scheme his father had employed. Dozens of noblemen refused and were jailed. When he called still another Parliament, it offered funds only on the condition that he sign the Petition of Right, a document written largely by Sir Edward Coke that objected to forced loans, unlawful imprisonments, the quartering of soldiers in private homes, and other abuses in which Charles had engaged. The king yielded to that demand, but when Parliament prepared a follow-up, protesting his illegal taxes, he once more shut down their meeting.

Parliament reassembled in 1629, with tensions still running high. Disputes between the Puritans and other Christian sects (especially the more moderate Arminians) became heated when Charles sided with the latter and appeared ready to declare Arminianism official Church of England doctrine. Outspoken Puritans in the House of Commons insisted it was Parliament's job, not the king's, to "establish true religion and to punish false."[36] Charles responded by ordering the House to adjourn, but several Puritan members refused to go home, and even physically held the Speaker of the House in his chair so they could continue reading out their protests. Charles had nine of the troublemakers thrown in jail.

Exasperated, the king decided he was through with Parliaments. For more than a decade—between 1629 and 1640—he governed the country by himself. Because he could not impose new taxes without parliamentary approval, he fashioned various ruses to finance his expenditures, instead. The most controversial of these was "ship money," an obsolete medieval form of taxation traditionally imposed on oceanside towns to defend the realm against pirates. Although ship money had fallen into disuse, Charles revived the practice, claiming that the country was at risk of invasion. This time, however, he demanded payment not just from port cities but from the entire realm. The tax was collected by the direct seizure of assets, overseen by an army of bureaucrats and sheriffs; it therefore represented an unprecedented degree of intrusion into private life.[37] The English hated it.

In 1637, a member of the House of Commons named John Hampden refused to pay and was arrested. Hampden had been arrested before—he was among the many noblemen jailed for refusing to lend Charles money—and he had helped draft the Petition of Right. This time, he argued in court that ship money was an illegal tax because Parliament had never approved it. The judges ruled against him seven to five, but the dissenting opinions of those who agreed with him circulated widely. Charles's ship money, wrote one judge, "is against the common law of the land, which gives a man a freedom and property in his goods and estates, that it cannot be taken from him, but by his consent . . . in Parliament, or by his particular assent."[38] Hampden became a hero of the resistance.

Charles was more successful at raising funds by selling monopolies. This, too, was illegal—it violated the Statute of Monopolies adopted just a few years earlier—but he nevertheless gave contributors exclusive permission to sell a variety of goods, including everything from salt and playing cards to hats and combs. In 1631, he even declared that only the Company of Soapmakers could legally sell soap. The company's product was of poor quality, because it was made from vegetable oil instead of the more effective whale oil, and many people bought black-market soap instead, despite the fact that Charles made doing so a crime. The government started a propaganda campaign, enlisting famous noblewomen to claim that their maids preferred the official product, and even hosting a public demonstration in London to prove that it cleaned better than the illegal soap. But few were persuaded, and in the end the company lost its charter for failing to sell as much as expected.[39]

As for religion, Charles pressed forward with his plans for the Church of England. His archbishop, William Laud, began imposing a regime of censorship and control over the minutest details of religious ceremony. Even in modest community churches, he dictated what the stained-glass windows should look like, what the communion tables should be made of, and how parishioners should act when receiving the Eucharist. To Puritans, it all seemed like Catholicism and idolatry. And when Laud demanded that the Scottish Presbyterian Church follow the Anglican Book of Common Prayer, the Scots took up arms.

Faced with a major rebellion, Charles was finally forced to summon Parliament to raise taxes. But when the members convened in April 1640, they once more refused to provide funds—whereupon Charles dismissed them again. When he tried calling yet another Parliament in November, the House of Commons had finally had enough. The members demanded that Charles agree that they could not be dissolved without their own consent. They pronounced Laud a traitor and jailed him in the Tower of London. They abolished Star Chamber, declared "ship money" illegal, and adopted a lengthy catalog of complaints against Charles's abuses called the Grand Remonstrance. It listed monopolies, confiscations, forced loans, and excessive fines. "New judicatories," it said, had been "erected without law," and merchants had been "prohibited to [unload] their goods in such ports as were for their own advantage, and forced to bring them to those places which were much for the advantage of the monopolizers."[40]

Charles spurned the Grand Remonstrance, but the momentum of revolution was already overwhelming. On January 4, 1642, the king led a group of 300 soldiers into the House of Commons to arrest leaders of the opposition, including Hampden. But when he entered the chamber, he found that they had fled. And when he asked the Speaker of the House where they were, the Speaker refused to tell him. "I have neither eyes to see nor tongue to speak in this place, but as this House is pleased to direct me."[41] Charles stormed out, with the members shouting "Privilege! Privilege!" at his back, to protest his violation of Parliament's traditional autonomy. It was effectively a declaration of war, and Charles soon left London to recruit an army to fight against the forces loyal to Parliament.

SUCH FREEDOMS AS BELONG TO THE FREEBORN PEOPLE OF ENGLAND

The issues that sparked the English Civil War will sound remarkably familiar to any student of the American Revolution: taxation without consent, the use of juryless courts, the manipulation of the economy to serve the king's cronies, and efforts to undermine the independence of judges. Charles's opponents argued that monarchs were law enforcers, not law creators, and that their rule was only legitimate if—in the words of parliamentary leader John Pym—they "observe [the] . . . ancient laws and liberties of the kingdom."[42] In other words, the law makes the king, not the other way around—and that means his authority is limited both by the English common law and by fundamental principles of justice, principles that originate not in man-made legislation, but in reason and human nature.

Kings only have "derivative" power, wrote the poet and political philosopher John Milton, who supported the rebellion against Charles. That power was "transferred and committed to [kings] in trust from the people, [for] the common good of them all, in whom the power yet remains fundamentally." Milton cited Aristotle for the idea that "a king . . . governs to the good and profit of his people," whereas a tyrant "regarding neither law nor the common good, reigns only for himself and his faction." The Bible, ancient history, and common sense all testified to the legitimacy of overthrowing tyrants. "By the very principles of nature," Milton concluded, the people "lawfully may do [the same thing to a tyrant as they do to] a common pest and destroyer of mankind."[43]

It's no surprise that when war began in August 1642, Puritans in the colonies tended to side with Parliament. Many had left Europe out of contempt for the Stuart kings and their established church, and they welcomed efforts by their fellow Puritans back home to institute a new, more Christian order in place of the hubris of monarchy. Hundreds of New Englanders even sailed back to join Parliament's New Model Army, including the sitting governor of Connecticut, a future governor of Massachusetts, and six of the nine members of Harvard's first graduating class.[44] Although Massachusetts remained officially neutral during the war—indeed, no colony provided material support for either side—its lawmakers followed Parliament's example by issuing their own bill of rights, called the Massachusetts Body of Liberties.[45] Among other things, it pledged that nobody's life, liberty, or property would be taken except through due process of law; that nobody would be forced to accept a religious creed against his will; and that all would be given equal justice and compensated for taken property. It forbade monopolies, restrictions on immigration, and the beating of women by their husbands.[46]

Virginians, by contrast, showed little support for Parliament. Officially a "Crown colony"—meaning it was directly governed by the monarch—its inhabitants tended to be Anglicans, not Puritans, and they supported King Charles, although under the circumstances they found it wise to remain officially neutral. Governor William Berkeley did work with the Burgesses to pass a law declaring it treason to question the king's legitimacy, but he allowed colonial planters to trade with Parliament's supporters.[47] That neutrality collapsed, however, when Parliament's army defeated Charles, took him to London, and put him on trial for treason. Scoffing at the idea of being brought to answer, the king insisted that "no earthly power can justly call me, who am your king, in question as a delinquent."[48] But he was convicted and beheaded before a crowd at the Palace of Whitehall on January 30, 1649.

Parliament abolished the monarchy and inaugurated the Commonwealth—a republic governed under a written constitution. Virginia's leaders, however, refused to accept Parliament's legitimacy. Governor Berkeley called the king's execution "horrid, monstrous, impious, and heretical," and pledged the colony's allegiance to his heir, 19-year-old Charles II, then living in exile in France.[49] Charles II would eventually give Virginia the nickname "the Old Dominion" for this act of loyalty. But for now, Parliament was in control, and it was not pleased by the colony's defiance. It ordered a halt to all trade between England and Virginia and adopted a law revoking its charter and proclaiming Parliament's authority to govern the colony—a power previously exercised only by the king and the colonial legislature. "We are forsooth their worships' slaves," Berkeley complained, forbidden "to buy or sell but with those they shall authorize."[50]

When Parliament learned what he said, it dispatched the navy to Chesapeake Bay. Berkeley prepared for a showdown. He even called out the militia—over 1,000 strong—to confront the ships when they arrived. It did not take him long, however, to recognize that the military situation was hopeless. Virginia was entirely dependent on European imports, and the royal cause had been vanquished in England. Berkeley therefore quickly folded, and the two sides patched things up peacefully with an agreement called the Articles of Surrender to the Commonwealth, or the Treaty of Jamestown.

In language that proved important a century and a half later, the treaty declared that Virginia was yielding to Parliament by "a voluntary act not forced," and that Parliament would, in return, let Virginia continue enjoying self-rule. It would allow the House of Burgesses "as formerly [to] convene and transact the affairs of Virginia," and would maintain no military bases or troops in the colony without the Burgesses' approval. It would impose no "taxes, customs [or] impositions whatsoever . . . without consent of the [legislature]," and residents would "have and enjoy such freedoms and privileges as belong to the free born people of England." Finally,

Virginians would enjoy the right of "free trade as the people of England do enjoy to all places and with all nations."[51]

Those were extraordinarily lenient terms. By "voluntarily" yielding on this limited basis, Berkeley's people could maintain their separate lawmaking jurisdiction. (Berkeley also insisted that he be allowed to write to the king to personally apologize for giving in.) Although Parliament would exercise a general authority over the colonies, it would leave local lawmaking to the local legislature.

Massachusetts, too, effectively insisted that its own lawmakers, not those in London, held that colony's legislative authority. Its initial charter had declared that "Great and General Court" would have the lawmaking power, and in 1634, the General Court reiterated that "none but [it] has power to make and establish laws" or "to raise money and taxes."[52] Now, with Charles's overthrow, the colony's leaders wrote to London to remind Parliament that their charter promised them "liberty and power . . . to live under the government of . . . magistrates of our own choosing, and under laws of our own making," and to ask that "our government shall not be changed."[53] Parliament responded by largely leaving Massachusetts to govern itself.

The English republic soon degenerated into dictatorship under the military general Oliver Cromwell. Cromwell occasionally blustered about controlling America, and he particularly hoped to make war on other European colonies in the New World, but he was too busy fighting enemies in England to spend much time on these efforts. When he tried sending recruiters to Boston to raise an army to fight the Dutch in New York, Massachusetts leaders gave a polite but firm reply: "No war may be undertaken" without their own consent, they said, and they chose "to forbear the use of the sword." Still, as a sign of respect (and to avoid outright confrontation), the lawmakers "consented" to allow Cromwell's agents "to raise 500 volunteers . . . within *our* jurisdiction."[54] New Englanders had found a way to profess their loyalty while preserving their autonomy.

THE MONARCHY RETURNS

Colonists understandably viewed both sides of the home country's civil war with fear and suspicion. In moments of anger, James and Charles had sometimes threatened to revoke their charters, with unforeseeable consequences for how their societies would be governed. But Parliament, too, had demonstrated a willingness to overthrow their fundamental laws. The colonists liked being "in but not of" England, so to speak—especially Massachusetts, where the Puritans regarded themselves as a uniquely chosen people. Although culturally English, and entitled to the legal rights of Englishmen, New Englanders aimed to establish a model community—a new kind of political institution with power to implement rules based on their religious precepts. Now, it seemed, God had vindicated their principles by destroying the monarchy—and making Cromwell leave them more or less alone.

That did not last. In 1651, Parliament adopted the first Navigation Act, a law banning colonial trade with the Dutch and prohibiting ships from carrying goods to and from America unless manned by Englishmen.[55] That marked the first step toward a centralization of the colonial system. Where Americans had previously been regulated in a haphazard fashion, largely free to buy and sell as they chose, now they would have their trade restricted to serve London's desires—a direct betrayal of the Treaty of Jamestown and a radical intrusion on the autonomy assured by Massachusetts's charter. Colonists protested that this violated their rights as Englishmen, but Parliament ignored them. They therefore resorted to smuggling, often with the connivance of sympathetic local governments. When one sea captain captured a vessel trading in violation of the act and brought it into court for condemnation, the Massachusetts legislature rebuked him instead, for doing "such actings (without the consent or allowance of authority here established)," which "[tended] highly to the infringing of our liberties [and] discouraging of trade."[56]

It was understandable that colonists resented the Navigation Acts. They were intended to bar colonists from sending goods directly to European countries or their colonies. This increased prices considerably and, if followed, would have made it extremely difficult to obtain items needed in America because many of them were not made in England. Americans saw little sense in transporting their products there so that they could be loaded onto another ship and carried to their destinations, instead of going straight to market. But the acts enriched merchants and sailors in England by creating make-work jobs and outlawing competition.

The mercantilist system, combined with low demand for certain goods in the New World, also created trade imbalances for Americans. This would not have been a problem if they could have paid for purchases in cash, but England also restricted the availability of coin in the colonies and barred Americans from printing their own currency. That made it hard to pay debts or taxes, and it compelled colonists to resort to barter or to imperfect substitutes for money. It also encouraged piracy because pirates brought much-needed coin into Massachusetts. (English visitors were shocked to find that pirates were welcomed in the colony and treated like respectable citizens.[57]) Smuggling flourished, of course; the profits were so high, the need so great, and the chances of capture so small.

Historians still debate how much smuggling really went on, but according to one estimate, Boston alone traded directly with European ports, ignoring the requirement that ships stop in England first, to the tune of £60,000 per year.[58] Illicit trade became so common that colonists ceased to regard it as illicit. "Social acceptance of smuggling went beyond a begrudging acceptance of economic necessity," writes one scholar. "Smuggling may have been illegal, but it didn't make you a criminal."[59] Nevertheless, the penalty of forfeiture was severe. American merchants were forced to hazard tremendous losses just to engage in legitimate competition that Parliament banned for the sole purpose of fattening wallets in England.

Cromwell died in 1658, and his son Richard failed to keep a ruling coalition together. Two years later, the revolution collapsed, and Parliament decided to bring back the monarchy. The following April, King Charles's son was crowned Charles II. After only 11 years, the English republic was gone. Intellectuals had said all along that the people could not govern themselves, and the failure of the Commonwealth seemed to prove them right: The people had to be ruled by kings or they would destroy themselves. (A century later, opponents of American independence would nickname the Patriots "Oliverians," likening the colonial rebellion to Cromwell's failed experiment.)

The new king was a hedonist and a philanderer, as much a spendthrift as his father and grandfather, and soon at odds with Parliament just as they had been. Needing money for war with the Dutch, he sought increased taxes and licensing fees for businesses. The burden on ordinary Englishmen grew heavy. Diarist Anthony Wood noted in 1662 that Londoners had adopted a new saying: "The bishops get all, the courtiers spend all, the citizens pay all, the king neglects all, and the devils take all."[60]

Equally troubling were rising religious tensions. Charles II flirted incessantly with Catholicism and was married to a Catholic. His brother, James, was openly Catholic—and he was next in line for the throne. Could a Catholic serve as king of a Protestant nation and lead an established Protestant church? Englishmen would have been even more alarmed had they known that in 1669, Charles told James he was considering converting himself, and had even entered into a secret agreement with Louis XIV, the Catholic king of France, whereby he promised to convert in exchange for payment. Although Charles never officially joined the Catholic Church, Louis began sending him money—and if things continued, that might enable Charles to rule without having to ask Parliament for funds.[61]

When Parliament tried to enforce the Church of England's authority on the people—by imposing licensing requirements on preachers, for example—Charles issued an order of religious toleration that shielded non-Anglicans. Puritans did not see this as a benefit, however. Toleration seemed to them like a ruse for reintroducing Catholicism into the country. In theocratic Massachusetts, of course, religious toleration was anathema. Many religious refugees to the New World saw England's Anglican-versus-Catholic fight as proof that Americans should curse both sides of the mother country's political and religious crises, and keep their heads down.

But England was not about to leave the New World alone. Charles grew increasingly irritated at the Americans' defiance of the Navigation Act and other customs and import regulations. For decades, the colonists protested against—or blatantly ignored—these restrictions, considering them, in the words of Virginia's Governor Berkeley, "mighty and destructive."[62] The 1651 Navigation Act, and follow-up Navigation Acts in 1660, 1663, and 1673, barred foreign ships from doing business in America (with some exceptions) and prohibited anyone other than English subjects from "exercis[ing] the trade or occupation of a merchant or factor" in the colonies.[63] The acts also forbade colonists from selling sugar, tobacco, cotton, and other goods except to England or other English colonies, and required that crews on English ships be at least 75 percent English. Other laws required that European products bound to or from America be shipped first to England, to be inspected, taxed, and reloaded, before being sent on to their destinations. These laws were backed by severe penalties, including forfeiture of the vessels and cargoes. "We cannot add to our plantation any commodity that grows out of it," complained Berkeley, "for it is not lawful for us to carry a pipe stave or a barrel of corn to any place in Europe out of the king's dominions. If this were for his Majesty's service or the good of his subjects, we should not repine, whatever our sufferings are for it, but on my soul, it is contrary to both."[64] Yet Charles was determined to get money however he could, and that meant the goal of his colonial policy was to find ways to make America enrich the mother country—not to help refugee Englishmen build self-governing societies in the hinterlands.

Americans responded by simply disregarding the Navigation Acts, shipping products directly to European ports and smuggling things they needed into the country. Mighty as England's navy might be, it could hardly catch them all, and North America's vast landscape helped black marketeers evade detection on land. With no professional bureaucracy to enforce the acts—a person could buy a job as a customs inspector, then sell it again—the customs service was riddled with bribery, incompetence, and negligence. Colonial legislatures, meanwhile, were so hostile to trade restrictions that they were willing to indulge violators. Massachusetts in particular, already the major entrepôt in the colonies, resisted the Navigation Acts, arguing that Parliament had no authority to impose them. "We conceive the [colonial charter] . . . to be the first and main foundation of our civil polity," the colony's General Court told the king in 1661. That charter said it, not Parliament, had "full power and authority, both legislative and executive, for the government of all the people here."[65] Statements like these only exacerbated Charles's hostility toward representative government, which seemed to him a menace rather than an essential component of the constitution. Finally, the frustrated king decided to act.

In 1674, Virginians proposed a new colonial charter, which, among other things, would guarantee the authority of the House of Burgesses. Charles refused; the charter he gave them pointedly declined to accept the necessity of an elected legislature.[66] (Governors, however, continued to convene meetings of the assembly, which over the next century often resisted what they viewed as abusive acts by royal leaders.) Then, he looked for ways to discipline Massachusetts. He began by dispatching an agent named Edward Randolph to Boston to investigate that colony's refusal to follow the Navigation Acts.

Randolph was scandalized by what he found. He reported back that when he complained to the governor about disregard of the Navigation Acts, the response was, "That the laws made by your Majesty and your parliament oblige them in nothing but what consists with the interest of that colony; that the legislative power is and abides in them solely to act and make laws, by virtue of a charter from your Majesty's royal father, and that all matters in difference are to be concluded by their final determination, without any appeal to your Majesty, and that your Majesty ought not to retrench their liberties."[67] When the Crown officially demanded to know why Massachusetts was disobeying the acts, the colonial assembly answered that it had not realized it was supposed to follow them. "According to the usual sayings of the learned in the law," it said, Parliament's statutes "do not reach America" because Americans were "not represented in Parliament."[68] Assuring London that it had never meant to cause trouble, the colonial assembly added a promise to "repeal with all convenient speed" any colonial laws contrary to those of England. Still, it added, the assembly would *not* agree to undo any laws "such as the repealing whereof will make us renounce the professed cause of our first coming hither."[69]

ROYAL DICTATORSHIP REACHES AMERICA

Massachusetts's audacious tone was probably inspired by news that Charles II was facing substantial opposition back in England. In 1673, when Parliament convened again after one of its periodic quarrels with the monarch, the king found himself confronted by forceful resistance in the person of Anthony Ashley Cooper, the Earl of Shaftesbury. The 52-year-old Shaftesbury had been born into a family with important political connections and had started his career by serving in the army of Charles I, before joining Cromwell's government. Then he became disillusioned with Cromwell and favored the restoration of the monarchy. He entered the House of Lords after Charles II was crowned, and rose to the highest ranks of government, even being named lord chancellor. But he gradually grew suspicious that Charles was planning to reintroduce Catholicism in England, and he eventually became the king's foremost political opponent. Gathering a retinue of dissenting intellectuals that included a young physician and philosopher named John Locke, Shaftesbury emerged as leader of the opposition party, known as the Whigs. Supporters of the monarchy were called Tories.

To forestall the possibility of a Catholic king, Protestant Whigs oversaw the enactment of the Test Act, a law that barred Catholics from important government roles. The act was primarily aimed at Charles's openly Catholic brother, because Whigs feared that James's potential succession gave agents of France or other Catholic powers an incentive to assassinate Charles. That fear was reinforced when documents were leaked in 1678 revealing that James had written to Louis XIV, soliciting money for some unspecified "mighty work."[70] Whigs began looking for potential alternative candidates to take the throne instead of James, or for legal ways to restrain his powers if he did become king. Charles fought back, however, and in 1681, he ordered Shaftesbury imprisoned in the Tower of London on charges of treason.

Yet when Shaftesbury was put on trial, the jury acquitted him. As soon as he was freed, he fled to safety in Holland, which was ruled by the Protestant monarchs William of Orange and his wife Mary (James's daughter). He took his protégé Locke with him. Meanwhile, the acquittal stiffened the spines of Charles's opponents, both in England and America. Shortly after Massachusetts insolently declared that it wasn't bound by British laws, Virginia's House of Burgesses sent the king a petition objecting to his veto of their legislation and to his assertion of power to decide legal appeals, which they thought belonged in their own courts. Overriding the colonial judiciary had "grievous and ruinous" consequences, they said, because it was "exceedingly difficult for a case of intricacy" to be relitigated in England. And depriving them of the right to make their own laws was unfair, considering that even "the most inconsiderable corporations within your Majesty's kingdom" enjoyed authority to make their own rules and policies. Why should Virginians, "out of whose labors and industry in the manufacture of our staple commodity tobacco accrues to your Majesty's revenue more than twice so much as we ourselves have for such our labor," be denied the same right?—especially given that the king had repeatedly promised to respect the lawmaking authority of the colony's legislature.[71]

Charles was unmoved. On the contrary, he saw all corporations as obstacles to his authority, and he was determined to make them into his puppets or destroy them. He started in England, filing lawsuits called quo warranto proceedings against several corporations, including cities, which were (and still are) a type of corporation. In 1684, he won a quo warranto against London, stripping it of its corporate status and taking the city directly under his personal rule. Then he brought similar cases against 39 professional guilds (that era's analogue to labor unions, which were also governed by charters). Dissolving their charters gave Charles power to choose their leaders, thus drawing every trade from haberdashers to weavers under his control.[72]

He then turned his attention to the New England colonies. Overriding the autonomy promised in their charters, he dissolved the governments of Connecticut, Massachusetts, New Hampshire, and Rhode Island, and combined them—along with part of Maine—into a single unit called the Dominion of New England. The Dominion would be placed under the command of a dictator named Edmund Andros, who would rule this vast territory without the involvement of bothersome elected legislatures. Andros would hold the executive, legislative, and judicial powers, and ensure that England's mercantilist trade restrictions were enforced.

He largely succeeded—and the predictable consequence was economic depression.[73] Yet as businesses closed for lack of inventory and ships began to lay idle, Andros turned to another assignment: establishing the system of quitrent landownership in America. Quitrent was a legal concept that reached back to the feudal age's system of "land tenures"—the categories of ownership recognized by the law, which often required landholders to provide the king with labor, including a certain amount of time in military service, to retain their property. Quitrent did not require personal service, but it did require the payment of an annual fee, thus resembling today's property taxes. Quitrent had never been established in New England, however, and Puritans viewed it with contempt. They thought they held their land free of any feudal tenures—through what lawyers called "allodial" ownership, instead—and that they could not be required to pay the government to keep it. Andros considered that attitude seditious. "Either you are subjects," he told New Englanders who objected, "or you are rebels."[74]

Andros had to engage in some clever scheming to introduce quitrent, however. He began insisting that any new deeds include a quitrent requirement, and then found ways to force landowners to obtain new deeds. Because many American title documents contained some technical defect, it was usually easy to find some pretext to require an owner to take out new paperwork for his existing holdings—which came along with a quitrent. Andros announced that many existing titles were simply invalid—especially purchases from Indians, or common land (property held and used collectively by citizens of towns)—and therefore that their owners needed new quitrent deeds. When the people of Lynn, Massachusetts, objected to being forced to request a new deed for the town's commons, on the grounds that they had bought it from the Naumkeag tribe and the colonial legislature had confirmed their ownership, Andros went even further: The town itself had never been properly chartered, he said, and therefore they did not own the commons. (Eventually, the townspeople were forced to accept a quitrent.)

Through actions like this, wrote one historian, "the seeds of hatred for the 'foreign government' which would take from them their means of livelihood were sown."[75] To clamp down on protests, Andros outlawed the traditional New England town meeting. He demanded that Puritans take oaths on the Bible (which they considered a sin), and forced them to let the Anglicans, who had not yet built their own church, use the Puritan meetinghouse for services. Most of all, he imposed taxes throughout the Dominion without legislative approval, raising tariffs on rum and other merchandise, and imposing a capitation tax on all men older than 16. Taxes on wine were doubled, and taxes on horses and cattle quintupled, all without a vote of the people's representatives.[76] When Reverend John Wise gave an impassioned speech encouraging parishioners to declare that "no taxes should be levied upon the subjects without the consent of the assembly chosen by the freeholders," Andros had him arrested, and when Wise asserted that the Magna Carta protected his rights, the reply came: "Mr. Wise, you have no more privileges left you than not to be sold for slaves."[77]

In what had once been Rhode Island, Andros and his followers regulated everything from the licensing of taverns to the building of courthouses—and imposed new taxes on Rhode Islanders to pay for it all. When he declared Connecticut's charter void, Nutmeggers were outraged—as well they might be, for their charter promised that they would "have and enjoy all liberties and immunities of free and natural subjects . . . as if they and every one of them were born within the realm of England."[78] Hoping to protect this promise against Andros's seizure, they hid the charter in a hollow oak tree in Hartford. That accomplished nothing, except to make the oak a cherished symbol of Connecticut. The colony was absorbed into the Dominion.

But probably the most striking instance of the Stuarts' attack on colonial legislatures came in New York. That colony was not originally part of the Dominion, but was instead governed by Charles's brother James, who ascended to the throne as James II after Charles died suddenly in 1685. New York had also long resisted the application of the Navigation Acts and customs duties; in fact, when the colony's governor left for a visit to England in 1680, New Yorkers ceased to follow the acts and arrested a customs collector named William Dyer who tried to enforce them, charging him with treason on the grounds that the customs duties violated the Magna Carta. Dyer was released, but colonial leaders followed up with a petition to the king that said that the incident proved their need for a colonial legislature.[79] A year later, a tax lawsuit set off a controversy when the defendant demanded to know by what authority the tax had been levied, since no colonial lawmakers had approved it.[80]

King James at first seemed willing to listen to New Yorkers' complaints. He sent a new governor to the colony with instructions to convene an elected assembly. That legislature immediately passed a "Charter of Liberties"—a proposed colonial charter listing the traditional rights of English law that New Yorkers expected to be observed. Among other things, it asserted that "the supreme legislative authority under his Majesty . . . shall forever be and reside in a Governor, Council, and the people met in General Assembly."[81] Yet although James appeared open to the proposal, the Charter of Liberties soon landed in bureaucratic limbo, and never received his royal assent. Instead, New York, and also New Jersey, were soon added to the Dominion.

Virginians fared little better. In 1672, they had asked London to exempt them from the Navigation Acts. That request was refused, of course. Although King Charles II did not add Virginia to the Dominion, he instead implemented a stringent new principle called Poynings's Law, named for a statute that the English governor of Ireland, Sir Edward Poynings, imposed on that country in the 15th century. Poynings's Law would restrict Virginia's assembly to adopting only laws written by the king and his ministers. Any bills the Burgesses might propose on their own would have to get royal preapproval.[82] Unanimous Virginian opposition managed to defeat the Poynings's Law scheme, but London did impose a hefty tax on tobacco exports, and directed that the money be sent to the king, not to the colony's own treasury.[83] In the Stuarts' eyes, Virginia, like all the colonies, existed solely to enrich the Crown.

THERE IS A TOTAL REVOLUTION AT HOME

Charles's death in 1685 meant that the moment Protestant Whigs had dreaded for so long now came to pass. The authoritarian Catholic James II was now King of England and head of the Anglican Church. And he proved every bit as dictatorial as feared. Not only did he persist in the Dominion scheme, and in the policy of direct royal control over corporations and colonies, but he also claimed that the monarch had a "dispensing power" that allowed him to exempt people from obeying the law. He needed this power to evade the Test Act that Parliament had adopted to bar Catholics from high government offices. When the archbishop of Canterbury petitioned against his efforts to undermine the Test Act, James had him arrested for sedition.

Protestants were right to be alarmed. Like his brother, James was being paid hundreds of thousands of livres by France's King Louis XIV—and six months after James's coronation, Louis revoked the Edict of Nantes, which for almost a century had provided toleration for Protestants (called Huguenots) in Catholic France. Protestant schools and churches closed across that country; Protestant gatherings for worship were made punishable by banishment, death, and forfeiture; and anybody who refused to convert to Catholicism was ordered to leave France within two weeks.[84] The result was a flood of refugees to England, Holland, and America. (Alexander Hamilton, John Jay, Paul Revere, and George Washington's wife, Martha, were descended from Huguenot exiles.) English Whigs saw little reason to doubt that James might do likewise, fully Catholicizing the Anglican church and outlawing all dissent.

The crisis came in late 1687, when news broke that James's queen was pregnant. With a new heir on the way, Protestants had no time to lose: The king must be overthrown, or England would be utterly transformed. When summer arrived, a group of English noblemen invited William and Mary, the Protestant leaders of Holland, to invade the country. The couple obliged. In November 1688, William led a massive invasion force into southwestern England, and James, realizing he was outnumbered, fled the country. He tried briefly to raise an army in Ireland and wrote to the pope, asking for help in exchange for bringing England and the "several colonies . . . in America" into the Catholic fold, but support quickly evaporated, and James remained in exile in France for the rest of his life.[85] Mary joined William in England in February 1689—arriving on the same vessel as John Locke, who had been living in Holland since escaping with Shaftesbury five years before. In April 1689, Parliament formally pronounced William and Mary king and queen of England.

James, the legislators declared, had abandoned the throne by fleeing the country. That left Parliament free to name a new monarch. It also meant Parliament could impose demands in exchange for the Crown. Accordingly, it required William and Mary to sign a new Bill of Rights, acknowledging that the Stuarts had abused their power, and promising not to do likewise. James's overthrow, called the "Glorious" or "Bloodless Revolution," ended a generation of conflict over the nature of England's political system. It ensured Protestant rule and established a bedrock constitutional principle: Parliament, not the king, is sovereign—*it* is the nation's supreme power, with authority even to break and remake the monarchy itself.

At the time, this principle seemed like an immense step forward for liberty. After all, it undergirded the new Bill of Rights, which, among other things, forbade the levying of taxes except by Parliament, protected the free election of members of the House of Commons, guaranteed the right to bear arms and the right to petition the king, and prohibited "the pretended power of dispensing with laws or the execution of laws by regal authority."[86] Yet in the decades that followed, the idea that Parliament holds such broad power would mutate into the notion that Parliament's rule is literally *absolute*, unlimited by historical tradition, written promises, or principles of justice. A theory of parliamentary sovereignty that began as a guarantee of freedom from royal oppression evolved into the theory of Parliamentary Supremacy, whereby Westminster held total power over the people and individual rights were viewed as mere permissions the legislature could grant or revoke at will. Had England simply exchanged one form of tyranny for another?

When word of the Glorious Revolution arrived in America, that question was far in the future. News of James's overthrow began trickling into Boston in February 1689. "There is a total revolution at home," wrote a friend to one of Andros's deputies. "Pray keep this private."[87] But New Englanders soon learned the truth, and on April 18, they staged a rebellion of their own. Seizing guns from the colony's storehouses, they arrested Andros and officially denounced him for "rais[ing] taxes as he pleased," governing "without any liberty for an assembly," conscripting "all persons residing in the territory as occasion shall serve," "extort[ing] [fees] from every one upon all occasions, without any rules but those of [his] own insatiable avarice," and telling New Englanders that they "were all slaves and the only difference between them and slaves is their not being bought and sold."[88] Then, the colonists voted for a new assembly as they had before the Dominion was created. In a letter to the new King William, they explained that they "humbly conceive[d]" that they had the right to make their own laws—a right gained "by prescription, which, according to [Sir Edward Coke] is one of those ways whereby corporations or bodies politic do commence and are established."[89]

Andros's arrest inspired other colonies to act. What followed was like a dress rehearsal for 1776. Rhode Islanders jailed one of Andros's deputies and resumed operating under their old system.

Connecticut held elections for a new legislature. In New York, a militia captain led a group of rebels to chase Andros's subordinate out of the colony. Marylanders went further—staging an armed uprising that ended the rule of Lord Baltimore, the colony's autocratic proprietor, and pledging the election of a colonial assembly. As for Virginia, the Burgesses had already sent James II a petition complaining about the "many unlawful and unwarrantable fees and other duties" and the "unlawful, unprecedented, and very burdensome and grievous ways and devices" that had "been of late made use of to the great impoverishing, vexing, and utter undoing of many of his Majesty's subjects."[90] James was overthrown before a reply could be sent—and the new king proved more receptive than James would have been. William appointed a new governor who soothed tensions, and all talk of Poynings's Law ceased. Parliament officially abolished the Dominion in 1691, and the colonial legislatures opened once again.[91]

These events were still vivid memories during John Adams's and Thomas Jefferson's lifetimes. When Adams went on a business trip in 1769, for example, he met with a client named Mr. Fisk, an elderly resident "born in the very month of the revolution under Sir Edmund Andros."[92] Another time he met a centenarian named Mrs. Poke. "She remembers the reign of King Charles II, James II, William and Mary. She remembers King James's wars, etc.," he wrote in his diary.[93] Like other Massachusetts men, Adams was proud of his colony's autonomy, however imperfect it may be, and often invoked the example of the Andros uprising.

In the century after the Glorious Revolution, many Americans viewed the crises of the 17th century as proof that they answered to the king, not to Parliament. Time and again, monarchs had taken the colonies under their own personal management, and although that often vexed them, it at least made clear that they were subject to *royal* authority, not that of the Lords and Commons. Instead, their own legislatures were miniature parliaments, with power to adopt laws that served local needs. True, they were required to pay "due respect" to Parliament when legislating, but "due respect" was not subordination.

Unfortunately, as is often true of revolutions, the Glorious Revolution of 1689 left many questions unanswered. For one thing, William and Mary turned out not to be as friendly toward assertions of colonial self-rule as Americans might have hoped. On the contrary, London repeatedly answered their appeals by holding that colonists were *not* the legal equals of Englishmen. In May 1691, when the restored New York legislature took the bold step of again adopting the Charter of Liberties and sending it to London for the new king's approval, William said no. Marylanders were bolder. Over the next decade, they repeatedly proclaimed similar declarations of rights, requesting royal confirmation—and these, too, were rejected, time and again. Colonists were informed that even the protections of the new Habeas Corpus Act did not extend to them. In 1691, as if to underscore their servile position, William appointed a new governor for Virginia: none other than Sir Edmund Andros, the same ruler whose management of the Dominion had proven so disastrous. Released from prison and forgiven by the Crown, he had grown no fonder of elected legislatures. He soon quarreled with the House of Burgesses, the local clergy, and even other governors, and eventually was recalled to England, where he died in 1714.

Not only did colonists find the new monarchs unreceptive, but Parliament also continued to pass laws restricting the New World's commerce. In fact, between the reigns of Charles II and George III, it adopted nearly 100 laws regulating trade with the colonies. But although Americans complained about these economic burdens—and often flouted them—they never disputed their constitutionality.[94] Much as Americans might not like Britain's trade restrictions, the principle now seemed settled that Parliament could regulate imperial commerce, even if it could not legislate for the colonists in other respects. This settlement would prove a major obstacle for Whigs of Adams and Jefferson's day, when Tories demanded to know how Americans could concede Parliament's authority to regulate their trade while objecting to its power to tax them.

In some ways, the Stuart years led to more liberalization: Most notably, Massachusetts's Puritan theocrats never regained the political monopoly they had enjoyed before Charles II forced them to accept religious toleration. But the Stuart theory of royal power was clearly at an end. William and Mary's coronation promised a reign of peace under the principle that monarchs are not above the law. Still, the problem remained: What exactly was the nature of this law?

— CHAPTER 3 —

NATURAL LAW AND SALUTARY NEGLECT

The Law of Nature says to individuals,
"Thou shalt do no injury to thy fellow;
thou shall do to him as thou wouldst be done by."
Nations being moral persons, the Law of Nations says to each of them,
"Thou shall do no injury to thy neighbor—
thou shalt do to him as thou wouldst be done by."
—John Adams[1]

As with any revolution, the uprising of 1689 required a theoretical justification. By what *right* could William and Mary and their supporters claim to rule? It wasn't enough to forcibly seize control; there must be some reason why their reign was worthy of recognition, and why they exercised not only power, but authority. Two Whig thinkers who devoted their energies to that subject would prove enormously influential for Americans in Jefferson and Adams's day. But what first inspired Algernon Sidney and John Locke to write their famous books—Sidney's *Discourses Concerning Government* and Locke's *Two Treatises of Civil Government*—were the arguments of one man, an obscure scholar named Sir Robert Filmer, who claimed that government is best seen as a kind of family, with kings serving as fathers and their subjects as children.

PATRIARCHA AND *LEVIATHAN*

Filmer was a man of widely varied interests, and in some ways remarkably advanced in his thinking.[2] Born in 1588, the son of a successful judge, he attended Trinity College, Cambridge, before studying law at

John Locke's Two Treatises of Civil Government *proved indispensable to the American Revolution almost a century after the book was published.*

Lincoln's Inn, one of England's most prominent law schools. He followed in his father's footsteps and became a justice of the peace. On the side, he wrote philosophical commentaries on Plato and Aristotle. In 1653, he became one of the first intellectual defenders of the practice of lending money at interest—something the Christian world considered a sin—anticipating the arguments Voltaire and Montesquieu would offer almost a century later. He also published a remarkable book attacking the idea of criminal prosecutions for witchcraft, which he thought represented hysteria and superstition and led to the abuse of women. He hoped science and reason would dispel such foolishness.

But sometime in the 1620s, Filmer began writing a book to defend the theory of absolute monarchy, making arguments that even by the standards of his day seemed primitive. Political society, he claimed, is effectively a large family with kings as the patriarchs. They have a right to rule not because of any kind of contract or agreement, as some philosophers believed, but because they are the heads of the national "household," a power they inherit from the biblical Adam. And because Adam enjoyed "absolute power of life and death, of peace and war, and the like," so modern kings, his heirs, "must of necessity be above the laws."[3]

When the English Civil War broke out, Filmer kept prudently quiet. Anti-monarchists searched his house for evidence of sedition, but could never prove him guilty of any crime, and he died peacefully in 1653. It was not until 1680, as efforts to exclude James II from the throne were reaching fever pitch, that his book defending monarchy was finally published under the title *Patriarcha*.

Algernon Sidney found *Patriarcha* laughable. Born in 1622, into a noble family that included the poet Philip Sidney, he grew up with a strong poetic streak of his own; his first philosophical work was an essay on love.[4] But he was no dandy. He was plainspoken and brave almost to a fault. "He had indeed studied the history of government in all its branches beyond any man I ever knew," wrote one acquaintance. "A man of most extraordinary courage . . . but of a rough and boisterous temper that could not bear contradiction, but would give foul language upon it."[5]

Sidney joined the army in 1644 to fight against Charles I, and was elected to Parliament a year later, but was forced into retirement when he denounced Cromwell as a dictator who had betrayed the

Algernon Sidney's Discourses Concerning Government *remained unpublished when he was executed in 1683 for plotting against the king.*

revolution. During the brief period between Cromwell's death and the restoration of the monarchy, he returned to government to serve as a diplomat in Scandinavia, and was therefore conveniently out of the country when Charles II took the throne. When Charles offered to let him come home if he renounced his revolutionary beliefs, Sidney refused. He lived in exile for two decades.

In 1677, however, he returned to England to deal with a lawsuit, and once back, he could not resist joining the Whig opposition to King Charles. He became involved in a conspiracy known as the Rye House Plot, the details of which remain unclear, but which apparently aimed to assassinate both the monarch and his brother on their way home from a horse race. The Earl of Shaftesbury and his deputy John Locke were also implicated, and when the plan was foiled, they managed to evade arrest by fleeing to Holland. Sidney was not so lucky. He was jailed and charged with treason.

He had not yet finished his *Discourses Concerning Government*, but the manuscript was read into the record as proof of his subversiveness. "It was a very large pamphlet and took a great deal of time," wrote one person who attended the hearing. "The substance . . . was that the sovereign power was in the people, and that the king was but only the people's trustee, and that if [the king disregarded the law] . . . he might depose himself, and if he would not they might by force depose him, and chastise him for misgovernment."[6] Sidney refused to take back these heresies. "We live in an age that makes truth pass for treason," he told the court.[7] He was convicted and beheaded in December 1683, going to his death, in the words of another witness, as "a perfect monarch-hater."[8]

Not until a dozen years later, with the Stuarts overthrown and a new king crowned, was the book finally published. Refuting Filmer's claim that royal authority is "patriarchal" in nature, Sidney argued that governments are more like a contract than a family. Kings are not inherently marked out to rule the people in the same way that parents are inherently suited to govern their children. In fact, "no man by birth has a right above another, or can have any, unless by the concession of those who are concerned."[9] Because "no government is imposed upon men by God or nature," people must be presumptively free unless and until some rational justification is given for ruling over them.[10]

This was not a matter of faith, but a logically provable fact. "Liberty being only an exemption from the dominion of another, the question ought not to be, how a nation can come to be free, but how a man comes to have a dominion over it; for till the right of dominion be proved and justified, liberty subsists as arising from the nature and being of a man."[11] More simply, Sidney believed that any person who asserts the right to rule others bears the burden of justifying that claim—as opposed to Filmer's view that people are presumptively unfree, until given freedom by the government. If Filmer was right, people "are born under the necessity of perpetual slavery," eking out their freedom by begging tyrants to toss them a few crumbs of independence.[12] But where Filmer scorned "the desire of liberty"—which according to his reading of the Bible was "the first cause of the fall of man"[13]—Sidney held that freedom is "the gift of God and nature," and one to which all people were entitled.[14]

Sidney did not focus his attacks exclusively on Filmer, however. He also set out to refute the arguments of another defender of royal absolutism: Thomas Hobbes. Born in 1588 and educated at Oxford, Hobbes was an ingenious physicist and philosopher whose 1651 book *Leviathan* offered a radical new theory of politics, shorn of any appeal to Christian teachings. He had worked as a tutor and accountant for a wealthy family before becoming fascinated with geometry and logic at the age of 40. A devoted monarchist, he fled to France when the English Civil War began, and got a job teaching mathematics to England's exiled crown prince Charles. There he remained until after the war, writing his book on politics in hopes of vindicating the principle of absolute monarchy on terms as rigorously logical as the mathematics he so admired.

Where Filmer based his patriarchal theory of monarchism on the Bible, Hobbes seems to have rejected virtually everything recognizable as Christianity.[15] He also had no interest in Filmer's claim that royal power is patriarchal rather than contractual—that kings are like fathers, not hired agents. On the contrary, Hobbes accepted the idea that government is a kind of contract whereby the people consent to be ruled in exchange for protection. But where others saw this as proof of mankind's fundamental freedom, Hobbes's version of the contract was extraordinarily stringent, and left subjects essentially helpless against the all-powerful state.

Hobbes began by imagining a society with no government. In this so-called state of nature, the only "law" applying to human beings would be the rule of self-preservation. That law, however, contains no principle of *justice*—it contemplates a crude scramble for survival at any cost. Justice, Hobbes thought, can only come into existence when government creates it: "Where there is no common power, there is no law; where no law, no injustice."[16] Nor can there be any rights in the state of nature, since these, too, exist only when enforced by the ruler. "The notions of right and wrong, justice and injustice, have . . . no place" before the existence of political authority. "There [can] be no propriety, no dominion, no mine and thine distinct; but only that to be every man's that he can get, and for so long as he can keep it."[17]

Because such a life would be miserable ("nasty, brutish, and short"[18]), the people eventually sicken of the state of nature and come together to choose a ruler who can establish peace and order. This is the social contract that gives the king his authority. But in joining that contract, the people hand over to the king all their rights, surrendering themselves entirely into his protection. This empowers him to establish justice, but it also means the people can have no rights against the king himself. Such things would be illogical; since the king's dictates are the very source and meaning of justice and rights, those dictates can never be unjust or violate rights. Consequently, the people have no way to enforce the social contract against the king. They can only trust that he will abide by that agreement and treat them fairly. And because the people have surrendered all their rights to him, their descendants are also bound to accept his absolute control, and that of his heirs.

Hobbes's disdain for Christianity put him on the fringe of intellectual respectability in his day, but his book did offer an intellectually rigorous case for absolutism—a remarkable blend of the "liberal" notions of government by consent and the domination and despotism advocated by the Stuart monarchs. And its apparent logic made it a formidable challenge for Whigs to refute. Sidney, however, zeroed in on Hobbes's claim that the people can give the king total power through a contract. That was absurd, he thought. The ruler cannot be the sole judge of whether he is fulfilling the agreement that entitles him to rule, because "the liberty of perjury cannot be a privilege annexed to crowns."[19] If Hobbes's social contract was a promise, it only made sense to expect the king to honor it. "If none will accept a crown unless they may do what they please," wrote Sidney, with his characteristic snark, "the people must bear the misfortune of being obliged to govern themselves."[20]

JOHN LOCKE

Sidney may have been a brash monarch-hater, but the same could not be said of John Locke. A retiring, scholarly man, Locke was born in 1632 and was a teenager when Charles I was executed. In fact, he was attending school just down the street when the king was beheaded. After graduating from Oxford with a medical degree, he would have happily spent his life in scholarly pursuits, but his plans were interrupted in 1666, when the Whig leader Lord Shaftesbury consulted him about an abscess he had developed in his side. Locke is said to have saved Shaftesbury's life by surgically installing a metal tube in his flesh to drain the fluid. True or not, it earned him Shaftesbury's lifelong gratitude.[21]

The earl hired him as his personal physician, but also as an all-purpose intellectual. Their conversations about philosophy led Locke to write his enormously influential *Essay Concerning Human Understanding*. Being the foremost Whig opponent to Charles II, it was natural that Shaftesbury also would discuss political questions with Locke. And in 1679, the earl seems to have inspired his protégé to start writing a philosophical critique of absolute monarchy. The result was a long manuscript refuting Filmer and Hobbes and setting forth a carefully argued case for individual liberty, limited constitutional government, and the right to rebel against tyranny.

Such writings were seditious, of course, and Locke kept them hidden, even disguising his manuscript under the sly false title *De Morbo Gallico*, "the French disease"—a medical term for syphilis that could also mean political despotism (which Whigs considered a characteristically French malady). That was wise. The king's officers searched Shaftesbury's and Locke's papers while investigating the Rye House Plot, and they did not find the evidence they were looking for. Still, during their search, a large part of Locke's manuscript was destroyed—probably more than half—with only the beginning and ending saved. These sections were eventually released as two separate (and noticeably incomplete) essays, instead of the single work Locke had planned.

First published anonymously in 1690—indeed, Locke never admitted his authorship—the *Two Treatises* opened with a furious attack on Filmer's notion that political power is paternal in nature. On that point, Locke agreed with Hobbes: Government resembles a contract more than a family. But where Hobbes thought the state of nature was a chaos in which no rules of justice apply, Locke thought it was governed by an implicit law: the law of reason, which prescribes rules of justice even in the state of nature. That means that political authority, to be legitimate, must satisfy universally applicable, objective standards of validity. *Political authority* may be a man-made artifact—a rationally chosen institution, unlike the rule of parents over families—but *rights* are not.

In other words, Hobbes thought government *creates* the principles of right and wrong by establishing and enforcing rules—but Locke argued that morality prescribes rules even before the people establish government, and these rules limit the kinds of governments they can form and the kinds of things those governments may do: "The state of nature has a law of nature to govern it, which obliges every one: and reason, which is that law, teaches all mankind, who will but consult it, that being all equal and independent, no one ought to harm another."[22]

What is the source of this natural law? Locke answered by quoting the 16th-century Anglican priest Richard Hooker. "Those things which are equal, must needs all have one measure," wrote Hooker. "If I cannot but wish to receive good, even as much at every man's hands, as any man can wish unto his own soul, how should I look to have any part of my desire herein satisfied, unless myself be careful to satisfy the like desire, which is undoubtedly in other men, being of one and the same nature?"[23] If these words seem familiar, that's because they describe the Golden Rule: Do unto others as you would have them do unto you. The Golden Rule is the basic "rule of reason" governing the state of nature. It applies to everyone, because all are equally responsible for their own survival and each properly seeks to persist and thrive. It also implies other rules—don't murder; don't steal; don't break promises—none of which exist by the say-so of any authority figure. Hobbes's idea that government *creates* justice was therefore a fallacy; instead, it merely *enforces* justice, a justice that has its roots in each person's natural state as a self-directed being. The king implements the basic rules of social life. He does not generate them. And because the people cannot give government more power than they themselves possess, the government they create must obey the rules, too. The people cannot write a social compact that empowers it to do wrong in their name.

Locke also argued that Hobbes's theory that the people give the king absolute power by signing the social contract is logically impossible.[24] Human beings do not actually own themselves *outright,* he contended; they are ultimately God's property, since He creates human beings. True, He gives people the right to use themselves during their lifetimes (a type of ownership lawyers call a "life estate"), but on death, ownership of their selves reverts to God. So just as the Golden Rule limits how people ought to treat each other, so moral law also limits what they may rightfully do to themselves. They may not commit suicide, for example—long recognized as a sin—and cannot sell themselves into slavery, because that would be stealing from God. Hobbes's idea that people effectively turn over their lives in toto to the king is therefore absurd.[25]

As for Filmer, Locke easily dispatched his argument that freedom is only a gift from the king, who inherits the power God gave Adam. Filmer's theory, he said, "[is that] 'we are all born slaves, and we must continue so'; there is no remedy for it; life and thralldom we entered into together, and can never be quit of the one till we part with the other."[26] This was plainly irrational. After all, God also gave Adam the right to eat all the animals in Eden—did that mean kings could *consume* their subjects, too? If the answer was no, royal authority must have *some* limits—limits that derive from the principles of logic and human nature. Even assuming Filmer was right that royal power is analogous to Adam's authority, it was still clear that this power was finite. Had not God Himself punished Adam for a transgression?

The bottom line was simple: The real reason people create governments is to specify and protect the rights they already have by virtue of their humanity. Since people own themselves (at least in "life estate"), they also own their own abilities and intelligence, and that means they have the right to the fruits of their own labors. The purpose of life is to pursue and obtain happiness—to thrive—but to achieve that, people must provide for themselves and be assured of safety in doing so. All government, therefore, exists to protect property—both the property people have in themselves, and the property they acquire in the world. True, people will be tempted to steal and commit violence, and that's why they create government: to secure, not to create, their rights. Kings and Parliaments must *respect* the rights they are bound to *protect*. That same principle, of course, also justifies changing or even overthrowing the government if it becomes inimical to those rights.

By the time John Adams began studying for the bar in the 1750s, the natural law theories that Sidney, Locke, and their allies advanced had become ubiquitous in America, found in everything from newspaper columns to Sunday sermons, and particularly in the extraordinarily popular *Cato's Letters*, originally published in the 1720s by British intellectuals Thomas Gordon and John Trenchard. Combining those ideas with the writings of Sir Edward Coke and other Whigs, 18th-century American lawyers came to see rights as divided into "natural" and "acquired"—with the former being those rights people are entitled to by virtue of their humanity, and the latter being those derived from historical practice and legal precedent. Natural law thus served as an intellectual foundation for more legalistic and technical debates over the scope of acquired rights. Because common-law lawyers ground their arguments less on general assertions of political theory—which can sometimes be vague and contentious—than on specific precedents and statutes, attorneys like Adams would initially respond to the conflict with Britain by focusing on questions of law and policy rather than on the philosophical matters Sidney and Locke addressed. But as the conflict deepened, they found themselves increasingly forced to resort to natural law arguments instead. When it finally became clear that their defense of acquired rights was proving fruitless in the face of the doctrine of Parliamentary Supremacy, they abandoned their claims to the protections of the British law, and rested their case on the ideas of human rights that Sidney and Locke had expressed so well.

THE DOMINION, BUT NOT THE REALM

If Americans hoped that the Glorious Revolution would halt London's meddling with their economy, they were quickly disappointed. In the years after William and Mary were crowned, Parliament pursued even more aggressive restrictions on colonial commerce, intended to benefit favored industries—what would today be called cronyism. In 1698, it adopted a law forbidding colonists from exporting wool, even to other colonies, so that Britain's own wool producers would not have to face competition.[27] In 1732, it adopted the Hat and Felt Act, restricting the manufacturing of hats in America, and limiting the number of employees hatmakers could hire, to protect English businesses from having to compete.[28] A year later, it adopted the Molasses Act, taxing imported sugar so that colonists would be forced to buy from British producers.[29] And in 1750, it passed the Iron Act, barring them from manufacturing retail goods out of iron; instead, they had to ship the metal to Britain to be made into finished products and then sent back, doubling the transportation expenses.[30] Meanwhile, the Navigation Acts still outlawed direct trade between the colonies and Europe, requiring instead that most items be transported to England first, to be unloaded and then reloaded for shipment to their final destinations. As historian David Ramsay observed, these laws imposed "immense" costs, but "served no other purpose but to procure jobs for British coopers and wharfringers."[31]

London also imposed other intrusive demands on the colonies, which Americans often resisted. In 1728, the king appointed a governor for Massachusetts and ordered the legislature to pay him an annual salary. The representatives refused, on the grounds that they could not be commanded to impose a tax. In the 1750s, when Virginia's royal governor sought to require a fee for certain legal documents, that colony's legislature objected that the fee was actually a tax, and therefore could only be imposed by the people's representatives. British subjects, wrote Virginia legislator Richard Bland in a pamphlet opposing the fee, "are so secured by law that they cannot be deprived of the least part of their property without their own consent. Upon this principle of law, the liberty and property of every person who has the felicity to live under a British government is founded."[32]

But while colonists resisted efforts to impose *taxes* on them, they raised no constitutional objections to the Navigation Acts and other limits on trade. Part of the reason was that British enforcement of these rules was relatively lax during the first two-thirds of the 18th century. During this period—which historians, borrowing a phrase from the British statesman Edmund Burke, call the era of "salutary neglect"—the Board of Trade that King William had created was largely distracted by bureaucratic wrangling and infighting. No armies were deployed to colonial cities to ensure compliance with trade restrictions, and the Royal Navy was not tasked with enforcement. Americans were largely left alone. When Parliament tried to change this, William resisted, unwilling to cede his power over America to the Lords and Commons.

Meanwhile, few Englishmen cared enough about Massachusetts smugglers or Virginia tobacco farmers to spend much time on the matter. Anyone showing such initiative was quickly dissuaded by the Americans' prickly attitude. In 1737, North Carolina's royal governor counseled another politician about attempts to control the colonists: "I imagined like most young beginners that with a little assistance from home, I should be able to make a mighty change in the face of affairs," he wrote. "But a little experience of the people, and reflection on the situation of things at home has absolutely cured me of this mistake."[33] "Governors," observed one Pennsylvania Quaker, "seldom . . . consider anything further than how to sit easy."[34]

What Americans found "salutary" about this neglect was that it enabled (or forced) them to develop the habits of self-government. Their forebears in the previous century had cherished their autonomy from Britain, and during this period, colonists became even more accustomed to viewing themselves as separate. They stopped even asking London to formally acknowledge their colonial legislatures as permanent lawmaking bodies. Instead, as historian Jack Greene writes, they pursued an "unstated strategy" of obtaining legitimacy for their own legislatures "through practice and usage that with the implicit acquiescence of [the British government] would gradually acquire the sanction of custom."[35]

The home government seemed to play along. It never tried to govern the colonies without the involvement of the provincial legislatures, and it never imposed direct taxes. Instead, it submitted requisitions, politely asking American lawmakers to gather revenues and forward them to England. Although Parliament imposed duties on imports, these were generally viewed as trade regulations, not as ways to raise revenue. So as the years passed, Americans gradually grew comfortable with the idea that their legislatures were miniature parliaments, and either bit their tongues about the Navigation Acts or ignored them entirely.

The end of the Seven Years' (or French and Indian) War, however, brought about a fundamental change in the unwritten constitution. British leaders began embracing the theory of Parliamentary Supremacy, arguing that the Lords and Commons were not just lawmaking bodies, but the holders of absolute, limitless power throughout the empire.[36] Legal thinkers such as William Blackstone and his mentor, Chief Justice Mansfield, considered it only logical that if Parliament could create a new king and queen, as it had done with William and Mary, it must have total authority over everything. British law was whatever it commanded. No customary legal protections, or written promises in statutes, charters, or bills of rights, could restrain it.

American Whigs did not agree. They preferred the theory of Prescriptive Right, which viewed the law not as will, but as reason; not as authority, but as *rightful* authority. Under this doctrine, no claim to absolute or arbitrary rule was justifiable, whether by the king or by Parliament. Instead, law was a limit on power, a limit that has its sources in abstract principles discovered over time through reason, custom, tradition, and important documents such as the Magna Carta, court decisions, and bills of rights. These writings were not themselves the law, but *evidence of* the law; they helped reveal the principles that together make up the unwritten agreement between the ruler and the ruled.[37] The principle "no taxation without representation," for example, was part of the constitution, not because it was created by any particular document, but because it could be derived from traditional practice, was reflected in charters such as the Magna Carta, and was consistent with reason and justice.

Under English law, "representation" or "consent" were not literal, and they could take different forms; many people in England could not vote in parliamentary elections, for example, but were still viewed as having "consented" by accepting the advantages of the law. That, however, made it all the more essential that the people be vigilant in voicing opposition to any government action that might interfere with their rights, lest their inaction be interpreted as acquiescence. As Pennsylvania Whig John Dickinson explained during a debate over Parliament's power to tax Americans:

> Some persons may imagine the sums to be raised by [the tax] are but small, and therefore may be inclined to acquiesce under it. A conduct more dangerous to freedom . . . can never be adopted. Nothing is wanted at home but a precedent, the force of which shall be established, by the tacit submission of the colonies. . . . If the Parliament succeeds in this attempt, other statutes will impose other duties. Instead of taxing ourselves as we have been accustomed to do from the first settlement of these provinces, all our useful taxes will be converted into Parliamentary taxes on our importations, and thus the Parliament will levy upon us such sums of money as they choose to take, without any other limitation than their pleasure.[38]

In other words, because the empire's unwritten constitution was a matter of habit and tradition, it was crucial to resist any "innovation" that threatened to upset the political balance. Failure to object would be interpreted as a concession.

Of course, if the Lords and Commons wielded the kind of supreme, irresistible power that the Parliamentary Supremacy theory supposed, none of that mattered. No customary rights, no long-standing practices, and no objection, however vociferous, could truly protect the people. "A resolution of the British Parliament can at any time set aside all the charters that have ever been granted," wrote one Massachusetts Loyalist in the 1760s.[39] This meant the contract between ruler and ruled could be unilaterally altered by a legislature thousands of miles away, subject to no limit beyond its own will. As the prime minister, Lord North, declared: "Parliament themselves are the only persons to judge the propriety of their measures."[40] In other words, the law, far from being a protection against arbitrary power, was merely an *instance* of arbitrary power.

The conflict between these two theories—Parliamentary Supremacy and Prescriptive Right—might have remained purely academic were it not for the dramatic events that followed Britain's 1763 victory in the Seven Years' War. The nation suddenly found itself controlling an enormous expanse of North American territory, including French Quebec and Spanish Florida, as well as expansive portions of India. It was, in fact, the largest empire since the days of ancient Rome. Yet her constitutional scheme had never been intended for such a thing. And fitting this new domain into a system that evolved for a small island nation would prove a formidable task—eventually an impossible one.

To advocates of Parliamentary Supremacy, the answer was clear: force the whole empire to accept the Lords and Commons as supreme. But adherents of Prescriptive Right, such as John Adams, were not prepared to accept that. "[Britain] has, after 150 years, discovered a defect in her government," he wrote in 1775. That defect was that she had "let colonies be planted, until they are become numerous and important, without ever having wisdom enough to concert a plan for their government consistent with her own welfare." The solution "ought to be supplied by some just and reasonable means, that is, by the consent of the colonies." But instead, Britain decided "to make [the colonies] submit to the authority of Parliament, and because there is no principle of law or justice or reason by which she can effect it, therefore she will [accomplish it with] war and conquest."[41]

Americans had a different vision. To their way of thinking, the colonies were constitutionally bound to the throne—since they operated under royal charters—but not to Parliament, which did not represent them. They pointed to a 1608 court decision called *Calvin's Case*, in which Sir Edward Coke had ruled that Ireland stood within the king's "dominion," and therefore within his governing authority—but outside the "realm" of England, and therefore beyond Parliament's reach.[42] In the years before the revolution, Adams, Jefferson, and other Whigs would cite *Calvin's Case* to show that the colonies, too, were subject to the king's rule, but not

Parliament's. That explained why they were not protected by statutes Parliament passed, such as the Habeas Corpus Act, and why, in 1696, King William had thwarted Parliament's effort to create a council with authority over the colonies, instead establishing the Board of Trade, appointed entirely by himself.[43] It also explained why Americans were ruled over by governors chosen by the king, and by colonial legislatures convened by order of those governors. "Allegiance to the king, and obedience to Parliament are founded on very different principles," wrote future Supreme Court Justice James Wilson in 1774. "The former is bounded on protection; the latter on representation."[44] Because Americans claimed royal protection, they owed allegiance to the monarch. But because they were not represented in Parliament, they owed it no obedience.

In London, this sounded like dangerous nonsense. The government's leaders considered the principle of Parliamentary Supremacy crucial because it alone prevented any repeat of the Stuarts' abuses. Parliament had to have absolute power, because otherwise the king might claim authority *not* derived from, or limited by, the people. That would divide political power between the representatives and an autonomous monarch, who might rule as a tyrant—just what had happened under the Stuarts. If colonial legislatures had their own inherent power to tax and spend, they might someday send tax money directly to the king, or even proclaim some other person to be monarch, thus risking civil war—and Parliament could do nothing about it.[45] The only safeguard against that fate was for Parliament to wield total authority throughout the empire.

Little wonder that London lawmakers clung with such tenacity to the principle that they were supreme over colonial legislatures as well as the Crown. But that also meant advocates of Parliamentary Supremacy were caught in a philosophical trap: They could never back down from any quarrel about their authority without risking the empire's very existence. Parliament's powers could expand, but never contract. It was all or nothing. Here were two not only different, but contrary, views of the British constitution—as incompatible as the pro- and anti-slavery views of the US Constitution a century later.

What in England seemed like a necessary safeguard against the king—Parliamentary Supremacy—looked to Americans like a recipe for oppression. It has sometimes been thought strange that in the run-up to independence, Americans typically focused their complaints against Parliament but not the king—directing their political protests only at his supposedly wicked advisers. But this is not actually surprising, because by that time, one overriding lesson had been drilled into colonists' heads for a century and a half: Their connection to Britain was through the king, not Parliament. He was the fountainhead of British authority over them. That was why they were not represented in Parliament and were, instead, governed by administrators chosen by the Crown. It was natural, therefore, that they would look to him for protection from what they viewed as Parliament's unjustified interference—and that they would ask why, if they did not enjoy the benefits of Parliament's laws, they should have to shoulder the burdens it imposed. These considerations all reinforced their view, expressed as far back as the 1620s, that they stood in the same position with respect to Britain as Commonwealth nations such as Canada do today: The king was their head of state, but when it came to making laws, they looked to their own legislatures.

And yet for decades, Parliament had passed scores of laws governing the colonies—on subjects from the cutting of pine trees to the establishment of post offices—and the colonists had raised few constitutional objections. The most obvious examples were the Navigation Acts. Under the "prescription" principle, their acquiescence seemed to prove Parliament's right to legislate. In the decade before 1776, Adams, Jefferson, and their colleagues would labor to explain why those laws did not disprove their contention that American legislative power resided in the colonial legislatures, not Westminster.

THE NEW POLICY

The constitutional crisis that separated America from Britain began not with the bitter, but the sweet—specifically, with taxes on sugar. The problem with the 1764 Sugar Act, however, was not its financial burden, but the change it represented in the nature and scope of Parliament's power. As to the *nature* of that power, the question was whether it was limited by colonial charters and constitutional principles that had evolved over the centuries, or whether it was so vast that it superseded even the ancient constitution. As to the *scope* of that power, the question was whether London lawmakers could govern the colonies directly, and if so, where its reach ended.

American Whigs pointed to eight decades of "salutary neglect" as well as 17th-century disputes over their charters to show that Britain had accepted a significant degree of colonial autonomy. Although Parliament had imposed duties on imports and exports to maintain mercantilist trade policies, it had never imposed a tax *within* the colonies for purposes of raising revenue. This, the colonists argued, proved that no such power existed. But in London, distinctions between duties and "internal" taxes, or between regulations of trade and taxation for revenue, seemed like childish wordplay.

In 1733, Parliament had adopted the Molasses Act, the first tax it ever imposed directly on the colonies.[46] The act applied to sugar imported from the French West Indies, and it was adopted at the behest of British sugar exporters who sought to prevent Americans from buying molasses from the Dutch or French. It aroused little opposition at the time—for an ironic reason: Its tax was so high that it was effectively a total ban, so Americans mostly resorted to smuggling or bribery to get around it.[47] Still, some colonies did speak out against the Molasses Act—only to encounter a withering reaction that was a hint of the rupture to come. When the House of Commons began debating the bill on March 8, 1733, a spokesman for the colony of Rhode Island submitted a petition opposing it on the grounds that such taxation violated the colony's charter. But instead of considering the argument, the members began debating whether to accept the petition in the first place.[48] The colony's missive was "very extraordinary," said Sir William Yonge, a poet and philanthropist then halfway through his four-decade career in the House. To suggest that the Lords and Commons lacked power to tax the colonies was so impertinent that "if there were no other reason for our not receiving their petition, I should on this single account be against giving leave to bring it up."[49]

Yonge's view prevailed: The House refused even to read the Rhode Islanders' complaints. In the years that followed, the Commons repeatedly shut its ears to colonial protests. Americans naturally viewed this as a violation of the English Bill of Rights, which specified that "it is the right of the subjects to petition the king," and that Parliaments existed "for redress of all grievances." But to Parliamentarians, accepting such petitions would mean implicitly conceding that their power *could be* limited—an idea they refused to countenance.

There was another reason the Molasses Act failed to arouse widespread outrage. Even during the debate over whether to receive Rhode Island's petition, members of the Commons themselves disagreed over whether the act actually imposed taxes to begin with, or just regulated imperial commerce. If Rhode Islanders objected to Parliamentary taxation, said one member, then they were misunderstanding the bill. "The tax to be thereby laid on, is no tax upon them, but a tax which is to be laid upon the French," because by banning French imports, it "encourage[d]" Britain's own sugar producers.[50] That was a dubious economic argument, but it was an important constitutional argument, because Americans generally conceded that Westminster *did* have authority to regulate imperial trade, including through import duties. In that mercantilist era, most Britons thought *some* authority *had* to superintend the empire's commerce, and it was logical for Parliament to perform that task.

Revenue-raising taxes were another matter, though. Unlike trade restrictions, they were intended to fund government operations. That meant tax money was held in trust by representatives answerable to the citizenry. If Parliament could generate income by taxing a distinct segment of the people—those residing far from the capital—and then spend the proceeds at will, it could operate without answering to those who paid. That violated the bedrock principle of British constitutionalism—embraced by Whig and Tory alike—that subjects could not be justly taxed without their consent or that of their representatives. In which category did the Molasses Act belong? It wasn't clear. These considerations blunted American opposition to the act. Colonists might not like having their trade restricted, but it wasn't unconstitutional.

They came to regret their complacency. Three decades later, when the act expired, Parliament pointed to it as a precedent to support their authority to tax Americans. With the end of the Seven

Years' War, and the nation facing a crushing load of debt, the new prime minister, George Grenville, saw the act as an opportunity. He would exploit that precedent as grounds for drawing revenue from the colonies. He knew that would be controversial; when a similar proposal had been aired in the 1750s, Benjamin Franklin himself had warned that it "would probably give extreme dissatisfaction" in America, because "compelling the colonies to pay money without their consent"—that is, without representation in Westminster—"would be rather like raising contributions in an enemy's country than taxing of Englishmen for their own benefit . . . treating them as a conquered people, and not as true British subjects."[51] Parliament had listened, then. But not this time.

A 50-year-old graduate of Eton and Oxford, Grenville belonged to a prestigious family; his four brothers all served in Parliament, and his sister married William Pitt, one of England's most renowned politicians (and who, incidentally, opposed taxing the colonies). Wordy, dogmatic, jealous, arrogant, and stubborn, he was not a man to be dissuaded by ignorant provincials.[52] His first step was a crackdown on smuggling, using the military to enforce trade restrictions in North America, and enforcing those restrictions in juryless vice-admiralty courts, where contraband was confiscated and sold to profit the informants and judges. His second step was the Sugar Act, which substantially reduced the financial penalty imposed by the old Molasses Act.[53] It may seem ironic that this *reduction* would spark colonial anger—Grenville certainly thought so—but the reason was that reducing the cost made it no longer a prohibition. Instead, it transformed the Molasses Act's trade limit, which Americans found annoying but constitutional, into the Sugar Act's revenue-generating tax (or "internal tax") that would collect funds for London.

Then Grenville took his third step: a set of resolutions proposing a new, unambiguously direct tax. "It may be proper," the resolutions declared, "to charge certain stamp duties in the said colonies."[54] Now, Parliament's plans became clear. It was abandoning the old "requisition" system, whereby it asked the colonists for funds, and was taking the money, instead.

A stamp tax was an old device. First used in England in 1694, it required people to pay for stamps and then affix the stamps to certain documents in order for those documents to be considered legally valid.[55] The stamp system was convenient and easy to administer, but it also removed any uncertainty: Parliament was asserting authority to extract funds from Americans. It was, as Grenville's deputy Thomas Whately wrote in a pamphlet published in 1765, "chosen, not only with a view to the revenue which [it] will produce, but for other, and in my opinion, greater political purposes."[56] Those "greater purposes" included ensuring that the colonies were subservient to London's plans.

The Sugar Act alone was enough to alarm some colonists. Rhode Island Governor Stephen Hopkins called it "a manifest violation of the [the Americans'] just and long-enjoyed rights." People who can be "taxed at pleasure by others" are not free, he wrote, because they "cannot possibly have any property, can have nothing to be called their own." As for Grenville's assertion that London was taxing them for their own good—to pay for the military to "protect" colonists—that was offensive. "To take the money of the Americans, which they want continually to use in their trade, and lay it up for their defense at a thousand leagues distance from them when the enemies they have to fear are in their own neighborhood, has not the greatest probability of friendship or of prudence."[57]

Massachusetts's Samuel Adams was equally offended. Chairing a committee of Boston's town meeting, he demanded to know where Parliament got the authority to impose the Sugar Act:

> This, we apprehend, annihilates our charter right to govern and tax ourselves—it strikes at our British privileges, which as we have never forfeited them, we hold in common with our fellow subjects who are natives of Britain. If taxes are laid upon us in any shape without our having a legal representation where they are laid, are we not reduced from the character of free subjects to the miserable state of tributary slaves?[58]

The members of the Massachusetts House of Representatives agreed, and they sent the Commons a petition protesting the act, particularly the provisions involving vice-admiralty courts, which took away "one of the most valuable of English liberties, trial by juries."[59] In fact, nine colonies ultimately submitted protests, arguing against unconstitutional revenue-raising taxes and unjust enforcement in vice-admiralty courts.[60] But, as with the Molasses Act 30 years before, Parliament refused even to read these petitions. "This country have the right to impose an inland tax [on the colonies]," Grenville told the Commons. "The very sovereignty of this kingdom depends on it."[61]

In Rhode Island, resistance to the Sugar Act even became violent: When one customs collector learned that a ship called the *Polly* was preparing to sail without complying with the act, he seized it and ordered it secured under guard while he looked for a crew to sail her back to Newport. A local mob stole the molasses and wrecked the ship before the customs collector returned. (The owner then arranged to have the sheriff arrest the collector and charge *him* with £3,000 in damages to the ship.[62]) Yet most Americans accepted the act. Notwithstanding Adams's and Hopkins's arguments, it seemed to most of them to be merely a continuation of the Molasses Act. Even Parliament seemed to view it as a regulation, not a tax. The act itself said it was designed to "improv[e] and secur[e] the [imperial] trade."[63] However problematic tariffs or import duties might be as a policy matter, they were still constitutional, because Westminster had regulated colonial commerce for more than a century. And because the act only taxed imports, not domestic products, it didn't look like an "internal" tax. Given this ambiguity, Americans mustered little outright opposition to the Sugar Act. The same would *not* be true of the Stamp Act.

THE STAMP ACT

The bill that became the 1765 Stamp Act was carefully designed as a test vehicle to establish a constitutional precedent. Because the constitution was understood with regard to custom and practice, Parliament's leaders recognized the importance of staking out their claims to authority. If they could successfully impose a tax, of even a small amount, that would help prove the constitutionality of doing so again going forward.

Therefore, although the Sugar Act had, at least arguably, been a mere regulation of commerce, the Stamp Act was an unmistakable attempt to directly tax the colonies. When introducing the bill in the Commons, Prime Minister Grenville made clear his intention to refute the "hint[s]" of those who denied London's power to impose taxes on Americans. "Mr. Grenville strongly urged not only the power but the right of Parliament to tax the colonies," according to one witness. "And hoped in God's name . . . that none would dare dispute their sovereignty."[64] He and his supporters explained in the ensuing debate that they thought Parliament had the supreme power to legislate for every aspect of the empire, and that the revenues the act would generate were less important than the precedent it would set.[65] "The House of Commons, say they, . . . is a part of the supreme and unlimited power of the nation," reported another person watching the discussions. "They say a power to tax is a necessary part of every supreme legislative authority, and if they have not that power over America, then they have none."[66]

Grenville faced some eloquent opponents, but they were hindered by their inability to settle on a persuasive constitutional theory. His brother-in-law, William Pitt, for example, argued that Parliament could *legislate* within the colonies in all respects, but could not *tax* them to generate revenue. Legislation and taxation were different, Pitt claimed, because taxation fell within the legal fiction of "voluntary gift and grant" and legislation did not. But while he was a brilliant speaker, and colonists embraced him as their champion, Pitt's obscure distinction persuaded few. Nor was another defender of colonial rights, Isaac Barré, any more successful. He ridiculed those who argued that the colonists should pay Britain back for the costs incurred during the war. "[Americans] protected by *your* arms?" he cried. "They have nobly taken up arms in *your* defense." Equally laughable was the idea that Britain had paid to create the colonies in the first place. "Children planted by your care? No! Your *oppressions* planted them in America. They fled from your tyranny. . . . They grew by your neglect. . . . [A]s soon as you began to care about them, that care was exercised in sending persons to rule over them . . . and to prey upon them." Barré told the House that the colonists were "truly loyal," but also "jealous" of their self-rule. Some called them England's children, he said, but it was more accurate to call them "sons of liberty."[67] Americans immediately embraced the term with delight.

Barré's powerful oratory changed no minds in Westminster, however. It seemed obvious that Parliament was the supreme imperial authority, and no historical precedent could stand in its way. And it only seemed fair that Americans help pay down the debts incurred by the Seven Years' War, since it had been fought for their benefit.

That argument infuriated Americans. They pointed out that the British government had also sent money and troops to foreign countries such as Prussia to aid in their military defense, and nobody thought that entitled Parliament to tax those countries. Why was it any different for Americans? Anyway, colonists had fought in the war, too—and in other British conflicts—and their legislatures had already paid what they could toward military protection. Parliament had even *refunded* money to the colonists, on the grounds that they had already paid more than they could afford.[68] To now accuse them of not paying their fair share was unjust and hypocritical. In any event, the taxes Britain was imposing were not intended solely for the defense of the 13 colonies, but were also for the defense of places like Canada, which competed economically against them. Why should they be forced to pay for that?

It was also unfair to call the war an "American" war. It had been an imperial war fought in France, Germany, Poland, and even India; North America had just been one theater of combat. And the war had actually served British interests; Americans had been forced to participate. "The people of America are chiefly farmers and planters," said Benjamin Franklin. "They were before in perfect peace with both French and Indians. . . . [T]he war, as it commenced for the defense of territories of the crown, the property of no American, and for the defense of a trade purely British, was really a British war—and yet the people of America made no scruple of contributing their utmost towards carrying it on."[69] It was wrong to characterize them as the ungrateful beneficiaries of Britain's sacrifice.

Colonists also argued that Americans were *already* being effectively taxed by the Navigation Acts. Those restrictions barred them from selling their products at market prices, and instead forced them to sell at a discount to Great Britain. That alone was equivalent to a tax, because it transferred wealth from Americans to the mother country. Americans couldn't even make their own hats or nails; they had to buy them from the British. To impose taxes on top of that meant essentially double taxation.

Even more galling was that at least some of Grenville's supporters did not actually want to use the revenues raised from taxation to pay for military security in America. Despite their pretenses, their true intention was to raise funds to be applied directly to the salaries of imperial officials stationed in the colonies. That, at least, was Massachusetts Governor Francis Bernard's goal. In his 1764 letters to London, he had argued that "there should be a certain and sufficient civil list laid upon perpetual funds for the support of all his Majesty's officers"—that is, a permanent bureaucracy controlled from London—"so that they may not be too much dependent upon the people."[70] In other words, Parliament should tax the colonists, and use the revenues to pay the salaries of the governor, judges, and customs inspectors, who could then manage the populace without being accountable to voters.

Even aside from the tax issue, the Stamp Act raised serious constitutional concerns. It worsened the objectionable provisions of the Sugar Act that deprived colonists of their right to jury trials by declaring that alleged violations could be tried either in the ordinary common-law courts or in the juryless vice-admiralty court based in Halifax. In England, violations of tax laws were tried before juries. But now, Parliament was discriminating against the colonists—depriving them and them alone of the right to a jury, by giving jurisdiction over colonial tax cases to non-common-law courts that had originally been created for the very different job of deciding cases involving ships at sea. "A customhouse officer may make a seizure in Georgia of goods ever so legally imported, and carry the trial to Halifax at fifteen hundred miles distance," complained Rhode Island's Stephen Hopkins. And even if the owner managed to win his case, "he may return to Georgia quite ruined and undone."[71]

The biggest problem with the Stamp Act was that it threatened to push aside the colonial legislatures entirely. For generations now, those assemblies were where colonial laws were made. But now, the Lords and Commons in Westminster were deliberately seeking to establish a precedent that would vindicate the theory of Parliamentary Supremacy. If that theory gained a foothold in British law, no individual rights would be safe. The stamp proposal was therefore a far greater threat than the import tariffs or the Navigation Acts. It represented an *innovation*—an attempt to overthrow the customs and traditions that made up the British constitution and to deprive colonists of rights they had enjoyed for over a century and a half. It was therefore critical that they not be viewed as acquiescing. If Parliament could get away with this, it could ignore the principles of consent and representation entirely, and govern the Americans like a conquered, captive populace rather than equal members of the empire. Their rights would be mere privileges that Westminster could revoke at will.

But on March 22, 1765, the British government approved the Stamp Act by an overwhelming vote—205 to 49 in the House of Commons and unanimously in the House of Lords. Beginning November 1, everything from newspapers to playing cards, as well as nearly all legal documents—mortgages, bills of lading for ships, permits to sell alcohol, licenses for attorneys to practice law—would have to be printed on paper bearing a special stamp as proof that the tax had been paid. The act, said Grenville's deputy Whately, deserved "the appellation of a great measure on account of the important point it establishes, the right of Parliament to lay an internal tax upon the colonies." Indeed, where the Sugar Act's language had been ambiguous—so that it straddled the line between revenue-raising tax and trade-regulating duty—the Stamp Act was carefully written to expressly declare that its purpose was to raise revenue. London was unmistakably asserting that it was the supreme controlling power in North America. "This," Whately predicted, "puts an end to all opposition to the principle."[72]

— CHAPTER 4 —

THE REVOLT AGAINST THE STAMP ACT

The English manifestly think mankind
and the world made for their use. Americans don't think so.
—John Adams[1]

In May 1765, six months before the Stamp Act was to go into effect, a young member of Virginia's House of Burgesses rose to introduce a set of resolutions protesting the act. Just turning 29 on the day he spoke, Patrick Henry was lean and blue-eyed, and wore a wig to conceal his premature baldness. His family was respectable, but not wealthy; his father was a college-educated Scottish immigrant who had served as a teacher and a justice of the peace. Patrick had worked as a storekeeper and bartender before becoming a lawyer. And although he had practiced law for only five years, he had already earned a reputation as a superb orator, thanks to his argument in a 1763 case challenging the constitutionality of King George III's veto of a Virginia law relating to the payment of debts. That case had won him enough acclaim to get him elected to the House, where he had taken his seat nine days earlier. Now, he poured his extraordinary eloquence into opposing the Stamp Act.

Henry had cleverly taken the opportunity of a day when many members had gone home, so few were present when he began speaking in favor of a motion that the House declare the Stamp Act unconstitutional. But those who were there got quite a show. Henry had a habit of stooping slightly, then gradually rising to full height, even standing on his tiptoes when carried away by the passion of a speech. Now, he was growing impassioned, indeed. "The General Assembly

Painter John Singleton Copley chose to portray Samuel Adams at the moment when, a day after the Boston Massacre, he demanded that Governor Thomas Hutchinson order British troops out of Boston. (Hutchinson refused.)

of this colony," he proclaimed, "have the *only and sole exclusive* right and power to lay taxes and impositions upon the inhabitants."[2]

Word of Henry's speech quickly circulated through Williamsburg, and a crowd began gathering in the Capitol building to watch. Among the faces was a 22-year-old law student named Thomas Jefferson, then living just down the street with his teacher, the celebrated lawyer George Wythe. Jefferson had probably learned of Henry's motion from Wythe himself, who was also a member of the House and who also opposed the Stamp Act. Wythe, however, was less brazen about it than Henry. A few months earlier, he had joined with other legislators to draft three separate protests, addressed to the king and each house of Parliament. "[We] entreat your Majesty," they told George III, "to protect your people of this colony in the enjoyment of their ancient and inestimable right of being governed by such laws respecting their internal polity and taxation as are derived from their own consent . . . a right which as men, and descendants of Britons, they have ever quietly possessed since first by royal permission and encouragement they left the mother kingdom."[3] But London had ignored those messages, as well as similar pleas from other colonies. And now that the act had passed, Henry was taking a far more aggressive step.

Virginians, he said, had emigrated to North America with all their natural and traditional rights, including the right not to be taxed except by their own representatives. For Parliament to disregard that autonomy was an act of despotism. As his denunciations of London's actions became more intense, some of the older Burgesses, probably including Wythe, began trying to calm him down. Yet Henry's rhetoric only grew more heated. Soon, other members were shouting their disapproval. At last, he reached a climax. "Caesar had his Brutus!" he cried, "Charles the First, his Cromwell—and George the Third—" at this point his opponents interrupted, yelling "Treason! Treason!" Without hesitation, Henry called back, "—may [he] profit by their example!" When the cries continued, he was ready. "If *this* be treason," he roared, "make the most of it!"[4]

Just as James Otis's challenge to the writs of assistance in Massachusetts had sparked the awed enthusiasm of John Adams, so Patrick Henry's attack on the Stamp Act now inspired the young Jefferson. Decades later, he could still remember the goosebumps

Henry's boldness brought to all listeners. "He appeared to me to speak as Homer wrote."[5]

Wythe and other moderates in the House stood firm against Henry's resolutions, however, and managed to vote down the most drastic of them—the one asserting that Virginia's legislature had the "only and sole exclusive right" to impose taxes. The next day, when Henry abruptly left for home, the moderates even scrambled to find ways to repeal those resolutions that had passed. Again, Jefferson walked to the Capitol, and stood watching as one member—his highly respected cousin Peyton Randolph—ransacked the legislature's compendious library for some precedent that would enable the House to expunge Henry's resolutions from the official journal. At last Randolph found one, and the House rescinded the resolutions—an indication that most Virginians were not yet prepared for a direct showdown with the mother country.

It made little difference, though. As Henry traveled through the countryside, he distributed copies of his original resolutions, leading newspaper editors to think they had been adopted in full. Soon, they were reprinted up and down the coast, and Americans north and south began applauding the Virginians for taking a bolder stand against the Stamp Act's constitutionality than they actually had.

THE STAMP ACT REACHES BOSTON

John Adams was enjoying the summer of 1765. Approaching his 30th birthday, he and Abigail had just welcomed their first child, a daughter they named Abigail, but called Nabby. His legal career was taking off, and he loved participating in the prestigious Sodalitas club, where he and the colony's other top lawyers exchanged scholarly papers and conversed about legal theory. He was not particularly interested in politics, but he could not help but follow the controversy over the Stamp Act, particularly as his idol James Otis and cousin Samuel Adams began organizing opposition to it.

When news of the act first reached the colony, Otis drafted a petition to Parliament urging the Commons to reject the bill as unconstitutional. Employing the same forceful language he had used two years earlier in his pamphlet *The Rights of the Colonies Asserted and Proved*, the petition he wrote denounced not only parliamentary taxation, but the vice-admiralty courts and the writs of assistance, too. Yet just as Patrick Henry found many Virginians reluctant to challenge the mother country, Otis also met with powerful opposition when he turned in his draft. Specifically, he ran into the colony's lieutenant governor, Thomas Hutchinson.

Fourteen years older than Otis, Hutchinson was a member of one of Massachusetts's most distinguished families. He was a superb scholar and writer, but sensitive about his lack of legal education—a serious handicap for a man who became chief justice of the colony in 1760. He was a skilled politician, however, adept at nepotism and at avoiding principled stands that might later come back to haunt him. He amassed many official titles, some simultaneously, serving in the House for several years, and even becoming Speaker, before being appointed to the Governor's Council and then chief justice and lieutenant governor. Those jobs he did not acquire for himself he typically obtained for relatives.

Otis and Hutchinson could not have been more unalike. Conniving, rather than principled, shrewd rather than idealistic, Hutchinson was, in his biographer's words, "bland, constrained, realistic, unromantic, ambitious, and acquisitive," one of those men who thinks entirely in clichés, and considers himself pragmatic because he evades the moral dilemmas of his times.[6] In a word, he was banal. His sole unwavering belief was in Parliamentary Supremacy. "[The Whig doctrine that] no act of Parliament can deprive us of the liberties of men, citizens, and British subjects," he wrote, "[is just] big sounding words."[7] John Adams loathed him. "Rather too craving," he wrote in his diary.[8] "Very ambitious and avaricious."[9] "A vile serpent."[10] "His death in a natural way would have been a smile of providence upon the public, and . . . the most joyful news to me that I could have heard."[11]

Hutchinson agreed with Otis in opposing the Stamp Act, but on practical grounds, not as a matter of right. Trying to steer what he considered a strategic course, he wrote to friends in London that the colonists "claim a power of making law and a privilege of exemption from taxes except by their own representatives," and that he considered their concerns legitimate—but at the same time, he "readily acknowledge[d] that it is in the very nature of a colony they are to remain the appendage of the mother state." Still, he was sure Parliament would be magnanimous enough to refrain from "the exercise of certain powers. . . . It does not seem to be an unreasonable proposition, that the inhabitants of [this] colony are entitled to all the privileges they enjoyed in their mother country which will consist with their dependence upon it." Although he expressed confidence that "the wisdom and justice of a British Parliament" was such that it would always show "a tender regard" for "all rights natural and acquired of every subject," he conceded that it might decide "that the natural right of a colonist is not the same with the natural right of an inhabitant of Britain," and that "whatever opinion we have of our rights the Parliament must be the final judges."[12]

Otis's draft petition against the Stamp Act was, of course, far more direct than that, and when Hutchinson saw it, he immediately cautioned against what he considered its extreme language. He particularly objected to the use of the word "rights." That was impractical, he told Otis. Parliament would refuse to read such a petition.[13] For 10 days, the two men negotiated over the wording, finally compromising on the word "liberties," instead of "rights." "Your petitioners acknowledge with all gratitude the tenderness of the legislature of Great Britain of the *liberties* of the subjects in the colonies," the final version declared, "who have always judged by their representatives both of the way and manner in which internal taxes should be raised within their respective governments, and of the ability of the inhabitants to pay them."[14]

Hutchinson was proud of watering down Otis's language. The compromise petition, he boasted later, asserted that the colonists "enjoyed the liberties and privileges which English subjects claim, of being taxed by their representatives, but not as a right."[15] Otis, however, made sure to explain to the colony's agents in London what had really happened. In a letter accompanying the petition, he told the colony's unofficial representatives that although the House had been "induced" to use mild language "to avoid giving offense," the members still thought "the people of the colonies have undoubtedly by charter [the right] to tax themselves," and that Parliament's efforts to tax them "will deprive them of this right."[16]

None of this made any difference in the end. The Commons did read the Massachusetts protest, but passed the Stamp Act anyway.

Then Henry's Virginia Resolves appeared in the Boston newspapers, as did the petitions of other colonies. None of these employed the timorous language Hutchinson had so carefully and pragmatically insisted on. Otis, Samuel Adams, and other Whigs were humiliated to find that other Americans had been bolder in defending their rights than the notoriously defiant Bay Colony. It seemed that Hutchinson's excessive caution had undermined colonial unity. Perhaps if Massachusetts had insisted unapologetically on its rights, Parliament might have been persuaded to back down.

That was unfair—George Grenville and his colleagues would never have been dissuaded—but the experience taught many Americans that mealymouthed appeasement of the Lords and Commons would accomplish nothing. It also taught Massachusetts Whigs that Hutchinson's alleged pragmatism was foolhardy. A decade later, Adams mused in his diary about the "Machiavellian dissimulation" employed by men like Hutchinson who changed their opinions like the moon changes phases.[17] For him, as for many New Englanders, Chief Justice Hutchinson would become a permanent symbol of the temporizing attitude that compromises with the enemy, only to be devoured by the logic of justice and the inertia of events.

THE TRUST INSIDIOUSLY BETRAYED

Massachusetts Whigs were not about to give up, however. Otis and his fellow representative Samuel Adams now arranged for the House to dispatch messages to other colonial legislatures urging them to attend an intercolonial meeting where the Americans could fashion a united opposition to the Stamp Act. Nine colonies agreed, scheduling a convention to begin in New York that October, just a month before the act was to go into effect. Otis was selected to represent Massachusetts.

Meanwhile, John Adams was focusing on bigger things. He had started writing a paper for the Sodalitas club comparing the English common law with the legal systems of the medieval world. Given the intimidating title *A Dissertation on the Canon and Feudal Law*, and published in August 1765, it turned out to be more of a meditation—Adams called it a "rhapsody"—on the past and future of freedom.[18] For centuries, he argued, Europe had been mired in tyranny and ignorance as a result of two overlapping forces: feudal legal doctrines—especially the rules of land ownership, such as quitrent, by which property was said to be held through the king's favor—and the obscure mysticism of Christian canon law, which used hocus-pocus to bewilder the populace and make them obey. In the 17th century, Adams claimed, these two forces had been overthrown by the self-reliant Protestant founders of New England.

Rejecting the "servile dependencies" of the Old World, they had asserted "that government [is] a plain, simple, intelligible thing founded in nature and reason and quite comprehensible by common sense."[19] When they fled England for the American wilderness, they brought with them an individualistic, down-to-earth realism, which they bequeathed to their descendants in the form of thrift, candor, skepticism, and protectiveness toward their rights. Unawed by government's obscure and pretentious ceremonies, they also had taught their children that "rulers are no more than attorneys, agents, and trustees for the people, and if the cause, the interest, and [the] trust is insidiously betrayed or wantonly trifled away, the people have a right to revoke the authority that they themselves have deputed, and to constitute abler and better agents."[20]

Economist Deirdre McCloskey has referred to the social transformation Adams was describing as the rise of "bourgeois values"—the emergence of a culture rooted in the experience of commerce and trade rather than in the religious or martial ethics of feudal or aristocratic societies.[21] Where the latter prioritized such warlike virtues as honor, courage, and disdain for labor, the merchant class of 18th-century New England focused more on commercial virtues, such as trustworthiness, moderation, prudence, thrift, and responsibility. This gradual transformation had already been noticed by writers such Montesquieu and Voltaire, who argued that trade tends to break down nationalistic and religious prejudices. And by the 1760s, the change was so pronounced that Boston, once capital of the Puritan "New Jerusalem," had become one of the commercial centers of British America—a place where bankers, merchants, and even smugglers were considered respectable.

One of the most remarkable characteristics of New England's revolutionaries was that although they cherished the moral teachings of the ancient Romans and Christians, they wedded those ideals to the entrepreneurial virtues of productivity and exchange. Colonists saw work as ennobling, and financial success through diligence and the smart application of one's abilities as well deserved. One reason they resented taxation so deeply, and defended private property so fiercely, was that their culture prized self-reliance and the conquest of nature—that is, the pursuit of happiness—and scorned those who lived at the expense of others. They tended to be stiff-necked, and disliked taking or giving orders. In 1777, when Prussian General Friedrich Wilhelm von Steuben took charge of drilling colonial troops, he expressed wonder at the way the Americans' temperament differed from that of Europeans. A German or French commander, wrote von Steuben, could "say to [a] soldier 'Do this, and he does it'; but I am obliged to say 'This is the reason why you ought to do that,' and then he does it."[22]

Adams considered this a kind of maturity. In New Englanders, the "love of power" that all people feel, which sometimes drives people to seek military glory, had mellowed so that they "aspire[d] to independency" instead—not political independence (at least, not yet), but personal independence, obtained by peaceful social and commercial pursuits and secured by laws that preserved individual rights. In short, Americans were growing up. The only thing holding them back now was that they were too "cautious and diffident" about asserting their rights against colonial rulers.

The *Dissertation* reflected Adams's lifelong fascination with the connection between politics and culture, but it ended on a far more practical note. The "timidity" he worried about was being exploited at that moment by political leaders in Boston and Britain who preached a doctrine of deference and subservience in the face of government power and viewed the very word "rights" as "offensive." "We have been told," Adams wrote, with a glance at Thomas Hutchinson, "that 'the king in his ministry and Parliament will not endure to hear Americans talk of their rights.'"[23] But weren't those who said such things actually insulting Parliament, by portraying the mother country "as deaf to the cries of her children?" Echoing Patrick Henry's speech in Virginia, Adams closed with a desire that "the same great spirit that once gave Caesar such a warm reception [and] . . . severed the head of Charles the first from his body" would prove itself "still alive and warm" in Boston.[24]

I WOULD THEY WERE EVEN CUT OFF WHICH TROUBLE YOU

By the time this essay appeared in print, John's cousin Samuel had been hard at work organizing public opposition to the Stamp Act. His efforts proved fruitful on August 14, only two days after the first installment of the *Dissertation* was published, when an effigy appeared hanging from a limb on a tree beside Boston Common. Pinned to its arm was a note: "What greater joy did New England see / Than a stampman hanging on a tree?"[25] It quickly began drawing a crowd. When one observer asked Samuel who had hung it there, he answered with a straight face that he didn't know.

The dummy swinging from the tree was no idle threat. Boston was not only a merchant capital, it was also a busy seaport teeming with sailors, pirates, and gangsters, and home to a "mob" legendary for its violence. Every year on November 5—Guy Fawkes Day, or "Pope's Day"—gangs from the city's north and south ends would celebrate with raucous festivities that regularly degenerated into large-scale street fights. But the mob could also explode over perceived injustices, as they had two decades earlier, when an effort to "impress" a crew of sailors into service touched off the worst riots the city had ever seen.

Impressment was an ancient English practice whereby naval commanders could seize civilians and conscript them on the spot to serve on navy vessels. It was not just sailors who were liable to be impressed; fishermen or local boaters who knew the geography of American rivers could also be arrested and forced to help navigate ships. This legalized kidnapping was often a thuggish business—press-gangs frequently beat men with clubs, got them drunk, and dragged them unconscious aboard vessels, or simply forged their signatures on enlistment documents. If violent abduction were not bad enough, the Royal Navy was a brutal institution, with only primitive sanitation and medical care. Discipline was maintained by whipping. Some 75 percent of impressed men died within two years of conscription, the typical victim being not a random bystander, but a well-trained "able seaman" with the skills to enjoy a lucrative career in the merchant service, and therefore good reason to avoid the military life.[26] Residents of port cities dreaded their fathers, brothers, or husbands being snatched onto a ship and never seen again.

After the Glorious Revolution, when wars broke out between the British, French, and Dutch, the number of sailors impressed into the British Navy skyrocketed, totaling perhaps 250,000 over the course of the 18th century.[27] Colonials were therefore relieved when Parliament exempted them from impressment in 1707, with a law called "An Act for the Encouragement of Trade to America."[28] Four decades later, it reinforced that act with "An Act for the Better Encouragement of the Trade of His Majesty's Sugar Colonies in America," which extended the exemption to residents of the West Indies.[29] Yet British naval commanders frequently ignored those laws and impressed Americans into service anyway. Political leaders backed them up, claiming that the 1707 ban had only been temporary and was now expired (although it included no express time limit).

Impressment often sparked violent resistance in seaport towns. Boston had erupted in November 1747, when Admiral Sir Charles Knowles—a ruthless boor who despised colonists generally—sent press-gangs ashore to round up 46 crewmen for a voyage back to Europe. A crowd of perhaps a thousand Bostonians retaliated by kidnapping some of Knowles's officers, menacing the governor's house, breaking the windows of the colonial assembly building, and dragging a barge onto Boston Common and then setting the barge on fire. Violence and fear reigned for three days while the local militia, siding with the mob, ignored instructions to restore order. When militiamen finally reported for duty, both sides backed down—Knowles released the impressed sailors, and the mob went home.[30]

A few days after that, a pamphlet had appeared in Boston bookshops, anonymously written by a 26-year-old Harvard graduate who lauded Bostonians for fighting back. Using Lockean principles, he argued that impressment "could never yet have the force of law," even if it were an age-old custom, because it violated natural law. "When [people] are suddenly attacked without the least warning by those unknown to them, I think they are treated as if they were in a State of Nature, and they have a natural right to [fight back against] their oppressors."[31]

That writer was Samuel Adams, whose father was then serving in the colonial legislature and was a member of a committee "to consider some method to prevent the distress brought upon the inhabitants of the Province by the impressing of seamen."[32] The Knowles Riot did not bring an end to impressment—nor did later riots, including ones in Rhode Island in 1764 and 1765—but they signaled an increasing willingness by colonists to use direct action to resist having their liberty taken by the arbitrary dictate of a distant government. In fact, according to one historian, impressment was "the most consistent cause of violence against British imperial officials in North America before the American revolutionary era."[33] Now, 20 years later, Samuel's indignation at British arrogance had only increased.

Samuel and John Adams had not been particularly close. John was a country boy, 13 years younger than his cousin. Samuel was so thoroughly city-bred that he didn't even know how to ride a horse. John had a grave sense of law and order, and a love for the English law's obscure disciplines, whereas Samuel was, in the words of one disapproving acquaintance, "born a rebel."[34] Where John was diligent and driven, Samuel failed at every business endeavor he attempted, ending up by 1765 a tax collector, the only steady job he ever had. That might seem ironic, but the explanation is simple: Tax collectors were elected, and Samuel Adams, notoriously lenient toward those who failed to pay, was repeatedly rewarded with their votes.

Also, where John wrote incessantly in diaries, letters, newspapers, and legal briefs, all of which he carefully preserved, Samuel took pains to cover his tracks—an important skill for a revolutionary. In fact, he was so good at concealing his political machinations that biographers are still thwarted in their efforts to tell his life story. He was deeply educated—he held a rare master's degree in political theory from Harvard—and he wrote and published a great deal. But his version of politics was more a matter of personal relationships and conversations. As John later put it, Samuel "made it his constant rule" to seek out and "court [the] friendship" of anyone who might be helpful in preserving the colony's freedom.[35] He became especially adept at coordinating with the leaders of local trade organizations—something like the union bosses of later days—who could arrange for laborers and mechanics to appear on short notice for the purposes of protest, intimidation, or even violence, if necessary. These groups, whom many scorned as "the Boston Mob," would prove instrumental time and again in the 1770s. In short,

Samuel Adams was that rarest of creatures: an effective and practical politician with a deep understanding of philosophy and an unyielding devotion to principle.

Among the most valuable of Samuel's acquaintances was shoemaker Ebenezer Mackintosh, leader of Boston's South End gang.[36] In 1764, the annual Pope's Day row between the South End and North End gangs had been especially violent, leading to several injuries and the death of a young boy. Now, by coincidence, the Stamp Act was scheduled to go into effect on November 1, 1765, only four days before Pope's Day. Samuel and his allies seem to have arranged to take advantage of this timing by uniting the two gangs under Mackintosh's leadership. It was just days later that the effigy appeared on Boston Common. It had Samuel Adams's and Ebenezer Mackintosh's fingerprints all over it.

The "stampman" in question was Thomas Hutchinson's brother-in-law, Andrew Oliver. When his official commission arrived, the 59-year-old Oliver would become responsible for selling the stamps and remitting the proceeds to London. But now he was understandably terrified by the threat the effigy conveyed. When Hutchinson ordered Boston's sheriff to take it down, the crowd—now grown to some 3,000 people—barred his way.[37] That afternoon, the mob began an impromptu procession, removing the effigy and carrying it through the streets toward a small brick building Oliver owned, which they assumed he would use as his tax office. Within minutes, they had torn the structure to the ground. The sheriff recommended that Oliver not spend the night at home.

That was good advice. The crowd soon headed to his house, building a bonfire in the yard and burning what was left of the effigy in the twilight. Then, they wrecked his garden, demolished a gazebo, smashed the windows, and by morning had destroyed the structure. Oliver announced his resignation the next day. This was an extraordinary step, as he had not yet received his commission—in fact, it would not arrive for another four months. Bostonians, however, remained restive.

The following Sunday, preacher Jonathan Mayhew drew his sermon from a text in Galatians: "I would they were even cut off which trouble you, for, brethren, ye have been called unto liberty."[38] Oliver's brother Peter, who served on the colony's Supreme Court, wrote that Mayhew's words were "so seditious" that some who attended "declared while [Mayhew] was delivering it [that] they could scarce contain themselves from going out . . . and beginning their [violent] work."[39] Because he spoke extemporaneously, we cannot know exactly what Mayhew said, but he tried days later to reconstruct his words in a memorandum:

> If [Americans] are to possess no property, nor to enjoy the fruits of their own labor, but by the mere precunious [*sic*] pleasure of the mother [country], or of a distant legislature in which they neither are, nor can be represented, this is really slavery, not civil liberty. Only slaves are bound to labor for the pleasure and profit of others, and to subsist merely on what their masters are pleased to allow them, though they may possibly have kind masters, who treat them with tenderness and humanity, still they are really in a state of slavery, as those who have hard and cruel masters.[40]

A few days later, Ebenezer Mackintosh's gang—now calling themselves "Sons of Liberty" after Isaac Barré's speech opposing the Stamp Act—descended on the home of a vice-admiralty official responsible for reporting smugglers to London. After vandalizing his house and burning his papers, they moved on to the home of a customs collector, breaking in and stealing wine and clothes, and destroying his documents, too. Then, they headed to Thomas Hutchinson's mansion.

Chief Justice Hutchinson was sitting down to dinner with his three sons and two daughters when they arrived. He rushed his family out the back door as the crowd broke in with crowbars and hammers and, over the course of eight hours, obliterated the house. The mob even destroyed his fruit trees and the priceless antique documents he had collected for the multivolume history of the colony he was writing. Mackintosh was arrested for his role in the violence, but it was obvious no jury would convict him. On the contrary, his jailer was politely informed that the mob was prepared to raze the jail to free their leader, if necessary. The sheriff promptly let him go.

The next day, Hutchinson arrived in court to take his seat on the bench without his judicial robes. "Some apology is necessary for my dress," he said, with tears in his eyes. "I had no other. Destitute of everything—no other shirt—no other garment, but what I have on." People were accusing him of supporting the Stamp Act, he said, but that wasn't true. "All the charges against me are false. . . . I can't help feeling—and though I am not obliged to give an answer to all the questions that may be put [to] me by every lawless person—yet—I call God to witness—and I would not for a thousand worlds call my Maker to witness to a falsehood—I say, I call my Maker to witness, that I never in New England or Old, in Great Britain or America, neither directly nor indirectly, was aiding, assisting or supporting, in the least promoting or encouraging what is commonly called the Stamp Act."[41]

Like many colonists, John Adams was stunned by the violence of the riots, and by the injustices done to Oliver and Hutchinson. "Is there any evidence, that Mr. Oliver . . . ever advised the Ministry to lay internal taxes upon us?" he asked his diary. He detested Hutchinson, but there was "no proof at all of any such injury done to the people by that gentleman. . . . To have his garden torn in pieces, his house broken open, his furniture destroyed and his whole family thrown into confusion and terror, is a very atrocious violation of the peace and of dangerous tendency." Still, he continued, it was understandable that Hutchinson and his brother-in-law would be targeted. The legislature had "labored to the utmost of [its] ability, to obtain a resolution to send home some petitions and remonstrances to the king, Lords and Commons vs. the impositions," and Hutchinson had "all along been the very gentleman who has prevented it." He had not only "wiped . . . every spirited, if not every sensible expression out of those petitions," but, in his typical fashion, had professed opposition to the acts while at the same time getting the lucrative job of stamp-master for his brother-in-law.[42]

THE STAMP ACT CONGRESS

As the Stamp Act's opponents began crafting plans for resistance, they saw two alternatives: They could do no business that required a stamp—which meant virtually any legal business or shipping, because vessels could not leave port without stamped documents—or they could defy the act and proceed as if it had never been passed. Meanwhile, Bostonians began hearing of riots in other colonies. Mobs forced the resignation of stamp distributors in New York, New Jersey, New Hampshire, and South Carolina. Rioters in Maryland destroyed the home of that colony's stampman. A crowd in Rhode Island hung effigies of tax-gatherers from gallows, then proceeded to destroy the homes of two of the colony's most outspoken Tories and loot the house of a third. On the island of St. Kitts, a crowd of 300 forced two royal officials to burn the stamps in their possession, then chased a third to Nevis, setting fire to houses along the way.[43] A Pennsylvania newspaper even carried a sensational story from the Bahamas: A mob had shoved a stamp collector into a coffin, lowered it into a grave, and began covering it with dirt before the terrified man begged to be released and resigned his commission.[44] When Virginia's newly appointed stamp distributor arrived in Williamsburg, he found angry colonists ready to meet him. He was lucky, though. He encountered Governor Francis Fauquier sitting on the porch of a tavern, and the governor coolly guided the man safely through the crowd to his mansion, where the two spent a night in conversation. The next morning, the bureaucrat resigned.

When the Massachusetts House of Representatives reconvened, Governor Francis Bernard opened their meeting with a somber address, warning the members of "the consequences if you should suffer a confirmed disobedience of this act of Parliament to take place." Courts would be shuttered, endangering all property and personal safety. The ports would also be closed, and "what will become of the seamen who will be put out of employment? What will become of the tradesmen who immediately depend upon navigation for their daily bread?" Most of all, Bernard stood firm against the idea that the Stamp Act exceeded Parliament's authority. "I trust that the supremacy of Parliament over all the members of their wide and diffused empire never was and never will be denied within these walls." If it were questioned, "who shall determine [the answer] but the Parliament?"[45]

While the legislators considered their response, the intercolonial meeting in New York City was gaveled to order on October 7. Although records of the debates at the "Stamp Act Congress" are intentionally vague, the 27 delegates apparently agreed without hesitation that taxes imposed on the colonists without the consent of their representatives were unconstitutional. And since "the people of these colonies are not, and from their local circumstances cannot be, represented in the House of Commons," the proper legislative authorities were their own colonial legislatures. They also agreed that the vice-admiralty court provisions of the act "have a manifest tendency to subvert the rights and liberties of the colonists," because they violated the right to trial by jury.

The members had more difficulty agreeing about the precise limits of their subordination to Parliament. They eventually settled on an ambiguous acknowledgment that colonists "owe the same allegiance to the crown of Great Britain, that is owing from his subjects born within the realm, and all due subordination to that august body, the Parliament of Great Britain." What exactly "due" subordination meant was left unexplained. Still, the delegates agreed that Westminster had the rightful authority to superintend the empire's commerce, and they made no constitutional objection to the Navigation Acts. Although complaining that these restrictions "render [colonists] unable to purchase the manufactures of Great Britain," they did not denounce them as infringements of the constitution—reflecting again a crucial, if elusive, distinction between trade regulations, which they considered legitimate, even if excessive, and taxes and vice-admiralty courts, which they considered violations of constitutional rights.[46]

While the Stamp Act Congress was drafting its resolutions in New York, John Adams was taking action in his hometown. At a local meeting on October 10, he took the first step in his political career, proposing that the citizens draft a set of instructions for their state representative—a common practice that placed citizens' sentiments on the record in an age before public opinion polls. They agreed, and gave him the task of writing the instructions. The young lawyer wasted no time in pronouncing the Stamp Act unconstitutional. "We have always understood it to be a grand and fundamental principle of the constitution that no man should be subjected to any tax to which he has not given his own consent, in person or by proxy," he wrote. It was therefore "inconsistent with the spirit of the common law, and of the essential fundamental principles of the

British constitution, that we should be subjected to any tax imposed by the British Parliament."

Parliament had not only violated that principle; it had done worse, by expanding the power of the vice-admiralty courts, in which "no juries have any concern," and where judges were paid a commission on items they decided to confiscate. "We have all along thought the [Navigation Acts] in this respect a grievance, but the Stamp Act has opened a vast number of sources of new crimes . . . and all these are to be tried by such a judge of such a court!"[47] This legislation violated the Magna Carta, and demoted Americans to a status little better than slaves, whose property could be taken at any time through an "alarming" parody of due process. Thus, Braintree's citizens demanded that the colonial legislature make "the most clear and explicit assertion and vindication of our rights and liberties"—none of the milquetoast language Hutchinson had foisted on the legislature the previous year—so that "all future generations" would know that Massachusetts had not taken the Stamp Act lying down.

Two weeks later, the House published its answer to Governor Bernard's speech about the riots. Written by Samuel Adams, it was a masterpiece of that era's baroque style, perfectly blending defiance and deference. "Your Excellency tells us that the right of the Parliament to make laws for the American colonies remains indisputable," the lawmakers declared. But "the charter of the province invests the General Assembly with the power of making laws for its internal government and taxation." Even if that weren't true, "there are certain original, inherent rights belonging to the people, which Parliament itself cannot divest them of, consistent with their own constitution; among these is the right of representation in the same body which exercises the power of taxation." No patriotic Briton would dispute this point, because to claim that Parliament enjoyed "despotic power" would be "most disrespectful" to the Lords and Commons themselves. Honorable legislators would disclaim such pretensions.

As for the Stamp Act, it "tend[ed] to destroy" the constitution's principles, including the right to trial by jury and the right not to be taxed without consent.[48] Along with this message, the House approved resolutions declaring that "the inhabitants of this province are unalienably entitled" to the "essential rights of the British constitution of government, which are founded in the law of God and nature, and are the common rights of mankind."[49] It was now late October. Bernard, Hutchinson, and other leaders had no idea what the Sons of Liberty were planning for November 1, the date the act would officially go into effect.

When that day came, however, the Whigs ensured that the town greeted it not with tumult, but with solemn silence. An angry but orderly crowd gathered at the Liberty Tree, hanged a portrait of Prime Minister Grenville, then cut it down, carried it in a calm procession to the city's public gallows, and hanged it again. Then they took it down and shredded it. But they remained calm. Four days later, on "Pope's Day," Ebenezer Mackintosh saw to it that there was no gang violence. Still, the message was clear. The Sons of Liberty would not let the stamps be sold or used. When the stamps arrived, Bernard ordered them locked in a warehouse, away from Mackintosh's mob. Andrew Oliver was terrified of withdrawing his resignation and selling them, and when his official commission as distributor finally arrived on November 30, he refused to act.

Now, with massive resistance and the threat of violence having paralyzed trade and government, merchants in New England and elsewhere announced a plan to boycott British imports until Parliament repealed the tax. Beginning with New York in late October, colonists signed agreements promising not to buy tea, linen, or other goods from Britain, and to shun anyone who did. In some cities, merchant groups began hosting public markets of American-made alternatives to encourage the boycott. When a cargo ship arrived in Philadelphia from Liverpool, the local Merchants Committee seized its cargo and locked it in a storehouse rather than allow it to be sold.[50] Colonists even ceased to wear mourning clothes to funerals, because most black clothing came from overseas. When some shipowners in Savannah did pay the tax and were cleared to leave port, some 600 Sons of Liberty armed themselves and began marching toward the city, forcing Georgia's governor to stash the remaining stamps on a warship in the harbor.

That Savannah incident would prove to be the only sale of stamps in the colonies. Otherwise, commerce froze. Because ships could not sail without stamps, ports began shutting down along the entire coast. If this continued, it would wreck the seaside economy and threaten the colonies with shortages. Not only would shipments be indefinitely stalled, but vessels would begin to deteriorate if they could not sail. And their crews, men with well-deserved reputations for violence, were left wandering colonial streets jobless, or unable to return home. "Nothing is more certain than that so great a number of seamen, shut up for that time in a town destitute of all protection to the inhabitants . . . would commit some terrible mischief," wrote one customs official.[51] In America, traders were already stockpiling grain. The ripple effect would soon be felt in England.

The shutdown was—and remains—the most successful mass protest in American history. Anti-stamp forces brought the economy and the law to a standstill. From Maine to Georgia, stamps had to be held under lock and key, certain to be destroyed if anyone tried distributing them. In the end, of the £100,000 worth of stamps sent to North America, the government sold only £45 worth, all in Savannah. In the West Indies and Canada, it did slightly better, but raised less than £3,300 in total.[52]

As fall turned into winter, colonial governors were forced to choose. No stamp officers were willing to serve, and no stamps were available for sale. Ships had to put to sea. Would they be allowed to depart without stamped paperwork? At last, Virginia's Governor Fauquier answered yes, and leaders in New Jersey, New York, and Pennsylvania soon did likewise. In Massachusetts, however, Governor Bernard stayed put.

OUT OF HIS PROTECTION

"How long we are to remain in this languid condition," wrote John Adams in his diary in mid-December, "is not certain. But such a pause cannot be lasting." Bernard, Hutchinson, and other royal officials "trembled" at the public's wrath over the Stamp Act, "afraid to speak and ashamed to be seen." Yet by refusing to reopen courts or to issue ships passes, they were managing to impose a sort of "passive obedience" to Parliament. That could not continue. If Bernard did not yield to the necessity of letting business proceed without the stamps, Adams predicted, "public offices will soon be forced open."

Adams was thrilled by the display of resistance, even though it was a hardship to have his legal career stalled just as it was taking off. "That enormous engine, fabricated by the British Parliament for battering down all the rights and liberties of America, I mean the Stamp Act, has raised and spread through the whole continent a spirit that will be recorded to our honor with all future generations."[53]

He also mused about what the "pause" might mean in constitutional terms. If "the king is the fountain of justice," how could the courts remain closed indefinitely? If that fountain ceased to flow, were the people not being denied the monarch's protection? "And if we are out of the king's protection, are we not discharged from our allegiance[?]"[54] Colonial judicial systems could not just stop forever; if they did, Americans would eventually be forced to create some new system for resolving disputes, and that would be tantamount to independence. If the monarch's job was to provide a structure of authority to keep the peace among the people, then the closure of the courts presented a major constitutional crisis.

Adams's phrase "out of the king's protection"—which would appear a decade later in the Declaration of Independence—was an old one. Shakespeare even used it in *Henry VIII*, which Adams read during the weeks he was pondering the shutdown.[55] But it traced back much further, to Christian theology and the feudal law of treason.[56] Since the relationship between king and subject was an exchange of obligations—with the Crown giving protection in return for loyalty—the king traditionally punished treason by withdrawing that protection. When that happened, the person was literally "outlawed," meaning that nobody would be held to account for killing him, taking his goods, or committing other crimes against him. The traitor was thrown out of the law's protective arms. Being barred from the king's courts was therefore a kind of punishment. On one notorious occasion, King Edward I (who ruled from 1272 to 1307) cast clergymen out of his protection for refusing to pay taxes, specifying that they would consequently be barred from access to the judiciary.[57] In the 1350s, Parliament adopted its first statute governing treason, which declared that anyone guilty of that crime would be denied the right to legal process in court.[58] Four decades later, under the Statute of Praemunire, certain political subversives were "put out of the king's protection," with all their property forfeit.[59]

For the king to *falsely* condemn people for treason, and undeservedly deny them royal protection, was therefore the worst abuse he could commit. In fact, it was just how the Stuarts had behaved.

In 1642, the people of London had asked King Charles I to return to the city after he fled to raise an army in preparation for civil war. Charles answered that he would only do so if his opponents ceased to resist him. Anybody who refused to submit, he announced, was a traitor, and "his Majesty shall likewise deny [such a person] the benefit of his protection, and . . . proceed against him as a public enemy."[60] Now, it seemed, George III—by refusing to stand up for his colonial subjects—was depriving them of his protection. If so, why should they render him obedience?

What Adams did not know when writing this was that, a day earlier, the Sons of Liberty had determined to reopen the port, come what may. The *Boston Gazette* published an announcement on December 17 that Andrew Oliver would resign his position as stamp distributor again—officially, this time—at noon under the Liberty Tree, where his effigy had swung months before. To ensure that he complied, a messenger was sent to knock on his door and inform him that the mob was prepared to riot again if he did not. Marched to the tree through the pouring rain, Oliver was forced to renounce his commission for good this time, before a crowd of 2,000 people. Then, since there were no stamps and no stampman, the town leaders simply pronounced the harbor open. Governor Bernard could do nothing. True, sailing without stamped papers meant risking interception by the Royal Navy, as well as confiscation and trial before one of his Majesty's vice-admiralty courts—but with most courts closed because of the lack of stamps, that risk was minimized.

Next, Bostonians met to prepare a petition asking Bernard to open the courthouses and allow other businesses to operate without stamps, too. Seeking legal assistance in writing their request, the city's representatives summoned a group of lawyers, including John Adams. "The reasons which induced Boston to choose me, at a distance, and unknown as I am," he wrote in his diary, "I am wholly at a loss to conjecture." Nor could he guess "what the future effects and consequences will be."[61] But the nervous attorney began planning what arguments to present. He thought it best to declare that because the Stamp Act was unconstitutional, it had never been law in the first place, and thus presented no obstacle to the port's operation. On a more practical level, the stamp-master had now resigned, and no stamps were available (being kept under lock and key), which made compliance impossible.

Yet when the governor at last agreed to meet with Adams, James Otis, and others to hear their arguments, the result was anti-climactic. Bernard and his council listened, said they would think about it—and then did nothing. Weeks began to pass.

Hoping to goad them into action, Otis turned to the newspapers. Under the pseudonym "Hampden," he published a series of articles arguing that the closure of the courts amounted to a declaration of war, and, in principle, to an abandonment of the throne. "The giving up the administration of justice in the colonies, by the several governors, judges, and other officers in the [Stamp Act] scheme," he wrote, equated to "giving up, as far as is in their power, his kingship and majesty."[62] Adams agreed. "Shutting up the courts is an abdication," he wrote in his diary. "A discharge of the subjects from their allegiance, and a total dissolution of government and reduction of all men to a state of nature."[63]

Adams decided to publish a series of articles of his own. Using the pseudonym "Clarendon" (which, like "Hampden" was the name of a famous English Whig), Adams lauded the British constitution for its guarantees of freedom—then complained of the way it was being perverted into an instrument of tyranny. "All men are born equal, and the drift of the British constitution is to preserve as much of this equality as is compatible with the people's security." Two institutions—the right to vote and the right to trial by jury—were the principal guarantees of this equality and liberty. "[The people] have no other fortification against wanton, cruel power; no other indemnification against being ridden like horses, fleeced like sheep, worked like cattle."[64] Yet the new vice-admiralty courts, which operated without juries, and where the judges themselves profited if they ruled for the government, were replacing these traditional constitutional protections with instruments of "insolence and rapacity."[65] Things could not go on this way.

As weeks became months, other colonies began opening their courts. Yet the Bay Colony's still remained idle. In part, this was the lawyers' fault; fearing the consequences for themselves and their clients if they proceeded to decide legal disputes without some official sanction, they hesitated to file lawsuits in the first place. But Adams feared that the closure of the courts was a tacit concession of the Stamp Act's legitimacy. Only by actually doing business in outright defiance of the act could its nullity be established as a constitutional matter. For that very reason, Chief Justice Hutchinson and other judges dragged their feet. Even after the legislature passed a resolution urging the courts to open, the justices chose not to convene until spring—and then Hutchinson managed to be out of town. His colleagues used his absence as an excuse to delay another month. "So Hutchinson is to trim, and shift, and luff up and bear away," growled Adams in his diary. "And elude the blame of the ministry and the people."[66] A month later, Adams returned to the courtroom, only to hear the justices announce still another two-week postponement. "What insolence and impudence and chicanery is this?" he raged.[67] At last, some county courts agreed to resume business as if the Stamp Act had never existed. But by then, rumors were circulating that Parliament was planning to withdraw the act, and most lawyers decided it was safer to await official news of repeal before proceeding with business.

In London, negotiations over undoing the stamp tax had been tedious and frustrating. Businessmen throughout England flooded the House of Commons with petitions begging for repeal, their work suffering from the American boycott. The tax was gathering practically no revenue, and was only alienating the colonists. That winter, William Pitt told the House that the time had come to recognize that Americans were "equally entitled with yourselves to all the natural rights of mankind and the peculiar privileges of Englishmen . . . equally participating in the constitution of this free country. The Americans are the sons, not the bastards, of England."[68] But few members were willing to go that far. In their eyes, undoing the tax meant conceding the constitutional point and abandoning Parliamentary Supremacy. Thus, the ministry spent the winter searching for some way to repeal the act without seeming to concede its illegitimacy.

They finally found a way on March 18, 1766. That day, Parliament revoked the Stamp Act by a nearly two-thirds vote. When the news arrived in America, it set off rejoicing from north to south, as colonists celebrated with parades, bonfires, and fireworks. Boston's church bells began ringing at sunrise, and townspeople started decorating the Liberty Tree with lanterns. Yet in the midst of that dawn, a stormy cloud appeared. To avoid seeming to acquiesce in colonial protests, Parliament had combined its repeal with a new law: a statement of power called the Declaratory Act, which asserted that the colonies "are, and of right ought to be, subordinate unto, and dependent upon the imperial crown and parliament of Great Britain; and that the king's majesty, by and with the advice and consent of the lords spiritual and temporal, and commons of Great Britain, in parliament assembled, had, hath, and of right ought to have, full power and authority to make laws and statutes of sufficient force and validity to bind the colonies and people of America, subjects of the crown of Great Britain, *in all cases whatsoever*."[69]

— PART TWO —

ALL CASES WHATSOEVER

The earliest known portrait of Thomas Jefferson depicts him about a decade after the signing of the Declaration of Independence.

— CHAPTER 5 —

JEFFERSON AND LIBERTY

I was bold in the pursuit of knowledge.
—Thomas Jefferson[1]

Word of the Stamp Act's repeal was greeted with jubilation up and down the American coast. In Williamsburg, Governor Francis Fauquier hosted a formal ball, followed by fireworks.[2] New Yorkers held a feast, rang church bells, and resolved to erect a new statue to George III. (A decade later, it would be melted down and made into ammunition for the revolutionary army.) In Boston, city leaders declared it a day of thanksgiving, and Jonathan Mayhew delivered a joyful sermon on the text "Our soul is escaped as a bird from the snare of the fowlers; the snare is broken."[3] "The course of justice between man and man is no longer obstructed," he announced. "Commerce lifts up her head, adorned with golden tresses. . . . Blessed revolution! glorious change!"[4] In Maryland, the legislature adjourned so members could spend the day drinking toasts to the king to the sounds of celebratory cannons.[5]

One visitor from Virginia who joined in the Annapolis festivities was the young law student Thomas Jefferson. Taking a break from his almost-completed studies, he was on his way to Philadelphia to be inoculated against smallpox. The disease had killed his beloved sister Jane only a year earlier, and he was determined to try the relatively new immunizing technology. He may have reached his destination in time to witness its revelries too; when the ship carrying news of repeal reached Philadelphia, the people paraded its captain through

Jefferson's original plan for Monticello was probably never completed before he revised the design to incorporate the dome that tourists see today.

the streets, plied him with punch, and presented him with a fancy new hat before lighting celebratory bonfires around the city.[6]

Soon afterward, the tall young Virginian proceeded to New York, where he probably enjoyed more parties before returning to Virginia. He had been too young to participate in resistance to the Stamp Act himself, but he honored the event in his characteristically studious way: In his commonplace book—a sort of diary where he kept detailed notes of everything he read—he began jotting down scholarly references to the law of treason and riot.[7]

THE WESTERNER

Born on April 13, 1743, Thomas Jefferson was a child of what was then more or less the westernmost edge of European civilization. British America's largest cities were hundreds of miles to the east of his family's Virginia plantation, called Shadwell, and to the west were forests, forts, and unmapped plains that were home to a handful of European traders and trappers and countless Native Americans. Among his early memories were occasional visits from tribesmen who stopped while journeying to and from the colonial capital of Williamsburg. Although Jefferson's intellectual pursuits would always flourish in eastern cities such as Philadelphia and New York, and European cultural centers such as Paris, it was the West, with its lure of independence, that always exerted the most powerful influence on his personality.

The spirit of the West was embodied in his father, Peter Jefferson, who was 35 when Thomas was born and seemed to his son an awesomely strong and intelligent figure. According to a family legend that the son credulously repeated years afterward, Peter could lift a hogshead of tobacco under each arm (an impossibility, as a hogshead would weigh about 1,000 pounds). He was also self-taught. "My father's education had been quite neglected," Jefferson later wrote. "But being of a strong mind, sound judgment and eager after information, he read much and improved himself."[8] In 1749, Peter left the six-year-old boy behind and traveled with mathematician Joshua Fry into the wilds of Virginia on a surveying expedition that produced a famous map of the colony. Three decades later, the son would proudly reprint the father's map in his book *Notes on the State of Virginia* and would display a copy in the entrance hall of his home.

Jefferson never expressed equal pride regarding his mother, Jane Randolph Jefferson (born in 1720), and his reticence about her has led biographers to detect hostility between the two. For example, around the time he retired from the presidency, he told a grandchild that after his father's death in 1757, he had been left "without a relative or friend qualified to advise or guide me," which implies disdain for his mother's capacities.[9] But the truth is that we know remarkably little about her, or about many other members of Jefferson's family. For example, hardly anything is known for sure about his younger brother, Randolph Jefferson (born in 1755), except for some letters that reveal him to be a marginally literate farmer. Jefferson was especially discreet about his relationships with women; for example, no letters or portraits of his wife survive.

He was the eldest of seven children. Among his siblings, he was closest to Jane, who was three years older, and was devastated when she died of smallpox in 1765. He would, in fact, suffer an excruciating amount of family loss; all his siblings except one predeceased him, as would his best friend, five of his six children, and his wife. "I have often wondered for what good end the sensations of grief could be intended," he told John Adams when they were both old men. "I wish the pathologists . . . would tell us what is the use of grief."[10]

His father's death meant Jefferson would grow up to be the legal head of the family, responsible for managing the estate. That was a significant obligation, given his mother's connection to the Randolphs, who passed for aristocracy in the colony. Virginia followed many feudal traditions, including the legal system of entail and primogeniture, which gave preferences to eldest sons—a practice Jefferson himself would later abolish. But the connections this future hero of democracy enjoyed with the colony's pseudo-aristocratic families brought him many advantages. Not only would he be related by blood to some of the most important people in American politics, but he would also have an opportunity for education that was truly special by the day's standards.

The education of an upper-class Virginia boy focused heavily on languages: English spelling and grammar, followed by studies in Latin and Greek, as well as French. In the end, Jefferson was to learn the classical languages well enough to correct typos in his textbooks. He also learned French and some Spanish and Italian, and became an early expert on Anglo-Saxon.

In addition to the Bible, Shakespeare, John Milton, and Alexander Pope, the young Jefferson read the Greek and Roman poets and playwrights, and copied extracts from Euripides and others into his commonplace book. "I thank on my knees him who directed my early education, for having put into my possession this rich source of delight," he once said of his knowledge of ancient languages. "I would not exchange it for anything."[11] He enjoyed Homer most of all. He was fond of poetry all his life—in old age he clipped poems out of newspapers and shared them with his granddaughters—but aside from Laurence Sterne's zany comic novel *Tristram Shandy*, he cared little for prose fiction.

His favorite writers were the Roman historians, especially Publius Cornelius Tacitus, the first-century author whom he considered the finest writer of all. The distinctive qualities of Tacitus's style are concision, subtly poetic phrasing, and a sardonic attitude toward the corruption and moral laxity of Roman society. Where other Romans—notably Cicero, who lived a century and a half earlier—used long, elaborate sentences, sometimes consuming entire paragraphs, Tacitus had a clipped, epigrammatic style. *Corruptissima re publica plurimae leges*, he wrote in *The Annals* (Laws are most numerous when the state is most corrupt).[12] Or in his *Germania*, *Ibi boni mores valent quam alibi bonae leges* (Good habits here are more effective than good laws elsewhere).[13]

A common theme of Tacitus's writings is the manner in which moral decay can erode the foundations of the state by softening citizens' character, rendering them eager to accept servitude—and how tyrants encourage such decay for that reason. For example, in describing how the Romans subdued the Britons in the first century, Tacitus explained that the general Gnaeus Julius Agricola accustomed the natives to Rome's riches, thereby undermining their willingness to resist the empire: "Step by step, the Britons were led to things which dispose to vice: the lounge, the bath, the elegant banquet. All this, in their ignorance, they called civilization, when it was but a part of their servitude."[14] Tacitus depicted the Roman Empire as a society rotting with treachery, debauchery, and terror, in which emperors punished virtue and wisdom and rewarded vice and ignorance. The anti-monarchist poet John Milton called Tacitus "the greatest possible enemy to tyrants," and all his life, Jefferson would admire the historian's contempt for despotism and its accompanying immorality—as well as his evocative, streamlined prose.[15]

The collapse of the virtuous Roman Republic into the tyranny and excess of the Roman Empire was among the most familiar lessons to educated Anglo-Americans in the 18th century, and the one that most readily came to mind when Great Britain in the 1760s became the largest empire since ancient days. The Romans inaugurated their republic in 507 BCE, when they overthrew their king and established a system that balanced the power of a public-spirited aristocracy with the needs of the "plebian" or common class. Under that well-adjusted constitution, the republic became a dominant power in the Western world, and, although savage and oppressive in many ways, it instituted an admirable rule of law that made it prosperous and successful. Yet prosperity also spelled its doom. As the people grew accustomed to a high standard of living, they began to disregard the stern discipline that self-reliance requires, and rallied around politicians who promised to keep the wealth flowing, even if that required sacrificing their liberty.

In the 80s BCE, after a series of wars wracked the Italian Peninsula, the victorious general Sulla arranged for the Senate to declare him dictator for life. That ended with his death in 78, but the precedent he set was easily imitated by Julius Caesar three decades later. Caesar had learned to manipulate ordinary Romans by handing out money. His successes as a military leader enabled him to distribute the spoils of conquest, thereby securing the loyalty of soldiers on the frontier and civilians back home. Plebians lost respect for Roman legal institutions and historical traditions, switching their loyalty to him personally and away from Rome in the abstract.

When, in 51 BCE, Caesar returned from a foreign military campaign and asked permission to enter the city at the head of his army, in violation of a long-standing law, the Senate said no. Caesar used that as a pretext—claiming the Senate had personally insulted him and his army—and led his men across the boundary of the Rubicon River, to start the war that eventually won him the dictatorship and destroyed Roman freedom. Although he was assassinated in 44 by a group of aristocrats who despised the damage he had done to the republic, it was too late. Rome remained unfree until its collapse five centuries later. True, some of the emperors had admirable qualities, and the Roman Empire achieved glorious feats; its legal system worked well, and architects and poets produced lasting masterpieces. But Tacitus chronicled how its rulers became increasingly crooked—even insane—transforming a once-admirable nation into a decadent society ruled by brutes.

The whole sordid tale seemed to vindicate the theory proposed by the historian Polybius, who lived a century before Caesar, and who argued that societies go through a cycle from freedom to tyranny that he called "anacyclosis." Pointing to the violent experiences of ancient Greek democracies—which were constantly wracked by civil war whenever the have-nots rose up against the haves—Polybius argued that the pattern begins when the people, exhausted by tyranny, overthrow their rulers, and, "remember[ing] with terror the injustice they suffered," refuse to select a new king, but establish a democracy instead. This lasts "as long as some of those survive who experienced the evils of oligarchical dominion." But in the next generation, people forget what tyranny was like and lose their appreciation for freedom. "They begin to lust for power" instead, and the easiest way to obtain power is to give people money—either their own, or money seized through taxes or foreign conquest. This practice ultimately wrecks the democracy, because the populace, "having grown accustomed to feed at the expense of others," seeks out a demagogue who "institute[s] the rule of violence," confiscating the property of the rich for redistribution to his own supporters. This causes the people to "degenerate again into perfect savages and find once more a master and monarch."[16]

In short, Greek and Roman history illustrated many of the dangers that had ruined nations in the past: the tyranny of the majority on the one hand, the greed and oppression of dictators and oligarchs on the other. By the dawn of the 18th century, those histories—and failed attempts at republicanism such as the rule of Oliver Cromwell—had persuaded most European intellectuals that, as bad as the tyranny of a single king could be, democracy was worse. It inevitably degenerated into a war between rich and poor, or the many and the few. Whereas a monarch could at least hand down laws to the people and create order, it seemed absurd to suggest that the people could give order to themselves.

As the political philosopher Henry St. John, First Viscount Bolingbroke (whom Jefferson deeply admired) wrote in an influential 1738 pamphlet, the king's role was, "instead of putting himself at the head of one party in order to govern his people, [to] put himself at the head of his people in order to govern, or more properly to subdue *all* parties."[17] There was always a risk of a bad monarch's abusing his power, but a virtuous ruler could stand uninfluenced by the people's infighting, to arbitrate their disputes and bring peace. That seemed far more likely than the foolish democratic notion that the people could establish their own laws. History proved to most political theorists that the majority would never be able to resist the temptation to ignore or rewrite the laws whenever that seemed convenient. They would inevitably use their power to steal each other's property, nullify their financial obligations, and rationalize foolish, cruel, and irrational policies by claiming that the majority is always right. Then they would be attracted to demagogues who promised to enrich them by confiscating the wealth of merchants, bankers, farmers, and landlords—and then used the people's loyalty to become despots.[18]

William Shakespeare's satires of democracy—from the "Friends, Romans, countrymen" scene in *Julius Caesar* to his portrayal of Jack Cade's rebellion in *Henry VI, Part 2*—reflected this intellectual consensus. Jonathan Swift, too, wrote that the histories of Greece and Rome proved that the people are "generally led and influenced by the very worst among themselves" and will, in the "spirit of cruelty and revenge, of malice and pride," overthrow the laws, rally around a dictator, and implement despotism.[19] Even the poet Milton—who had supported Cromwell in the English Civil War—agreed. After England's experiment with republicanism failed, he wrote in *Paradise Lost* that "tyranny must be," because the people cannot rule their "upstart passions."[20]

Jefferson's generation would strive to overturn this consensus. They hoped to prove that the majority in a society can be loyal not to any particular ruler, but to the law itself; that they can establish rules *and* obey them. But to achieve that feat would require a precise attention to the nuances of legality and virtue—especially the classical virtues of self-reliance and civic responsibility. Nothing else could prevent democracy from degenerating into covetous and violent mob rule.

RELIGION AND PHILOSOPHY

Along with languages and history, the young Jefferson received religious instruction consistent with the doctrines of the colony's established Anglican Church. Virginians were legally required to attend services and support the Church with their taxes, and while the British rule of "toleration" meant people could profess and even practice different religious viewpoints, the colony nevertheless outlawed meetings by groups such as the Baptists. Although Jefferson would later emerge as a champion of freedom of conscience, his own religious education was conventional.

It's unclear when he decided that organized Christianity was not for him. He once told a granddaughter of a time when, as a child, he sneaked out of class and prayed that school might end early; the fact that his prayer went unanswered might have helped him toward his later skepticism.[21] However that may be, Jefferson's mature religious views settled into deism. "It is impossible for the human mind not to perceive and feel a conviction of design, consummate skill, and indefinite power in every atom of [the world's] composition," he thought."[22] He did not, however, believe in a creator who interfered with human affairs or violated the laws of nature. God to him was more an engineer than a divine personality.

Still, Jefferson combined this deism with what he considered "genuine" Christianity—that is, an adherence to the nonsupernatural elements of the teachings of Jesus, whom he saw as a great philosopher on a par with Cicero or Socrates, rather than the son of God. He thought Christianity's mystical elements had been illicitly added to the scriptures by St. Paul and other early followers, who were influenced by Plato, a philosopher Jefferson hated. "The doctrines which flowed from the lips of Jesus himself are within the comprehension of a child," he once told John Adams. "But thousands of volumes have not yet explained the Platonisms engrafted upon them, and for this obvious reason: that nonsense can never be explained."[23] Such concepts as the Virgin Birth, the Trinity, or the separation of the soul from the body were figments of the imagination and inessential to Jesus's true teachings, which were "the most sublime morality which has ever fallen from the lips of man."[24]

Worse, Platonic supernaturalism was a dangerous political tool, used by kings and priests to delude the populace into sacrificing their liberty. If people could be made to believe, say, that three and one are the same thing, they could also be made to accept the irrational dictates of arbitrary political authorities. Thus, Jefferson concluded, the miraculous elements of organized religion were legacies of, and gateways to, despotism. He therefore formulated a version of Christianity that was comprehensible by reason and purged of all supernatural elements. "I am a Christian in the only sense [Jesus] wished any one to be," he remarked. "Sincerely attached to his doctrines, in preference to all others, ascribing to himself every *human* excellence, and believing he never claimed any other."[25]

In formulating this creed, Jefferson relied on Greek and Roman philosophers, especially the Epicureans and Stoics. Epicurus, who lived from 341 to 270 BCE, authored numerous philosophical and scientific treatises, but his writings were largely lost over the centuries. Instead, his doctrines—such as his belief that morality is principally concerned with seeking personal serenity or calm (ataraxia)—were best known through the book-length poem *De rerum natura*, written two centuries later by his Roman admirer, Lucretius. Lucretius praised reason and science, and he spurned religion, which, he said, "hath bred the foul impieties of men."[26] Only rationality could bring about ataraxia, by dispelling the fears that superstition and mysticism breed. Life should be spent not in seeking to serve the gods, but in the thoughtful enjoyment of the natural world, or what Jefferson called "well-regulated indulgences."[27] Or, as the philosopher John Locke put it in a passage heavily influenced by Lucretius, "The highest perfection of intellectual nature lies in a careful and constant pursuit of true and solid happiness."[28] Years later, when Jefferson would use the phrase "pursuit of happiness" in the Declaration of Independence, he would have this Epicurean notion in mind.[29]

Jefferson, like other 18th-century Epicureans, sought to merge the concept of ataraxia with traditional Christian ethics. He thought Jesus offered "a supplement" to Epicurus's doctrines: Where the Greek had described the "laws for governing ourselves," the

Nazarene had added "the duties and charities we owe to others."[30] Yet it was not easy to reconcile Jesus's directive to "go and sell that thou hast, and give to the poor . . . and come and follow me" with the worldly materialism of Epicurus.[31] Jefferson seems to have found at least a partial resolution in the writings of the Stoic philosophers.

The Stoics differed from the Epicureans in important ways. Although they, too, preached the virtues of self-control and argued that the goal of life was a sense of tranquility, the philosopher Epictetus—Jefferson's favorite Stoic—added the principle of *philanthropia*, or love of humanity.[32] A rightly ordered person, wrote Epictetus, would see himself as part of the human community, and would therefore "never . . . think about anything as though he were detached, but [would] be like the hand or the foot, which if they had the power of reason and understood the order of nature, would direct every impulse and every process of the will by reference to the whole."[33] Appreciating his connection to others, the rational man would see that it is in his own interest "to guard [his] character for good faith, honor, forbearance, self-control, and service."[34] He will be "friendly to his neighbor, always and absolutely, if he be like himself, and if he be unlike, he will bear with him, be gentle and tender with him, considerate to him as one who is ignorant and in error about the highest matters; not hard upon any man."[35]

Philanthropia never fully resolved the tension between the Christian ethic of service and the rational self-interest preached by Epicurus. "If we are made in some degree for others, yet in a greater are we made for ourselves," Jefferson once wrote, when exasperated by the demands of public duty. "It [would be] contrary to feeling and indeed ridiculous to suppose a man had less right in himself than one of his neighbors or all of them put together."[36] Still, Epicurean and Stoic thought, leavened with a deistic sense that the universe is organized with a purpose, would give order and meaning to his life through decades of public service. It's obvious why it appealed to someone who suffered so much personal loss in the deaths of his wife, children, family, and friends, and who often struggled for rational control over his emotions.

The Stoic and Epicurean influences probably also explain a feature of Jefferson's personality that frustrates many biographers: the sense of personal detachment one encounters in his writings. His letters could be eloquent, persuasive, charming, and erudite, but rarely self-revealing, and anyone who reads his correspondence soon detects the tone of someone striving to imitate a classical model of self-control instead of candidly jotting down his thoughts. This detachment is particularly evident in his famous correspondence with John Adams during their retirement. There, Adams's Yankee candor contrasts strikingly with Jefferson's self-consciously disciplined style. Jefferson would never have written, as Adams did, "Let me now ask you, very seriously my friend, where are now in 1813, the perfection and perfectibility of human nature? Where is now the progress of the human mind? . . . I know not whether [there can be] . . . more terrors than the present state of the world."[37] And it is equally unimaginable that Adams could have written, as Jefferson did, "It is a good world on the whole. . . . It has been framed on a principle of benevolence, and more pleasure than pain dealt out to us. . . . My temperament is sanguine. I steer my bark with Hope in the head, leaving Fear astern."[38]

That hopefulness was carefully cultivated—the sculpted self-representation of a gentleman raised on the ancient model. But it was also a response to emotional strain. Living in the age of Beethoven and Goethe, Jefferson's own life and ideas reflected the same transition from classicism to romanticism that theirs did. He channeled his emotional energies into a high idealism that inspired his admirers and maddened his critics, and that sometimes led him into incautious moments, such as when he cheered on violent revolutions that alarmed his countrymen. Even in private, the Apollo of his reason sometimes wrestled with the Dionysus of his feelings. He was one of those people for whom everything is either the best or worst thing ever. Music was "the favorite passion of my soul," he declared.[39] But he also "[could] not live without books."[40] And at the same time, "No occupation is so delightful to me as the culture of the earth, and no culture comparable to that of the garden."[41] He once told a dinner companion that "the unnecessary killing of a tree" was "a crime little short of murder."[42] It was after his death that his closest friend, James Madison, offered the most insightful comment ever made about him: "Allowances also ought to be made for a habit in Mr. Jefferson, as in others of great genius, of expressing in strong and round terms impressions of the moment."[43]

WILLIAM SMALL

By 1760, Jefferson's schooling was advanced enough for him to enter the colony's only institution of higher learning, the College of William and Mary in Williamsburg. But while the 17-year-old was eager to dive into his studies, he also found the school disappointing. It was unimpressive even by the standards of the day, consisting only of the (still-extant) Wren and Brafferton buildings, along with some smaller structures. With one exception, it was staffed entirely by clergymen. Shortly before Jefferson's arrival, a dispute within the college led to the termination of half the faculty, forcing the sole nonclerical professor to take over the teaching of a wide variety of subjects, including mathematics, ethics, physics, and "natural philosophy," or what we now call biology.

That teacher's name was William Small, and he became Jefferson's mentor. A Scottish immigrant who had arrived only two years earlier, Small was "profound in most of the useful branches of science," Jefferson recalled, "with a happy talent of communication, correct and gentlemanly manners, and a large and liberal mind."[44] Small's intellectual stature is revealed by the fact that when he returned to England, he joined the Lunar Society—the middle-class counterpart to the Royal Society—which numbered among its members such luminaries as Matthew Boulton, James Watt, and Erasmus Darwin. Darwin (grandfather of evolution's discoverer) said Small's learning and integrity "[had] no equal."[45]

Small remained in Williamsburg only until 1764, two years after Jefferson's graduation (or rather, matriculation, for in keeping with the practice of the day, he received no degree but moved directly to other studies). During that time, however, Small introduced Jefferson to the writings of Isaac Newton, which brought the young prodigy such a love of mathematics and geometry that he often turned to math puzzles in times of stress. It was probably under Small's tutelage, too, that Jefferson first encountered the writings of John Locke and Francis Bacon, whom he grouped with Newton as "the three greatest men that have ever lived."[46]

Locke's influence on Jefferson's political ideas is obvious. Also an admirer of Epicurus, Locke had argued that the purpose of life is the pursuit of happiness, as regulated by reason. Just as the laws of diet and exercise prescribe the means by which people can attain physical health, so moral law prescribes what is good or bad for people's moral health. And part of that prescription is political liberty. Everybody has "a property in his own person" that "nobody has any right to but himself," Locke wrote, and this includes the right to use one's faculties, to employ one's labor, and to enjoy the rewards.[47] The pursuit of happiness, of course, did not mean sensuality or mindless pleasure, but the steady application of one's gifts to honest productivity and to relishing the full experiences of life. The state's role was not to provide these things to people, or to force them to be morally good—it does not *own* the people or give them rights. Rather, its job is to furnish the framework within which each person can pursue the good life in accordance with his or her unique talents and tastes:

> The necessity of pursuing happiness [is] the foundation of liberty. As therefore the highest perfection of intellectual nature lies in a careful and constant pursuit of true and solid happiness; so the care of ourselves, that we mistake not imaginary for real happiness, is the necessary foundation of our liberty. The stronger ties we have to an unalterable pursuit of happiness in general, which is our greatest good, and which, as such, our desires always follow, the more are we free from any necessary determination of our will to any particular action.[48]

Alongside Newton and Locke, the third member of Jefferson's trinity was the 17th-century polymath Francis Bacon. A lawyer, scientist, poet, and philosopher, Bacon is remembered today as a pioneer of the "scientific method," thanks to his insistence that observation, experimentation, and analysis—not introspection and contemplation—are the keys to discovery. He shunned appeals to authority or mysticism and adopted as his motto "knowledge is power"—a slogan Jefferson was fond of quoting. In 1620, Bacon published his pathbreaking *Novum Organum* to promote his epistemological theories.[49] Genuine knowledge, he argued, must always be tested against reality, and even the oldest traditional knowledge must be open to challenge. In fact, Bacon was such an enthusiast for experimentation that he once stuffed a dead chicken full of snow to see whether freezing could preserve food. His theory was correct, but his method flawed; he contracted a chill and died of pneumonia a week later.[50]

But while Bacon rejected the Scholastic philosophy that emphasized deduction and contemplation over experimentation, he was not an empiricist—the term for those who entirely rejected speculative theorizing and held that only demonstrable facts qualify as knowledge. Instead, he defended what he called the "middle way"—namely, the process of induction, whereby one draws general conclusions from particular examples, to develop testable models of the world. True scientists, Bacon wrote, should imitate the honeybee, who "draw[s] her material from the flowers of the garden or the field, but transform[s] it by a faculty peculiar to herself."[51] Through a careful process of inductive reasoning and experimentation, mankind could come to know the hidden laws of nature—including human nature—and use these laws to cure disease, eliminate drudgery, and improve human life.

This was amazingly prescient. In his utopian novel *New Atlantis*—one of the earliest works of science fiction ever published—Bacon even envisioned a technologically advanced society that enjoyed airplanes, artificial light, tall office buildings, "engine-houses, where are prepared engines and instruments for all sorts of motions" (power plants), and even air-conditioning.[52] Most importantly, he thought the purpose of human reason was not to construct "a tower of state for a proud mind to raise itself upon," or to seek "a couch whereupon to rest a searching and restless spirit," but instead to develop "a rich storehouse for the glory of the Creator and *the relief of man's estate*."[53] The latter phrase was crucial: Bacon was a champion of scientific progress, who believed in seeking ways to alleviate disease and poverty, as opposed to stern resignation in the face of inevitable suffering. It was an attitude Jefferson was to embrace with fervor.

Much of Bacon's philosophical writing is complex, but he also prepared works for ordinary readers, most famously his *Essays*, published in 1597. In a pithy, epigrammatic style reminiscent of Tacitus, Bacon addressed subjects as diverse as marriage, envy, revenge, and superstition, and his commonsense plainness lodged deeply in Jefferson's mind. "It were better to have no opinion of God at all than such an opinion as is unworthy of Him," Bacon wrote. "The one is unbelief, the other is contumely, and certainly superstition is the reproach of the Deity."[54] In the 1780s, Jefferson likewise advised his nephew to "question with boldness even the existence of a God; because, if there be one, He must more approve of the homage of reason, than that of blindfolded fear."[55] "Travel, in the younger sort, is a part of education," wrote Bacon, "in the elder, a part of experience. He that travels into a country, before he has some entrance into the language, goes to school, and not to travel."[56] Jefferson, writing to the same nephew, said: "Traveling makes men wiser, but less happy. When men of sober age travel, they gather knowledge, which they may apply usefully for their country, but . . . young men who travel . . . do not acquire that wisdom for which a previous foundation is requisite, by repeated and just observations at home."[57]

Not all of Bacon's ideas appealed to Jefferson; the 16th-century monarchist had been an archenemy of Sir Edward Coke, the judge and legal scholar Jefferson admired. Yet his belief that there are natural laws governing the world and human beings—rooted in nature rather than revelation and grasped not by meditation but by reason and experiment—had a profound effect on Jefferson's outlook. He shared Bacon's drive to remake the political world along rational lines. He also admired Bacon's multiplicity of interests and accomplishments and was likely inspired by the fact that he combined a successful legal career with scientific and literary pursuits. When, in 1776, Jefferson undertook a project to compile and revise all the laws of Virginia, he likely had in mind the fact that Bacon had proposed a similar scheme for revising English law a century and a half earlier.[58]

A FAITHFUL AND BELOVED MENTOR

By his own admission, Jefferson was "a hard student" during his days at William and Mary, but he was not anti-social.[59] He even joined a student organization called the Flat Hat Club, which, he said, had "no useful object."[60] It may have been members of the club who one night overturned the desk on which he was studying in order to get him to accompany them on a frolic. His letters from this time to his dearest friends, John Page and Dabney Carr, reveal a deeply intellectual but friendly young man, who enjoyed showing off his learning and had a tendency to excessively romanticize the young ladies of Williamsburg. One night, when rain leaked through his roof and destroyed a paper silhouette that 16-year-old Rebecca Burwell had given him, the melodramatic Jefferson told Page that it was "the last stroke Satan had reserved for me."[61]

He was especially close to Carr, who later married Jefferson's sister Martha. On holidays, the two youths often hiked up the mountain west of Shadwell to study together under a tree. Called Monticello—Italian for "little mountain"—the hill became a favorite place of retreat, and Jefferson announced his plan to someday build a house there. He and Carr pledged that if one should die, the other would have his friend buried at that spot. Jefferson honored that promise when Carr passed away in 1773. The location is still Monticello's graveyard.

Bookish as Jefferson was, there's little reason to believe that he devoured the college library. We know, for example, that he did not read Plato during those days—a remarkable omission for a student of the classics. Biographers have sometimes been misled about his studiousness by a letter he wrote to an in-law in 1771 who had asked what books he should buy for his library. Jefferson, by then a 28-year-old practicing lawyer, answered with an ornate list of recommendations that included everything from Dryden and Pope to Montesquieu and Voltaire. A few years later, he designed an even more extravagant schedule for a prospective law student. Aspiring attorneys, he said, should first master mathematics, natural philosophy, astronomy, and geography. After that, they should spend from dawn till 8 a.m. reading "physical studies, ethics, religion, natural and sectarian, and natural law"; followed by law from 8 a.m. until noon; politics from noon to 1 p.m.; history in the afternoon; and "belles lettres, criticism, rhetoric, [and] oratory" until bedtime.[62] There's no evidence that Jefferson ever followed such a rigorous plan himself, however, and although a man of strict habits, he cannot have adhered to so demanding a schedule during his Williamsburg days, let alone during the busy years that followed.

In fact, he confessed that he learned less from his classes than from the conversations in which he was privileged to participate thanks to William Small's influence. In about 1762, Small introduced his protégé to the prominent attorney George Wythe and to the colony's governor, Francis Fauquier. Fauquier was an aspiring intellectual—a member of the Royal Society, in fact—and hosted convivial dinner-time discussions at the Governor's Palace, often followed by music. Small and Wythe were regular guests. Jefferson, who was a competent violinist, joined these weekly salons, where he "heard more good sense, more rational and philosophical conversations, than in all my life besides."[63]

It was Wythe, however, who exerted the greatest personal influence on his thinking. Born in Virginia in 1726, Wythe had begun practicing law at the age of 20 and, by the 1760s, had risen to the top rank of the profession. Alongside his legal practice and his service in the House of Burgesses, he took on students, who typically lived with his family in a substantial brick house still standing in Williamsburg. He eventually became tutor to many of America's most illustrious legal minds, including President James Monroe, Senator Henry Clay, Virginia Supreme Court Justice St. George Tucker, and US Supreme Court Justices John Marshall and Bushrod Washington. Jefferson moved into his house in 1762 and stayed for five years—an extraordinarily long period of study even by today's standards. Wythe became a "faithful and beloved mentor" to Jefferson, and he remained a "most affectionate friend." He would eventually add his signature to the Declaration his student wrote.[64]

Wythe's first assignment for law students was Coke's *Institutes*. Slogging one's way through Coke's four volumes was not easy. "I never was so tired of a dull old scoundrel in my life," an exhausted Jefferson complained after one long day of reading.[65] Yet he came to appreciate Coke's view that the law is a fundamentally rational enterprise and that English law provided a uniquely precious framework for a free society. "A sounder Whig never wrote," Jefferson said of Coke, "nor of profounder learning in the orthodox doctrines of the British constitution, or in what were called English liberties."[66]

After Coke, Jefferson carefully scrutinized the works of a dozen other thinkers, including Henry Home, Lord Kames, the Scottish judge whose writings on the theory of equity explored the relationship between the general rules that make society function and the specific exceptions necessary to serve the needs of justice; the reformer Cesare Beccaria, whose 1764 book *On Crimes and Punishments* was lauded by liberal minds for condemning severe criminal penalties such as death, torture, and confiscation; and Baron de Montesquieu, whose 1748 book *The Spirit of the Laws* was probably the single most influential work on politics in revolutionary America, aside from Locke's *Treatises*.

Montesquieu is best remembered today for advocating the principle of separation of powers. The unique genius of the English constitution, he claimed, was that it divided the executive, legislative, and judicial roles among different officials, thereby preventing any one person or group from acting as a tyrant. This insight would prove invaluable as Americans first critiqued parliamentary rule and then sought to create new governments to replace it. But Montesquieu also advanced another argument that, although less emphasized by today's historians, had an equally pronounced impact on Enlightenment intellectuals.

In *The Spirit of the Laws*, he argued that the poverty of the Middle Ages had been caused by the Christian world's hostility toward economic freedom, especially moneylending. Medieval theocracies considered lending with interest a sin, based on their interpretation of certain biblical passages and the writings of Aristotle and St. Thomas Aquinas. The Christian taboo on lending did not apply to Jews, however, which led them to take up banking as a traditional profession—many others being closed to them. At the same time, Montesquieu wrote, the delegitimization of banking fostered stereotypes of the ruthless, greedy Jew, "for whenever a thing is forbidden, which nature permits or necessity requires, those who do it are looked upon as dishonest."[67] Yet every economy—not to mention every royal family—needs capital, which is best obtained through loans. Thus, Christian rulers found it necessary to borrow from those they viewed as enemies. This mix of tensions led the Christian world to view Jewish bankers with contempt and fear—which gave those same Christian rulers an excuse to arrest and plunder Jewish businessmen for being "greedy" and accumulating "too much." Meanwhile, Jews themselves were effectively denied access to the courts, since Christian judges refused to enforce loan contracts, which sometimes forced Jews to resort to violence to ensure repayment.[68] The consequence was a cycle of bigotry, persecution, organized crime, and legalized robbery that impoverished Jew and Christian alike. If societies would instead eliminate anti-usury laws and let people borrow and trade freely, society would become more peaceful and more productive. "Peace," Montesquieu concluded, "is the natural effect of trade."[69]

Other writers shared this view. "Enter the Royal Exchange of London," wrote Voltaire in 1720, "[and see] there the Jew, the Mahometan, and the Christian bargain with one another as if they were of the same religion, and bestow the name of infidel on bankrupts only."[70] In short, Montesquieu and other Enlightenment thinkers came to view commerce as a civilizing force, which breaks down racial, religious, and national prejudices and encourages cooperation and construction instead of war and depredation. In the fifth century, St. Jerome had declared that "a merchant can seldom if ever please God," but Enlightenment intellectuals now came to see economic exchange as pacifying, constructive, and ennobling.[71] "The spirit of trade produces in the mind of a man a certain sense of exact justice," wrote Montesquieu.[72] This embrace of bourgeois values set the stage for the revolution Adam Smith would inaugurate in the principles of political economy, and it would bolster the arguments of American revolutionaries that British mercantilism was both unwise and unjust—a violation of the colonists' natural right to earn a living. Jefferson would become one of the most notable spokesmen for economic freedom during the American Revolution.[73]

THEY WILL OPPOSE IT TO THE LAST

By the autumn of 1765, Jefferson was ready to take the bar exam. Yet the test was scheduled for October—just as the Stamp Act crisis was reaching its climax—and it may have been difficult to concentrate on studying. It was that month that his sister died. With the courts closed, and a legal rule that in any event imposed a one-year waiting period between passage of the bar and work as a lawyer, Jefferson had time to travel to Philadelphia to be inoculated against smallpox, where he witnessed the celebrations over the act's recission the following May. What neither he nor the colonists carousing in the streets acknowledged at the time was the poison pill accompanying repeal: the Declaratory Act of 1766, formally asserting Parliament's authority to legislate for the colonies "in all cases whatsoever."

It was this law, more than any other single piece of legislation, that would precipitate the American Revolution. Colonists may have groaned under the expense of taxes and the unfairness of trade restrictions, but their disputes with the mother country only raised the risk of civil war when they touched on bedrock issues of constitutional law. Throughout the conflict over the Sugar and Stamp Acts, Americans had made it clear that they thought lawmaking in America was a job for their own legislatures, not a distant Parliament where they were not, and could not be, meaningfully represented.[74] Neither Prime Minister Grenville nor his allies could accede to that objection, however, without sacrificing what they considered the basic principle of the imperial constitution: Parliamentary Supremacy. By pronouncing that doctrine to be the law of the land, the Declaratory Act drastically raised the stakes.

When the idea of repealing the Stamp Act came up for debate in early 1766, Britain's chief justice, Lord Mansfield, told the House of Lords that American arguments against the act's constitutionality were baseless and that repeal would endanger the empire. Parliament's power was either complete or nonexistent, he said. There was no middle ground. That was a characteristic assertion for Mansfield, who, although born into a noble Scottish family that remained loyal to the Stuarts, had rejected his family's politics and had become a stalwart champion of Parliamentary Supremacy. He had been made chief justice 10 years earlier, while serving simultaneously in Parliament, and now he argued that Westminster could and should control colonial economies to serve British domestic interests.[75] The idea that Americans were constitutionally entitled to their own legislatures, or that they were within the king's dominion but outside the realm of Parliament, was foolishness. Americans were actually "*more* emphatically subjects of Great Britain than those within the realm"—that is, they were even more subject to Westminster's power—because their ancestors had "migrated with [the British government's] leave," and therefore the colonies existed solely by parliamentary grace. The principle of government by representation was a mere privilege. The idea that it was a *right* was "merely ideal."[76] What's more, it was "settled" that "there is no restriction on the legislative authority of Great Britain." Sovereignty was all-or-nothing. To repeal the Stamp Act therefore risked "giving up the total legislature of this kingdom." It might even lead Americans to "think they have a right to an open trade and establishment of manufactures."[77] Parliament must never yield on the question of its supreme power. "Take care, my lords," Mansfield warned his colleagues, "that you do not abdicate your authority."[78]

While these debates went on, the House of Commons invited Benjamin Franklin to testify about American public opinion and the potential consequences of repeal. Already a celebrated figure, Franklin had been born to a poor English emigrant who had 16 other children. At the age of 12, he had been apprenticed to his brother James, who ran a Boston printshop. The two did not get along, however, and when James beat him once too often, Benjamin ran away. In violation of Massachusetts law—which bound apprentices to service for a term of years—he fled to Philadelphia, arriving virtually penniless in the fall of 1724. Through hard work and the diligent cultivation of personal relationships, he rose to prominence, publishing newspapers and almanacs, managing community improvements such as the first lending library and first fire insurance company, and conducting experiments with electricity that brought him fame throughout the empire. By the 1760s, he was the most renowned American of all, universally called "Doctor" despite having no formal education. Now 60, he had been living in London for nearly a decade, working as an "agent," or lobbyist, for the colonies of Pennsylvania, Delaware, and New Jersey. In explaining American protests against the Stamp Act, he would be combining the role of diplomat and advocate for the entire continent.

Franklin had warned British officials as early as 1754 that taxing the colonists directly was a bad idea. Americans considered themselves entitled to the same rights as all other Britons, he said, and that included the right not to be taxed except by legislatures in which they had a voice. They would blanch at the idea "that by hazarding their lives and fortunes in subduing and settling new countries, extending the dominion and increasing the commerce of their mother nation, they have forfeited [their] native rights."[79] Now, as de facto ambassador from North America, he repeated that point again and again as members of Parliament (MPs) subjected him to a four-hour barrage of questions about resistance to the stamp tax.

"Was it an opinion in America before 1763 that the Parliament had no right to lay taxes and duties there?" asked one MP.

"I never heard any objection," Franklin replied, "but a right to lay internal taxes was never supposed to be in Parliament, as we are not represented there."[80]

Would Americans accept *any* tax Parliament imposed? No, he answered. They thought that if Britain needed funds, it should request them from colonial legislatures "according to the old established usage." Colonists considered it "extremely hard and unjust that a body of men, in which they have no representative" would try "giving and granting what is not its own, but theirs, and deprive them of a right they esteem of the utmost value and importance."[81]

Several MPs tried to pressure Franklin into compromising. "Do not you think the people of America would submit to pay the stamp duty, if it was moderated?"

"No, never," he said.

Asked if Americans in general had lost respect for Parliament, Franklin replied that they had. "Demanding a new and heavy tax by stamps, taking away, at the same time, trials by juries, and refusing to receive and hear their humble petitions" had made Americans, once proud of their English heritage, begin to sour on that relationship. When another MP asked if he had heard about Parliament's idea of adopting a formal statute asserting its power to legislate for America, Franklin said that such a thing would be "unconstitutional and unjust."

The questioning gradually became more heated, taking on the tone of a cross-examination. Some members tried to back Franklin into conceding that American arguments against Parliament's power were "innovations"—that is, new ideas not rooted in constitutional tradition. He carefully framed his replies to avoid that trap and to make clear that it was actually Parliament that was engaged in "innovations." When one member asked if Franklin could "name any act of assembly, or public act of any of your governments" that before now had distinguished between unconstitutional taxation and constitutional trade restrictions, he answered that "there was never an occasion to *make* any such act, till now that you have attempted to tax us. That has occasioned resolutions of assembly, declaring the distinction, in which I think every assembly on the continent, and every member in every assembly, have been unanimous."[82]

Groping for some face-saving expedient that would enable Parliament to withdraw the tax without conceding the constitutional point, one member asked, "If the Parliament should repeal the Stamp Act, will the assembly of Pennsylvania rescind their resolutions [declaring it unconstitutional]?"

"I think not," Franklin replied.

"Is there no means of obliging them to erase those resolutions?" asked another member.

"None that I know of; they will never do it unless compelled by force of arms."

"Is there a power on earth that can force them to erase them?"

"No power," the American answered, "can force men to change their opinions."[83]

Yet Franklin did offer one important concession. Asked what colonists would think were Parliament's "motives" if it did repeal the Stamp Act, he tried to reassure the House that colonists would not view it as a *constitutional* concession. "I suppose they will think it was repealed from a conviction of its inexpediency," he said, "and they will rely on it, that while the same inexpediency subsists, you will never attempt to make such another."[84] Would Americans object if Parliament reiterated its constitutional authority to legislate for the colonies? No, he replied. "I think the resolutions of right will give them very little concern, if they are never attempted to be carried into practice."[85]

That last phrase was critical. Franklin was taking a diplomatic, and potentially misleading, step. As a lobbyist seeking repeal, he was offering Parliament a way to retreat with honor. It was better to obtain repeal now, and argue about constitutional theory later. Maybe a pro forma assertion of Parliamentary power—if never actually enforced—would soothe British tempers without giving away anything of substance. For Americans to demand that Parliament admit it was wrong would be futile. So, contradicting what he had said only moments earlier, Franklin seemed to accept the idea of a Declaratory Act.

Advocates of Parliamentary Supremacy feared that a merely abstract assertion of power would be pointless. Surely it would be wiser to substitute a new tax for the Stamp Act, instead of just repealing it. Yet when this was suggested, Franklin again warned the House: "As to any internal tax, how small soever, laid by the legislature here on the people there, while they have no representatives in this legislature, I think it will never be submitted to. They will oppose it to the last."[86]

Two months later, Parliament chose its course. It would repeal the Stamp Act, while making clear that it did so exclusively on account of the "inconveniencies" of enforcing it.[87] And although it would not replace that tax with a new one, it would formally assert authority to make laws for the colonies if it chose to. It had done something like that before. In the Great Britain Act of 1719, also known as the Irish Declaratory Act, it had officially proclaimed that Ireland "is, and of right ought to be subordinate unto and dependent upon" the Westminster Parliament, which "had, has, and of right ought to have full power and authority to make laws . . . to bind the kingdom and people of Ireland."[88] Now it did the same for America. In a new Declaratory Act, it pronounced all resolutions by colonial legislatures that denied its taxing power to be "utterly null and void" and decreed that Parliament "had, has, and of right ought to have, full power and authority" to legislate for Americans "in all cases whatsoever."[89]

In hindsight, it seems remarkable that this broad language did not immediately provoke a backlash in the colonies. It was exactly the principle Americans had opposed, stated in the starkest possible terms. Some colonists were indeed alarmed by it; Maryland's legislature refused even to pay a printer to publish the official text of the Declaratory Act because doing so "might hereafter furnish an argument" that the people "acquiesce" in Parliament's authority.[90] But most colonists viewed the law as an empty gesture. After all, despite the 1719 act, the London Parliament had seldom tried to interfere in Irish affairs.[91] In any case, colonists were too busy celebrating their win. Compromise was so welcome in light of the grave risks entailed by American defiance that all sides were willing to quietly overlook what seemed like abstract concerns, if that would help ease tensions. "The Stamp Act was repealed and the Declaratory Act was passed," John Adams recalled four decades later. "As we expected [that the Declaratory Act] would not be executed, good humor was in some measure restored."[92]

Such a sigh of relief was understandable. The threat of violence had never been far from the minds of those opposing the Stamp Act. It had even come up during Franklin's testimony. "What do you think is a sufficient military force to protect the distribution of the stamps in every part of America?" one MP asked him.

"A very great force," Franklin answered.

"What," his questioner shot back, "is the number of men in America able to bear arms?"

The question caused an uproar. As Franklin opened his mouth to respond, voices called out objections. Such a question was inappropriate, some said. As the members began to argue, Dr. Franklin was asked to kindly step outside for a moment. He left the room and waited in the hall. When, at last, he was called back in, calm had been restored, and talk of military intervention ceased.[93] The message, however, was clear: Legalistic disagreements over the constitution could rapidly escalate into something much more dangerous. Little wonder that Americans rejoiced at what seemed like a compromise. As Franklin left the building that day, one moment in particular must have stuck in his memory. "Can anything less than a military force carry the Stamp Act into execution?" one member had asked.

"A military force sent into America," he replied, "will not find a rebellion; they may indeed *make* one."[94]

— CHAPTER 6 —

SWARMS OF OFFICERS

We had been so long in the habit of seeing [Britain] consider us merely as objects for the extension of their commerce, and of submitting to every duty or regulation imposed with that view, that we had ceased to complain. . . . But when they proposed to consider us as objects of taxation, all the states took the alarm.
—*Thomas Jefferson*[1]

While Jefferson and other colonists cheered the Stamp Act's repeal in the spring of 1766, conflicts still remained. For one thing, Parliament wanted the Americans to reimburse officials, such as Massachusetts Chief Justice Thomas Hutchinson, whose property had been damaged in the riots. It also began rewarding those who had tried unsuccessfully to enforce the act, giving them new titles and salaried positions, including appointments as judges of the vice-admiralty courts. This upset people like John Adams, who regarded the act as unconstitutional and considered anyone responsible for enforcing it an unprincipled lackey of London politicians. When Bay Colony legislators finally agreed to pay for the damage, they combined compensation with a general pardon for the rioters. That was promptly vetoed in London, which commanded the colony to pass a new law for compensation "unmixed with any other matter whatsoever."[2]

Also, while Parliament repealed the Stamp Act, it left in place the other laws that infringed on colonial rights. This included the Mutiny and Quartering Acts—adopted at the same time as the Stamp Act—which forced colonial legislatures to furnish supplies to

This portrait of Thomas Hutchinson was painted in 1741,
30 years before he became governor of Massachusetts.
(Collection of the Massachusetts Historical Society)

British soldiers stationed in North America and empowered officers to commandeer inns, warehouses, or uninhabited houses to shelter troops who could not be accommodated in existing barracks.[3] The Quartering Acts did not, as is often believed, require people to take soldiers into their homes, but they did compel farmers to let soldiers live in "outbuildings" such as barns and stables. This legislation was not just a confiscation of private property, but a form of surveillance every bit as intrusive as "general warrants." Soldiers were expected not just to keep order, but to seek out and punish suspected smugglers. As for laws compelling colonies to equip the army, those were indistinguishable from imperial taxes, and they, too, had not been repealed.

These laws were not entirely new—there had been Mutiny and Quartering Acts in the 17th century—but colonial legislatures had never accepted their validity. Instead, American lawmakers had found ways to provide supplies while calling them "gifts" or "loans," so as not to concede that such demands were constitutional.[4] But when 1,500 red-coated British troops marched ashore in New York in May 1766 in response to that colony's Stamp Act riots (a mob had burned the stamps and even destroyed the governor's carriage), the legislature refused to make any payment except for barracks, and then only after the costs had been incurred, not up front, as Parliament demanded. London sent the New Yorkers a letter reminding them of their duty to obey the acts, and remonstrating that it only seemed fair for the colonists to comply, given that the mother country had been so kind as to withdraw the Stamp Act. But the Americans only replied with more petitions against Parliament's authority.

At this, London lost its patience. In the summer of 1767, it retaliated with a law called the New York Restraining Act, which effectively shut down New York's government.[5] It barred the governor or legislature from "pass[ing] any bill, order, resolution, or vote," or taking any other action "of any kind, for any other purpose whatsoever," until the colony obeyed the Mutiny Act.[6] Parliament was making clear that it meant what it said by "all cases whatsoever."

New York legislators were not prepared to back down. Instead, they passed a bill that did not provide the required supplies, but gave funds directly to British officers to buy items for their men. The bill also made no mention of the Mutiny Act. This meant the colonists could accommodate the soldiers' needs while still appearing to give the money "voluntarily," rather than in obedience to Parliament's dictates. In London, George Grenville—no longer prime minister, but still in Parliament—was not pleased. "I do not see how the conduct of the Assembly of New York in giving a sum of money to the crown but refusing to take the least notice of the Mutiny Act can be called a submission to that law," he wrote to his friend Thomas Whately. "It seems to me the very reverse . . . . [Americans] must feel before they believe, and I think that period of conviction is not far off."[7] But the Board of Trade ruled that New York's actions were good enough and pronounced the "restraining" of the legislature at an end.

That did not mean Westminster was backing down, however. The Restraining Act was just one of four laws passed between June 29 and July 2, 1767, that, along with a fifth law adopted the following spring, proved that Parliament was taking its claim of absolutism seriously. Known as the Townshend Acts after Chancellor of the Exchequer Thomas Townshend, who supported Grenville's American policy, these statutes were intended to raise revenue from taxes on the American colonies, just as the stamps had been.

First, the Revenue Act imposed taxes on tea, glass, lead, paper, and paint, and included harsh enforcement provisions: authorizing the use of writs of assistance and specifying the penalty of forfeiture, with informants being rewarded with a portion of the proceeds.[8] Hearings, of course, would be held in vice-admiralty courts. The act also provided that the funds raised through the taxes would be paid directly to colonial governors and their deputies—meaning colonial legislatures would lose all power over these officials' salaries—and that the revenues would be spent "for defraying the charge of the administration of justice and the support of civil government, in *such provinces where it shall be found necessary*"—meaning that taxpayers in Massachusetts or Virginia would be paying for the governments of New Jersey, Delaware, Canada, or the West Indies.[9] "What justice is there in making us pay for 'defending, protecting and securing' these places?" demanded one Pennsylvanian. "None of them was conquered for us; nor will [they] 'be defended, protected and secured' for us."[10]

The second Townshend Act created a new American Board of Customs headquartered in North America, in order to streamline enforcement of trade restrictions.[11] Its officials would not be subject to the governor's authority, or paid by the elected legislature, meaning they were unaccountable to the people and exercised the power of an occupying force instead. Indeed, the commissioners who arrived in Boston in November 1767 turned out to be the loudest voices goading London to dispatch more soldiers to America. Still another law, the Indemnity Act, reduced the taxes that the East India Company had to pay for its business exporting tea to Americans—effectively a subsidy no colonial merchants enjoyed.[12]

Next, Parliament adopted the Colonial Trade Act, which created new vice-admiralty courts in Boston, Philadelphia, and Charleston, with power to hear cases involving tax violations, even if they had nothing to do with the sorts of maritime matters that vice-admiralty courts traditionally heard.[13] Because these juryless tribunals did not follow such traditional common-law rules as the presumption of innocence or the right to counsel, a colonist might find his property seized for alleged nonpayment of taxes, and then be forced to prove to a judge that the property was not contraband. Worse, in some colonies—including Massachusetts and Virginia—the same person who served as vice-admiralty judge also served as attorney general, creating a clear conflict of interest. London did fix one objectionable feature of the courts by providing salaries to the judges, so they were no longer paid a percentage of whatever they confiscated. But the salaries seemed exorbitant, and the judges often left the colonies for long periods, appointing deputies in their places and thus turning their jobs into sinecures. (This was a common source of complaint in places like Virginia, which between 1756 and 1768 was ruled by royal governors who never even visited the colony.)

The Townshend Acts enraged colonial Whigs. Yet most Americans seemed to shrug. When, in October 1767, Samuel Adams arranged for the Boston Town Meeting to announce another boycott of British imports to protest the acts, the plan aroused little enthusiasm. And although Massachusetts and other colonies did form a general nonimportation agreement in the months that followed, it was never as effective as the Stamp Act protest had been.[14] To maintain the boycott, Sons of Liberty organizations in port towns monitored the markets for goods that violated the agreement, and they intimidated businesses and consumers who evaded the ban. They also frequently "rescued" ships from potential confiscation when seized by customs officers—either by threatening the inspectors or by taking over captured vessels and sailing them away before the government could act. But sporadic protests like these proved a poor sequel to the united front Americans had put up against the Stamp Act, and when Pennsylvania merchants refused to join the boycott, it seemed the colonists might actually be forced to give in.

MASSACHUSETTS CALLS FOR UNITY

Massachusetts's Whigs would not let that happen. After sending another protest to London seeking repeal of the acts, the House of Representatives asked Samuel Adams and James Otis to write a "circular letter" to the other colonies, arguing that the Townshend Acts violated both the British constitution and the basic principles of political legitimacy and urging all Americans to unite in opposition. "It is an essential unalterable right in nature, ingrafted into the British constitution as a fundamental law and ever held sacred and irrevocable," the letter said, "that what a man has honestly acquired is absolutely his own, which he may freely give, but [which] cannot be taken from him without his consent." The Townshend Acts were shoving that principle aside. Adams and Otis conceded that Parliament could impose tariffs and duties to regulate trade, but laws that seized the colonists' wealth for "the sole and express purpose of raising a revenue" were "infringements of their natural and constitutional rights."[15] On February 11, 1768, the House approved the letter and sent it to the other colonies.

Virginia's House of Burgesses agreed without hesitation. "Applaud[ing]" the Yankees "for their attention to American liberty," and assuring Massachusetts of their "fixed resolution to concur with the other colonies in their application for redress," the Virginians dusted off the protests they had sent to London against the Stamp Act (and that Parliament had refused to consider) and again sent three separate documents—a petition to the king, a memorial to the House of Lords, and a remonstrance to the House of Commons—arguing that the Townshend Acts were contrary to "the natural rights and first principles of the English constitution."[16]

By emphasizing natural rights and first principles, the colonists were making clear that this was not a mere constitutional dispute, but a moral one. The essence of ownership is the power to decide how to dispose of one's belongings. To take Americans' earnings without their consent or that of their representatives was to violate the very concept of private property. Almost a century earlier, John Locke had written, "I have truly no property in that which another can by right take from me, when he pleases, against my consent." Thus, even a government with "good and equitable laws," would still be illegitimate if it could "take from any private man, what part [it] pleases of his property, and use and dispose of it as [it] thinks good."[17] Now, the Burgesses reiterated that point, arguing that if Parliament could "give and grant, at their pleasure, the properties of the people in the colonies" or "impose an internal tax of any kind on them, who are not, and cannot from the nature of their situation, be represented in their House of Commons," then no person could truly *own* anything—their property would instead be subject to seizure at any moment on orders from London. If that were the law, Americans might as well "bid Adieu to their natural and civil liberties, and to prepare for a state of the most abject slavery."[18] That, the Burgesses added, seemed to be the direction things were heading. If Westminster could suspend New York's legislature by fiat, just for protesting on behalf of the people's rights, then "what advantage could the people of the colonies derive from their right of choosing their own representatives . . . ?"[19]

The most striking thing about this language was that American protests were demanding repeal of the Townshend Acts not as a favor but as a matter of right. Equally brazen, many colonies sent their petitions not to Parliament but exclusively to King George, which represented a deliberate refusal to acknowledge Parliament's power and an implicit assertion that they were governed only by the king and their own legislatures, not by the Lords and Commons. As Rhode Island's governor explained to the Earl of Hillsborough, who became secretary of state for the colonies in February 1768, his colony's legislature was sending the king a "dutiful and loyal address" asking him to "interpose" between Parliament and themselves to protect the colonists' "exclusive right of giving and granting their money themselves, or by representatives chosen by them."[20]

To some observers, this boldness indicated a new, more resolute approach to the imperial crisis. "During the regal government," wrote Thomas Jefferson years later, "our minds were circumscribed within narrow limits by a habitual belief that it was our duty to be subordinate to the mother country in all matters of government, [and] to direct all our labors in subservience to her interests. . . . The difficulties with our representatives were of habit and despair, not of reflection and conviction."[21] Now, that was beginning to change. By calling for a united front against the Townshend Acts, the Massachusetts Circular Letter seemed to indicate the birth of an American nationalism.

Equally alarming to Lord Hillsborough and other ministers was a series of essays that began appearing in newspapers that winter, making an unusually strong case that Parliament lacked authority to tax Americans. Published as a pamphlet the same month that Hillsborough assumed office, the series was called *Letters from a Farmer in Pennsylvania*, and it was the work of Philadelphia lawyer John Dickinson (who was not a farmer). The Townshend Acts, he wrote, represented an effort to "supersede [the] authority in our respective assemblies, which is most essential to liberty." If Parliament could tax and spend without the involvement of American legislatures, then "what taxes will remain to be imposed by our assemblies. . . ? What must become of [those legislatures], and the people they represent?"[22] Dickinson urged Americans to "unanimously join in this sentiment, that the late act of Parliament is injurious to their liberty," and to "unite . . . in a firm opposition to [the Townshend Acts], in the same manner as the dread of the Stamp Act did."[23] His *Letters* became a sensation.

Lord Hillsborough was startled by such impudence. A strutting mediocrity whom one colleague called "a man of more pomp than solidity, very ambitious, changeable, and false to his friends," the 50-year-old Hillsborough was fabulously rich and a member of both the British House of Commons and the Irish House of Lords.[24] He was a friend of former Prime Minister Grenville, and he had firm views about the relationship between Britain and her colonies. His inflexibility was not leavened by understanding. King George once said of him, "I do not know a man of less judgment."[25]

Now, Hillsborough wrote to all the colonial governors, warning them of the subversiveness of Dickinson's *Letters* and instructing them to make sure their own legislatures did not endorse the Massachusetts Circular Letter. In a separate note to Governor Francis Bernard, he issued an even harsher command: Bernard was to order the Massachusetts House to repudiate the Circular Letter or face suspension, just as New York's legislature had been nullified months before.[26]

As if that were not enough, a new crisis erupted that summer, when the *Liberty*, a ship owned by the rich colonial merchant John Hancock, was seized by customs officials who suspected Hancock of smuggling and were determined to make an example of him. Hancock's wealth and prominence—he was not only a member of the colony's legislature but also commander of the local militia—gave his open opposition to the Stamp and Townshend Acts particular significance, and he compounded this with overt rudeness toward customs officials. When members of the new Board of Customs Commissioners arrived in the colony, he declined to let his militia company participate in a welcome parade, and he later refused Governor Bernard's express order to bring the company to a celebratory banquet in their honor. Hancock added further insult when his ship the *Lydia* arrived in Boston with a cargo of wine. When inspectors went aboard, he barred them from going below decks—which was technically his right under the law, but raised suspicions to such a degree that the Board asked their supervisors for permission to prosecute him for interfering with a customs inspection. London said no, but a month later, the commissioners found a different way to punish Hancock.

In early June, they waited until his employees had loaded the *Liberty* with a cargo of tar and whale oil, and then seized the ship for failing to obtain a permit before loading. Although the law technically required that the paperwork be filled out before placing cargo on board, most Boston shippers found it easier to fill out the paperwork *after* loading, and the government had never considered that a problem before. This time, however, the commissioners decided to exploit this minor infraction to seize Hancock's £1,000 vessel and its £1,000 cargo, with plans to sell it and divide the proceeds.

Because the Sons of Liberty had by now become adept at "rescuing" confiscated ships, the government decided to immediately have a navy vessel called the HMS *Romney* tow the *Liberty* out into the harbor, where it could be safely impounded. But when the colonists realized what was happening, they erupted in violence. A crowd of perhaps 3,000 Bostonians attacked customs officers, beating them in the streets and throwing rocks at their houses. The bureaucrats only escaped lynching by taking refuge in Castle William, the garrison controlling the port, which would soon become a regular sanctuary for British officials fleeing enraged Bostonians. Meanwhile, the mob managed to board the *Romney* and set it on fire. The riots, which lasted all weekend, proved ferocious even by Boston standards.

When calm was finally restored, one of the inspectors filed a statement with the Customs Board claiming that when he first went aboard the *Liberty*, Hancock's employees had tried to bribe him and, when he refused, had locked him in the hold for hours, presumably while removing contraband. The story was a lie, but the Board seized upon it as grounds for prosecuting Hancock criminally. Seeking £9,000 in penalties—the triple damages allowed under the Sugar Act—prosecutors filed their case in the vice-admiralty court, where no jury would be available and where Hancock would be presumed guilty until proven innocent. Thus began what historian Oliver Dickerson calls "the most unusual suit in the entire history of British revenue laws in America."[27]

Needing a defense attorney, Hancock turned to his friend John Adams. John and Abigail (who had just given birth to a son named John Quincy) had recently moved into a rented home in Boston to be closer to court, and John had become increasingly involved in defending merchants against customs officers. The Hancock case, however, took more work than any lawsuit he had yet litigated. He was called to the courthouse nearly every day that winter to examine witnesses and present arguments—all a "painful drudgery."[28] Eventually, Adams—who considered the vice-admiralty courts "the most grievous innovation" of all the abuses that led to the American Revolution—put together a powerful defense, arguing not only that the witnesses had perjured themselves but that the laws under which Hancock was being prosecuted were unconstitutional.[29]

"[The law] was made without our consent," he argued. "My client, Mr. Hancock, never consented to it. He never voted for it himself, and he never voted for any man to make such a law for him. In this respect, therefore, the greatest consolation of an Englishman . . . is torn from him, I mean the reflection, that it is a law of his own making." The idea of prosecuting a man under such a law was "a hardship . . . scarcely to be endured." The decision to try the case in a vice-admiralty court was even worse. In England, Hancock would have been entitled to a jury trial—but not in America. "Is there not in this . . . a brand of infamy, of degradation, and disgrace, fixed upon every American? Is he not degraded below the rank of an Englishman? Is it not directly, a repeal of Magna Carta, as far as America is concerned[?]"[30] The *Liberty* trial would drag on until the following spring.

In the meantime, the Massachusetts House took up the question of whether to rescind the Circular Letter as Hillsborough had demanded. Their answer was a resolute no—by a vote of 92 to 17. Instead, the House sent the colonial secretary an address—written, as usual, by Samuel Adams—expressing its confidence that "Your Lordship surely will not think it a crime in [this] House, to have taken a step, which was perfectly consistent with the constitution."[31] The House then created a committee to draft a new petition to the king, this time asking that Governor Bernard be removed from office.

Thrilled by the boldness of the legislators who refused to rescind the letter, Samuel Adams's friend, the silversmith Paul Revere, hammered out a commemorative silver bowl, 11 inches in diameter—enormous by the standards of the day—and engraved it with the names of "the glorious ninety-two" along with a picture of a torn-up general warrant. A few days later, the bowl was used at a party whose guests gathered to sing "The Liberty Song," America's earliest patriotic tune. "In freedom we're born and in freedom we'll live," it declared.

> Swarms of placemen and pensioners soon will appear
> Like locusts deforming the charms of the year;
> Suns vainly will rise, showers vainly descend,
> If we are to drudge for what others shall defend.
> Then join hand in hand, brave Americans all,
> By uniting we stand, by dividing we fall;
> In so righteous a cause let us hope to succeed,
> For heaven approves of each generous deed.[32]

The song was the work of John Dickinson of *Letters from a Farmer* fame. His Bible-inspired lyrics—"by uniting we stand, by dividing we fall"—would become a staple of American political rhetoric, and his reference to "swarms of placemen and pensioners" struck with particular force. The "swarms" metaphor, borrowed from the book of Job, had long been used by Whig thinkers such as Thomas Gordon and John Trenchard, who often remarked on the way political authorities surround themselves with "hirelings" subsidized by taxes taken from the people. Just two weeks before Dickinson's song was published, John Adams, attending the Boston Town Meeting, had written on the city's behalf a set of instructions to representatives in the colonial legislature, expressing the people's "mortification" at witnessing "one Act of Parliament after another passed for the express purpose of raising a revenue" and then seeing the money "appropriated to the maintenance of swarms of officers and pensioners in idleness and luxury."[33]

The "swarms" image would eventually make its way into the Declaration of Independence, where it would spark resentment from Loyalists, especially Thomas Hutchinson. In a 1776 pamphlet responding to the Declaration, Hutchinson called it an exaggeration, because the Townshend Acts had only created "thirty or forty" customs commissioners, which hardly amounted to "swarms."[34] That was a rhetorical trick on Hutchinson's part, however, because the customs collectors were not the only "officers" Dickinson, Adams, and others had in mind. The forfeiture system behind the tax laws provided that informants, judges, and colonial governors also got to share in the proceeds of tax seizures. Customs enforcers freely hired deputies of various ranks, and they, too, were paid from the spoils of seized cargoes. The Grenville government had added some 20 Royal Navy ships to the patrol of the American coastline, charged with catching tax evaders; their crews were entitled to share in confiscated property, as well. Even more oppressively, the Mutiny and Quartering Acts forced colonists to pay for the equipping, feeding, and lodging of whatever armies Britain might send to America. At the same time, governors and other officials who never even visited the colonies were paid sinecures and salaries out of the pockets of hardworking Americans. All of this gave weight to colonial complaints that they were forced to subsidize "swarms of officers and pensioners."

Massachusetts's refusal to rescind the Circular Letter did not amuse the imperial government. As soon as Governor Bernard learned of the House's vote against rescinding, he ordered the representatives to meet him in his office. He was shutting them down, he said. They should go home. "I should have thought myself blamable," he told Lord Hillsborough, "if I had suffered five minutes to intervene between receiving the answer and dismissing the House."[35] For more than a year, Massachusetts would operate without a legislature.

The lawmakers were nevertheless determined not to comply. They arranged for the Boston Town Meeting to call on all Massachusetts towns to send representatives to a special "convention" instead—the word "convention" being typically used for a parliament not legally sanctioned by the king. Ninety-six towns agreed, sending delegates to a weeklong meeting in Boston that September. Although the convention accomplished little beyond petitioning the governor to reopen the legislature (a request he immediately rejected), it represented a new step toward independence: In the years to come, colonists would simply hold such conventions whenever imperial representatives closed their assemblies, and these would gradually take on the role of de facto legislatures—just as the Boston Town Meeting would now substitute for Massachusetts's shuttered House of Representatives.

Lord Hillsborough and his allies in London were starting to think the Bay Colony's government was hopeless. Riots were regular occurrences, defiance to the Townshend Acts was consistent and overt, and Boston juries refused to convict violators. Instead, they often threatened to convict imperial officers for executing customs laws that jurors considered unconstitutional. As for Governor Bernard, he seemed incapable of keeping order; his executive council—chosen by the House, not the king—hampered him by refusing to declare the existence of riots, which made law enforcement impossible. To deal with this mess required a show of strength.

Parliament therefore took a grave step. It created "a special commission for enquiring of, hearing, and determining" whether the leaders of the *Liberty* riot were guilty of treason "pursuant to the provisions of the statute of the thirty-fifth year of the reign of King Henry the Eighth."[36] That statute, called the Treason Act—already more than two centuries old—enabled imperial prosecutors to try people accused of treason in England, far from obstinate colonial juries.[37] Then, resolving that a military force was necessary for "the preservation of the public peace, and the due execution of the laws" in America, Parliament ordered thousands of troops to Boston.

Within months, the city resembled an armed camp. Scarlet-clad soldiers (or "regulars") marched down Beacon Street, drilled in the marketplaces, pitched their tents in public parks, and took over warehouses on the wharves.[38] Many locals despised them, and fist-fights between soldiers and citizens became common. When Governor Bernard ordered that troops be quartered in an old factory near Boston Common, the poor tenants living in it refused to leave. The infantrymen spent weeks trying to starve them out, only to see Bostonians tossing bread through the windows to encourage their resistance.

Through the fall and winter of 1769, hundreds of regulars met at reveille in Brattle Square just outside John Adams's rented house. "The ear-piercing fife aroused me and my family early every morning," he recalled, marching and training on the village green.[39] It was not just the noise of their assemblies, or their frequent brawls with the townspeople; rumors also swirled about theft and rape, and the men were often disciplined by brutal whippings, which took place in public view. When Adams grumbled about such sights to a friend—a clergyman fond of puns—the man wryly answered that despite their petitions, the colonists' grievances had not been "redressed," but merely "red-dressed." Adams, however, could not laugh as he watched the blood-colored uniforms crossing back and forth on the avenues. "Their very appearance in Boston was strong proof to me, that the determination in Great Britain to subjugate us, was too deep and inveterate ever to be altered."[40]

THE VIRGINIA RESOLVES

Far to the south, Thomas Jefferson was spending the summer planning his new home. The eight square miles of land he had inherited from his father was divided into four sections—Shadwell, Lego, Tufton Farm, and Monticello, the latter located about five miles from Shadwell and named after the 850-foot mountain that had been Jefferson's favorite place to study during his college days. Now 26 years old, he had long ago settled on the idea of building a residence of his own atop that hill—the Shadwell farmhouse was old and small, and he seems to have wanted to live away from his mother—so in May 1768, he had a team of enslaved workers begin leveling the site to prepare a foundation.

The mountain offered a sublime view of the valley where the new city of Charlottesville was being built. Yet the idea of constructing a house there—far from convenient river access—reveals more than anything else the impractical and romantic side of Jefferson's personality. Every household item would have to be carted up the incline—including water when the wells went dry, as they sometimes did for whole years at a time. Jefferson's architectural tastes were also more aesthetic than realistic: He fancied the designs of the Italian Renaissance builder Andrea Palladio rather than the workaday styles most colonial plantation owners used. Where other Virginia farms were plain rectangular wooden structures, sometimes adorned with classical ornament, Monticello would be a symmetrical two-story edifice built out of brick made on-site, with columns inspired by Palladio's Villa Emo and Villa Barbaro. (The version he originally designed was never actually completed, however. In the 1790s, before it was finished, he radically revised the plan, adding a dome as its central feature—again inspired by Palladio—and it is this version of the house that tourists visit today.)

In the meantime, Jefferson began buying land elsewhere in Virginia, including 300 acres in Bedford County, about 50 miles from Monticello, where he later built a second home, called Poplar Forest. Real estate speculation was an obsession with upper-class Virginians, and Jefferson had spent the first two years of his legal career traveling the western countryside, working on property disputes. Between 1767 and 1774, he managed nearly 1,000 cases, specializing in those involving "caveats"—a scheme that enabled landowners to avoid paying quitrents by arranging for a friend to file paperwork claiming the land had been abandoned, and then postponing resolution of the abandonment claim. The delay could last for years before a court finally threw out the case, and in the interim, the owner had avoided payments.[41]

Jefferson's legal practice gained him the admiration of many prominent Virginians, including the wealthy William Byrd, who kept him on retainer. But it did not pay well, and obscure real estate disputes were hardly as interesting as the controversies now roiling British America. When, in December 1768, the colony's new governor, Lord Botetourt, called for elections to the House of Burgesses, Jefferson announced his willingness to serve. He was easily elected in a campaign that consisted mostly of shaking hands and serving punch at town meetings.

He cannot have expected a peaceful scene when he took his seat in the House in April 1769. Governors throughout America, in obedience to Lord Hillsborough's instructions, had started shutting down colonial legislatures whenever they responded positively to the Massachusetts Circular Letter. The assemblies of Delaware, Georgia, Maryland, New Jersey, New York, and South Carolina had all been closed, and not only was the Bay Colony's legislature dissolved, but thousands of troops were now occupying Boston.[42] Two months earlier, Parliament declared the Massachusetts resolutions against the Townshend Acts "illegal, unconstitutional, and calculated to excite sedition and insurrections." It also pronounced the Massachusetts convention illegal and encouraged the king to use the Treason Act to extradite Boston troublemakers to England for trial.[43]

Remarkably, the ministers in London were actually more worried about Virginia than the other colonies. Norfolk residents had rioted in September 1767 against the impressment of sailors, even seizing some members of the press-gang. They rioted again the following June, only two weeks after the Boston *Liberty* riots, when a local Whig leader led a mob to chase a Tory physician out of town for providing inoculations against smallpox.[44] (They feared the inoculations were actually causing an epidemic, which was not an unreasonable suspicion, given the crude quality of medicine at the time.) Then, London learned about Virginia's positive response to the Massachusetts Circular Letter. Lord Hillsborough thought the Virginians' "indecent remonstrances" against the Townshend Acts were proof that they were in "a much worse state than even the colony of Massachusetts."[45] That had led him to send Lord Botetourt to

Williamsburg as the colony's new governor, in hopes that he might rein in the Old Dominion.

Norborne Berkeley, Fourth Baron Botetourt, was the bankrupt son of a rich English family that had important connections in Virginia—he was distantly related to Governor William Berkeley who had presided there during the Stuarts' reign—and his appointment as governor proved a convenient way to evade his creditors. In his early 50s, proud to show off the horses that the king's uncle had given him as a farewell present, Botetourt was convivial and well-liked in Williamsburg. His arrival marked the first time in a decade that Virginia's governor would actually reside there. But behind the scenes, he was encouraging London to exert its power to the fullest. "Opinions of the independency of the legislature of the colonies are grown to such a height," he told Lord Hillsborough, "that it becomes Great Britain, if ever she intends it, immediately to assert her supremacy in a manner which may be felt."[46]

He was prepared to do that himself. On May 16, 1769, the House approved resolutions prepared by the respected elder statesman George Mason, which asserted that the Virginia legislature had "the sole right of imposing taxes on the inhabitants of this his Majesty's colony and dominion" and that it was "highly derogatory of the rights of British subjects" to send people accused of crimes "to places beyond the sea to be tried," a reference to Parliament's threat to use the Treason Act in response to the *Liberty* riots. Mason's resolutions also pointedly declared that all subjects had the right to petition "their sovereign"—not Parliament, but the king—for redress of grievances.[47] As soon as Botetourt learned what the House had done, he did as Hillsborough had commanded: He called the Burgesses before him, and said: "I have heard of your resolves, and augur ill of their effect. You have made it my duty to dissolve you, and you are dissolved accordingly."[48]

Like their New England brothers, the Virginians coolly decided to meet anyway. They marched down the street to the Raleigh Tavern, which had a ballroom large enough to accommodate the Burgesses, and unofficially reconvened to weigh their options. Not long before, Massachusetts had proposed an economic boycott modeled on the Stamp Act protests, but it had received little support.

Now, the Virginians were more interested. Mason and his protégé, a 37-year-old military veteran named George Washington, drafted "articles of association" in which they pledged not to buy or use imported British goods. Jefferson, like the other Burgesses, signed his name. "[Our] spirit," he recalled years later, "manifestly displayed [our] considering the cause of Massachusetts as a common one."[49]

It was around this time that dissenters who had previously called themselves Whigs began calling themselves "Patriots" instead—lovers of the *patria,* or homeland—whereas former Tories came to be called "Loyalists." Benjamin Franklin had warned Parliament that sending troops to Massachusetts might cause a revolt; now his prediction was coming true. Rather than dissuading the Americans, Hillsborough's efforts to enforce the Townshend Acts were helping generate a new, nationalistic spirit of resistance.

Meanwhile, Jefferson was busy forming his own views about the nature of the British constitution. His mentor, George Wythe, had taught him that "the only link of political union between us and Great Britain was the identity of our executive; that that nation and its Parliament had no more authority over us than we had over them, and that we were co-ordinate nations with Great Britain."[50] But if that were true, would it not mean that Parliament had no power to legislate for the colonies *at all*?—that the Navigation Acts, too, were unconstitutional?

That was a radical idea, one few older Virginians were willing to entertain. But Jefferson found support for it in the writings of another member of the House of Burgesses, Williamsburg attorney Richard Bland. More than 30 years older than Jefferson, and one of his many Randolph cousins, Bland was more a legal scholar than a practicing lawyer, and he was much admired for his extensive collection of antique legal documents. One acquaintance said he had "something of the look of the musty old parchments which he handles and studies so much."[51] And during the Stamp Act crisis, he had put his collection to good use by publishing a pamphlet called *An Inquiry into the Rights of the British Colonies*.

Bland started with the idea that among the natural rights of all human beings is the right to "quit the [political] society of which they are members, and to retire into another country" to start a new one.[52] Virginians had done that a century and a half earlier—arriving not as "fugitives," let alone as deputies of Parliament, but as "private adventurers" under a charter granted by the king. That charter formed the original contract of government for Virginia, and, along with subsequent declarations and agreements, it made Virginia's legislature, *not* Parliament, the supreme lawmaker in the province. "I will not dispute the authority of the Parliament, which is without doubt supreme within the body of the kingdom," Bland argued, "but may not the king have prerogatives which he has a right to exercise without the consent of Parliament? If he has, perhaps that of granting license to his subjects to remove into a *new* country, and to settle therein upon particular conditions, may be one." That was just what had happened. Virginia was "a distinct state, independent, as to their *internal* government, of the original kingdom, but united with her, as to their *external* polity, in the closest and most intimate LEAGUE AND AMITY, under the same allegiance, and enjoying the benefits of a reciprocal intercourse." It was not *dependent* on Parliament at all.

Bland's argument implied that even the Navigation Acts were illegitimate. They "deprived the colonies, so far as [their] restrictions extended, of the privileges of English subjects," he wrote, "and constituted an unnatural difference between men under the same allegiance, born equally free, and entitled to the same civil rights." Of course, to deny the legitimacy of the Navigation Acts meant taking a drastic step toward literal independence, but Bland seemed at times prepared to take that step, even likening the acts to robbery. "I say that *power* abstracted from *right* cannot give a just title to dominion," he declared. Such language might sound bold, even insolent, but when "speaking of the *rights* of a people," one must put the case "without respect to the dignity of the persons concerned." But Bland then appeared to sense that his argument was too advanced for the times, and he abruptly backtracked, ending his pamphlet by insisting that he did not wish for independence. "May the colonies ever remain under a constitutional subordination to Great Britain!" he wrote. "It is their interest to live under such a subordination, and it is their duty . . . to advance the grandeur and the glory of the nation."

Jefferson lauded Bland's *Inquiry* as the first attempt to make sense of Britain's colonial relationship that had "any pretension to accuracy," but he regretted Bland's moderate conclusion.[53] He himself would be bolder. Five years later, he would argue that the colonies were entirely "exempt" from Parliament's power. They were united with Britain exclusively through the king, who served as chief executive of both countries, but when it came to lawmaking, every provincial legislature was the equivalent of Parliament. The Lords and Commons, he thought, had "no right to exercise authority over us."[54]

America's intellectual leaders were not prepared to embrace that doctrine in 1769. Instead, Jefferson wrote, they "stopped at the half-way house," and concluded that London could not tax the colonies, but could control their commerce.[55] It would be a long time before they were ready to take the leap and declare that their right to trade should be as respected as their right not to be taxed without consent.

JOHN ADAMS FOR THE DEFENSE

John Adams had been busy defending John Hancock in the *Liberty* trial throughout the spring of 1769. But after exhausting rounds of argument and testimony, that case ended anti-climactically in March, when the prosecutor suddenly dropped the charges. Exactly why was never made clear, although it probably had to do with the publicity the lawsuit had generated throughout America. Only weeks later, however, Adams was asked to take up yet another case involving colonial policy, this time turning on the question of impressment. The outcome of this case would be much more dramatic.

That April, a British naval vessel off the coast of Marblehead, Massachusetts, intercepted a merchant ship called the *Pitt Packet*, which was carrying a cargo of salt. Intending to impress some of the crew into service, Royal Navy Lieutenant Henry Panton boarded the *Pitt Packet* and began searching it. He found four sailors hiding in a crawl space under the deck, armed and determined to resist. "You have no right to impress me," said their leader, an Irish sailor named Michael Corbet. Coolly drawing a line in the salt with a harpoon, Corbet added, "If you step over that line . . . by the eternal God in Heaven, you are a dead man."

Panton showed little fear. "Aye, my lad," he said, "I have seen many a brave fellow before now"—and took a step over the line. Without hesitation, Corbet drove the harpoon into his throat.[56]

Charged with murder and piracy, Corbet and the other sailors were tried before a vice-admiralty court, even though British laws were unclear regarding whether they were entitled to a jury trial. John Adams and James Otis took up their defense, arguing that colonists were exempt from impressment—so that the men had been legitimately defending themselves—and that the case should be tried before a jury. Otis's mental illness was growing worse, making him unable to appear in court, so Adams stood alone in a packed Boston courtroom to make his case. "You may easily believe I was anxious," he recalled afterward. "The lives of four honest men in my hands, and a sympathizing world looking at me for exertions to preserve them."[57]

As in the Hancock case, Adams argued that resistance to unlawful government action was itself lawful—a position backed by arguments drawn from natural law. If the difference between government and a gang of robbers is that the former acts under the ambit of public-spirited principles (such as rationality, intelligibility, and security for individual rights), whereas the latter acts capriciously and without the sanction of justice, then any government action that violates those principles is not *law*, but an arbitrary act of force. That, Adams argued, made it lawful for Corbet to resist such actions, even though committed by public officials. He was acting in self-defense just as surely as if Lieutenant Panton had been a highway robber.

Adams's argument was strengthened by the fact that law enforcement in the colonies was largely a private affair: Without a professional police force, order was typically maintained by deputized citizens and by jurors who could punish public officials if their actions were legally unjustified. The line between lawful authority and unlawful power was therefore primarily drawn by citizen jurors themselves, based on a variety of legal, historical, and moral considerations. That was one reason the colonists resisted inroads on the right to trial by jury. Undermining that right threatened to deprive Americans of the power to hold their officials accountable. It also threatened to break down the distinction between constitutional order and the arbitrary or unjustified commands of misguided or even corrupt officers—the distinction, that is, between authority and power. Natural law theory enabled Adams to argue that mere power—force without right—was literally *not law*, and consequently that to oppose it was not to defy, but to vindicate, the law. Panton and his men, he asserted, were the ones actually rioting. Corbet was acting legally.[58]

The judges rejected Adams's request for a jury, however, and ordered the testimony to begin. As the evening wore on, Adams questioned a series of witnesses about the violence and injustice of impressment. He finally finished near midnight and rose to deliver his closing argument. "I had taken more pains in that case than in any other," he remembered. "I vainly felt as if I could shake the town and the world." But no sooner had he started speaking than Chief Justice Thomas Hutchinson interrupted with a bang of the gavel. The judges needed a moment to confer privately, he said. Adams watched with alarm as they stood and marched out. "Alas, for me, my glass bubble was burst!" Now he was sure his clients would be condemned. But he could only wait.

At long last, the judges returned. Shocking the crowd, they announced a unanimous verdict: not guilty. The stunned Adams could only think of one explanation: The justices were terrified of public reaction if they convicted the men. "Hutchinson dreaded . . . the public investigation, before the people, of the law applicable to that case," he wrote. "It would have accelerated the revolution."[59]

Things did indeed accelerate in the months that followed. It was inevitable that the presence of 4,000 troops in Boston—one for every four citizens—would lead to conflict, and troops and townspeople repeatedly clashed. Sullen colonists accused redcoats of not paying their bills. Fistfights broke out in taverns. Rumors circulated of soldiers raping wives and daughters. That fall, James Otis got into an angry confrontation at a coffeehouse with customs officers who beat him in the head with a heavy cane. Finally, in August 1769, Governor Bernard threw up his hands at the Bostonians' ungovernability and sailed for London to request more support. As his ship departed, the townspeople celebrated by ringing church bells. The House refused to pay his salary, and the Boston Town Meeting officially pronounced him "a pimp rather than a governor."[60] Thomas Hutchinson, who in addition to his position as chief justice was also the colony's lieutenant governor, would substitute during Bernard's absence.

Six months later, a Loyalist customs informant named Ebenezer Richardson was attacked by a mob who stoned his house. He pulled a gun and fired into the crowd, killing a child and wounding two adults.[61] A few weeks after that, a street fight erupted after a worker at a local rope-making business cursed a passing infantryman.[62] Then, on the evening of March 5, 1770, a group of Bostonians started shouting at a sentry stationed outside the headquarters of the Board of Customs Commissioners. The dispute—which may have started with a disagreement over payment for a wig—quickly attracted a crowd of as many as 300 people, who began pelting the guardsman with ice and cobblestones. Terrified, he called out the soldiers in the barracks, who marched to his defense armed with muskets. In the chaos that followed, they opened fire, killing three and wounding eight, two of whom later died from their wounds. It would eventually be known as the Boston Massacre.[63]

Acting Governor Hutchinson was thrown into despair. "How far the affronts and abuses offered by the inhabitants may avail to excuse this action is uncertain," he wrote to Lord Hillsborough, "but it is certain that nothing more unfortunate could have happened, for a very great part of the people are in a perfect frenzy."[64] The soldiers, including their captain, Thomas Preston, were arrested and charged with murder. Given the city's "frenzy," they understandably feared the prospect of being tried by Boston jurors. But the Sons of Liberty saw a chance to make a political point. Given the recent talk of using the Treason Act to send colonists to England for trial, if Boston could give Preston and his men a scrupulously fair hearing—or, better yet, acquit them—London would be deprived of any pretext to interfere with colonial courts.

Thus, when Preston sought counsel, he was immediately encouraged to call on Josiah Quincy, a prominent Son of Liberty—and Quincy recommended John Adams.[65] It was the perfect choice. Although Adams was an unimpeachable Patriot, he was genuinely disturbed by the Boston mob's violence. Crowds of violent and manipulable men in the streets were threats to public order, he thought. When, during the Stamp Act riots, a mob burst into the home of a wealthy farmer named Richard King, who supported the act—terrorizing his wife and five children with axes, destroying the furniture and burning the family's papers—Adams represented King in a lawsuit against the perpetrators. "The distress, the distraction, and horror of this family," he told Abigail, was "enough to move a statue. . . . These tarrings and featherings, these breaking open houses by rude and insolent rabbles" could not be rationalized "upon any principle which can be entertained by a good citizen."[66] Now he was certain to give the Boston Massacre case his best efforts.

The trial, held in October 1770, cost him two weeks of "most exhausting" labor.[67] The work paid off, however, when the jury acquitted six of the eight soldiers entirely and convicted two of the lesser charge of manslaughter. John endured some nasty remarks for defending the redcoats, but the case actually boosted his reputation. That spring, he was elected to the House of Representatives to replace the now-incapacitated Otis. Adams appreciated the honor but felt no joy in the election. He was now Boston's most famous attorney, with a wife and three young children to support (a new son, Charles, had been born in May). Joining the legislature would be a costly, time-consuming distraction from work. He would be exchanging "as bright prospects as any man ever had" for "endless labor and anxiety."[68]

FATIGUING THEM INTO COMPLIANCE

Attending legislative sessions was indeed a hassle. For the previous six months, members of the House had been protesting the presence of troops in Boston, especially when the regulars aimed two cannons at the legislature's front door as an unmistakable threat to the Patriots inside.[69] In the wake of the Boston Massacre, Samuel Adams had met with acting Governor Hutchinson to demand that the redcoats leave the city and move to Castle William. Hutchinson answered that he had no authority to issue such an order. That was a lie—as acting governor, he was commander-in-chief—but Hutchinson clung to it. Still, he had an idea. If the House objected to meeting in occupied Boston, he would simply order them to move. In June 1770, he declared that the House would convene in Cambridge instead.

If Hutchinson thought that would settle things, he was soon disabused of that notion. On John Adams's first day in office, the House met in a room rented from Harvard and immediately began protesting that Hutchinson had no authority to order them to meet in a different city. The distance from the capital made it hard to consult constituents or examine government files, they complained, and requiring them to pay a private owner for meeting space undermined their independence. The only precedent for the governor's moving the legislature—except in cases of true emergencies such as smallpox epidemics—had been in 1729, when Governor Jonathan Belcher had forced lawmakers to meet in Salem, in hopes that by making their meetings inconvenient, he could pressure them into granting him more funding. "But," the House now declared, "that arbitrary and injurious [action] . . . savoring more of despotism than a due exertion of the prerogative of a British prince, will never be mentioned as a constitutional precedent by any friend to the British Constitution."[70]

Hutchinson thought it absurd for lawmakers to complain about relocating to Cambridge. "It was within four miles of the town of Boston, and less distant than any other town fit for the purpose," he wrote.[71] But these excuses fell flat. There was no epidemic—there was a military occupation which Hutchinson had the power to halt. Tensions only worsened when he told lawmakers that he had ordered their move based on instructions from London—but then added that he was not at liberty to show them those instructions. This only "awakened and fixed our attention," the House replied. Why would the king govern the colony through secret commands?[72]

The legislators thought it obvious that Hutchinson had sent them to Cambridge to "insult" them and make them "meanly compliant." After all, when they had complained about the cannons pointed at their doors, "[we], and not the soldiers, were made to give way. Can freedom and dignity then exist in an assembly that can tamely brook such usage?"[73] In any event, it was a matter of principle. If the governor could order them about based on classified directives from London, then "are we not . . . in a state of vassalage[?]"[74] The governor might "carry the Assembly from one extreme part of the province to another, adjourning them from place to place, till the year expires, or perhaps till he shall have worried them into a compliance with some arbitrary mandate, to the ruin of their own and their constituents' liberties."[75]

That, in fact, was exactly what South Carolina's royal governor, Lord Charles Greville Montagu, decided to do not long after Hutchinson's action. In the autumn of 1772, after an angry dispute with that colony's legislature over whether he or they had the authority to decide how tax money was spent, Montagu sent the lawmakers home and called for new elections. After the elections, when the new representatives met, he told them at their opening session that he would immediately adjourn them if they questioned his authority again. They responded by refusing to meet at all under those conditions, whereupon Montagu shut them down and ordered elections for another meeting—this time to be held not in the capital city, but in Beaufort, 75 miles away. He boasted to superiors in London that this was a clever move, because his political opponents would find it hard to attend sessions there. But the plan was foiled when Patriots managed not only to make it to the Beaufort meeting, but to cram the hall with a record number of attendees. When Montagu saw this, he shut down the legislature yet again and ordered them back to Charleston.

To their credit, the Colonial Office in London rebuked Montagu for this gamesmanship, telling him that he had only placed "new difficulties in the way of an accommodation."[76] But the damage had been done. When they resumed business, the lawmakers formed a Committee of Grievances, which prepared resolutions complaining of Montagu's manipulation of their meetings. When he learned of this, Montagu prorogued the legislature yet again. At last, the embarrassed Colonial Office had had enough. It arranged for the governor to resign.[77]

Like the Carolinians, the angry Massachusetts lawmakers declared that they "refuse[d] to proceed to business in Cambridge."[78] A four-month standoff ensued, with daily arguments between the governor and the House over his authority to send them out of Boston. In the end, however, Hutchinson wore the lawmakers down. Exhausted and pressed by "absolute necessity," they agreed to proceed to business.[79] John Adams, absent on the day that decision was made, was furious at the cave-in and insisted, upon his return, that he place his disagreement on the record.[80] Not until 1773 would the Massachusetts General Court return to Boston—only to be moved again a year later, when General Thomas Gage was made governor in the wake of the Boston Tea Party and ordered the legislature to meet in Salem. Once again, the House replied with indignation, leading Gage to order their adjournment.[81] That would be the last time the colonial legislature ever met.[82]

When Adams helped write the Declaration of Independence in 1776, he would ensure that it included a reference to governors "call[ing] together legislative bodies at places unusual, uncomfortable, and distant from the depository of their public records, for the sole purpose of fatiguing them into compliance with his measures." Hutchinson and other Tories might roll their eyes at this complaint, but Adams and his colleagues, living in a city occupied by the military and governed by leaders who did not hesitate to intimidate the people's elected representatives, took it seriously.[83] "This House has the same inherent rights in this province, as the House of Commons has in Great Britain," they declared. For the royal governor to "harass us, in order to bring us into a compliance with some arbitrary mandate" would mean "the ruin of our own or our constituents' liberties."[84]

ALL MEN ARE BORN FREE

While Adams and his colleagues were quarreling over Hutchinson's power politics, Thomas Jefferson was in Virginia, delving into philosophy. In the fall of 1769, he ordered more than a dozen books on government and politics from London, including works by Locke, Montesquieu, and Adam Ferguson.[85] Having just been elected to the colony's legislature, he felt a responsibility to study not only practical matters such as the rules of parliamentary procedure but also the theoretical foundations of government, and especially constitutions. He had read these thinkers before, but now he started focusing more carefully on their theories about how and why government comes into existence in the first place, and what limits natural law imposes upon its power. What he learned would lead him to push the boundaries of justice in the Old Dominion.

Locke and his contemporaries held that all people are equally entitled to rule themselves—that they are inherently and inescapably self-responsible, and that they therefore must be entitled to make decisions for how to live their lives. In other words, they are naturally free and have the right to pursue happiness, meaning the right to engage in the pursuits they believe will benefit them, as long as they harm no other person. Wholly internal matters, too, such as one's religious beliefs, are simply not political concerns. "The legitimate powers of government extend to such acts only as are injurious to others," Jefferson later said. "But it does me no injury for my neighbor to say there are twenty gods, or no god. It neither picks my pocket nor breaks my leg."[86] Government's role is only "to restrain men from injuring one another" and "leave them otherwise free to regulate their own pursuits of industry and improvement."[87]

The challenge for the statesman is to devise political institutions that will protect people not only against harms by other citizens, but also against those caused by the government itself. One critical protection is the separation of powers. The "definition of despotic government," Jefferson wrote, paraphrasing Montesquieu, comes from "the concentrating [of legislative, executive, and judicial powers] in the same hands"—and that was true even if those "hands" consisted of a majority of the people.[88] An "*elective despotism*" is just as oppressive as a monarchical one. Instead, what is needed is a government "in which the powers of government should be so divided and balanced among several bodies of magistracy, as that no one could transcend their limits without being effectually checked and restrained by the others."[89]

At its best, the British constitution implemented such a balance of powers. Yet it also contained a major defect. If, as its leaders maintained, the Lords and Commons in Westminster were the supreme sovereign, able to override even the deepest principles of common law, then they could decide for themselves how much power they enjoyed—and that meant there was really no constitution at all. Under the theory of Parliamentary Supremacy, the people's rights existed solely at Westminster's mercy, and their lives, liberty, and property could be despoiled and plundered at any time by lawmakers who enjoyed literally limitless power. Yet Locke had written that no legislature could ever justly claim such sovereignty. Parliament could only have the powers that the people gave it. And since no person "has an absolute arbitrary power over himself, or over any other, to destroy his own life, or take away the life or property of another," then no group of people could confer such authority on

Parliament.[90] If the Lords and Commons had power to act however they pleased, on the theory that whatever they decreed just *was* the law, then that really meant they were claiming the right to act *lawlessly*—or, in the word Jefferson's generation used, "arbitrarily."

That seemed exactly the path Parliament was headed down—and not just in America. In 1769, the House of Commons expelled John Wilkes, a troublemaking MP who reveled in satirizing the authorities and who had attacked the king in a newspaper article some years before. When his constituents reelected him, the House refused to accept him and seated his opponent instead, sparking a wave of protests by voters who claimed Parliament had no right to disenfranchise them and to swear in a member who lost at the polls. Instead of heeding the voters, however, Parliament seemed to regard them as enemies. It even began punishing reporters who dared to print transcripts of its debates. When, in 1771, Wilkes encouraged two London newspapermen named Wheble and Thompson to publish transcripts in their papers—violating a long-standing but generally ignored law against reprinting the proceedings of the Commons—Parliament responded by ordering their arrest. Wheble and Thompson went into hiding in London, however, so Parliament's deputies began searching for them, whereupon London's indignant mayor, Brass Crosby, intervened. Parliament's actions violated the city's rights under its royal charter, he said—and he ordered the House of Commons' deputy arrested. The House reacted to that by having Crosby and one of his fellow city aldermen arrested and sent to jail without trial. (They were released weeks later when judges refused to preside over the case.)[91]

Such clashes reflected Parliament's increasing aggressiveness regarding its allegedly boundless power. And to American Patriots, being ruled by an absolute legislature appeared no better than being ruled by an absolute monarch.[92] As legal historian John Phillip Reid puts it: "Sometime between 1765 and 1774, Americans realized that parliamentary government, at least for them, was arbitrary government. The discovery could be called the kingship of Parliament . . . or, looking back to the Glorious Revolution, the Stuartness of Parliament."[93] Jefferson appears to have made that discovery himself in late 1769, thanks to his self-directed course in political philosophy.

We cannot know for sure, however, thanks to a catastrophe that befell him the following February: His mother's home, Shadwell, burned to the ground. All of Jefferson's papers went up in flames, including documents crucial for his legal practice, along with about £200 worth of books. "Would to god it had been the money!" he told his friend John Page.[94] Not enough of Monticello had been finished to enable him to move there, so the family probably took shelter in outbuildings at Shadwell until November, when the first small structure was finished on Jefferson's little mountain.

Among the documents destroyed in the fire were those relating to a remarkable lawsuit Jefferson argued around this time, one that challenged the legitimacy of the colonial system of chattel slavery and that taught the young politician important lessons about Virginia's tolerance for radicalism. The case, called *Howell v. Netherland*, began in October 1769, when a poor man named Samuel Howell approached Jefferson to ask for help in defending his freedom against the claim that he was a slave.[95] Howell's great-grandfather had been a black man who had a baby girl with a white woman. Under Virginia laws of that time, the daughter was bound to servitude until the age of 31—and during those years, she gave birth to Howell's mother. She, too, was enslaved until the age of 31—and during that time, she gave birth to Howell himself. Then, the owner of Howell's mother and grandmother, thinking that Virginia law also rendered Howell a slave until the age of 31, sold him to a man named Joshua Netherland.

Two Virginia laws governed Howell's case. The first provided that if "any woman servant" or "free Christian white woman" were to "have [a] bastard child by a negro," the resulting child would be "a servant until it shall be thirty-one years of age." The second provided that if a "female mulatto . . . obliged to serve till the age of thirty or thirty-one years shall, during the time of her servitude, have any child . . . such child shall serve the master . . . until it shall attain the same age the mother of such child was obliged by law to serve unto." The first condemned Howell's grandmother to servitude, and his mother might also have been subject to that statute, because she could qualify as a "woman servant." If so, and if Howell's father were black (which is not clear from the surviving documents), Howell would also have been condemned to servitude for 31 years. If his mother did not fall within the first statute, she still came within the second, because she would have been considered a "female mulatto." Howell was born during her period of servitude, so he too would be bound to serve until the age of 31.

Nevertheless, Jefferson agreed to argue for Howell's freedom. His anti-slavery sympathies were well-known in Williamsburg; he had likely absorbed them from George Wythe, whose hostility to slavery Jefferson called "unequivocal."[96] And during these years, Jefferson took six "freedom cases," including Howell's, charging nothing for his services.[97] On Howell's behalf, he argued, first, that the fact that Howell's purported owner had sold him rendered the servitude mandate void. "Bond servants"—that is, temporary, as opposed to lifetime slaves—were not saleable, he asserted, because they were properly classified as a kind of apprentice rather than chattel property or slaves for life. The reason for the 31-year enslavement rule, he claimed, was actually to ensure that the parents of illicit children cared for them instead of abandoning them. Allowing people to sell these "bond servants" would give the parents a way to evade the law and escape their paternal responsibilities. But if Howell was a bond servant, his master could not legally sell him, which meant the attempted sale voided Howell's bondage status and rendered him free.

It was a creative argument, but there was more. Jefferson claimed that the two statutes only governed the cases of Howell's grandmother and mother, not Howell himself. Although they might seem to apply to every succeeding generation automatically, they could not actually do so because that would violate natural law. "Under the law of nature, all men are born free," he told the court. "Everyone comes into the world with a right to his own person, which includes the liberty of moving and using it at his own will. This is what is called personal liberty, and it is given him by the law of nature, because [it is] necessary for his own sustenance."[98] The statute enslaving the grandmother was bad enough, but to inflict bondage on generation after generation of innocent children was untenable. And, Jefferson added, the Virginia legislature must have realized this, because the very fact that it had passed the second act—specifying that children "shall be bond or free according to the conditions of their mothers"—proved that lawmakers never believed that the first act would inflict slavery on every descendant of the initial liaison. "It remains for some future legislature," Jefferson concluded, "*if any shall be found wicked enough,* to extend [slavery] to the grandchildren."[99]

Jefferson's case was idealistic, even naive, and it did not impress the judges. When the opposing lawyer—Jefferson's own mentor, George Wythe—rose to present the counterargument, they waved him back into his seat. They did not need to hear what he had to say. They had already made up their minds. With a bang of the gavel, the presiding judge—none other than Governor Botetourt himself—declared that Howell would remain in servitude.

It was a humiliating lesson for the 27-year-old attorney. Slavery's evils might be an interesting subject for coffeehouse debate, but colonial authorities were not prepared to upset a century and a half of economic policy. Still, as biographer Willard Sterne Randall observes, the *Howell* case marked "the first time Jefferson had spoken the words in public—'all men are born free'—six years before he wrote the Declaration . . . and he had said them first in the legal defense of a black slave."[100]

Slavery and other forms of compulsory servitude were ubiquitous in America. Aside from the approximately 450,000 slaves in the colonies at the time of the revolution—not counting the West Indies—about half of the colonial population fell within some category of unfree labor, including apprenticeship, indentured servitude, and convict labor. Workers in these categories were subject to sometimes brutal forms of control and discipline. Benjamin Franklin himself had suffered so severely as an apprentice that he had run away, breaking colonial law. But where apprentices and convicts might look forward to eventual freedom, most chattel slaves were held in lifetime bondage, relegated to a bizarre legal twilight zone where they were treated partly as people and partly like livestock.

The ownership of black people had been introduced into Virginia a century and a half before the *Howell* case, but the English had practiced it since at least the 1550s, and African slaves had been employed in the New World for half a century before that. Egypt, Greece, Rome, and tribal nations in America had engaged in slavery too, and it remains common in some parts of the world even today. Although the Anglo-American variety was unique in some respects—particularly its heavy reliance on race—the claim by some historians that slavery in the colonies differed fundamentally from previous iterations of the practice is misleading. Race played at least some role in Roman slavery, for example; although Romans did not observe the same color line Americans came to use, they tended to believe that Syrians and Jews were natural-born slaves.[101] Nor was American slavery distinctively crueler than its ancient counterparts; the slaves who labored in Rome's mines or latifundia (farms) experienced the severest misery of "social death." The 19th-century Industrial Revolution would magnify slavery's brutality and lead its defenders to seek pseudoscientific and pseudophilosophical rationalizations for it, but those developments were still in the future when Jefferson formed his views about slavery's injustice.

According to the classical liberalism that he and his allies embraced, all people are fundamentally individual beings, responsible for their own actions and consequently endowed with the right to direct their own lives. This quality of self-responsibility, shared by all normal adults, makes people "equal" in an important sense: None is inherently entitled to control another's actions the way grown-ups are inherently entitled to oversee and discipline children. Nor is this inherent liberty a function of tradition or culture. It is an unavoidable feature of human life. A person's individuality and self-possession are inalienable. Slavery, by contrast, is not natural, but artificial, a man-made institution that can be tested against the standards of justice—by the same reasoning Locke and others used when evaluating the institution of monarchy—and found wanting. Just as Locke showed that all people are inherently entitled to freedom, so Jefferson saw that slavery could not be reconciled with the principles of equality and liberty for which the Patriots were contending.

As the imperial crisis accelerated in the 1770s, Tories would be quick to accuse the revolutionaries of hypocrisy for practicing slavery while protesting in defense of their own freedom. Samuel Johnson, of dictionary fame, sneered: "How is it that we hear the loudest yelps for liberty among the drivers of negroes?"[102] But it was not at all surprising that Americans who every day witnessed the horrors of slavery would dread—to the point of paranoia—the possibility of experiencing the same fate themselves.[103] What is actually remarkable about the Patriots is the degree of candor with which they confessed that slavery conflicted with their principles. No Patriot of stature ever defended the practice. And no considerable political movement in the English-speaking world had ever before condemned slavery as candidly and as often as the Patriots did.

Franklin, for example, anticipated Johnson's accusation and offered a reply in a 1770 newspaper article in which he imagined a dialogue between an American and two Britons. When the British characters call the American a hypocrite, he replies that this "seems to me not quite fair" because "many thousands [in America] abhor the slave trade as much as [any Englishman] can do, conscientiously avoid being concerned with it, and do everything in their power to abolish it." Relatively few colonists own slaves, he continues, and it would be wrong to "stigmatize us all with that crime." Notably admitting that slavery was evil, Franklin—who, a few years later, would become president of the world's first anti-slavery society—went on to point out that the hypocrisy charge cut both ways: "[England] began the slave trade," and while Americans were certainly blameworthy for buying slaves, "you bring the slaves to us, and tempt us to purchase them." This rhetorical move—which Jefferson would employ in the Declaration of Independence six years later—might seem disingenuous to historians, but it's no more so than the language of today's political leaders who blame oil companies for climate change, tobacco companies for lung cancer, or fast-food companies for obesity, even though these businesses, too, merely serve consumer demand.

Worse, Franklin continued, when colonial governments tried to limit or prohibit slave importation, the imperial government "disapproved and repealed" those laws "as being prejudicial, forsooth, to the interest of the [Royal] African Company."[104] He had in mind efforts by the assemblies of Pennsylvania in 1712, South Carolina in 1760, New Jersey in 1763, and Virginia in 1710, 1727, and 1766 to ban or restrict slave imports—all of which had been overridden by London officials.[105]

British policy was to prop up the Royal African Company, which had been chartered by Charles I and was now the world's largest slave trader. In 1770, the same year Franklin published his article, George III vetoed yet another attempt by Virginians to tax slave imports, declaring that it would "prejudice and obstruct as well the commerce of this kingdom as the cultivation and improvement of [Virginia]." He even went further, instructing the governor "upon pain of our highest displeasure" to veto "any laws whatever . . . by which the importation of slaves shall be in any respect prohibited or obstructed."[106] Similar instructions were sent to the governors of Connecticut, Georgia, Maryland, Massachusetts, New Hampshire, New Jersey, New York, North and South Carolina, and the Caribbean colonies.[107]

It was also illegal to manumit slaves except for "meritorious services." Around the same time that he represented Samuel Howell in court, Jefferson had taken another quixotic step against slavery by seeking to change this rule, by drafting a bill to let masters free their slaves when they chose.[108] Thinking himself too young and unknown to offer such a major proposal, he asked Richard Bland to sponsor it in the House. The older man agreed—and soon regretted it. When he rose to speak, the Burgesses shouted him down so ferociously that Bland dropped the subject. "He was denounced as an enemy to his country," Jefferson recalled, "and was treated with the grossest indecorum."[109] The message was clear: Neither the royal government nor the planter class controlling the colony would tolerate outright attacks on slavery, and even modest efforts to limit it could destroy a man's political reputation. "I soon saw that nothing was to be hoped" on the subject of slavery, Jefferson wrote afterward. Many Virginians engaged in "little reflection on the value of liberty" even while willing to fight for their own. "It was not easy to carry them the whole length of the principles which they invoked for themselves."[110]

True, efforts to limit the slave trade or allow manumission were not the same as attacking slavery in toto. But leaders who wanted to eradicate the practice itself thought the first steps must be gradual. Prohibiting importation and letting owners free their bondsmen would not cut off the supply of victims—the children born into slavery every year soon outnumbered those arriving from abroad—but it could influence public opinion against the institution in general. Because the slave trade was held in such opprobrium, campaigning against it was the most politic way to introduce the idea of prohibiting slavery itself.

This approach did have an element of disingenuousness, since cutting off the importation of slaves from abroad would likely increase the market value of those already in North America, thus creating an incentive to preserve slavery, rather than eradicate it. And there was another, more severe element of disingenuousness: the fact that many, including Jefferson, shared the racial prejudices that appeared to substantiate the claims of those who viewed Africans and their descendants as biologically doomed to servitude. Only a few years after the Declaration, Jefferson published *Notes on the State of Virginia*, in which he set forth his "suspicion . . . that the blacks . . . are inferior to the whites."[111] A later generation seized on his words to justify slavery, and although Jefferson himself denied this connection—"whatever be their degree of talent, it is no measure of their rights," he said[112]—he did come to the conclusion that biological as well as historical differences between the races made it impossible for them to live together permanently in North America.

Jefferson was one of many white Southerners who, while regarding slavery as evil, found it impossible to imagine a peaceful multiracial democracy. Such a thing had no historical precedent; the record with which the American Founders were familiar suggested that racially and religiously diverse societies could only be governed by emperors, as with Rome, or through legal segregation, as with medieval Jerusalem. No civilization known to man had ever successfully abolished slavery; history seemed instead to prove that mass emancipation led inevitably to deadly reprisals and civil war. Even Yankees such as John Adams agreed on this point. Immediate emancipation, wrote Adams, "would probably excite insurrections among the blacks to rise against their masters and imbrue their hands in innocent blood."[113]

Southerners were haunted by that prospect whenever they contemplated slavery, and when Jefferson tried to envision the future of racial diversity in America, he found it more likely that "deep-rooted prejudices entertained by the whites" and "ten thousand recollections, by the blacks, of the injuries they have sustained" would "divide us into parties, and produce convulsions which will probably never end but in the extermination of the one or the other race."[114] Quoting a line by the Roman playwright Terence, he was later to remark that "we have the wolf by the ear, and we can neither hold him, nor safely let him go."[115] How, then, to address the problem? Eventually, Jefferson and his followers—notably including James Madison and James Monroe—decided that America's enslaved population should be freed on a gradual plan, and that black Americans should then agree to emigrate to Africa or Central America.

This was not a realistic scheme; indeed, it was almost delusional, and its very impracticability resulted in political paralysis on the slavery question until after Jefferson's death. The only thing that could have broken that impasse was some dramatic gesture by a universally admired leader that would signal that the time had come to end slavery. George Washington took one step when he freed his slaves in his will in 1799. But years later, the elderly Jefferson was offered the chance to make a similar move and declined. In 1814, when his neighbor Edward Coles freed his slaves and paid to set them up in farming in Illinois, he wrote to urge the retired president to likewise. The Sage of Monticello—by then in despair over the threat slavery posed to the nation's future—said no.

That choice represented a singular failure of leadership by a man who, at the age of 27, had summoned the courage to tell Virginia's royal governor to his face that all men are created equal. The aged Jefferson told Coles that only "the younger generation" could resolve the slavery problem—as indeed they did.[116] But his silence deprived that rising generation of the moral guidance that could have opened their eyes and hearts to doing so peacefully and thoroughly. Only the efforts of the abolitionists, especially those of constitutional abolitionists such as Frederick Douglass and Samuel Chase, would begin the process of fulfilling the principles that the Virginian himself articulated in the Declaration of Independence.

All of that was far in the future when Jefferson, Franklin, and others discussed the question of slavery in the years before the revolution. Almost to a man, the Patriots agreed that slavery was evil, and irreconcilable with their principles. Yet they were stymied by the practical politics of the situation, particularly given that their focus at the time was not slavery but the problem of colonial rule. These factors led many Patriots not only to direct their attacks against the slave trade instead of human ownership itself, but also to blame the British government in ways that strike the modern ear as dubious. The accusatory fingers Franklin and Jefferson pointed at Britain for "tempting" Americans to buy slaves, or preventing them from restricting the slave trade, look today like efforts to deflect the charge of hypocrisy. In truth, there was plenty of hypocrisy, and plenty of blame, to go around. What is extraordinary—indeed, unprecedented—about the American revolutionaries was that time and again, they conceded that the principles for which they fought would require the liberation of the enslaved, even if racial prejudices (including their own) still seemed like an insuperable barrier.

For their part, leaders in Parliament showed no interest in freeing the empire's bondsmen. When Pennsylvania Quakers petitioned London to abolish the slave trade, the prime minister simply replied that it was "impossible" to do so, "for it was a trade which had, in some measure, become necessary to almost every nation in Europe."[117] It would be decades before Britain changed its collective mind and took up a national crusade against slavery.

Five years before he died, Jefferson expressed frustration with his countrymen's lack of vision on the matter while simultaneously demonstrating his own. In two sentences that perfectly encapsulate the slavery dilemma at the time of the revolution, he wrote: "Nothing is more certainly written in the book of fate than that these people are to be free. Nor is it less certain that the two races, equally free, cannot live in the same government."[118] Within a lifetime of his writing these words, slavery would be abolished. Only then would Americans begin to answer the question of whether the two races could live together in the same free country.

— CHAPTER 7 —

BLOOD AND TEA

An exasperated people, who feel that they possess power, are not easily restrained within limits strictly regular.
—Thomas Jefferson[1]

It was clear by early 1770 that the Townshend Acts were not working. This was due less to the colonists' nonimportation agreements, which were only sporadically effective, than to the difficulty of enforcing the taxes. The thousands of soldiers stationed in Boston were costing far more than the Townshend duties raised, and those soldiers had not pacified the locals. Some English commercial leaders also feared that the duties were actually too *favorable* to Americans, because by encouraging them to make their own products instead of buying imports, Parliament was nursing Britain's future competition. "Every family has become a little manufactory," one Connecticut visitor told John Adams. "They raise and make within themselves many things for which they used to run in debt to the merchants and traders."[2] Little surprise, then, that petitions for repealing the acts arrived not only from America but also from businesses throughout England.

The House of Commons began discussing a repeal in April 1769. The members took no action at the time, but everybody noticed that no member spoke in favor of keeping the taxes. Soon afterward, the Customs Board reported that it had collected only a little over £11,000 in revenue—far less than the government had spent enforcing the laws.[3] Yet in seeking some face-saving way to abandon the Townshend Acts, London's politicians were stuck with the same problem they had confronted during the Stamp Act crisis: how

In December 1773, the Boston Sons of Liberty donned disguises and destroyed 46 tons of tea in a matter of hours, leaving behind no clue as to their identities.

to retreat without appearing to concede to American claims that parliamentary taxation was unconstitutional. The colonial secretary, Lord Hillsborough, told the House of Commons that he had "no particular fondness" for the Townshend Acts, and he admitted that the Revenue Act in particular was "so anti-commercial that he wished it had never existed," but he was determined not to repeal them in a way that might look like a precedent against Parliament's authority. It was frustrating that Americans refused to ask for repeal "upon the ground of its inexpediency," he thought. Instead, they kept insisting that Parliament had no constitutional power to impose taxes. The Lords and Commons could not even "think of repealing [the acts] . . . until the colonies had properly submitted to the authority of Parliament and dropped the point of right."[4]

The new prime minister, Lord North, who took office in January 1770, agreed. He would not consider abandoning the Townshend taxes, he said, "until he saw America prostrate at his feet."[5] That summer, his cabinet finally decided on a way to accomplish that. They would repeal the acts, but instead of repeating the empty boast of the Declaratory Act, Parliament would continue to implement its taxing authority—albeit in a small way—thereby ensuring that it did not abandon its claim to power. And it was easy to do that because only one of the Townshend taxes actually proved profitable: the tax on tea.[6] Retaining that tax while repealing the others would preserve the constitutional claims of Parliamentary Supremacy and keep the money flowing in.

Lord Frederick North, the Second Earl of Guilford, was a graduate of Eton and Oxford and had first been elected to Parliament in 1754, at the age of 22. Rumored to be George III's bastard son, he had a moderate temperament, conservative politics, and distaste for confrontation that might have led one to expect him to favor American claims. But he shared the constitutional views of George Grenville, Lord Hillsborough, Lord Mansfield, and others. So when he rose in the House to move for repeal on March 5, 1770, he made clear that he did so only because the Townshend Acts were not proving effective. They had "created so much dissatisfaction among the merchants trading from the mother country to the continental colonies," he said, "that I conceive it very proper for this House to give the matter a serious consideration." Yet in view of the Americans' "vehemence," outright repeal was unthinkable. "The properest time to exert our right of taxation is, when the right is refused," he thought. "To temporize is to yield." Americans would try to spin repeal as proof "that we were to be terrified into [a] concession," just as they had with the Stamp Act repeal. "[Our] very lenity has encouraged them to insult our authority, to dispute our rights, and to aim at independent government." So the best thing to do was to retain the tea duty, while declaring that the other taxes were only withdrawn because they were "contrary to the true principles of commerce."[7] His colleagues agreed, and partial repeal was adopted on April 12.[8]

At first, it seemed to work. With all but one of the taxes gone, many colonists were indeed content to call it a win, and in the months that followed, Patriot leaders felt the momentum beginning to wane. "Our countrymen," wrote Jefferson, "seemed to fall into a state of insensibility to our situation."[9] Philadelphia and New York chose to officially end the boycott on everything except tea. In Boston, Samuel Adams lost an important election to an outspoken Tory—and when he tried rallying the public with a series of provocative newspaper articles recalling all the troubles since the Stamp Act, it had little effect.[10] Even the angry dispute over Governor Hutchinson's order moving the Massachusetts legislature to Cambridge fizzled out. "How easily the people change, and give up their friends and their interest," John Adams grumbled in his diary.[11] By April 1771, he had decided to quit the movement entirely. He would concentrate on his farm and his legal practice, instead. "Farewell, politics," he announced.[12]

THE BURNING OF THE *GASPEE*

Yet even as Adams wrote, American resentment toward British trade restrictions was still simmering. That month, a government inspector boarded a ship at Newport, Rhode Island, to search for contraband, only to be beaten nearly to death. When asked about the incident, the colony's governor, Stephen Hopkins—the outspoken opponent of the Sugar and Stamp Acts—denied that Rhode Islanders were responsible and blamed "a company of lawless seamen" instead.[13] In London, Benjamin Franklin agreed. It was no big deal, he wrote. "If . . . the drubbing of an informer or low custom-house officer were rebellion," then "England, Scotland, and Ireland might be said to be in rebellion almost every week."[14] In fact, such incidents were so frequent in Britain that "one would think riots part of the mode of government."[15]

But a little over a year later, a Royal Navy schooner called the HMS *Gaspee* suffered a more violent fate, one that proved impossible to ignore. On June 9, 1772, the *Gaspee* started chasing a suspected smuggler off the coast of Rhode Island, only to run aground near Warwick, south of Providence. The stranded ship had to wait for the tides to change to float off. But before that could happen, night fell, and a gang of colonists sneaked aboard. They shot the commanding officer and set a fire that destroyed the vessel. When London demanded an investigation, Governor Hopkins found ways to procrastinate. But the new secretary of state for the colonies—William Legge, Lord Dartmouth—was not willing to let the matter die down.

Dartmouth, who had succeeded the disliked Hillsborough in August, was an amiable and devout man—people called him "the Psalm Singer"—and, in Franklin's estimation, "a truly good man, [who] wishes sincerely a good understanding with the colonies."[16] But whatever his private desires, it was his duty to implement the policies of Lord North (who happened to be his brother-in-law). And these showed no leniency toward colonial resistance. When he learned of the *Gaspee*'s destruction, Dartmouth demanded not only that those responsible be brought to justice but that they be sent to England for trial under the Treason Act.[17] To track them down, he created a commission of inquiry, staffed by the chief justices of Massachusetts, New York, and New Jersey, as well as a Boston vice-admiralty judge.

Yet despite lengthy meetings and the offer of a £500 reward, the commission never found any suspects or witnesses, in part because local attorneys refused to acknowledge the commission's authority.[18] Meanwhile, the Sons of Liberty howled in protest. "The persons who are the commissioners of this new-fangled court are vested with the most exorbitant and unconstitutional power," declared one, who concluded that such a violation of the right to trial by jury was an "alarming star-chamber inquisition."[19]

When Jefferson learned of the *Gaspee* commission, he, too, was alarmed. Yet he doubted whether the "old and leading members" of Virginia's House of Burgesses were "up to the point of forwardness and zeal" needed to formulate an effective protest.[20] Thus, he and a group of younger Burgesses—including Patrick Henry and Dabney Carr—decided to offer a resolution calling for the establishment of a Committee of Correspondence, which would maintain communications with the other colonies and fashion ways to deal with the imperial government's incursions. The committee would also ensure that the Burgesses could meet and plan even after the legislature adjourned—convenient in case the governor dissolved the House again. The resolution passed, and Jefferson, Henry, Carr, Richard Bland, and others were chosen to serve on the committee.[21] Within a few months, every colony had its own Committee of Correspondence, and their members would likely have been pleased if they had known of a report from London that this maneuver "struck a greater panic into the ministers than anything that has passed since the Stamp Act."[22]

The committee idea had also occurred to the members of the Massachusetts House. In the summer of 1772, news arrived from London of the ministry's decision to pay the salaries of the governor and the colony's judges directly, thus taking away the House's power to decide on payment (or to refuse payment to officials it disliked). The colonial charter guaranteed the legislature "full power and authority to name and settle annually all civil officers" and to "impose and levy proportionable and reasonable assessments, rates and taxes" for the "support of [the king's] government." Moreover, as the House explained in an indignant resolution that July, such a power was "necessary to preserve the freedom of the constitution," because it was the only effectual way to ensure both the independence of the courts and the accountability of public officials.[23] To make their displeasure clear, Massachusetts lawmakers followed up that remonstrance with a note refusing to pay for repairs to the governor's official residence. If Thomas Hutchinson—now officially promoted to governor—was going to get his paycheck from London, then he might as well ask Parliament to fix his house, too.[24] Hutchinson responded by closing down the legislative session, but not before lecturing the members about their "erroneous opinion" regarding the British constitution and reasserting Parliament's "supreme legislative authority."[25]

In October, the Boston Town Meeting also passed resolutions objecting to the Crown's decision to pay judges directly. Yet Hutchinson ignored these, privately mocking the way "the inhabitants of Boston" thought they had the right "to concern themselves with all the affairs of government."[26] So, a month later, the town meeting agreed to Samuel Adams's proposal to form a Committee of Correspondence within Massachusetts, enabling the colony's cities to communicate with one another. The Bostonians immediately wrote to the other towns about the threat posed by the direct-payment plan, which made judges "not only independent of the people . . . but absolutely dependent on the crown (which may hereafter be worn by a *tyrant*)."[27]

London's willingness to curtail judicial independence especially aroused John Adams's anger. He thought it obvious that an independent court system was the keystone of any free government. He was therefore shocked to hear William Brattle—former colonial attorney general, and once a reliable Whig—endorse the proposal at a town meeting in Cambridge. Brattle thought Parliament's new rule would actually *reinforce* judicial independence, and he offered to debate Adams on the subject in the newspapers. Adams agreed, fearing the man's "ignorant doctrines" might take "root in the minds of the people." Taking the unusual step of signing his own name instead of using a pseudonym, he unloaded a torrent of scholarship showing that for Parliament to pay judges' salaries would make them subservient to London.[28] If the plan were implemented, he warned, "our lives, liberties, reputations and estates" would exist only "at the mercy of a majority [in Parliament], and of a triumphant party."[29]

But merely arguing the issue in the newspapers was not enough to ensure the rule of law in Massachusetts. Something more direct had to be done, and quickly. If London made the province's judges into paid sycophants, Adams believed, "the liberties of the province would be lost."[30] So one night, when the subject came up at a dinner with some prominent colonial lawyers, he proposed an idea: what if the House impeached any judges who accepted Parliamentary salaries?

That suggestion startled the other attorneys. No such thing had ever been done before; did the House even *have* the power to impeach?

Of course it did, Adams answered. It was a miniature Parliament—or so all good Patriots believed—and if the Commons in Westminster could impeach, so could the House in Boston. Eventually, the members decided to try it. First, they asked the judges if they intended to accept a salary from London. After a lengthy delay, the colony's new chief justice, Peter Oliver—brother of the Andrew Oliver who had been hanged in effigy during the Stamp Act protests—answered yes. Immediately, the House drew up articles of impeachment against Oliver and sent them to Governor Hutchinson.

"This proceeding," Hutchinson told his superiors in London, "is a most explicit declaration against the just authority, as I conceive, of the king as well as the Parliament."[31] He refused to even acknowledge the articles of impeachment. But they were published in the newspapers, and when the court next met, the jurors, much to Adams's delight, refused to participate in any hearings. "They answered to a man that the chief justice of that court stood impeached of high crimes and misdemeanors," he recalled, "and they would not sit as jurors while that accusation was pending."[32] The courts were forced to shut down. The next time they opened, it would be under the authority of an independent Massachusetts.

THE BOSTON PAMPHLET

No sooner had the Bay Colony's Committee of Correspondence been established than it released an extraordinary document at the Boston Town Meeting of November 20, 1772.[33] Written by Samuel Adams, Boston doctor Joseph Warren, and James Otis—in what proved to be Otis's final public act, given his now crippling mental troubles—the report was a Patriot's manifesto. It consisted of three parts: a statement of basic philosophical principles, a sketch of the Whigs' Prescriptive Right theory of the British constitution, and a concluding "list of the infringements and violations" of the colonists' rights. Copied and circulated throughout America, the report came to be known as "the Boston Pamphlet," and it would become one of the earliest templates for the Declaration of Independence.

"Among the natural rights of the colonists are these," it began. "First, a right to life; secondly to liberty; thirdly to property;

together with the right to support and defend them." People form governments "for purposes of common defense," not by instinct or destiny or even divine command, but "by voluntary consent"—and that meant the people "have a right to demand and insist upon the performance of [certain] conditions." The citizens do not, and cannot, enslave themselves to the government, as Thomas Hobbes had believed, because "it is not in the power of man to alienate" his own freedom. Instead, the people remain free, with government officials their servants, rather than their masters.

The Pamphlet went further. Expressly citing John Locke, it explained that no legislature can claim absolute power, because that would effectively transforms the citizens' rights into mere permissions given by the rulers and make the people into slaves. Instead, lacking any *inherent* right to govern, Parliament could have that power only by consent, and consent has limits. Since the colonists weren't represented in Westminster, and "from their local situation and circumstances" could not be, they could give it no consent to tax them. And if Parliament *did* have the power to tax the colonists unilaterally, what would happen as America's population grew? If it could legislate for Americans in all cases whatsoever, the empire's "haughty and relentless" aristocrats would soon be able to "ride at ease" by taxing Americans to fund their desires, even after the New World became more populous than Britain.

The Boston Pamphlet's concluding list of grievances, apparently drafted by Warren, began with Parliament's claim to "the power of legislation for the colonists in all cases whatsoever." Second was the taxation of the colonists "without consent or representation." Third, Parliament had sent "a number of new officers" to Massachusetts to implement the taxes and customs regulations, and these were not chosen by the voters, even though the colony's charter gave the people "the sole right of appointing all civil officers." These officials were empowered to search homes and businesses and to seize property without warrants, using writs of assistance. Parliament had also decided to pay the salaries of governors and judges, taking the power of the purse out of the hands of the people's representatives and making the judiciary, which ought to be neutral, "altogether dependent" on Westminster.

In addition, the ministry had ordered Governor Hutchinson to close the Massachusetts legislature when it protested against illegal actions, and it had forbidden the official Governor's Council from meeting, even for informal conversations, without Hutchinson's permission.[34] This all had the consequence of making the colonial government "merely a ministerial engine." And as if to prove that, Parliament had sent an army to occupy Boston, whom the colonists were forced to equip and house. Now, Governor Hutchinson, who by virtue of his office was commander-in-chief, was claiming that "he had no control" over the troops. If that were true, Boston was really run by the military.

Expansion of the vice-admiralty courts was also a violation of constitutional rights—such an "enormous" one, in fact, that it alone was "sufficient to rouse our jealousy." In Britain, defendants were entitled to trial by jury. But the Townshend Acts took that right away from Americans, "and that, too, with every mark of indignity, insult, and contempt." Along the same lines, talk of using the Treason Act to send colonists to England for trial also "deprived [us] of our grand right to trial by our peers *in the vicinity*," violating the long-standing rule that a defendant should typically be tried in the same locale where the crime occurred. Even if English juries were not biased against American colonists, which they probably were, forcing Americans accused of crimes to voyage to Europe—an expensive, dangerous, potentially months-long trip in those days—made trial a burden rather than a protection, especially if the accused had to persuade witnesses to come along.

The Boston Pamphlet also expressed concerns about news that the Church of England planned to establish a diocese in America. Rumors of such a step had been circulating since at least 1763, and in 1771, James Horrocks, president of Jefferson's alma mater William and Mary—who was also the bishop of London's representative in Virginia—petitioned Parliament to create an Anglican bishopric in that colony.[35] Such a step would make a drastic change in American religious culture. Colonial churches were unusually democratic, being governed not by appointed leaders as in Europe, but by local parishioners and vestrymen. Most colonists regarded this organizational structure as more in harmony with the spirit of Protestantism; as historian Gordon Wood writes, "Religious life never flowed from the top down" in America.[36] To replace this decentralized system with a chain of command controlled by London would upend that democratic ethos.

Also, religious diversity worked as a crude form of checks and balances in the colonies, fostering a strong sense of individualism and political resistance. To reinforce Anglican control in the New World would weaken that spirit, because established churches invariably ally themselves with political authorities and preach the false virtues of subservience. Indeed, there were growing signs of such a trend. In 1775, Anglican clergyman Jonathan Boucher would even deliver a sermon based on the ideas of Sir Robert Filmer. "The leading idea, or principle, of Sir Robert Filmer's *Patriarcha* is, that government is not of human, but divine origin," Boucher declaimed. "And this principle, notwithstanding Mr. Locke's answer, is still (in the opinion of the author of these sermons) unrefuted, and still true. . . . All government, whether lodged in one or in many, is, in its nature, absolute and irresistible."[37] A powerful Anglican establishment in America would certainly serve as a conduit for such absolutist propaganda. (Boston's Congregationalists likely also feared that an Anglican bishop would threaten the power of their own established church.[38])

When viewed together, the Boston Pamphlet declared, these "innovation[s]" revealed a "constant, unremitted, uniform aim to enslave us"—to treat Americans not like fellow members of the empire, but like a subject populace whose role was to pay taxes, obey orders, and keep quiet. It was therefore "of the utmost importance that we stand firm as one man, to recover and support" the true principles of the constitution and the rights it protected.

Benjamin Franklin made sure the pamphlet was published in London, where it joined a flood of writing now pouring out of America. Imperial officials were already alarmed about such publications. A month before the pamphlet appeared, the *Massachusetts Spy* printed a shocking article titled "To the King," which Governor Hutchinson considered "so seditious and treasonable" that he forwarded it to London asking what to do.[39] Its anonymous author accused George III personally of "plung[ing] your countrymen into a labyrinth of confusion, from which, were it not for the angelic virtue of a few whom you can neither corrupt nor intimidate, your empire [would have] been a scene of slaughter and desolation long before this day."[40] Hutchinson—who for years labored in vain to suppress the Sons of Liberty's publications by bringing criminal charges of "seditious libel"—thought this so incendiary that he asked for permission to arrest the publisher.[41] But Lord Dartmouth thought that would do no good. He, too, wished such writers could be punished, he told the governor, but Massachusetts juries were dominated by the Sons of Liberty and always refused to convict dissenters. "In the present temper of the times," he sighed, "prosecutions will be of no effect."

Anyway, the article was just a small symptom of "the unhappy mistake" that "possesse[s] the minds of so many of the people . . . concerning the connection between the different parts of the dominions of Great Britain and the authority of the British legislature." In other words, the basic problem was the colonists' Prescriptive Right theory, which held that Americans owed allegiance only to the king and their own legislatures, not to Parliament. That doctrine, wrote Dartmouth, "would leave the assemblies of America possessed of a power that is absolutely incompatible with the supreme authority of the Mother Country and utterly inconsistent with every idea of subordination and dependence."[42] The correct principle was "that in every society there must be somewhere a supreme uncontrollable power, an absolute authority to decide and determine; that wherever such power is found, there is, of necessity, independent sovereignty."[43] That supreme authority was, of course, held by the Lords and Commons.

THE GREAT CONTROVERSY

Immediately after this letter arrived, Hutchinson learned of the Boston Pamphlet. "I am sorry that I am obliged to acquaint your lordship with the extravagant principles in government which are still avowed not only by the writers in newspapers but by the inhabitants of towns, who assemble together and call themselves a legal town meeting," he told Dartmouth, sending him a copy. "It is very dangerous to tolerate such publications tending to mutiny and rebellion."[44] But the secretary's letter had given him an idea. Still stung by the House's criticisms for accepting a salary from London, he decided to show the legislators the errors of their ways. Summoning them to an emergency session on January 6, 1773, Hutchinson delivered a diatribe, explaining their legal errors and defending the theory of Parliamentary Supremacy.

He began by denouncing the "repugnant" publications that denied the principle of the Declaratory Act. American legislatures, he insisted, were subordinate to Parliament, not its equals. They did not have the "sole power of making laws," and to suggest otherwise must logically result in "the total independence of the colonies." After all, Chief Justice Mansfield had said that it was "impossible there should be two independent legislatures in one and the same state." As for the argument that Parliament's taxing the colonies deprived Americans of the rights other British subjects enjoyed, the colonists would just have to accept their inferior position. "It is impossible the rights of English subjects should be the same, in every respect, in all parts of the dominions."[45]

The governor might have thought he was settling things, but he was actually playing into the Patriots' hands. The ensuing showdown, known as the "Great Controversy," would put on paper, in the most unambiguous way, the basic conflict between Britain and the colonies. To ensure that they offered the strongest possible reply, members of the House of Representatives turned to the colony's most respected Patriot lawyer, John Adams. Although no longer serving in the House, he agreed to join Samuel Adams and another Patriot attorney, Joseph Hawley, to prepare the official response.

The crisis, they began, was not caused by any misunderstanding of the constitution on their part, but by the unconstitutional acts of the House of Commons, particularly its notion that Parliament could bind the colonies "in all cases whatsoever." Massachusetts's first settlers had never agreed to be ruled by such "supreme authority." They had bought the territory from the Indians, which meant the colony was "not annexed to the realm of England, [but was] at the absolute disposal of the crown." After that, England's monarchs had repeatedly promised Americans the *same* rights as all other Englishmen, "as if they had been abiding and born within the realm." And that meant they had the right to a legislature of their own choosing.

True, colonial charters limited the Massachusetts legislature's power to making laws "not repugnant to those of Britain," but that only meant their statutes had to be "as much as possible conformant . . . to the principles and fundamental laws of the English constitution"—it did not "bind the colonies to a subjection to the supreme authority of the English Parliament." On the contrary, one of the most basic rights of political society was the right to have a say in legislation. The theory of Parliamentary Supremacy contradicted that principle and would make Americans slaves, "for nothing is more evident than that any people who are subject to the unlimited power of another must be in a state of abject slavery."

Hutchinson had likened the colonies to private corporations, operating pursuant to charters from the legislature. Those charters let companies make their own internal rules, but they were still subject to parliamentary control. Adams and his colleagues rejected that analogy. "The members of those corporations are resident within the kingdom," they wrote, but the Bay Colony had been founded by people who left Europe precisely because they wanted to be "governed by laws made by themselves." Their charter allowed them to create a legislature and courts of their own, something no mere corporation could do. If they had been told that Parliament would make laws for them, the first settlers would have objected "that their design might and probably would be frustrated." Instead, they considered themselves "distinct states from the mother country" from the beginning.

Adams concluded his argument with a shocking statement. The governor had tried to frighten the people of Massachusetts with the "terrors" of independence, claiming that the colony would collapse; laws would go unenforced; Indians and Frenchmen would take over. But that was all nonsense. Britain and the colonies could easily live together, sharing the same king, but with different legislatures. Nevertheless, if forced to choose, they would prefer separation. "There is more reason to dread the consequences of absolute uncontrolled supreme power, whether of a nation or a monarch, than those of a total independence."[46]

A few weeks later, Hutchinson submitted a rejoinder. He started by appealing to the basic dogma of European monarchy: feudal land tenure. "As English subjects," he wrote, "all our lands and tenements are held mediately, or immediately of the crown." That meant the argument that Massachusetts was part of the "dominion" but not the "realm" was legally meaningless; everything colonists owned was theirs due to their subjection to government authority—and that meant Parliament. The ancient colonial charters Adams cited were irrelevant, because Parliament had replaced them with new charters after the 1689 revolution. "Surely, then . . . it was the sense of our predecessors, as well as of the king and of the nation, that there was, and would remain, a supremacy in the Parliament." As for the notion that Massachusetts was within the king's jurisdiction but outside Parliament's, the whole point of the Glorious Revolution was that the monarch *had no power* except what he derived from the Lords and Commons. "If you should disown [their] authority, which has power even to change the succession to the crown, are you in no danger of denying the authority of our most gracious sovereign, which I am sure none of you can have in your thoughts?" As for Adams's vague threat of independence, he might shrug at the dangers involved, but the truth was that it would bring "inevitable distress and misery" for all. The best course was to admit that "the British empire [is] one entire dominion, subject to one supreme legislative power."[47]

Again, the House turned to John Adams to help write a reply.[48] He began by attacking the feudalist theory Hutchinson took for granted. The notion that all land was held through the government's grace was an obsolete "system of iniquity" that, fortunately, was now being increasingly recognized as obsolete. "The constitution has been gradually changing for the better, and upon the more rational principle that all men by nature are in a state of equality in respect of jurisdiction and dominion," he wrote.

This represented something of a contradiction in Adams's argument. The whole point of the exchange had been to condemn Hutchinson's notion of Parliamentary Supremacy as an "innovation"—a newfangled idea out of step with long-standing constitutional principles. Adams had also appealed to ancient precedent in arguing that Americans owed allegiance exclusively to the king, on the grounds that their colonies had been founded under the monarch's autonomous authority. Yet now Adams was distancing himself from ancient precedents and appealing to the innovative idea that feudalism was contrary to natural law. Yet however inconsistent that might seem, Adams was able to turn the charge of self-contradiction back against Hutchinson. Even if the governor was right that the principles of feudalism should guide Massachusetts, that only strengthened the colonists' cause because Feudal law allowed kings to give away their dominions—and they had done just that in the colonial charters. What's more, the "feudal system admits of *no idea of the authority of Parliament*." Feudalism therefore proved once more that the colonies were subject to the monarch, but not the Lords and Commons.

Feudalism aside, the colonies had never been intended to fall within Parliament's power. "Our ancestors considered the land which they took possession of in America as out of the bounds of the Kingdom of England, and out of the reach and extent of the laws of England." King James I had agreed, memorializing that understanding in the Massachusetts charter. True, the colonists later acknowledged the legitimacy of William and Mary, who had been made king and queen by Parliament's act. But that did not prove, as Hutchinson claimed, that the colony conceded Parliament's supremacy. "There had been a revolution here as well as in England," Adams wrote, referring to the overthrow of Edmund Andros. Those who rebelled against Andros had accepted William and Mary on their *own* accord, not because Parliament forced them. Hutchinson certainly couldn't point to any admission by the people of Massachusetts "of [Parliament's] supreme authority to make laws binding on us *in all cases whatever*." On the contrary, William and Mary had been crowned on the condition that they respect "the laws and customs" of England—and the most crucial of those was the rule that laws could be made only by the consent of the governed. Parliamentary Supremacy violated that principle.

Most fundamentally, Westminster's power to make laws could never include the power to alter the constitution itself. That's just how constitutions work. "The fundamentals of the constitution [are] excepted from the commission of the legislators." To say otherwise—that Parliament could supersede the constitution—would mean it could wipe away all customs, all statutes, and all principles of justice. It would mean that Britons were "subjects of absolute, unlimited power," whose rights could be "superseded and nullified" at the will of London lawmakers. Parliament would then be a many-headed tyrant, even worse than the Stuarts.

THE HUTCHINSON LETTERS

The Great Controversy of 1773 was a complete triumph for Adams and the House of Representatives. Shaking his head at Hutchinson's decision to provoke such a duel, Lord Dartmouth wrote to reprimand him for having "so unhappily agitated" his constituents.[49] It was "in vain to hope that [Americans] will be induced by argument and persuasion," he said. He ordered Hutchinson to "avoid any further discussion whatever upon those questions." From now on, if the House denied Parliament's authority, he should not try to argue, but simply "prorogue or dissolve it."[50]

Then, only weeks after that humiliating rebuke, Hutchinson suffered another bombshell. Benjamin Franklin in London had obtained a group of confidential letters that Hutchinson and Andrew Oliver (now lieutenant governor) had written in 1769, which revealed that the military occupation of Boston had actually been proposed by Hutchinson himself. Franklin sent these to Boston with strict instructions that they were not to be published, only handed around discreetly to trustworthy Patriots.[51] John Adams saw them in late March 1773, whereupon he exploded in indignation in his diary. He had long thought Hutchinson unprincipled, self-serving, and ignorant of the law, but these letters proved he was also a "cool, thinking, deliberate villain, malicious and vindictive, as well as ambitious and avaricious."[52]

It turned out that Hutchinson had urged London to demonstrate its "resentment" against the upstart colonists after the Stamp Act's repeal. The Declaratory Act was not enough, he wrote. "If no measures shall have been taken to secure [Massachusetts's] dependence, or nothing more than some declaratory acts or resolves, it is all over with us." Most of all, there would have to be "an abridgment of what are called English liberties," because it was preferable to lose freedom than to disturb the connection with Britain. "I doubt whether it is possible to project a system of government in which a colony 3,000 miles distant from the parent state shall enjoy all the liberty of the parent state." So much for the charter's promise of equal rights.

Hutchinson had also urged the Lords and Commons to punish opponents of parliamentary taxation and to unilaterally change the Massachusetts charter to reduce the power of voters. Oliver had agreed. "While [Parliament's] friends and the officers of the crown are left to an abject dependence on these very people who are undermining its authority," he wrote, "it cannot be expected that you will ever again recover that respect which the colonies had been wont to pay."[53]

The letters seemed proof of Hutchinson's and Oliver's treachery. These men were Massachusetts natives, occupying the highest levels of government. Now, they were revealed as not merely preaching bad constitutional doctrine but actively conspiring to undermine the colony and betray its people at the very time that Americans had been rejoicing over the peaceful resolution of the Stamp Act crisis. An enraged Adams drafted a newspaper article addressed to Hutchinson and purporting to be signed by Crispus Attucks, the first victim of the Boston Massacre: "You are chargeable before God and man with our blood," it declared. "The soldiers were but [your] passing instruments."[54] After he calmed down, he decided not to publish it. But his cousin Samuel was not so restrained. He began publicly hinting at the letters' contents during speeches in the House of Representatives, and at last ordered them read aloud by the clerk—technically complying with Franklin's instruction not to reprint them. After that, copies began circulating throughout America.

In June, the House resolved that Hutchinson and Oliver were responsible for "the severe and destructive measures which have been taken against this province." While pretending to love and care for the people, they had actually encouraged "measures destructive of our constitutional liberty." Hutchinson in particular was to blame for the military occupation and for "the great corruption of morals, and all that confusion, misery, and bloodshed which have been the natural effects." The House ended its resolution with a plea that King George remove Hutchinson and Oliver "forever from their places in this government."[55]

Some historians have found the Patriots' fury over these letters exaggerated, but there was method to the outrage. With Lord Dartmouth replacing Lord Hillsborough as colonial secretary, there might be a way for the new administration to adopt a face-saving compromise. If both sides could come to see the legal and political tensions of the previous decade as a giant misunderstanding caused by Hutchinson's and Hillsborough's poor leadership, the new, more easygoing colonial secretary might retreat from his predecessor's policies and say it had all been just a little family quarrel. That, at least, was Franklin's plan. In the guileful cover letter accompanying the letters to Boston, he told the Massachusetts Patriots that after reading them, he was persuaded that Britain's "arbitrary measures" had been "advised and called for by men of character among ourselves, and whose advice . . . [was] misleading." This revelation, he said, "exceedingly abated" his own "resentment" toward Parliament.[56] Maybe all Americans would feel the same.

But if Hutchinson was being made a scapegoat, that doesn't mean he was an innocent victim of Patriot trickery. The governor's sympathetic biographer characterizes him as "sincere, industrial, and profoundly loyal to the community of his birth," as well as "more tolerant and reasonable" than the Patriots, but this description would have stunned Americans who expected their leader to defend their rights and were incensed to learn that he instead championed parliamentary absolutism beyond the limits of law and logic.[57] Ignorant and craven, thirsting for money and political advancement, Hutchinson was an opportunist whose notion of political wisdom was to pursue what he considered pragmatic solutions at a time when only a forthright defense of principle would do. Had the colonists seen other letters he wrote—ridiculing the idea of liberty, encouraging the arrest of newspaper publishers, and repeatedly accusing his opponents of treason, sedition, and mutiny (all capital crimes)—they would have been far more scandalized than they were.

Above all, they would have considered it misleading to call Hutchinson a "conservative" opposing "radicals."[58] To the extent that these anachronistic labels are useful in describing 18th-century debates, the Patriots considered *themselves* "conservatives," appealing to a time-honored English constitution, the meaning of which was discerned through traditions dating back to medieval times. Even London regarded the Patriots' ideas as old-fashioned and reactionary, not new and radical. Lord North himself said so when he characterized the colonists' claim that the king enjoyed power separate from that of Parliament as "the language of Toryism."[59] He was right. North and his allies, by contrast, took the "radical," innovative position that law was not, as previously believed, a principle of reason by which the rightfulness of government power was discerned, but instead a mere matter of command, by which Parliament—the supreme and absolute sovereign—exerted its unconstrained will over a populace halfway around the globe. That Thomas Hutchinson emphatically defended this drastic new theory of Parliamentary Supremacy and secretly urged London officials to back it up at gunpoint not only denies him any claim to conservatism but fully deserved the Patriots' scorn.

DIGNITY, MAJESTY, SUBLIMITY

When the scandal over his letters broke, Hutchinson asked for permission to visit England to vindicate himself. But his request arrived too late in the year for him to make the voyage. And with winter came still another crisis, when New England learned of the latest legislation from London: the Tea Act. Adopted in May, that act did not itself impose a tax on tea, but was artfully designed to reinforce the tea tax that had been left in place when the Townshend Acts were partly repealed, and to prop up the ailing East India Company.[60] The company—in which many members of Parliament were investors—had suffered from the colonial boycotts and was on the verge of bankruptcy. Parliament therefore fashioned a bailout.

The Tea Act effectively exempted the company from the Navigation Acts' prohibition on direct shipments. Instead of being required to send tea first to England, to be unloaded and reloaded before its ships proceeded to their final destination—as all other merchants were required to do—the act allowed it to carry tea straight to America, drastically reducing its transportation costs. The act also gave it the exclusive right to sell tea in America through its own licensed "consignees" instead of auctioning it to colonial retailers, as had been done previously. By giving the company a monopoly and reducing its business costs, the act ensured that the company's tea would be cheaper than the smuggled Dutch variety Americans were drinking during their boycott. (True to form, Hutchinson made sure that two of his sons and two close friends got licenses as consignees.)

Consignees would pay the import tax when they accepted a shipment and would naturally incorporate that cost into the retail price. That meant, as an anonymous Philadelphia writer observed, that the act was "more dangerous" than the Stamp Act, because it was "more insidious in its operation":

> The Stamp Act was sensibly felt by all ranks of people, and was therefore opposed by all, but the Tea Act . . . required some pains to discover its malignity. Under the [Stamp Act] no man could transfer his property, he could not even read a newspaper, without seeing and feeling the detestable imposition. . . . But under the Tea Law, the duty, being paid on importation, is afterwards laid on the article, and becomes so blended with the price of it, that . . . every man does not know it, and may, therefore, not object to it.[61]

In short, the act was ingeniously devised to entice Americans into paying Parliament's taxes, and to deny them the opportunity to boycott the product. Nor could the tea be sent back to England unsold, because customs officers would have to give ships permission to leave port—and that was not allowed if the tax had not been paid. Hutchinson had the power to override that rule, but he would certainly refuse. And the law further provided that any shipment not unloaded within three weeks of arrival would be confiscated by the governor and sold at auction—which, again, would result in the tax being paid.

If Americans paid, they would be charged with having conceded Parliament's authority to tax them—thereby establishing the rule they had long sought to resist. It was crucial to avoid looking like they acquiesced in the tax. That had been the point of the boycotts of the previous five years. Those had been difficult to enforce, though, as merchants and consumers had often been tempted to cheat. And although Sons of Liberty groups tried to name and shame anyone who bought British imports, or even to intimidate them through threats and violence, those efforts had only been moderately successful. They would certainly collapse if the East India Company took advantage of this new law to deliver tons of delicious bohea, hyson, and souchong that cost less than the black-market alternatives. Samuel Adams candidly admitted that he "could not trust the private virtue of his countrymen in refraining from the use of [tea]."[62] Thus the conflict over tea was not, as historians have often claimed, a matter of mere "symbolism," but a question of constitutional precedent.[63]

When the Committees of Correspondence learned in July 1773 that the company was preparing cargoes for Boston, New York, Philadelphia, and Charleston, some tried warning London not to send the ships. That autumn, however, 11 vessels departed for America carrying more than half a million pounds of tea. The first arrived in South Carolina on December 1. After weeks of debate, the local Sons of Liberty decided to move 257 chests of the stuff to a warehouse and lock it up. (There it remained for three years, finally being sold to fund the revolutionary army.) Other ships were on their way, and it was crucial that something be done.

The first to reach Boston was the *Dartmouth*, which made port on November 28, followed by the *Eleanor* and the *Beaver*. The November 28 date started the clock running, because if the tea was not unloaded by December 17, Governor Hutchinson would confiscate it and auction it off. Samuel Adams therefore convened a town meeting on November 29 to announce that the people could not and would not let the tea be unloaded. Yet it wasn't clear what he and his fellow Sons of Liberty could do. They could not force the ships to return to England, because no vessel could leave without Hutchinson's permission, and the navy, expecting resistance, stationed gunships at the harbor's mouth with orders to fire on any vessel that tried.[64]

That left no alternative. On the night of December 16, the Sons of Liberty concealed their identities with crude Native American disguises, boarded the three vessels, and threw 92,000 pounds of tea into the water. They were organized and superbly skilled; by now, they were fully experienced at "rescuing" ships from customs officers. Nobody was hurt, and other than the tea, no property was damaged, beyond a single broken lock that the Sons of Liberty politely replaced the next day.

The Boston Tea Party was a carefully orchestrated operation, and the most remarkable fact was the secrecy with which the participants acted. No objective evidence has ever surfaced connecting

Samuel Adams with the scheme, which he almost certainly oversaw. On the contrary, as his biographer remarks, the night of December 16, 1773, is one of the few dates for which historians can say exactly where he was—because that master of intrigue took care that witnesses could testify he was *nowhere near* the waterfront that evening.[65] That was wise; the ministry immediately opened a treason investigation.[66]

Over the course of the next year, "tea parties" broke out in at least a dozen cities, as crowds impounded cargoes, burned ships and their contents, and forced captains to take their merchandise back to Europe. When Philadelphia's shipment arrived, the city's official Committee for Tarring and Feathering went aboard and, with a great show of courtesy, invited the captain ashore. He immediately agreed not to unload the tea, and sailed home with his payload three days later. In Manhattan, local Patriots met the captain of a tea ship at the dock, marched beside him into town to buy supplies for a return voyage, and sent him back to London within a few hours, all in a festive mood, to the ringing of church bells and the singing of "God Save the King." Things went differently in Annapolis. That city's consignee paid the tax after the local Sons of Liberty warned him not to. Days of public debate ensued, which concluded with a command that he set fire to the tea ship, cargo and all, and publicly apologize for "deservedly incur[ring] the displeasure of the people."[67] Even in places far from seaports, colonists joined in the protest; villagers burned tea in their town squares throughout America.[68] Never again would tea be the nation's beverage of choice.

When John Adams heard of the Boston Tea Party, he was ecstatic. "There is a dignity, a majesty, a sublimity in this," he declared. He even fantasized about seeing Governor Hutchinson's body floating beside the tea chests in the harbor.[69] But many colonists disapproved of Boston's act. The sanctity of private property was a cardinal Whig principle. The destruction of the East India Company's merchandise therefore seemed shockingly excessive to those outside the city. Towns across Massachusetts passed resolutions condemning the Bostonians, even while sympathizing with their goals. Even George Washington and Benjamin Franklin complained that the Tea Party was counterproductive. Tories had claimed all along that autocratic government was necessary to protect property rights against the ungovernable "mob." Boston's Sons of Liberty seemed to be proving them right.

That tension between the will of the people and the rule of law was poignantly expressed in an argument between merchant John Greenough and his father, Thomas. John had managed to obtain a chest of tea from a shipwreck and wanted to sell it; Thomas was a member of the Sons of Liberty, which threatened violence against John if he sold the tea. Both men supported the colonial cause. But John thought there was nothing wrong with selling this tea, which had been acquired without paying taxes, and he was furious about his neighbors' bullying. Was mob rule "not a greater infringement of our rights and liberties and more dangerous than any act of the British Parliament[?]" he demanded of his father. "Thus [are] our liberties destroyed, so far as such men who have no lawful power and right do govern and control our private lawful actions or the public acts of government and our properties are become precarious and uncertain, being at the disposal of these Indian Liberty Sons."[70] Thomas was unpersuaded. "When our liberties are invaded," he replied, "a mob is as requisite to the body politic as a portion of [medicine] is to a foul stomach."[71] (The Sons of Liberty eventually decided to let John sell his tea.)

To John Adams, the Tea Party was justified by necessity. "To let [the tea] be landed would be giving up the principle of taxation by parliamentary authority, against which the continent have struggled for ten years," he wrote.[72] Hutchinson could have let the ships take their freight safely back to England, as some colonial governors, blessed with "more wisdom than ours," had done. His sons could also have resigned their licenses as consignees or refused to accept the tea. But instead, their hearts had been as hardened as Pharaoh's, thus forcing the citizens' hands. It was a blessing that nobody had been hurt and no property other than the tea damaged. Of course, he knew London would exact revenge. "Military execution—charters annulled—treason—trials in England and all that," he predicted. Nevertheless, he thought, these things "had better be suffered [rather] than the great principle of parliamentary taxation given up."[73]

— PART THREE —

PATIENT SUFFERANCE ENDS

The "battle" of Lexington in April 1775 was a minor skirmish that left eight Americans dead. By the end of the day, colonial militia rallied and killed more than 70 British troops on their march back to Boston.

— CHAPTER 8 —

THE RIGHTS OF BRITISH AMERICA

There is so much of a republican spirit among the people, which has been nourished and cherished by their form of government, that they never would submit to tyrants or oppressive projects.

—John Adams[1]

London was astounded at the Bostonians' audacity. Not even during the Stamp Act riots had the Americans been so defiant. The ministry swiftly concluded that the Tea Party was an act of treason, but the Sons of Liberty had concealed their identities so effectively that ministers saw no way to bring the perpetrators to trial. King George and Prime Minister North therefore decided to punish the entire city. General Thomas Gage, who for the past five years had commanded the British army in North America, told the king during a visit to London that winter that the colonists "will be lions while we are lambs; but if we take the resolute part, they will undoubtedly prove very meek." Passing this advice along to Lord North, George added his own conviction that "the fatal compliance of 1766"—meaning repeal of the Stamp Act—had only encouraged Americans "to increase in their pretensions" to their "subversive" plan of "thorough independency."[2] Now, he thought, the government must be stricter.

Its first target would be Benjamin Franklin. His scheme of blaming Governor Hutchinson for the imperial crisis had completely failed—American hostility toward Parliament only grew when the governor's letters were published. Now, Franklin would be the scapegoat instead. Summoned before the Privy Council on January 29, 1774, he was publicly humiliated in an hour-long tirade by Solicitor General Alexander Wedderburn, who accused him of plotting to

King George III was "the main driving force of the British war for America."

"incense the colonies against the mother country." Pounding the podium with his fist, the livid Wedderburn mocked Franklin as a liar and a thief who had "forfeited all the respect of societies and men." Worse, he claimed, it was Franklin, not Hutchinson, who had inflamed American tensions, and had turned "the whole province [of Massachusetts] against his Majesty's government."[3]

The American said nothing in reply, silently withstanding Wedderburn's insults. But he had no regrets. "If the ministry here had been disposed to a reconciliation, as they sometimes pretend to be," he wrote afterward, the publication of Hutchinson's letters had given them "a fair opening, which they might have thanked me for. But they choose rather to abuse me."[4] Franklin sailed back to America when spring came.

Next, Parliament decided on a punishment for the Bay Colony. It would be a severe one, indeed. The Boston Port Act closed the colony's harbor entirely until the populace paid for the destroyed tea and proved their "obedience to the laws" to the king's satisfaction.[5] The goal was not to compensate the East India Company. In fact, when London merchants offered to pay for the tea themselves to keep the port open, Lord North refused. Rather, Parliament's goal was to make a constitutional point. Americans "deny our legislative authority," North explained. "If they deny authority in one instance, it goes to all. We must control them or submit to them."[6] Anything short of the heaviest chastisement would be viewed as a concession. The issue was no longer about "the degrees of freedom or restraint in which [the colonies] were to be held, but whether they should be totally separated from their connection with and dependence on the parent country."[7]

North appears to have been goaded into these steps by the king. On March 7, George asked Parliament to "take such measures" that would ensure "the just dependence of the colonies" and put an end to the Bostonians' constitutional "pretenses."[8] The monarch was determined, as Lord Dartmouth explained to Governor Hutchinson, to do whatever was necessary "to vindicate the insulted authority of this kingdom."[9] One MP was even more bellicose. During debate over the Port Act, Charles Van, a Welshman known for hating Americans, told the House, "The town of Boston ought to be knocked about their ears and destroyed. *Delenda est Carthago*."[10]

Van's classically educated audience would immediately have recognized the Latin as the infamous slogan of the Roman Senator Cato the Elder, who ended every speech with the phrase "Carthage must be destroyed," to underscore his belief that Rome needed to eradicate its rival city. Cato eventually prevailed, and in the Third Punic War (149–146 BCE), the Roman army obliterated Carthage, rendering it uninhabitable for a hundred years.

Van may have meant his words as comic hyperbole, but the humor was lost on Americans. The Port Act clearly spelled Boston's doom. News of the act arrived in May, less than a month before it was to go into effect, and the colonists were astonished to learn that it not only halted the shipping of "any merchandise whatsoever," except for food and firewood, but also was backed up by penalties that included forfeiture, triple damages, and even—if a merchant sold anything imported in violation of the act—the loss of any "horses, cattle, and carriages" used to carry the contraband.[11]

By the end of the month, Boston was experiencing shortages. "We suffer much for want of fresh meat," wrote one citizen. The people's "anxiety indeed is so great to get out of town that even were we obliged to go naked, it would not hinder us."[12] By year's end, the city was subsisting on charitable donations sent by other colonies. Anyone who could escape started moving to the countryside, leaving behind the destitute, whose numbers doubled. By June 1775, Boston's population had fallen to fewer than 3,000—one-fifth of what it had been just five years earlier.[13] John Adams darkly predicted to his wife that the town would "suffer martyrdom. It must expire. And our principal consolation is that it dies in a noble cause."[14]

To ensure enforcement of the Port Act, London made General Gage governor, replacing Thomas Hutchinson. A veteran of the French and Indian War, Gage had served as military governor of Quebec in the 1760s, married an American woman, and lived in America for 20 years. But he, like Hutchinson, was a firm believer in Parliamentary Supremacy. "None but the most stubborn and factious spirits," he thought, "can refuse to submit the decision of their constitutional rights to the wisdom of the British legislature."[15] He was convinced that colonial unrest was just the work of a few noisy troublemakers—specifically, Samuel Adams and John Hancock—and that firm treatment would bring the Americans to heel.

The colonial secretary, Lord Dartmouth, wasn't so sure about that, but he instructed the general to see to it that the colonists made "full and absolute submission" to Parliament's authority.[16] Gage's orders not only made him governor, but also required "all officers and ministers, civil and military, and all other inhabitants" to render him full assistance in putting down the rebels. He was to "pursue and prosecute" them and, "if it shall so please God," to "vanquish, apprehend, and . . . put [them] to death or keep and preserve [them] alive at your discretion."[17] In short, Gage would serve as military dictator, with power to conscript the locals and instructions to capture or kill the Massachusetts "traitors."[18]

The Port Act and Gage's appointment were only the beginning. Parliament also adopted four new laws that together would become known as "the Intolerable Acts."

The first was the Administration of Justice Act, which provided that any customs official, magistrate, or deputy of the government who killed a colonist while engaged in "the suppression of riots or . . . the carrying into effect the laws of revenue" could be tried not in the place where the crime occurred, but either in another colony or in England, as the governor chose.[19] Patriots quickly labeled this "the Murder Act," because it made it far more likely that imperial officials who killed Americans would be acquitted by a biased imperial justice system. Witnesses to any homicide would have to travel to London to testify—at tremendous cost and delay—where they would find jurors far less sympathetic. This was not just a practical problem. It also violated a vital principle of the English common law, which guaranteed (and still guarantees) not only the right to trial by jury, but specifically a jury drawn from the "vicinage," meaning the neighborhood where the crime occurs.[20] The reason behind this rule is essentially the same as the reason for the principle of "no taxation without representation": to ensure that government and the governed share common interests as much as possible. Quoting Montesquieu's observation that "the inhabitants of a particular town [or colony]" are "much better acquainted . . . with its wants and interests than with those of other places," one anonymous colonial pamphleteer added that "the English constitution deems this a fundamental principle, and extends it beyond the legislative line, into the civil administration of justice. Juries . . . must come in a manner qualified for the office, by having lived in the neighborhood of the party. In the cases of taxations and verdicts, a man's neighbors alone . . . are the persons who have the exclusive right to determine all his questions."[21] But now Parliament was severing that connection, dividing society into those who commanded and those who obeyed.

Next, the Massachusetts Government Act voided the colony's charter and replaced it with a new one. From now on, the king would appoint and remove the governor's council and "assistants," thus taking that power away from the House of Representatives.[22] The governor would also appoint and remove all judges and sheriffs, and where jurors had previously been elected, the sheriffs from now on would choose jurors on their own. This meant the judicial and executive branches of the government would be entirely in London's hands. The act also outlawed any town meeting without the governor's written approval and provided that when meetings were allowed, they were forbidden to address any subject other than what the governor expressly permitted. That would put a stop to all the troublemaking resolutions, instructions, and circular letters. The act was truly unprecedented—Parliament had never before tried to alter a colonial charter by fiat.

Parliament also adopted a new Quartering Act, which let General Gage force colonists to accommodate soldiers on their property even if room was already available in existing barracks. And then there was the Quebec Act, adopted several months after the other Intolerable Acts, which established a new and highly autocratic government for the territory won in the French and Indian War.[23] Instead of the English common-law system, it would follow the continental civil law system—one more familiar to French Canadians—which lacked ancient English legal guarantees, such as the right to counsel, habeas corpus, freedom from ex post facto laws, a right to a jury in civil cases, and even the right not to be tortured for evidence.[24] The act also provided for no elected representative assembly. Deeming an elected legislature "inexpedient," it instead gave the lawmaking power to the governor and his council, who answered exclusively to London.[25] Although the Quebec Act did not directly apply to the 13 colonies, it offered a fearsome indication of what could be in store for them. Worse, one provision of the act expanded Quebec's borders so that people whose property had previously been located in western Pennsylvania now found themselves in Canada, subject to the act.

Lord North explained that the lack of an elected assembly was necessitated by the fact that Roman Catholics were barred by British law from holding office. But the king had issued a proclamation in 1763 promising that anyone emigrating to Quebec "may confide in our royal protection for the enjoyment of the benefit of the laws of our realm of England."[26] The act broke that promise by nullifying the Quebecois' basic English right to be governed by representatives of their own choosing—thus effectively punishing Catholics for their religion.[27] At the same time, however, it established Catholicism as the official church, meaning that even Protestants there would be forced to pay tithes to Rome.

Some scholars have viewed the Patriots' objections to the Quebec Act as disingenuous, arguing that American complaints about the law were motivated, as one writer puts it, by "ethnocentrism and anti-Catholicism."[28] But although the revolutionary movement was overwhelmingly Protestant, Patriot fears regarding the act were hardly a sign of bigotry. The 18th-century Catholic Church was profoundly anti-liberal, and Catholic governments were actively persecuting Protestants throughout Europe and South America. The Inquisition was still operating in Spain, burning Jews and other heretics at the stake. In what is now Italy, Catholic authorities exiled the Waldensian sect to ghetto-like villages in the Alps. In 1731, the Catholic ruler of Salzburg expelled some 20,000 Protestants from the country. In France, the persecution of Protestants was routine. Nineteen-year-old Jean-François Lefebvre de La Barre was tortured to death in 1766 for allegedly defacing a crucifix. That incident was widely publicized by Voltaire, whose books La Barre is said to have admired. At a time when the pope still commanded political as well as spiritual loyalty—he even directly ruled over a swath of territories in central Italy called the Papal States—and when American colonists were already surrounded by the Catholic French to the west and Catholic Spaniards to the south, it was understandable that they would be alarmed at the idea of erecting an established Catholic Church in Quebec. Indeed, the new borders of Quebec now encompassed the land that would become the states of Ohio, Indiana, Illinois, Michigan, and Wisconsin—essentially walling in the 13 colonies.

Americans realized that if Parliament could deprive French Canadians by ipse dixit of such long-standing rights as representative government and trial by jury, and could do so on the basis of their religion, then it could do the same to Calvinists in Massachusetts, Quakers in Pennsylvania, or Baptists in Virginia, who were already being persecuted by Anglican authorities. Combined with the Massachusetts Government Act, this new law looked like a revival of the Dominion of New England scheme—or worse. "By the Quebec Act," declared Connecticut preacher Ebenezer Baldwin, "we find the Parliament claim a power to establish in America the same arbitrary government that takes place in France."[29]

When the Boston Town Meeting learned of the Intolerable Acts, it dispatched a message to the other colonies. "The inhabitants of this town have been tried and condemned and are to be punished [for the Tea Party]," it declared, "without their having been called to answer . . . [or even being] accused of any crime."[30] Had Bostonians been given a fair hearing, they might have presented their arguments to King George—pleading that Parliament's actions were unconstitutional and that mass resistance was therefore justified. Instead, the Lords and Commons had inflicted summary punishment of the severest kind—peacetime blockade would later be deemed an act of war under international law[31]—and had followed that up with an implicit threat to destroy centuries of English common-law protections throughout America. If Parliament could do these things to Massachusetts, it could do the same to "every other colony who will not surrender their sacred rights and liberties."[32]

A SHOCK OF ELECTRICITY

Meanwhile, in Virginia, Thomas Jefferson was busy with his growing household. Four years earlier, he had met a widow named Martha Wayles Skelton, and the two quickly fell in love. Daughter of a wealthy lawyer and slave trader, Martha was fond of music and books, particularly sharing with Thomas an enthusiasm for the novels of Laurence Sterne. They married on New Year's Day 1772 and settled into the only structure yet completed at Monticello, a one-room brick building still called the "Honeymoon Cottage." They were destined, however, to share only a decade before Martha's death. The always-private Jefferson left virtually nothing in writing about her, saying only that their marriage had been "ten years [of] uncheckered happiness."[33]

The couple welcomed their first child, a daughter also named Martha, in September 1772, and enjoyed the prospect of their new family and a new home under construction on the mountaintop. But their life together was to be marred by frequent tragedy. Martha's son John died at the age of four the summer before their marriage, and in May 1773, they were stunned by the sudden death of Jefferson's closest friend, Dabney Carr, who passed away at the age of 29. He left behind a widow—Jefferson's sister Mary—and six children, all younger than 10. In keeping with their boyhood pledge, the devastated Jefferson had Carr's body brought to the little mountain and buried in a new graveyard at the far end of the long garden he called "Mulberry Row." To distract himself from his grief, he spent time calculating how long it took to dig the grave.

Only weeks after Carr's death, Martha's father died. John Wayles left behind a large estate, but also substantial debts, and Jefferson was forced to sell large sections of Wayles's land to pay them off. Still, even after the creditors were paid, the Jeffersons stood to inherit more than 130 slaves and enough land to effectively double their wealth. Among the enslaved people they transferred to Monticello that autumn was Elizabeth "Betty" Hemings, who may have been Wayles's concubine.[34] Hemings had six children, the youngest of whom was a girl named Sally, who historians now believe bore several of Thomas's children after Martha's death.

Then, in February 1774, Jefferson's sister Elizabeth died under dreadfully bizarre circumstances. Apparently suffering from an intellectual disability, the 30-year-old Elizabeth may have been frightened by an unusual series of earthquakes that struck the area that month. "Bet," as she was called, disappeared from Monticello, taking along an enslaved girl. Their bodies were discovered days later, having apparently drowned while trying to cross the Rivanna River in a boat.[35] Jefferson, who was, in the phrase often used to describe plantation masters, "land rich and cash poor," had to sell two bookcases to pay the preacher at the funeral.[36]

As he often did, Jefferson dealt with these losses by plunging into work. (Staying busy is "the grand recipe for felicity," he told his daughter. "The idle are the only wretched."[37]) He arranged extensive plantings along Mulberry Row and began studying Italian with the help of a new neighbor, an immigrant named Philip Mazzei, who came to Virginia hoping to establish a winery. Jefferson invited Mazzei to live at Monticello while his own house was being built, and the two cultivated everything from raspberries and watermelons to strawberries and rice—as well as grapes, of course. The winery experiment failed; although Charlottesville-area vintners are highly regarded today, Jefferson's own efforts at winemaking never prospered.

News of the Boston Port Act reached Virginia in May 1774. Frustrated at what he called "the lethargy into which [the people] had fallen as to passing events,"[38] Jefferson now left his vines to travel to Williamsburg, where he joined Patrick Henry and other Patriots in seeking the most effective way to respond. After ransacking old colonial records, they discovered that during a crisis 20 years before, the House of Burgesses had issued a proclamation calling for a public day of "fasting, humiliation, and prayer" as a means of protest. A similar proclamation now might be the perfect way to demonstrate their displeasure in a manner that even the severest critic would find difficult to condemn. The group therefore "cooked up a resolution" declaring the Port Act a "hostile invasion" of a "sister colony" and urging Virginians to pray for a way to avoid "the heavy calamity which threatens destruction to our civil rights and the evils of civil war." The resolution concluded with a request that all Burgesses attend a special service at Williamsburg's Bruton Parish Church on June 1—the day the Port Act was to go into effect—and that the public "oppose, by all just and proper means, every injury to American rights."[39] It was likely no accident that the resolution did not say *legal* means.

Jefferson's "day of fasting" scheme did not fool the colony's new governor, John Murray, Lord Dunmore. A Scottish veteran who had served as governor of New York for a year before being transferred to Virginia in 1771 after Governor Botetourt's death, the 47-year-old Dunmore was greedy, haughty, belligerent, and mercurial. He had pursued the governorship in hopes of making a fortune to support himself and his seven children, and although he could be an agreeable dinner companion, he was singularly unsuited to resolving complicated political disputes. He could not tolerate disagreement and became bitterly enraged when crossed even slightly. One acquaintance said that "as a governor" he was "the most unfit, the most trifling, and the most uncalculated person living."[40] It was "quite necessary," said his brother, "to have a person about him who is knowing and attentive, and who will remind him of business."[41] Dunmore even lost his temper with the king himself. At a royal audience in 1803, he accused George III to his face of fathering bastard children. The infuriated king stormed out of the room. Dunmore was hardly the man to negotiate with an organized and genteel colonial legislature.

When he learned of the Burgesses' "day of fasting," he reacted immediately. The proclamation "reflect[ed] highly upon his Majesty and the Parliament," he told them.[42] That was unacceptable. Perhaps its most alarming element was its references to "sister colonies" and "American" rights—language that implied the intercolonial unity that threatened British rule. This time, instead of merely proroguing the House, as governors had done in the past, Dunmore dissolved it entirely.

That was an extraordinary move, but the Burgesses had become accustomed to having their debates shut down. Once again, they walked a few blocks to the Raleigh Tavern, and with over a hundred members crowding into the ballroom, discussed their next move. Some firebrands, such as George Washington's mentor George Mason, wanted to halt all trade with Britain. But it was hard to imagine how such an extreme measure would actually work. Merchants and farmers had to earn a living, and if Patriot leaders really tried to stop imports and exports along the entire coast, they would either fail and look silly or succeed and generate public resentment. Any more moderate embargo, however, was likely to prove as equivocal in its results as the previous efforts at boycotting British trade. It had now been seven years since the Townshend Acts were passed, and colonial nonimportation agreements had accomplished only mixed results.

At last, the Burgesses decided on a modest ban on British imports and called for a meeting of all the colonies in Philadelphia that September to consider what additional steps to take. In the meantime, the Committee of Correspondence would continue to meet, enabling the colony to keep abreast of ongoing developments and express a unified opposition. Then, the Virginians turned to the courts. Dunmore had dismissed the legislature before it had agreed on a "fee bill," the annual legislation necessary for funding the colony's legal system. Could the courts continue to operate without a fee bill? Jefferson volunteered to research the question and eventually produced a detailed memo answering no: Virginia's judiciary would have to close. Once again, as during the Stamp Act crisis, the colony's justice system shut down.

On June 1, Jefferson and the other Burgesses were gratified to see that their day of prayer had its intended effect. It was "like a shock of electricity," he wrote, which immediately set Virginians talking about how to address the crisis.[43] The Burgesses quickly followed it up with another step: With the assembly officially dissolved, they called for the people to choose representatives for a colony-wide "convention" that would meet in Williamsburg that August to serve as an unofficial legislature. Jefferson was chosen to attend by citizens at an Albemarle County meeting that also adopted a series of resolutions he wrote condemning the Intolerable Acts. "It is an absolute right inherent in every British American subject to have and enjoy such freedoms and privileges as belong to the free people of England," they declared, and these freedoms included the right not to be taxed without their consent or that of their representatives.[44] Parliament's actions represented "a tyrannical exertion of power" that violated "the natural rights of the people of the province, as men, and . . . their constitutional rights as English subjects."

As August approached, Jefferson prepared for the Williamsburg convention by sketching out some ideas for resolutions that the substitute legislature should adopt. His first attempt was a brief memo titled "A Declaration of Rights and League for Their Support by the Inhabitants of Virginia," which set forth a basic statement of the moral and legal basis for colonial resistance.[45] "The people of the several states of British America," he began, "are subject to the laws which they adopted at their first settlement . . . [and] no other legislature may rightfully exercise authority over them." This was supported not only by traditional English legal practice, but also by the "common rights of mankind." Not only had Parliament violated that principle for a decade now, but its "frequent" violations of American autonomy had climaxed in an even more egregious wrong: the closing of Boston's harbor. Virginians should support their Yankee brothers by refusing to buy anything from Britain except fabric, gunpowder, lead, and the tools necessary for domestic manufacturing. Only when Parliament agreed to respect the constitutional rights of all the colonies should that boycott be dropped.

Jefferson's second draft was more elaborate. He revised his memo into a 7,000-word essay—nominally a series of resolutions—setting forth colonial grievances and refuting the arguments of Parliament's supporters. It was the longest official paper he had yet written and it was sprinkled throughout with striking and memorable phrases. But after he was finished and had mounted his horse to carry it to the convention, he was struck ill and had to return home. Taking to bed, he sent copies of his paper to Peyton Randolph and Patrick Henry in Williamsburg.

Henry, Jefferson later grumbled, took no notice of it—probably never read it, in fact, "for he was the laziest man in reading I ever knew."[46] Randolph, however, was impressed enough to share his copy with other delegates. Although Jefferson's language was too radical to be approved by the Williamsburg convention, Randolph and others admired Jefferson's firm phrases and sophisticated arguments. They decided to have the document published. Titled *A Summary View of the Rights of British America*, the essay soon began appearing in bookstores throughout the colonies.

THE STATES OF THE BRITISH EMPIRE

A Summary View was an impressive effort.[47] Its 31-year-old author tended to write with an enthusiasm that older and more respectable delegates avoided, but he combined that with learning and eloquence that commanded respect. He would later incorporate many of its phrases—sometimes verbatim—into the Declaration of Independence. But at the same time, he seems to have intended the essay as a refutation of Chief Justice Mansfield's theory of imperial-colonial relations.

Jefferson considered the 69-year-old Mansfield a baleful influence on the law—the judge's "object," he said, was "to render [law] more uncertain under the pretense of rendering it more reasonable"—and

As chief justice of Great Britain, Lord Mansfield was a leading champion of the theory of Parliamentary Supremacy. Thomas Jefferson wrote A Summary View *primarily to refute his arguments.*

he thought American lawyers should be banned from citing his rulings.[48] For years, the politically active Mansfield had been closely involved in shaping Britain's colonial policy; he had helped George Grenville craft his initial plan for taxing the colonies, and later had written the Quebec Act. But as a legal thinker, he also provided crucial intellectual support for the theory of Parliamentary Supremacy. In his 1766 speech opposing repeal of the Stamp Act and supporting the Declaratory Act, Mansfield characterized the colonies as little more than subsidiary corporations. The first colonists, he claimed, had "migrated with [Parliament's] leave," and that meant they had always been subordinate to Westminster's authority.[49]

Jefferson set out to refute that argument. The colonies had never been intended to serve England's financial interests, he wrote; they had always been separate bodies politic, whose founders were "free inhabitants," not government agents or feudal serfs. They had come not by Parliament's "leave," but by exercising their natural right of "departing from the country in which chance, not choice has placed them" and creating new governments "under such laws and regulations as to them shall seem most likely to promote public happiness." True, they had based their political institutions on English models, but that did not make them subservient to Britain. And far from being financed by the British government, the settlers had built their communities through their own toil. They owed Britain nothing.

Another cornerstone of Mansfield's argument involved the issue of feudal tenure. He had ruled in a 1759 case that places employing feudal principles were "under the government" of Parliament regardless of where they were located, and Tories cited that decision to prove that America, too, was subject to parliamentary control.[50] But Jefferson answered that feudal tenure did not actually apply in America. Instead, Americans held their land under the principle of "allodial" ownership, meaning they held it free and clear, not subject to feudal duties. Jefferson admitted that Virginia's founders had sometimes said the opposite, but they had been "farmers, not lawyers," and had therefore sometimes failed to appreciate that feudalism was inapplicable in America. In fact, he claimed, feudalism was not even authentically English. It had only arrived with the Norman invasion of the 11th century, and never totally supplanted the allodial principle even in England. In any case, the Normans had never invaded *Virginia*. Virginians could therefore claim a right to the authentic principle of allodial possession—not "the fictitious [feudal] principle that all lands belong originally to the king."

This argument seems technical, and some people disputed it even at the time. But Jefferson's antipathy to feudalism ran deep. He rebelled against every vestige of unchosen obligations imposed by the state—leading one scholar to call his opposition to feudal land tenure "the most revolutionary aspect of his republican vision."[51] Uprooting the theory that property is held at the government's pleasure, he worked, both in *A Summary View* and later in his career, to substitute a libertarian conception of property in which landowners were expected to respect each other's rights, but otherwise answered to no higher power—a theory he based on the cutting-edge historical scholarship of his day.[52]

Jefferson was certainly right that Mansfield's feudalism theory was out of place in the American context. But his objections were not just historical; they were also based on justice and prudence. Jefferson thought it was not "consistent with good policy or free government" to force property owners to pay annual taxes to retain their land. That would make government less dependent on the people by effectively denying them any opportunity to refuse payment if they were unhappy with the way public officials acted. Annual property taxes thus tended to become "an engine of immense oppression." History—especially the history of the English Civil War—proved that people tend to gradually neglect their liberty, and to "run into the idea" of monarchism even "after living many years under a republican government."[53] It was therefore crucial that Americans destroy the social and legal bases of tyranny while they could.[54]

Having dealt with Manfield's ownership theory, Jefferson disputed his other arguments for Parliamentary Supremacy. The fact that the colonies had been settled by English emigrants certainly did not prove that Americans were subject to parliamentary rule; after all, England had been settled in the fifth century by Saxons, who came from what is now Germany, Denmark, and the Netherlands, but nobody expected the English to "bow down the sovereignty of their state" to those countries. On the contrary, the Saxons had brought their traditional ideas of freedom to England—ideas that Jefferson's favorite historian, Tacitus, said were actually of German origin—but that hardly made modern England a German satellite. Now, American colonists were relying on their own political ancestry by invoking English traditions of freedom, but that did not make them subject to Parliament's absolute control.

It was also foolish to claim that Parliament's jurisdiction was justified by Britain's expenditures in defending the colonies from the French and Indians. After all, England had also sent money and troops to help the Portuguese fight the Spaniards, but that did not entitle Parliament to legislate for Portugal in all cases whatsoever. Anyway, Britain's financial investments in America were already recompensed by colonial purchases of British imports. The trade monopolies that forced colonists to buy items from Britain at higher prices, rather than from other countries at lower prices, were the equivalent of taxation.

In Mansfield's view, imperial power was all-or-nothing. Either Parliament's power was supreme, or America was not part of the empire. Jefferson, however, thought the best way to picture the relationship between Britain and America was to see them as distinct entities united by "the same common sovereign," the king forming "the central link connecting the several parts of the empire." They were still united—but as far as laws and taxes were concerned, Americans looked to their own legislatures. This idea was hardly Jefferson's invention; England and Scotland had that relationship before the 1707 Act of Union, as did England and Hanover—a region in what is now Germany that acknowledged George III as king. Today's British Commonwealth is organized this way: the same monarch serves as head of state for all, but each country governs through its own legislature. John Adams had characterized the British–colonial relationship this way in the "Great Controversy" in 1773, and future US Supreme Court Justice James Wilson offered the same argument in a 1774 pamphlet.[55]

Nevertheless, modern scholars have tended to reject or even mock Jefferson's arguments in *A Summary View*. Biographer Joseph Ellis, for example, claimed the pamphlet's historical assertions "bore the same relation to colonial history as a nursery rhyme does to a Jamesian novel."[56] What Ellis failed to appreciate was that Jefferson was not writing history; he was offering a historically informed legal argument about the nature of the connection between America and

Great Britain—one he admitted was radical even at the time, but which was well-grounded in the facts. Historians may quibble about details, but constitutional thinking is an exercise in crafting narratives that *normalize* history—that is, that draw the facts together within a normative framework. As legal philosopher Ronald Dworkin put it, constitutional theory "does not require consistency in principle over all historical stages of a community's law," but "aims rather to justify what [past generations] did . . . in an overall story worth telling now, a story with a complex claim: that present practice can be organized by and justified in principles sufficiently attractive to provide an honorable future."[57] Jefferson and his allies were seeking those principles in the messy history of the common law. The fact that the constitutional scheme they envisioned governs the British Commonwealth today is sufficient vindication of their efforts.[58]

A Summary View had another, far more original feature, although it's often overlooked today. Unlike John Adams or John Dickinson, who conceded that Britain could regulate and restrain colonial commerce, Jefferson denounced mercantilist policy in its entirety. "The exercise of a free trade with all parts of the world" was not only guaranteed to Virginians in the 1652 Treaty of Jamestown, he wrote, but is a "natural right" to which all people are entitled.[59] In some of his most heated rhetoric, Jefferson condemned the "spirit of tyranny" underlying the Steel Act, the Hat and Felt Act, and the Navigation Acts, which blocked Americans "from carrying [goods] in quest of other purchasers" and forced them to sell to Britain, instead. Mercantilist policy amounted to nothing more than British business owners "purchasing for themselves, by a sacrifice of our rights and interests, certain privileges in their commerce." Once again, Jefferson was making the moral and practical case for laissez faire against mercantilism, two years before Adam Smith's *Wealth of Nations*.

Parliamentary Supremacy was both impractical and immoral, Jefferson wrote. If English history taught that no monarch could be trusted with absolute power, then surely the same principle applied to the Lords and Commons: "Bodies of men, as well as individuals, are susceptible of the spirit of tyranny." If it was wrong for the people to be subjugated by a single king, it was equally wrong to adopt a constitutional theory under which Americans would "hold their political existence at the will of . . . a body of men whom they never saw, in whom they never confided, and over whom they have no powers of punishment or renewal." The record of the past decade proved just how dangerous the Parliamentary Supremacy theory was: Westminster had violated the colonists' rights so extensively that their impositions could no longer be regarded as merely misguided. London's actions since 1764 constituted "a deliberate and systematical plan of reducing us to slavery."

Consider the New York Restraining Act: "One free and independent legislature hereby takes upon itself to suspend the powers of another, free and independent as itself." Or the Boston Port Act, which reduced an entire city "from opulence to beggary" without a hearing and despite the fact that "not the hundredth part of the inhabitants" had been involved in destroying the tea. Actually, the Port Act went even further: It gave the king the unilateral power to decide when to reopen the harbor, which meant it delegated power not just to enforce, but to *make* law, in violation of the separation of powers that had long been one of the British constitution's distinctive advantages. This provision had been inserted into the act "for no other purpose than that of setting a precedent for investing his majesty with legislative powers." If allowed to stand, Jefferson warned, "another and another will be tried, till the measure of despotism be filled up" by laws that let the king decide in his own discretion when to allow or forbid commercial trade.

The taxes, the Navigation Acts, the Intolerable Acts, the occupation of Boston, and the rest were "acts of power," not of right—power "assumed by a body of men, foreign to our constitutions and unacknowledged by our laws." And George III was the only person who could set things right. Standing above the fray of partisan politics, he was the sole "mediatory power" between what Jefferson insisted on calling "the states of the British empire"—the only person who could fairly adjudicate the dispute between the advocates of Parliamentary Supremacy and the defenders of Prescriptive Right. Yet instead of resolving that dispute, he was taking Parliament's side, or simply neglecting his duties. He had repeatedly nullified colonial laws, for example, sometimes "for the most trifling reasons, and sometimes for no conceivable reason at all." At other times, he neglected even to review laws submitted for his approval. His royal governors had also taken to adjourning colonial legislatures whenever the representatives protested against Parliament's actions, and they often took so long to call for new elections that emergencies came and went without lawmakers being able to act.

The king had taken many other steps to weaken colonial assemblies. He vetoed bills for creating new legislative districts or increasing the number of representatives or liberalizing voter qualifications.[60] His deputies allowed colonies to create new towns only if the inhabitants waived their right to elect members to the legislature, and barred colonies from providing for annual meetings of their assemblies.[61] All of this indicated that the king was hostile to the very idea of representative government. "Does his Majesty seriously wish," Jefferson asked, "that his subjects should give up the glorious right of representation . . . and submit themselves the absolute slaves of his sovereign will?" Worse, George's dislike of elected legislatures seemed to apply only to Americans. When Londoners angered over the Wilkes controversy petitioned the king for the dissolution of Parliament, he had condemned that request as "disrespectful."[62] Yet he had no qualms about dissolving American legislatures, not only in New York, Massachusetts, and Virginia, but in North and South Carolina, Georgia, and elsewhere.[63]

To level criticism directly at the monarch represented a new step for Americans. For generations, they had viewed Parliament as a threat, and the Crown as a protector. The king had issued their charters and sometimes, to their dismay, interceded to take over colonies directly. But all along, kings had acted as the colonies' patrons. As a result, as historian Brendan McConville notes, Americans' "attachment to the monarchy was passionate," even "consuming."[64] Now, that began to change. If the king's job was to mediate between contending factions, the current occupant of the throne was abandoning his post—aligning himself with Parliament's claim of total power and implementing that idea at the point of a bayonet. Jefferson concluded with hope that the two sides might still reconcile, but that could only happen if the king stopped "sacrificing the rights of one part of the empire to the inordinate desires of another."

Although George III bought a copy of *A Summary View* for his library, there's no evidence that he or Lord Mansfield ever read it. In any case, they would not have been persuaded. Jefferson's insistence that the American governments were equal components of the empire contradicted the basic dogma of Parliamentary Supremacy, which viewed them as subsidiaries of an all-powerful Parliament. If George did read it, though, he was probably struck by its closing lines. Admitting that his language might seem prideful, Jefferson—in wording modeled on Richard Bland's *Inquiry*—concluded that the colonists would never "flatter" the king as if their rights were "gift[s]" from the government, when in reality they were "derived from the laws of nature." Kings "are the servants, not the proprietors of the people," Jefferson wrote. To beg their rulers for favors was "not an American art."

THE FIRST CONTINENTAL CONGRESS

At almost the same time that *A Summary View* was published, the *London Chronicle*—doubtless aware of the gravity of the Continental Congress that was scheduled to convene on September 5—reprinted an article Benjamin Franklin had published six years earlier, titled "Causes of the American Discontents Before 1768."[65] The years since its first publication had changed little; Franklin's complaints now seemed only more prescient.

The colonists, he wrote, thought the right way for Parliament to raise money in America was to request it from colonial legislatures, not to seize it through direct taxation. "Had this happy method of requisition been continued," there would have been no "heart-burning, offense, or breach of the harmony." But by taxing Americans directly and unilaterally asserting its absolute power, Westminster had now given them plenty of reasons to think that they "could not be said to have any property, anything they could call their own." Instead, they held their belongings merely by the government's permission. And although Parliament had tried to justify this with the Declaratory Act, Franklin wryly noted, "Not a single [American] . . . has been convinced of his error, even by that Act of Parliament."

On the contrary, when the Lords and Commons sought to vindicate their authority by adopting the Quartering and Mutiny Acts, occupying Boston, and dissolving the New York legislature, the message had seemed to be "obey implicitly laws made by the

Parliament of Great Britain . . . , or you shall enjoy no rights or privileges at all." And when Parliament decided to pay colonial officers directly, taking away the voters' most effective tool for holding officials accountable, the message was again clear: Colonial legislatures were "useless." They might as well be dispensed with. Franklin had predicted that London's next step would be to make every official—from judges to the most junior customs inspectors—answerable solely to Westminster, and to rule the colonists like conquered barbarians rather than fellow subjects. The Massachusetts Government Act now seemed to prove him right.

London's heavy-handedness, Franklin added, was causing Americans to question the legitimacy even of those laws they had long accepted. Increasingly, it seemed to them that Parliament regulated imperial trade not to benefit the public, but to enrich a few English tycoons. More than 100 members of Parliament, for example, owned stock in the East India Company's tea business.[66] And banning Americans from making and selling hats or nails; from importing wine, fruit, or oil from Europe; or from shipping lumber, tobacco, or sugar to European markets without first paying to ship these items through the home island, accomplished nothing but to enrich English businessmen at American expense.

Like Jefferson, Franklin concluded that there was still hope for restoring harmony, but only if the central government would return to "the old *constitutional* manner" of dealing with the colonies. If it continued to insist on absolute authority, though, "we cannot submit." Such demands would "sever us forever" from the empire.[67]

If John Adams read Franklin's "Causes" article or Jefferson's *Summary View* during his trip to Philadelphia to attend the Continental Congress, he made no mention of it. After all, his schedule left little time for reading. He had never been to Pennsylvania before, and his 300-mile journey had been full of excitement, as town after town greeted the delegates with parades, church bells, and lavish dinners. Months before, he had told Abigail that he was "full of fear" that Americans would lose interest in the controversy with Britain and abandon the resistance.[68] Now, he saw that colonists of every description were rallying behind the Philadelphia meeting. Americans, he wrote, "universally consider our cause as their own, and express the firmest resolution to abide by the determination of the Congress."[69]

As the opening gavel fell on a rainy September 4, Adams stood in Philadelphia's Carpenters' Hall, surrounded by some of the colonies' most illustrious men. Besides Samuel Adams, there was Rhode Island Governor Stephen Hopkins, Virginia's celebrated veteran George Washington, and, most famous of all, Pennsylvania's John Dickinson, author of the *Letters from a Farmer.* He was "tall, but slender as a reed [and] pale as ashes," Adams thought—so skinny he almost looked ill—but full of fascinating conversation.[70] Virginia's "spirited" delegates impressed him even more.[71] The quietly captivating Washington was already well-known for a rumor—apparently apocryphal—that he had offered to pay out of his own pocket to march a regiment to fight General Gage's troops in Boston.[72] There was also Patrick Henry, author of the inflammatory Stamp Act resolves, and the "learned and bookish" Richard Bland, whose pamphlet on colonial rights had so impressed Jefferson. They were accompanied by four colleagues.[73] Only New York sent a larger delegation.

The first important debate concerned how the representatives would vote. Henry moved that they vote in proportion to population, underscoring the populist nature of the resistance movement. More moderate delegates objected, partly out of a view that majority rule should be checked by the voices of wiser, more experienced leaders, and partly out of a belief that pure majoritarianism posed a threat to the smaller colonies. Henry, however, thought the Intolerable Acts had effectively erased the differences between the colonial governments, leaving Americans en masse with a natural right to organize government however they chose. "Government is dissolved," he claimed. "We are in a state of nature. . . . The distinctions between Virginians, Pennsylvanians, New Yorkers and New Englanders, are no more."[74]

Although the records are unclear, Henry probably meant that by taking such drastic measures against the colonial governments—especially dissolving their legislatures—London had wiped away their constitutional significance in theory, if not entirely in practice. That left no political institutions sufficiently secure to deserve the title of governments, which meant the Americans were free to establish substitutes. But whatever Henry's argument was, other delegates were unpersuaded. "I can't yet think that all government is at an end," declared New York's John Jay. "The measure of arbitrary power is not full, and I think it must run over, before we undertake to frame a new Constitution."[75] Jay's idea would find voice in the Declaration of Independence, with its acknowledgment that only a "long train of abuses" could justify overthrowing existing governments. In any case, it was a moot question: There was no way to determine the colonies' actual populations, anyhow. The members decided that each would get one vote.

Next, the delegates turned to an even more fundamental question: how best to make the case for American freedom. Until now, pamphleteers and journalists had employed a blend of legal and philosophical arguments against the theory of Parliamentary Supremacy. But if the representatives were to resolve the imperial crisis, they would need to settle on a single coherent constitutional theory and speak with one voice. To that end, two representatives from each colony were chosen to serve on a committee to draft a statement of rights. But should they assert the rights established in British law?—or the basic natural rights to which all human beings are entitled?

It was not an academic question. Because English law depended principally on tradition and habit, asserting *natural* law arguments appeared dangerously revolutionary—a step toward overthrowing *acquired* rights and long-established customs in the service of what a later generation would call "ideology." Americans generally shared a belief in the validity of natural law, but powerful political figures feared that invoking higher-law principles could unleash dangerous innovations. After all, slaves, women, and members of religious minorities could appeal to natural law, too. As one scholar puts it, invoking Lockean classical liberalism "threatened to swallow everything artificially contrived to assure order and society."[76]

Virginia's Richard Henry Lee, however, had no such reservations. A 42-year-old, England-educated military veteran from one of Virginia's most prominent families, Lee had blown off four fingers in a hunting accident six years earlier and now wrapped his left hand in a silk scarf as he gestured dramatically during speeches. Drawn early to the idea of American independence, Lee and John Adams immediately hit it off; one historian calls them "alter egos" of each other.[77] Now, Lee proposed four grounds for the American case: (a) natural law, (b) the British constitution, (c) the colonial charters, and (d) the precedents and practices of history. The delegates, he argued, should emphasize all four.

Legal precedents and the language of colonial charters were important, but focusing on them alone meant overlooking an important aspect of the colonial cause. After all, if Parliamentary Supremacy were true, statutes and charters were essentially useless; Parliament could override them at will. Connecticut representative Roger Sherman rose to second Lee's argument. A blunt Puritan whose manners struck Adams as "the reverse of grace," Sherman was firmly convinced that Parliament had no legitimate power to legislate for the colonies.[78] But he was also certain that no amount of legal or constitutional argument would persuade London of that fact. The Congress, he said, should rest its case on principles of justice, instead.

Others were not so sure. The argument from natural law was "a feeble support," argued New York's James Duane. People disagreed about the meaning of natural law, which was at best vaguely understood. It was safer to ground their protests on the charters, which were written legal documents and therefore less subject to dispute than were philosophical propositions about justice and human rights. Pennsylvania's Joseph Galloway agreed. "I have looked for our rights in the laws of nature," he said, "but could not find them in a state of nature, but always in a state of political society."[79] Months earlier, Galloway had published an article urging Americans to base their arguments on English law's "long known and securely trodden paths of prudence and regularity" instead of "wander[ing] into the maizy [*sic*] labyrinths of perplexity" that would elevate "anarchy above order" and—worst of all—might prove "the beginning of republicanism."[80] In any case, he thought it would be easier to resolve the dispute with Britain if Americans confined their arguments to those that were "defensible upon the principles even of our enemies."[81] New York delegate Isaac Low was more direct. "Gentlemen have been transported by their zeal," he said. Their talk of natural rights gave "too much reason . . . to suspect that independency is aimed at."[82] (When war came, Galloway and Low joined the Loyalist side, aided the British forces, and lived the rest of their lives in England.)

But while Galloway and Low might have been shocked by the idea of independence, others were already starting to think it unavoidable. Two weeks before the Congress began, an anxious Abigail Adams asked her husband if he could think of any example of a "kingdom or state regain[ing] their liberty, when once it was invaded, without bloodshed?"[83] Days later, citizens in nearby Ipswich adopted a series of resolutions proclaiming the Massachusetts Government Act unconstitutional and pledging that "if in support of our rights we are called to encounter even death, we are yet undaunted, sensible that he can never die too soon who lays down his life in support of the laws and liberties of his country."[84]

On September 9, the congressional committee sided with Richard Henry Lee: The Continental Congress would assert that Parliament's actions violated not just British law, but the natural rights of all Americans. Then, just days later, the dreaded threat of violence seemed to be realized, when word arrived that the Royal Navy had bombarded Boston, leaving six Massachusetts militiamen dead. New Englanders, it was said, were arming themselves for all-out war.

It turned out to be a false alarm, but when the rumor reached Philadelphia, John Adams was both horrified by the possibility of violence and gratified to see how the other delegates expressed support for his home colony. "Every gentleman seems to consider the bombardment of Boston as the bombardment of the capital of his own province," he told Abigail.[85] "WAR! WAR! WAR! was the cry, and it was pronounced in a tone which would have done honor to the oratory of a Briton or a Roman."[86]

What had actually happened was that a Massachusetts Tory had written to General Gage to warn him that city leaders in Medford were moving their town's store of gunpowder from its usual warehouse to Charlestown, instead. Worried about what that meant, Gage decided to transfer the colony's primary powder supply to a secure location at the Castle William fortress. When Bostonians learned of that, they panicked. Fearing that Gage was preparing for full-scale military action, mobs began assembling in Cambridge and outlying towns. Gage and his colleagues eventually calmed them down, but the people's readiness to defy the occupiers was a shock.[87] The incident proved that "the time for conciliation, moderation, reasoning, is over," the general told Lord Dartmouth. "Nothing can be done [to halt the rebellion] but by forcible means."[88]

Perhaps the most important consequence of the "Powder Alarm," as this event came to be called, was the reaction of the people of

Suffolk County. Suffolk was one of the many communities that openly defied the Massachusetts Government Act's ban on town meetings, and at a gathering chaired by John Adams's friend Joseph Warren, the people adopted a series of resolutions stating the colonial case in startlingly militant terms.[89] Massachusetts's first settlers had come not as agents of the Crown, they said, but as refugees—fleeing "the power, not the justice, the vengeance, but not the wisdom of Great Britain." They had built a civilization in a wilderness through their own "toil and treasure . . . valor and blood"—not with Parliament's assistance—and their heirs would not surrender that inheritance to the Lords and Commons, who had issued the "fatal edict which proclaims a power to frame laws for us in all cases whatever." Although they "cheerfully acknowledge[d]" the king's authority, they refused to concede that Parliament could legislate for Americans. In fact, "no obedience is due" to its pseudo-legislation, and any official who tried to implement Parliament's edicts "must be considered as under undue influence."

To that end, the Suffolk Resolves "recommend[ed]" that all royal officials "make [a] public resignation," and that tax collectors refuse to remit funds to the authorities until Parliament changed its ways. Colonists should also "acquaint themselves with the art of war as soon as possible, and . . . for that purpose, appear under arms at least once every week." Warren and his neighbors insisted that they were "determined to act merely on the *defensive*," but they concluded the resolves with a shocking recommendation: The colonists should arrest any officials who tried to confiscate colonial munitions, and hold such officers in "safe custody." Such strident language indicated the public's awareness that conflict was quickly approaching.

Thrilled as he was that the members of the Congress had greeted the Powder Alarm with a willingness to fight, Adams was even more delighted when word of the Suffolk and Ipswich resolutions arrived in Philadelphia and the Congress officially endorsed them. It was "one of the happiest days of my life," he said.[90] The resolutions "acquired unbounded honor" for his home colony.[91] Lord Dartmouth, on the other hand, announced that the Congress's endorsement of the resolves amounted to a declaration of war.[92]

The panic subsided, however, and the Congress began to settle on a more orderly plan. They would ban British imports, issue an address to the people of Britain, and petition the king for a redress of grievances—but not petition Parliament. Ignoring Parliament was crucial: To petition the Lords and Commons would be interpreted as acknowledging their authority. The Congress also officially resolved that if the government tried to implement the Intolerable Acts by force, "all America ought to support [their fellow colonists] in their opposition."[93] It further declared that any effort by British officials to take an American to Britain for trial was illegal and would "justify, and ought to meet with resistance and reprisal."[94] Finally, it announced that Americans would not pay for the tea destroyed in Boston.

Crafting an effective import ban was a challenge. The Continental Association, as it was called, would in some ways be stronger than previous no-purchase agreements. It would ban exports as well as imports. But that would work such severe hardships on American farmers that the Congress decided to implement it gradually—and that decision blunted much of the Association's force. The items on the list of prohibited imports also appeared haphazard. For example, the ban applied to the purchase of tools. But if the Congress wanted to encourage Americans to make their own products instead of buying from abroad, it seemed wiser to allow the importation of capital goods.

The Continental Association did, however, include one truly revolutionary innovation. Previous boycotts had been only partly successful because there was no formal means of implementation. Since the Stamp Act crisis, enforcement had been left to local Sons of Liberty groups, acting without coordination, who penalized offenders through ostracism, humiliation, or violence. But that resulted not only in the destruction of property, but also in the potentially deadly punishment of tarring and feathering—which Patriot leaders knew was both morally indefensible and strategically embarrassing.[95] Ad hoc enforcement was also inconsistent and violence tended to undermine colonial unity by setting neighbors, friends, and families against each other, as in the case of John Greenough and his father. As one Connecticut Patriot told a member of the Congress, if mobs were not "stopped in their first growth . . . dissensions will soon follow, and we soon should be, instead of a united, a broken body."[96]

Most of all, vigilantism sacrificed the moral high ground. Tories had long claimed that Parliamentary Supremacy was the only thing standing between British America and the anarchic tyranny of the majority. European philosophers had insisted for centuries that the people could never be expected to control themselves; they needed strong rulers to force them into conformity with the law. Otherwise, rebellions would follow the cycle Polybius called *anacyclosis*: The people's uprising might be justified, but eventually, through greed and ignorance, they would degenerate into a lawless mob, stealing from the wealthy, abolishing the obligation to repay debts, ganging up on religious minorities, obliterating formal legal protections like due process of law, and eventually embracing dictatorship. Were the Stamp Act riots, the burning of the *Gaspee*, and the Boston Tea Party not proof of the people's inability to control themselves? Direct action by the Sons of Liberty might be thrilling, but in the end, hardworking citizens had a right to expect a society governed by general rules, systematically followed. If denied that, they would eventually side with Parliament, which at least promised order instead of chaos.

The Congress's plan, therefore, was to formalize the Continental Association by calling on every community to establish a committee, staffed by elected members, that would investigate alleged violations, hold hearings to determine whether the accused were violating the rules, and punish offenders by denouncing them by name in the newspapers. Offenders were to be "universally condemned as the enemies of American liberty," and shunned, but not injured or stripped of their belongings.

Providing for elections gave these committees—and there were soon nearly a thousand of them—a degree of legitimacy that the Sons of Liberty lacked. And because the Congress instructed the committees only to name and shame transgressors, the Association plan deterred violence, or at least distanced the Patriot cause from any violence that did happen. At the same time, the label "enemy of American liberty" would stick with greater force because it was backed by an august intercolonial assembly.

This was not just a prudent step toward respectability; it was a move toward self-rule. The committees were, in historian Kevin Phillips's words, "the first institutions of independent local government in the future United States," and they represented a remarkable experiment in practical political philosophy.[97] According to Lockean theory, before the creation of government, people live in a "state of nature" in which rules of justice and principles of right do exist (because these are rooted in humanity) but are hard to enforce. People therefore establish formal governments, operating under the rule of law, to protect themselves in their pursuits of living and flourishing. They do this by forming an agreement or compact that sets forth the scope and limits of the governing authority. Now, the British government's closing of colonial legislatures was putting Americans into something like that position in real life. By the time the Continental Association was formed, legislatures had been shut down entirely in Massachusetts, New Hampshire, and Maryland—which were being governed by Patriot-run "conventions" or "provincial congresses" instead—and although official assemblies were still technically operating in Virginia, North Carolina, Pennsylvania, South Carolina, and Georgia, the real power there was being exercised by similarly unsanctioned assemblies. In other words, the American people were being deprived of their governments and thrown back into the ungoverned state Locke had described. When the Massachusetts convention, known as the Provincial Congress, began meeting in October 1774 in defiance of the Massachusetts Government Act, its president wrote to John Adams that it was "no longer a [theoretical] question whether any people ever subsisted in a state of nature. We have been and still remain in that situation."[98]

The Declaration of Independence would later address this point. Loyalists denied the legitimacy of the colonists' ersatz legislatures—including the Continental Congress—because these were not authorized by Parliament. But the revolutionaries insisted that the closure of their old legislatures had caused "the legislative powers, incapable of annihilation," to revert "to the people at large for their exercise." Indeed, the colonial conventions were actually *more* legitimate, because they were authorized by the people.

Those conventions were temporary institutions, however. To replace them with permanent new governments would represent a far greater step—one that was obviously the equivalent of declaring independence, because it meant discarding British sovereignty entirely. Some were already prepared to do that. But, as the president of the Massachusetts Provincial Congress told Adams, most people feared taking such a step without the approval of the Continental

Congress, "lest our attempts should be disapproved of."[99] Thus, while the Continental Association committees represented a breakthrough in the development of American sovereignty, the critical step was yet to come: asserting and exercising the natural right of self-government.

THE RIGHTS *YOU* ARE ENTITLED TO

The resolutions the Continental Congress finally adopted on October 14, 1774,[100] zeroed in on the basic problem: Parliament's assertion of the "power of right to bind the people of America by statutes in all cases whatsoever." That was the source of all British outrages, which the Congress listed with remarkable precision—in some cases identifying them by their statutory designations: "The several acts of 4 Geo. 3 ch. 15 and ch. 34—5 Geo. 3 ch. 25—6 Geo. 3 ch. 52," and so on.[101] These referred to the familiar grievances: the Intolerable Acts, trials without juries, payment of officials without the consent of colonial legislatures, the "unconstitutional powers" of customs commissioners to search and seize property without warrants, the repeated dissolutions of legislatures "when they attempted to deliberate on grievances"—and, of course, taxation.

"The inhabitants of the English colonies in North America, by the immutable laws of nature, the principles of the English constitution, and the several charters or compacts, have the following rights," the Congress continued. "They are entitled to life, liberty, and property, and they have never ceded to any sovereign power whatever a right to dispose of either without their consent." They had the right to trial by jury, the right to assemble and petition the government, the right to a constitution where separation of powers was respected, and where armies did not occupy cities in peacetime. Adams himself was particularly proud of one item he added to the list: "The foundation of English liberty, and of all free government, is a right in the people to participate in their legislative council," and since Americans "cannot properly be represented in the British Parliament," they had the right to rely on their colonial legislatures, instead, "in all cases of taxation and internal polity."

The Congress nevertheless "cheerfully consent[ed]" to Parliament's power to regulate trade "for the purpose of securing the commercial advantages of the whole empire to the mother country." This was due to "the necessity of the case" and "a due regard to the mutual interest of both countries." Still, this power only applied to "the commercial benefits" of the "respective members" of the British empire. It did not mean Parliament could impose "taxation, internal or external, for raising a revenue."

This passage in the resolutions was the result of a long and frustrating debate. The delegates could not decide where to locate the line between Parliament's unconstitutional efforts to tax the colonies and its legitimate power to oversee commerce. At some point in the interminable back-and-forth, South Carolina delegate John Rutledge approached Adams. "We must agree upon something," he said. "You appear to be as familiar with the subject as any of us, and I like your expressions 'the necessity of the case' and 'excluding all ideas of taxation external and internal.' . . . Come, take the pen and see if you can't produce something that will unite us."

Adams tried his best, and the committee reluctantly accepted his version, unable to fashion anything better. The problem was that Adams was trying, like a lawyer, to find language that "demanded as little as could be demanded, and conceded as much as could be conceded with safety."[102] Using the phrase "cheerfully consent" was meant to signify that Parliament had no *right* to control colonial commerce. That bothered some members, however. "The Parliamentary authority over our trade was co-eval with our settlements," declared New York's James Duane.[103] To deny that Parliament held this power of *right* was dangerously revolutionary.

Even worse, it was logically untenable to deny Parliament's power to tax the colonies while accepting—even "cheerfully"—its power to regulate trade. Such language reflected the same halfway position Jefferson had rejected in his *Summary View*. There was no principled distinction between revenue-generating taxes and trade-regulating duties; if Parliament could regulate colonial trade, it could do so by imposing taxes. The line between the two was "flimsy," Jefferson later explained, because "he who could put down the loom could stop the spinning wheel, and he who could stop the spinning wheel could tie the hands which turned it." Anyway, "who were to be judges whether duties were imposed with a view to burden and suppress a branch of manufacture, or to raise a revenue?"[104] Only articulating a clear principle would suffice. Yet a clear principle would inevitably commit the Congress to independence.

Days after adopting their resolutions, the representatives released their statement to the British people and their petition to the king. In the first document, they explained to their fellow Britons that they were proud of their shared heritage and cherished the protections of British law. "Reason looks with indignation," they said, upon the idea that colonists could be treated as subordinates, whose rights only existed as long as the Parliament "vouchsafe[s] to permit." It was precisely because they loved their Britishness that they had quietly endured even "grievous" limits on their trade.[105] But Westminster's policies since 1764 had shattered that patience. The laws now emanating from London were proof of a deliberate plan to reduce Americans to servitude. And if Parliament could do that to the colonies, it could do the same to the homeland. "Take care," the Americans warned their fellow Britons, "that you do not fall into the pit that is preparing for us." With parliamentary elections on the way, the Congress begged voters to do what they could to restore harmony between the two sides. But they also warned, "If you are determined that your ministers shall wantonly sport with the rights of mankind . . . we will never submit to be hewers of wood or drawers of water for any ministry or nation in the world."[106]

The petition to George III was more restrained.[107] Written by John Dickinson, this "loyal address" listed colonial grievances in succinct and unimpassioned terms: "Assemblies have been repeatedly and injuriously dissolved"; "the officers of the customs are empowered to break open and enter houses without the authority of any civil magistrate"; "commerce has been burdened with many useless and oppressive restrictions." The "bare recital of these acts," Dickinson declared, should shock any king who "enjoys the signal distinction of reigning over freemen." Yet the American cause had been so grievously misrepresented by Parliament's leaders that the colonists found it necessary to reiterate that they were *not* unwilling to pay for the support of government—they simply insisted that the taxes be imposed by their own legislatures. They were *not* seeking British military protection without paying for it—they had proved their willingness to serve in the army and navy themselves. They were *not* seeking "a diminution of the [royal] prerogative," or "the grant of any new right in our favor." They merely wanted Britain to honor its promises to respect their equal rights. Finally, they did *not* want independence. They just "implore[d]" the king to halt Parliament's abuses and prevent "the transcendent relation" between America and Britain from being "further violated."

The Congress finished two more documents before adjourning: an address to the American people and another to the people of Quebec, urging them "to unite with us in one social compact, formed on the generous principles of equal liberty."[108] The Quebec letter is particularly revealing, given that it represented neither a petition to a superior, as with the address to the king, nor a propaganda document, like the letter to the British people, but an effort to persuade a separate colony to join in resisting British impositions—a colony, moreover, made up of French Catholics, as opposed to the English Protestants who dominated the Continental Congress. Its authors therefore took greater pains to set out the argument for American liberty as objectively as possible.

Drawing on the works of Cesare Beccaria and Baron de Montesquieu—both famous Catholic liberals—the letter argued that the English constitutional tradition to which the Quebecois were now entitled, due to their incorporation into the empire, was grounded in five basic human rights, which Parliament was now disregarding.

The first was the right of the people to have "a share in their own government," being subject to "*laws* which they themselves approve, not by *edicts* of *men* over whom they have no control." This right formed the basic distinction between a free society and a tyranny, and it was manifested in the legal principle that taxation could only come through consent. As long as the people's representatives had the right to decide whether to impose taxes, the people could keep public officials in check. "If money is wanted by rulers who have in any manner oppressed the people, they may retain it, until their grievances are redressed, and thus peaceably procure relief." But without such guarantees, the people's lives, liberties, and property were held entirely at the government's mercy.

The second essential right was to trial by jury, which ensured that the accused were tried in public by independent fact finders. This prevents the government from resorting to summary punishment or extortion. A third and related right was habeas corpus, which ensures that if someone is arrested, he or she can demand a hearing before an impartial judge instead of being locked up without recourse.

The fourth basic right was property ownership "by the tenure of easy rents," as opposed to the feudal principles that forced people to render personal service or annual payment in exchange for keeping their land. Allodial ownership meant personal independence. And the fifth right was freedom of the press, which, along with promoting new discoveries and improving knowledge, also helped discipline political leaders. Freedom of expression meant "oppressive officers" could be "shamed or intimidated into more honorable and just modes of conducting affairs"—whereas censorship prevented the people from learning what their leaders were up to or calling them to account.

"These are the rights *you* are entitled to," the Congress told the Quebecois. Yet the Quebec Act deprived them of all these rights. It enabled royal officials to legislate for the province directly and even barred the people from adopting their own tax laws. Worse, the act violated the separation-of-powers principle by making the tenure of public officers depend entirely on the governor's will. In principle, the act was even more dangerous to Canadians than the other Intolerable Acts were to the colonies further south—because it set a precedent for Canadians to be deprived of all their rights. "What would your countryman, the immortal Montesquieu, have said to such a plan of domination as has been framed for you?" Would he not advise the Quebecois to "seize the opportunity" to reject Parliamentary Supremacy?

The Congress acknowledged that Catholics might hesitate to join with Protestants. But, the delegates argued, there was no reason they could not coexist in a free North America. "The transcendent nature of freedom" lifts people "above all such low-minded infirmities" as religious prejudice, they said. Look at the Swiss Confederation: It was made up of Catholics and Protestants who lived together in peace. Catholics in Maryland were treated as equal partners in the Patriot cause, too. If united under the "generous principles of equal liberty," different religious sects could live happily together on a free continent.

Yet the Congress's pleas proved ineffectual. Although some Canadian towns did hold meetings to discuss the letter, none supported joining with the Patriots. And although the Congress would continue lobbying the Quebecois in the years to come, relatively few rallied to the conflict with Britain.

The Congress's letter to the American people was more effective. Fearing that the public saw Massachusetts as a troublemaking outlier—as an effectively lawless territory whose mobs were arousing the mother country's wrath against them all—Adams and his colleagues took pains to reinforce American unity. Only if the colonies acted in unison could their protests succeed, they explained. If even a single one found it expedient to make a separate peace with Parliament, support for the American cause would peel away, colony by colony, leaving Massachusetts to fend for itself. In its address to the people, therefore, the Congress argued that everybody from New Hampshire to South Carolina had a stake in the Yankees' struggle. They had all suffered under the oppressions of the past decade. New York's legislature had been closed; Rhode Islanders were threatened with extradition to England; even Quebec had been deprived of the rights of representation and jury trials. And the severity of London's punishments proved the risk they were all facing. Massachusetts's legislature had been shut down merely for sending the Circular Letter—that is, for petitioning for a redress of grievances, which was something "deemed innocent even in slaves."[109] Westminster had followed that up by signing a death warrant for Boston in response to the Tea Party. If Parliament could do that, it could do worse to Virginia or Pennsylvania or New Jersey. American unanimity was therefore imperative. The Continental Association must succeed, or all the colonists would be forced "to choose, either a more dangerous contest, or a final, ruinous, and infamous submission."[110]

— CHAPTER 9 —

PETITIONING AND FIGHTING

We have pursued every lawful and every respectful measure. . . . We have reasoned, we have remonstrated. . . . But subsequent events have shown how vain was even [the] last remain [sic] of confidence in the moderation of the British ministry.
—*Thomas Jefferson*[1]

Thomas Jefferson was chosen to serve on one of the committees for enforcing the Continental Association. He was eager to participate in this new resistance effort, but in truth, he was disappointed in the Association plan. For one thing, it included an absurdly long grace period—not going into effect for more than a year—which gave colonists plenty of time to stockpile items. Stockpiling, of course, meant buying *more* from British sellers, and that undermined the whole scheme. The plan also exempted wine, coffee, and other items, even though these were subject to British taxation. And it did *not* exempt tools that were necessary for domestic manufacturing, which seemed foolish. If Americans were supposed to make things instead of importing them, the Congress should *encourage* them to buy tools.

Still, Jefferson intended to comply and to ensure that others complied. That commitment proved slightly embarrassing in December, when he realized that 14 pairs of windows he had ordered for installation at Monticello would likely violate the boycott. Discovering his mistake, he wrote to the committee in Norfolk, where the shipment was scheduled to arrive, to confess and concede to their being confiscated. "I mean to be a conscientious observer of the measures,"

Pennsylvania's John Dickinson opposed independence, but—contrary to Adams's claims—not because he was a Quaker or a pacifist.

he explained. "I submit to [their] disposal."[2] (The committee decided the windows fell outside the ban, however, and let Jefferson keep them.)

By this time, his legal practice had ground to a stop. The Virginia legislature's failure to adopt a new "fee bill" before being dissolved by Governor Dunmore threw the colony's legal structure into disarray. Such bills were necessary to set the rate of payment not only for lawyers, but for every other aspect of the justice system, from a coroner's inquests to the recording of deeds. At the Raleigh Tavern meeting the previous May, the Burgesses had been unable to decide whether the courts could operate at all without a fee bill, and Jefferson had written the report answering that they could not.[3] Now, counties were starting to close their courts—which some people welcomed for practical reasons, hoping the inability of British creditors to collect debts from Americans might increase the boycott's effectiveness. But this also left Virginia with an even more dysfunctional government.

Jefferson may not have been too distressed to end his legal practice, however. Although he enjoyed the intellectual challenge, he found the actual business of law frustrating. Only weeks before the shutdown, he had joined Patrick Henry, Edmund Pendleton, and the colony's attorney general—his Tory cousin John Randolph—in publishing a newspaper advertisement that complained about clients who failed to pay their bills. The four lawyers announced that except for pro bono cases, they would provide no legal services unless clients paid at least half the fee in advance.[4] There is no indication that clients complied, and when the courts shut down, Jefferson appears not to have regretted closing up shop.

DRIVE THEM INTO SUBMISSION

In Massachusetts, John Adams's legal practice was also coming to an end. That colony's courts were closed too, leaving him unable to argue cases, and he soon decided to shutter his Boston office. "There will be no business there nor anywhere, I suppose," he told Abigail.[5] Although he continued to do occasional legal work for a few more years, politics was already taking up most of his time. No sooner had the Philadelphia Congress adjourned than he was elected to the

Massachusetts Provincial Congress, the colony's unofficial government now meeting in Concord. Its most important decisions were to select Adams as one of five delegates to attend the next meeting of the Continental Congress, scheduled for May 1775, and to begin equipping and training the colonial militia in anticipation of hostilities. "We are in this province, sir, at the brink of a civil war," Adams told a British friend. "We have no council, no House, no legislature, no executive. Not a court of justice has sat since the month of September."[6] A decade earlier, he had wondered whether the court shutdown during the Stamp Act crisis was the equivalent of the king's withdrawing protection from his American subjects. Now, it seemed increasingly clear that the answer was yes.

The same week Adams wrote those words, Benjamin Franklin and other American agents in London handed the Continental Congress's "loyal address" to Lord Dartmouth, secretary of state for the colonies, who promised Franklin that he would show it to the king and to both houses of Parliament.[7] But George simply tossed the petition unread into a packet containing 148 other documents that he forwarded to the House of Commons. Its members also ignored it, and weeks later, when Franklin asked permission to address the Commons about it, his request was denied by a vote of 218 to 68.[8] Dartmouth meanwhile ordered the colonial governors to use their "utmost endeavors" to prevent a second meeting of the Continental Congress.[9]

The king was even more dismissive of the Americans' effort at reconciliation. More than a month before Franklin handed the petition to Dartmouth, he told the prime minister that the colonists were "in a state of rebellion" and that "blows must decide whether they are to be subject to this country or independent."[10]

George's modern apologist Andrew Roberts excuses this belligerent attitude, claiming that "throughout the crisis over America, the king behaved with constitutional propriety, going along with his government's measures rather than driving them."[11] But it was precisely because Americans looked to the king to guard them against Parliament's overreaching—to resist, rather than "go along with," its claims to absolutism—that his refusal to read their petitions proved so devastating to American public opinion. From George's perspective, reading the address would mean conceding the Continental Congress's legality—which would undermine the principle of Parliamentary Supremacy. Yet by refusing to hear their pleas, and supporting Parliament's purported authority to legislate for the colonies in all cases whatever, he was literally declaring the Americans outside his protection—or, more precisely, proclaiming that he had no constitutional protection to give. That message was made even clearer when both George and Parliament also ignored petitions in support of the Americans that were submitted by the City of London—hardly an illegal body.[12] Far from acting with "constitutional propriety," George was adopting an absolutist view of parliamentary power far removed from the traditions of English law, and summarily enforcing that vision on the Americans through military force.

The king's refusal to hear these appeals was, of course, consistent with Parliament's decades-long policy of ignoring any protest against its authority to tax the Americans. As long ago as the debates over the Molasses Act, the Commons had blocked such petitions, and even as late as May 1775, when Edmund Burke pleaded with the House to accept a message from New York, the prime minister refused, insisting that "the honor of Parliament required that no paper should be presented to that House, which tended to call in question [its] unlimited rights."[13] What this meant in practice was that Americans were barred from exercising their constitutional right to petition for redress of grievances unless they surrendered their constitutional right to be free from taxation without consent.[14]

In any event, George's mind was made up. In November, weeks before Franklin and his colleagues delivered the "loyal address," the king spoke to Parliament, decrying the "spirit of resistance and disobedience" that "still unhappily prevails" in Massachusetts, and pledging his "firm and steadfast resolution to withstand every attempt to weaken or impair the supreme authority of this Legislature."[15] In fact, he was prepared to do more than that. When his own prime minister suggested sending a group of negotiators to America to discuss a peaceable resolution to the dispute, George disapproved. "This looks [too much] like the mother country being more afraid of the continuance of the dispute than the colonies," he said. "I do not want to drive them to despair but to submission."[16]

MASSACHUSETTENSIS VERSUS NOVANGLUS

While Americans waited for an answer to their "loyal address," Boston newspapers began publishing a series of articles by an anonymous Tory calling himself "Massachusettensis."[17] The articles were written with a high degree of legal skill, and John Adams watched with alarm as they began moving public opinion away from the Patriot cause. When the series had been running for a month with no rebuttal, he finally decided to respond himself. The result was a series of 12 essays, totaling more than 66,000 words, that Adams signed with the pseudonym "Novanglus" and that mustered an extraordinary range of constitutional scholarship to argue the case for American freedom.

Adams was offended by Massachusettensis's stale assertion that Americans should help pay back the costs of the French and Indian (or Seven Years') War. They had already paid, he wrote—to the amount of "twelve shillings in the pound in taxes"—after having sent "a sixth or seventh part of her sons" to fight. On top of that, the Navigation Acts created monopolies that were tantamount to taxes because they forced American merchants to sell products to Britons at below-market prices. The truth was that Americans paid a disproportionate share of the British tax burden, more than any other similarly sized group within the empire. As for protecting the colonies by stationing forces there, the army's presence "has been nothing but a public nuisance"—climaxing in the Boston Massacre.[18] Tories claimed the army was there to protect against mobs, but the soldiers were *themselves* a mob—a mob "of the worst sort, with red coats, fuses, and bayonets."[19]

Even more maddening was Massachusettensis's snide remark that the Patriots had spun themselves into an "unaccountable frenzy" as a result of a trifling three-penny tax on tea. "This is so gross an attempt to impose on the most ignorant of the people, that it is a shame to answer it," Adams replied.

> Are we not in this province deprived of the privilege of paying our governors, judges, etc.[?] Are not trials by jury taken from us! Are we not to be sent to England for trial! Is not a military government put over us? Is not

> our constitution demolished to the foundation? Have not the ministry shown by the Quebec bill that we have no security against them for our religion any more than our property, if we once submit to the unlimited claims of Parliament?[20]

The imperial crisis was not a trivial argument about taxes. Tories in England and America were engaged in "schemes for enslaving this country" that differed little from "the designs of [Edmund] Andros," who a century earlier had established a dictatorship in New England.[21] Beginning in the 1760s, Governors Bernard and Hutchinson, along with Prime Ministers Grenville and North, had "conceived the design" of overturning the long-standing "fundamentals of the government" and "building their own greatness on its ruins."[22] Now, their allies were seeking to replace the constitutional principle of Prescriptive Right with the theory "that Parliament is the only supreme, sovereign, absolute, and uncontrollable legislative over all the colonies."

Adams denied that Parliament had any authority over the Americans, except to regulate imperial trade, and that was based "not [on] any principle of common law, but merely [on] the consent of the colonies, founded on the obvious necessity of [the] case."[23] Beyond that, Parliament could point to nothing in law, history, or morality that gave it power over Americans—except the Declaratory Act, and that "was made without our consent."[24] The colonists had protested against the Navigation Acts, had petitioned against the Molasses and Sugar Acts, and had defied some of Parliament's purported laws outright. For at least a decade, they had made their position plain: They had never been governed by Parliament and they never would be.

Adams and his fellow Patriots "acknowledge[d] a subordination to the king," of course, and "a *voluntary* subordination to Parliament, as far as the regulation of trade," but they would not concede that Americans were in "absolute dependence upon Parliament as their supreme legislative in all cases whatsoever."[25] Reiterating what he had said in his "Great Controversy" with Hutchinson the previous year, Adams explained that Americans were within the *dominion*, but not the *realm*. In fact, they were not part of the "British empire" at all—because, properly speaking, there was no such thing. An empire is a kind of despotism. But Britain's government was "a limited monarchy"—a kind of republic, in fact, which means "a government of laws, and not of men."[26] That was the opposite of an empire.

Certainly the colonies' founders had never considered themselves subject to Parliament's authority. For a century and a half, Americans had been governed by the king and their own legislatures. In any event, for land to be part of the realm, it had to be annexed, with their agreement, by an act of Parliament, and no act had ever been passed annexing America. Thus, as Sir Edward Coke had said of the Scottish in *Calvin's Case*, so it was true of colonists: They were free subjects, entitled to representation in their *own* parliaments, not subject to the whims of London lawmakers.

There was nothing absurd about regarding the British colonies as "distinct states" that were "united under one king."[27] Even ancient empires had operated that way: The Greeks and Romans had let their colonies govern their own internal affairs. Yet even those empires were not really analogous to the Anglo-American relationship, which was really unprecedented. The North American colonies were not connected to Great Britain by annexation (like Wales), or agreement (like Scotland), or conquest (like Ireland). And since there was "no precedent in point," the nature of the American-British connection could only be discerned "by eternal reason and the law of nature."[28] There, the argument was simple. The initial settlers were free to make their own laws not because Parliament allowed it, but because under natural law they "had a clear right to have erected in this wilderness a British constitution, or a perfect democracy, or any other form of government they saw fit."[29] They had chosen to accept England's king as their ruler, but their charter contained nothing that bound them to Parliament's control. The moment the pilgrims stepped ashore, "they got out of the English realm, dominions, state, empire, call it by what name you will, and out of the legal jurisdiction of Parliament."[30]

Massachusettensis's entire case seemed to boil down to "an apprehension that it was necessary [that] there should be some superintending power," Adams concluded.[31] But that was not really true. Even if it were true, it need not be a legislature 3,000 miles away; an intercolonial legislature could accomplish that. The real reason Parliament claimed jurisdiction was because it was trying to establish an oligarchy—that is, "a government of grandees, over whom the people have no control."[32] That explained why it was trying not just to tax the colonists, but also to control the payment of official salaries, and why it had adopted the Government Act, replacing the Bay Colony's 150-year-old constitution with autocratic military rule. Worse, the Quebec Act—which deprived Canadians of their right to government by consent, punished them for their religious beliefs, and obliterated trial by jury and habeas corpus—showed what London had in store for Massachusetts next.

OUR LAST HOPES OF RECONCILIATION

Adams's "Novanglus" essays ran through the winter of 1774 and the spring of 1775, thus coinciding with the circulation of Jefferson's *Summary View*. But in mid-April, while Adams was in the midst of writing the 13th installment and preparing to travel to Philadelphia for the Continental Congress's next meeting, his work was interrupted by terrible news.

General Gage in Boston had ordered a detachment of soldiers to march on Concord—site of the Provincial Congress and therefore the colony's de facto capital—to seize the colonists' gunpowder and, if the opportunity arose, arrest "the principal actors and abettors in the Provincial Congress," specifically John Hancock and Samuel Adams.[33] Just weeks before, the Provincial Congress had adopted a resolution declaring that "whenever the army under command of General Gage, or any part thereof to the number of five hundred, shall march out of the town of Boston . . . the military force of the province ought to be assembled . . . to act solely on the defensive."[34] Accordingly, a group of militiamen hastily mustered on the public square in Lexington to confront the redcoats en route. A firefight ensued, leaving eight Americans dead before Gage's regulars continued on toward Concord. Hancock and Adams escaped, but the soldiers destroyed some munitions before turning around to march 40 miles back to Boston. That was when colonial militiamen, gathering from the countryside, attacked. By the end of the day, more than 70 British soldiers lay dead. The war everyone had dreaded had arrived.

Gage had already closed Boston's city limits, prohibiting anyone still living there from leaving without his permission. To enable civilians to come and go, John Adams's friend Joseph Warren—author of the incendiary Suffolk Resolves—negotiated an agreement with Gage: Any Bostonian who handed over his guns would be allowed to depart. The civilian population accordingly surrendered more than 2,000 muskets, pistols, and other weapons—only to find Gage dragging his feet.[35] Eventually he reneged entirely, and the residents, now disarmed, found themselves hostages. "Poor Bostonians!" wrote John Adams. "My heart bleeds for them day and night."[36]

A few days after the fighting at Lexington and Concord, Adams rode out to see the battle site himself. He found it a scene of "great confusion and much distress." Colonial soldiers were ill-equipped, with no uniforms and little ammunition. Yet it was clear "that the die was cast, the Rubicon passed, and . . . if we did not defend ourselves they would kill us."[37] The idea of going to Philadelphia for the Continental Congress's next session was unnerving: He would be leaving behind his wife and children—of whom there were now five, all under the age of 10—while an army based only 15 miles away was raiding the countryside. Nevertheless, he departed only a week later. He tried to sound calm in a letter to Abigail, but his words cannot have been comforting: "Many fears and jealousies and imaginary dangers will be suggested to you, but I hope you will not be impressed by them," he wrote. Still, "in case of real danger . . . fly to the woods with our children."[38]

When word of the fighting reached Virginia, the rumor mill distorted the story into a massive engagement. "We have received the unhappy news of an action of considerable magnitude," Jefferson wrote to his mentor William Small in London. "It is said that 500 of the [British] with [their commander Hugh Percy] are slain."[39] Percy had not actually been killed, and casualties on both sides totaled about 300 killed, wounded, and missing, but either way, Jefferson—who was unaware that Small had died of an illness months before—wanted his former teacher to tell people in England that Americans would not yield. "This accident has cut off our last hopes of reconciliation," he said. The colonists had hoped King George would serve as a mediator between them and Parliament. Instead, he had chosen to "pursue the incendiary purpose of still blowing up the flames."[40] Very well; the Americans were resolute.

One problem, Jefferson added—in a passage he ended up deleting from his letter—was that the British seemed to think the revolutionary fervor was the work of a few demagogues manipulating the people. "The reverse of this is most assuredly the truth." American political leaders had been doing their best "to moderate" the public's "almost ungovernable fury."[41] In fact, just days after the Massachusetts fighting, residents in Williamsburg reacted ferociously to word that Governor Dunmore was moving Virginia's store of gunpowder from its storage facility in the capital to a ship in the James River. Insisting that the powder belonged to the colony, not the British government, a crowd surrounded the Governor's Palace, threatening Dunmore's safety until Patriot leaders managed to persuade them to disperse.

Days later, a force of 700 men gathered in Fredericksburg, planning to march on the capital and get the powder back. Among them was the Hanover County Militia. At their head was Patrick Henry, who had recently dazzled members of the Virginia Convention in Richmond with his famous "liberty or death" speech, warning Virginians that "the next gale that sweeps from the north will bring to our ears the clash of resounding arms!"[42] His words had helped persuade the convention to adopt resolutions for arming the colony. Then, he had rushed off to lead his own company of volunteers, aiming for a direct confrontation with Dunmore.

When the governor asked his council of advisers what to do, one of them, Jefferson's college friend John Page, recommended returning the powder. Enraged, the governor pounded his fist on the table—"Mr. Page, I am astonished at you!"—and removed Page from the council. Something had to be done, however. At last, a group of elder Patriots intervened, arranging a deal whereby Dunmore's treasurer would hand over a payment of £330 for the powder.[43] Satisfied, Henry's militia disbanded, but the governor quickly issued a proclamation declaring him an outlaw. Virginians regarded that as a badge of heroism.

Dunmore, convinced that the people were ready to lynch him, decided to run. A month after the gunpowder confrontation, he took his family and fled in the middle of the night to a British warship anchored off Yorktown.[44] North Carolina Governor Josiah Martin had already done the same; terrified after a local mob stormed his mansion and took away his guns, he had bolted for a vessel in the Cape Fear River in April.[45] In June, New Hampshire's governor, John Wentworth, rushed from his capital, too, when a mob pointed a cannon at his house.[46] Other governors ran away in the months to come: South Carolina's Lord William Campbell sneaked out of Charleston in September, followed a month later by New York's William Tryon, Georgia's James Wright in February 1776, and, just days before independence was declared, Maryland Governor Sir Robert Eden.[47]

Violent as the situation was becoming, there were still half-hearted signs from London of a possible compromise. In February 1775, William Pitt—the elderly member of Parliament who had championed the Stamp Act's repeal—offered a bill in the Commons called the "Provisional Act," which provided that in exchange for the colonists accepting Parliamentary Supremacy and pledging a perpetual grant of funds to London, the imperial government would renounce the use of military force, refrain from taxing the Americans, acknowledge the Continental Congress's legitimacy, and repeal the Intolerable Acts. The Commons, however, rejected Pitt's bill in a landslide.[48] Then, Lord North offered his own "conciliatory proposal," a vague, single-paragraph proposition that Parliament would consider it "proper" to "forbear" from imposing taxes on any colony—except those Westminster thought "expedient" for the "regulation of commerce"—if that colony would "propose to make provision . . . for contributing their proportion to the common defense (such proportion to be . . . disposable by Parliament)."[49]

News of this offer did not arrive in America until after fighting had broken out in Massachusetts and Dunmore had fled Williamsburg. By then, prospects for peace seemed slim. But before abandoning the capital, Dunmore had received instructions from London ordering him to convene the House of Burgesses to consider North's proposal. He had accordingly scheduled a meeting for June 1, and that meeting was still on, despite his absence. So Jefferson joined the other Burgesses in Williamsburg, where he was placed on a committee to write the colony's answer.

North's proposal did not fool the Virginians. It was obviously not a real effort to resolve their grievances. For one thing, Parliament accompanied it with a resolution proclaiming the colonies in rebellion, as well as two new laws—the Restraining Acts of

1775—the first of which barred Massachusetts ships from fishing off Newfoundland or engaging in trade with anyone other than Britain and the West Indies, and the second of which expanded that ban to encompass Virginia, New Jersey, Pennsylvania, Maryland, and South Carolina.[50] North may have thought he was taking a carrot-and-stick approach, but it gave the opposite impression: It looked like he was trying to oppress Americans while distracting them with illusory offers of compromise.

Jefferson drafted a reply that was polite and insisted yet again that Virginians wanted nothing more than to maintain their "union with Great Britain," but that rejected North's suggestion in terms that made clear just how far the colony had moved toward independence.[51] Parliament, he wrote, had "no right to intermeddle with the support of civil government in the colonies." It was not London's place to set policy for Americans; Virginia's government had been established "for us, not for them."

One objectionable feature of North's proposal was his insistence that Parliament would decide how to spend the funds raised by taxation. "We cannot conceive that any other legislature had a right" to tell Virginians when and how to pay public officials, Jefferson answered. That was contrary to the fundamental principle of private property, which included the right not to have one's wealth taken away without consent or the consent of one's representatives. Without that right, the colonists would be "stripped of the only means" of controlling the government and would "possess no check on the royal prerogative."

There was also the matter of free trade. North's proposal spoke of Americans paying "their proportion to the common defense," but if they were to pay the same that taxpayers paid in England, it was only fair that they enjoy the same freedom of commerce that English merchants enjoyed. Reiterating the point he had made in *A Summary View*, Jefferson wrote that Parliament should "either be content with the monopoly of our trade, which brings greater loss to us and benefit to them than the amount of our proportional contributions to the common defense [would]," or, if it insisted on taxing Americans, it should withdraw its trade restrictions, "lay[ing] open to us a free trade with all the world." Imposing taxes *and* mercantilist economic restrictions amounted to double taxation.

North's plan—if something so vague could be called a plan—was also silent about the Quebec Act, the vice-admiralty courts, and other grievances. "This seems to bespeak no intention to discontinue the exercise of this usurped power over us." It was clear that North's real goal was to dissolve colonial unanimity.[52] He was offering to withhold taxation of those specific colonies that agreed to "make provision"—which was obviously intended to entice wavering colonies (perhaps trade-dependent New York, which according to rumor was less than enthusiastic about the boycott) into breaking the unity the Americans had forged.[53] Virginians would have none of that. "We are now represented in General Congress," wrote Jefferson, and "bound in honor as well as interest to share one general fate with our sister colonies."

But while Virginia would leave it to the Congress to offer a definitive answer to North's proposal, the Burgesses could not resist pointing out that the prime minister was only offering more of the same high-handedness that the colonists had refused for a decade. Americans had repeatedly tried to petition Parliament for redress, only to be ignored. They had also sent the king numerous appeals, and he had "not deigned to answer us." They had even published an address to the British people, and that, too, had proved "ineffectual."[54] "What then remains to be done?" There seemed only one answer: "That we commit our injuries to the even-handed justice of that being who doth no wrong."

When Dunmore, aboard his warship, saw this response, he was disgusted. In a curt, single-sentence message, he told the Burgesses, "I can discover nothing in your address that I think manifests the smallest inclination to, or will be productive of, a reconciliation with the mother country."[55] This was a "severe and cruel" thing to say, the House replied. "We are sorry that your Lordship had so little feeling for [our] honor and integrity." Although the governor had been telling his superiors that Virginians were of a rebellious temperament, "the truth is, my Lord, that his Majesty's dutiful subjects in this colony have the utmost attachment to their sovereign; they admire, they love the constitution, and will risk everything most dear and valuable in support of it." But they would never "sit down supinely, and submit to yokes which neither they nor their forefathers were able to bear."[56]

Dunmore had told the Burgesses that he would not return to Williamsburg unless they agreed to North's proposal, which he called an "opportunity . . . of establishing the freedom of your country upon a fixed and known foundation."[57] But the House rejected the insinuation. They *already* knew what the foundation of their freedom was. "It is written, as with a sun-beam, on our hearts."[58]

THE SECOND CONTINENTAL CONGRESS

By the time this exchange took place, Jefferson, too, had left Williamsburg. The Virginia Convention where Patrick Henry had delivered his "liberty or death" speech had chosen a slate of representatives for the Continental Congress's May meeting in Philadelphia, and although Jefferson was not selected, he was named as an alternate in case Peyton Randolph—who was still the Speaker of the House of Burgesses—had to return to Virginia. Thus, when the Burgesses began their June 1 meeting, Randolph was required to travel to Williamsburg to preside, and Jefferson had to go to Philadelphia to replace him. Leaving behind his wife to care for their two-year-old daughter Martha and their new baby Jane, born on April 3, he began the 12-day journey to the Congress, now being held at Pennsylvania's own capitol building, today called Independence Hall.

He arrived at almost the same time that news broke of major developments in Massachusetts. On June 12, General Gage had proclaimed martial law there. "The infatuated multitudes," he said, had been seduced by "incendiaries and traitors" whose constitutional arguments were "the grossest forgeries, calumnies, and absurdities that ever insulted human understanding." These "traitors"—specifically John Hancock and Samuel Adams—had drawn the people into "avowed rebellion" against "the constitutional authority of the state" and even inspired them to attack the king's "unprepared" troops with a "wantonness of cruelty." If the colonists returned to their former loyalty, all would be forgiven—except for Hancock and Adams, whose crimes were so "flagitious" that they could expect only the most "condign punishment."[59]

Five days later, 2,400 Massachusetts militiamen clashed with 3,000 British infantry at Breed's Hill and Bunker Hill, overlooking

Boston. The colonials fought until they ran out of ammunition, then threw rocks at the attackers. Although finally forced to retreat, the Americans inflicted over 1,000 casualties on the British, at a cost of only 450 of their own—an impressive showing for untrained provincials. Among the Patriot casualties, however, was Adams's friend, Joseph Warren. "[He] fell gloriously fighting for his country," Abigail told John. "The tears of multitudes pay tribute to his memory."[60]

She and her young children had witnessed the fighting from their home and saw the flames sparked by British cannons begin to sweep through Charlestown, eventually reducing that community to ash. "My heart overflows at the recollection."[61] Still, awful as the battle was, the bravery of the defenders inspired the colonists, and the disproportionate losses shocked the king's commanders. "A few more such *victories*," wrote General Sir Henry Clinton sarcastically, "would have shortly put an end to British dominion in America."[62] That fall, London relieved General Gage from his post and sent another 20,000 soldiers to the colonies.

Jefferson reached Philadelphia just four days after the battle, to find the Congress deluged by the worst emergency Americans had ever faced. The representatives had already commissioned a new intercolonial army and made Virginia delegate George Washington its leader. John Adams had been given the honor of nominating him. Not only was Washington highly regarded for his military record, but Adams and his colleagues also knew that placing a Southerner in charge of a predominantly Northern army sent a powerful message of colonial unity. Two days after his arrival, Jefferson joined Adams and the other delegates in a parade bidding farewell to the general as he left to take command.

But if Adams and Jefferson met that day, they left no record of it. In fact, no document survives memorializing their first encounter. Adams certainly knew the Virginian's reputation; decades later, he recalled that "writings of his were handed about" that were "remarkable for the peculiar felicity of expression."[63] Those documents were *A Summary View* and the Burgesses' reply to Lord North's conciliatory proposal, which Jefferson brought with him from Williamsburg. His legal research skills swiftly impressed some delegates. New York's James Duane told Adams that Jefferson was "the greatest rubber off of dust that he [had] met with."[64] But Adams seems not to have spent much time in his company during the first months after their meeting. Serving on an astounding 90 committees—making him by far the busiest man at the Congress—left Adams little time to socialize.

When they did get to know each other, however, they found they had much in common. Both were lawyers, bibliophiles, and enthusiasts for farming and family life. And although they grew apart in later years—becoming angrily estranged during the presidential election of 1800—both were at this time "radical" revolutionaries, adherents of the classical liberal ideas of John Locke and Algernon Sidney, and willing to face war with the world's largest empire to vindicate those principles. They shared, in Jefferson's words, "a perfect coincidence of thought and action."[65] Adams was blunter. Jefferson "seized upon my heart," he remembered. "Not even Samuel Adams" was as "prompt, frank, explicit, and decisive" as the young Virginian.[66]

A persistent myth holds that Adams was more politically conservative, or even communitarian, than the libertarian-minded Jefferson. In reality, they shared what one scholar calls "a distinctively modern form of liberal individualism."[67] Both thought government should be confined to securing private property and freedom of commerce, while leaving people otherwise free—and both were willing to drastically change their societies to serve that principle. Their differences lay more in their views of the relative importance of culture as opposed to abstract principles. As far back as his *Dissertation on the Canon and Feudal Law*, Adams had argued that politics is an outgrowth of mores or social habits, which resist radical change—a view that would be regarded as pessimistic in years to come—whereas Jefferson tended to suspect that such habits were riddled with irrationality and prejudice and could and should be rationally reformed. This distinction would disrupt their friendship when the French Revolution broke out in the 1780s. But the bitterness of that later schism only testifies to the strength of their ideological and personal bond during the 1770s. Adams was "a great man," Jefferson told James Madison. He could be vain and short-tempered sometimes, but he was "profound in his views and accurate in his judgment. . . . You will love him forever if you become acquainted with him."[68]

By now, both men were convinced that there was no going back for America. Even if some rapprochement were possible, the relationship with London could never be what it had been. Yet even as the Continental Congress organized its army, some members still sought compromise, in ways that frustrated Jefferson and infuriated Adams. The leader of this group was John Dickinson, the Pennsylvania lawyer and author of the famous *Letters from a Farmer*, who arrived in Philadelphia determined to try yet another petition to George III.

A MEASURE OF IMBECILITY

Born in 1732 into a wealthy family that straddled Pennsylvania and Maryland, Dickinson had studied law in London for three years—he even met the king—before establishing a legal practice in Philadelphia. Elected to the Delaware legislature at the age of 27, he had risen within a year to Speaker of the House. Then in 1762, he was elected to the Pennsylvania legislature. After that, he served in the Stamp Act Congress, where he wrote the Declaration of Rights and Grievances, and in the First Continental Congress, where again he took a leading role in preparing a petition to the king. Shrewd and extraordinarily patient, Dickinson also had a lawyerly habit of splitting hairs and overthinking simple matters. Jefferson found him "honest" and "able," but thought he had "more ingenuity than sound judgment."[69]

Now, convinced that the bloodshed in Massachusetts would shock George III into action, Dickinson argued that the colonists should once again seek redress. Acknowledge Parliament's authority to regulate colonial trade, remain steadfast in opposition to parliamentary taxation, and surely the monarch would relent.

In his memoirs, written 30 years later, Adams recalled viewing this idea as foolish—a "measure of imbecility," he called it—but there's little evidence that he opposed it at the time.[70] On the contrary, he himself had expressed a desire for reconciliation with Britain as recently as his "Novanglus" essays, and later told Abigail that the Congress hoped to have "a redress of grievances."[71] The bloodshed at Bunker Hill might have changed his mind, but when Dickinson made his formal motion to petition the king again, Adams voted yes, and signed the petition when it was finished. He "dread[ed]" another petition "like death," he told a friend, "but it must be proposed. We can't avoid it."[72] If he thought it a waste of time, he at least yielded to the need for unanimity. Leading the colonies was like driving horses, he said: The faster ones must be slowed, and the slower ones hastened, to keep the team together.[73]

But his view of Dickinson did change during that stressful summer. When they had first met a year earlier, Adams had been starstruck. Now, he began to see Dickinson as hedging, even stonewalling. And by the time he composed his autobiography, this impression of Dickinson had hardened into downright hatred. The Pennsylvanian seemed in retrospect to suffer from a revolting moral paralysis, positively hindering the Patriot movement. He even had blood on his hands for Bunker Hill, Adams claimed, since his prevarications had prevented the formation of a continental army. As for the idea of petitioning the king yet again, Adams depicted it as little more than cowardice—a cowardice brought on by Dickinson's Quakerism, with its pacifist principle—something Adams considered both a recipe for slavery and positively un-Christian.

It was true that Quakers tended to be Loyalists, or, at least, by passively refusing to join the Patriot cause, they effectively undermined the rebellion. In January 1775, the Friends' annual meeting in Philadelphia adopted a "testimony" denouncing the Continental Congress and its supporters for acting "contrary to the nature and precepts of the gospel." Good Christians, the Quakers declared, should "demean themselves as peaceable subjects" and "discountenance and avoid every measure tending to excite disaffection to [Parliament]."[74] A year later they repeated this message, professing their "abhorrence of all such writings and measures as evidence a desire and design to break off the happy connection we have heretofore enjoyed with the kingdom of Great Britain."[75]

Nothing could inflame Adams more. During the Stamp Act crisis, he had expressed frustration about the "very absurd sentiment" of "passive obedience." "We have tried prayers and tears and humble begging and timid tame submission as long as trying is good," he wrote. "And instead of redress we have only increased our burdens and aggravated our condemnation."[76] He would forever bristle at Quaker nonviolence, as did other Patriot leaders, including George

Washington, who, while president, told the Quakers' annual meeting that he considered them "exemplary and useful citizens"—"*except* [for] their declining to share with others the burden of the common defense."[77] To a significant degree, Dickinson became a magnet for criticism less for his own views than as a symbol of a large faction in Pennsylvania politics that prioritized peace over freedom.

Yet this was unfair to Dickinson. For one thing, he was *not* a pacifist. He was actually a militia colonel who later served honorably on the battlefield. Indeed, he was not even a Quaker, although his wife and family were. And he certainly was no Tory. Rather, he argued that petitioning the king once more would help Americans generate sympathy in Europe and prove "that we are influenced not by timidity or despondence."[78] He opposed separation from Britain—but claimed that this was only on account of timing: He thought it best to delay while preparing for war.[79] Thus, even while he wrote his "Olive Branch Petition," as the document was later called, he also collaborated with Jefferson on a Declaration of the Causes and Necessity of Taking Up Arms. This, argues Dickinson's biographer Jane Calvert, proves he was not an obstructionist but "principled and pragmatic," and that he only wanted to postpone independence because "his countrymen were not prepared for it."[80]

That cannot be the whole story, however. While Adams's depiction of Dickinson was distorted, other delegates also found him a hindrance and saw fearfulness rather than prudence in his hypertechnical legalisms. One called him "cautious and timid," a man whose "nerves were weak."[81] Another complained that "all his productions" had "the vice of refining too much."[82] Still another blamed his "feeble politics" for "the disadvantages we now experience, for want of a full supply of every necessary for carrying on the war."[83] Yet another called his ideas "very timid" and even "disgust[ing]" in their extreme deference to Parliament.[84]

Like General George McClellan a century later, Dickinson seemed able at every critical moment to find some sophisticated reason why delay was strategic when what was really needed was action, or some plausible pretense for further negotiations even after the futility of such measures was obvious. A year later, after the Congress had opened American ports and the colonies had created new governments—both amounting to unofficial independence—Dickinson was still trying to postpone explicit separation. That struck Adams as pure malingering. Most of the Congress's deliberations were left off the record, which, as Adams noted, "was convenient to the party in opposition to [independence], who by this means evaded the appearance, on the journals, of any subject they disliked."[85] As a result, we cannot know exactly what was said in their debates—although we do know that the arguments grew so heated at one point that half the delegates left the room. Still, it's revealing that Dickinson was proud of the fact that his Olive Branch Petition "make[s] no *claim* and mention[s] no *right*."[86] That was a form of meekness he considered appropriate, but which most Patriots found grotesque.

In any event, Dickinson and Adams came to a personal clash in the summer of 1775. The specifics are unclear. In his notoriously unreliable memoirs, Adams recalled delivering a passionate oration against something in Dickinson's petition, only to be accosted by the author afterward. "What is the reason, Mr. Adams, that you New England men oppose our measures of reconciliation?" he demanded. "If you don't concur with us in our pacific system, I and a number of us will break off from you in New England, and we will carry on the opposition by ourselves in our own way."

If Dickinson actually said this, which is unlikely, it was the direst threat he could utter, and Adams was appalled. He would not be "threatened" into agreeing to measures he despised, he told Dickinson.[87] He would go along with the petition, if that was the majority's will, but he would not stop calling it a dumb idea. Around that time, he wrote a candid letter to a friend in which he said that Dickinson gave "a silly cast to our whole doings."[88] That letter fell into the hands of the British, who published it in the newspapers, much to Adams's humiliation. He and Dickinson were never on speaking terms again.

Jefferson's impressions of the "Pennsylvania farmer" were more favorable. He thought Dickinson a genuine patriot whom everybody respected so much that he was "greatly indulged even by those who could not feel his scruples."[89] The Virginian had long ago rejected Dickinson's belief that Parliament was entitled to regulate colonial trade, but, highly conscious of being one of the least experienced delegates—at 31, he was the Congress's second-youngest member, a decade junior to both Dickinson and Adams—he deferred to his elders. And unlike Adams, he retained a warm regard for Dickinson for the rest of his life. "His name will be consecrated in history as one of the great worthies of the revolution," Jefferson wrote when hearing of his death in 1808.[90] Still, by that time, Dickinson had joined the Jeffersonian Republicans—which probably further tainted Adams's recollection.

Dickinson worked on the Olive Branch Petition for weeks before it was approved and sent to London on July 8. It again pledged loyalty to the king, while complaining that Parliament was using "delusive pretenses, fruitless terrors, and unavailing severities" to extend its unconstitutional power over America. The colonists had been forced "to arm in our own defense" but felt "required by indispensable obligations to Almighty God, to your Majesty, to our fellow subjects, and to ourselves, immediately to use all the means in our power not incompatible with our safety, for stopping the further effusion of blood."[91]

Like Adams, Jefferson thought such language excessively deferential. Everyone was "disgust[ed]" by the petition's "humility," he wrote. In fact, as the Continental Congress was finalizing its wording, Dickinson spoke up to say that he wanted just one more thing changed: Perhaps they should remove the word "Congress." After all, one reason the House of Commons had refused to listen to colonial entreaties in the past was that it considered the Congress illegitimate. Maybe it would be more prudent to use some other term. That was too much for Virginia delegate Benjamin Harrison. "There is but one word in the paper, Mr. President, of which I approve," he cried, "and that is the word *Congress*."[92]

Harrison spoke for many Patriots, but Dickinson also represented a large number of Americans who still hoped George III would intercede to prevent all-out war. The New Jersey and New York legislatures, not content like other colonies to defer to the Continental Congress, even prepared their own separate peace petitions to the king.[93] New Jersey's largely echoed the Olive Branch Petition, pleading for protection against Parliament but reiterating that the colonists had "no thoughts injurious to the allegiance which, as subjects, we owe."[94] New York's petition also begged the king, "as the indulgent father of your people," to resolve the dispute peacefully. "We mean not to become independent of the British Parliament," it declared. "On the contrary, we cheerfully acknowledge our subordination to it as the grand legislature of the empire; we wish only to enjoy the rights of Englishmen and to have that share of liberty, and those privileges secured to us, which we are entitled to upon the principles of our free and happy constitution."[95] Protesting the taxes, the closing of Boston Harbor, and the other Intolerable Acts, the New Yorkers asked George to "ascertain and limit the authority claimed by the British Legislature" so that the "RIGHTS AND PRIVILEGES which all your Majesty's subjects are entitled to" would remain secure.[96] They did not yet appreciate that the king recognized no such limits and no such rights.

The Philadelphia Congress may have been willing to indulge Dickinson's doomed wishes for reconciliation, but it was not prepared to see colonies undermine American unity by communicating with London on their own. When the members learned of the New York and New Jersey petitions, they adopted a resolution declaring it "very dangerous to the liberties and welfare of America" for colonies to communicate with London separately, and followed that up by sending a committee to chastise the New Jersey legislators in person.[97] They appointed Dickinson himself to lead that committee. "Nothing [will] bring Britain to terms but *unity and bravery*," Dickinson told the New Jersey lawmakers. "It [is] necessary to convince Britain that we would fight and [are] not a rope of sand."[98] New Jersey quietly shelved its petition. Never again would a colony attempt to conduct its own foreign policy.[99]

THE CAUSES AND NECESSITY OF TAKING UP ARMS

At the same time, Dickinson was preparing another public statement, one that would accompany Washington's appointment as head of the new intercolonial army. This proclamation, which would come to be called the Declaration of the Causes and Necessity of Taking Up Arms, was intended to buttress American unity by explaining why something that might seem like a Massachusetts conflict should concern the entire continent. Yet the Congress was running late. It had hoped to issue the statement weeks earlier, but the committee charged with writing it had turned in an uninspiring draft. Now, the Congress added both Dickinson and Jefferson to the committee and asked them to try again. Busy with his other tasks, Dickinson let the young Virginian take the first crack, and Jefferson quickly produced a draft that was formidable, indeed.

Opening with words that foreshadowed the first line of the Declaration of Independence, he wrote, "As it behooves those who are called to this great decision to be assured that their cause is approved before supreme reason, so it is of great avail that its justice be made known to the world."[100] The colonists' cause was straightforward: America's initial settlers had fled "the evils of misrule" in Europe and established a foothold in the Western Hemisphere "at the expense of their blood [and] ruin of their fortunes." They had also exercised their natural right to create their own political institutions, vesting their provincial assemblies with "full and perfect powers of legislation." True, they looked to the same king as "the link of union between the several parts of the empire," but that made them copartners with England, not vassals.

In the 1760s, however, Parliament changed its tune, "for the first time assert[ing] a right of unbounded legislation over the colonies." The laws it had adopted since then proved its intention to establish "absolute government over us." These included the taxes, the vice-admiralty courts, and laws that "declared that American subjects charged with certain pretended offenses shall be transported beyond the sea for trial to be tried before the very persons against whose pretended sovereignty [the] offense is supposed to be committed." But at this point, Jefferson cut himself off: "Why should we enumerate their injuries in detail?" he wrote. "By one act they have suspended the powers of one American legislature and by another they have declared [that] they may legislate for us themselves in all cases whatsoever. These two acts alone form a basis broad enough whereon to erect a despotism of unlimited extent."

At every step, Americans had "reasoned" and "remonstrated" in the "most mild and decent language," sometimes speaking so humbly as to be "almost disgraceful to freedom."[101] But instead of hearing Americans' pleas, Parliament had sent thousands of soldiers to Massachusetts. Their general had now declared martial law and was using Boston's people as human shields. "We do then, most solemnly before God and the world declare," wrote Jefferson, "that, regardless of every consequence, at the risk of every distress, [with] the arms we have been compelled to assume, we will wage [war] with bitter perseverance . . . to preserve that sacred liberty which He committed to us."

When Dickinson saw this draft, he disapproved. In old age, Jefferson recalled that it "was too strong" for the Pennsylvanian, who "still retained the hope of reconciliation with the mother country and was unwilling it should be lessened by offensive statements."[102] But Jefferson, like Adams, was misremembering.[103] Dickinson actually thought his wording was not strong enough. Over the next two weeks, he revised the draft, giving it a tone that combined maturity, regret, and steadfastness in expert measure. Cutting out approximately half of Jefferson's initial attempt, he made the declaration smoother, more assured, and more philosophically grounded. Where Jefferson had started by reciting Parliament's abuses, for example, Dickinson began with a broader point—specifically, the Lockean principle of equality:

> If it was possible for men who exercise their reason in contemplating the works of creation to believe that the Divine Author of our existence intended a part of the human race to hold an absolute property in, and an unbounded power over, others marked out by His infinite goodness and wisdom as the legal objects of a domination never rightfully resistible, however severe and oppressive, the inhabitants of these colonies might at least require from the Parliament of Great Britain some evidence, that this dreadful authority over them has been granted to that body. But a reverence for our great Creator, principles of humanity, and the dictates of common sense must convince all those who will reflect upon the subject that government was instituted to promote the welfare of mankind, and ought to be administered for the attainment of that end.

The long opening sentence was a slightly sarcastic rephrasing of the natural law argument that all men are created equal—or, as Algernon Sidney had put it, that people are not born wearing spurs or saddles, destined to ride or be ridden.[104] Parliament was made up of men, not gods, and they had no natural or constitutional right to exercise boundless power over Americans and their property. Dickinson also repudiated the idea of nonresistance. If political authorities become "severe and oppressive" enough, the people have the right to rebel. Now that London was using military force to achieve its "cruel and impolitic purpose," it was necessary for Americans to defend themselves. "Yet . . . we esteem ourselves bound by obligations of respect to the rest of the world to make known the justice of our cause."

Next, Dickinson incorporated the list of grievances Jefferson had prepared for his first draft: Parliament was "plunder[ing]" the colonies, taxing them unconstitutionally, taking away their jury rights, suspending their legislatures, closing the Massachusetts fisheries, and more. The king had treated the First Continental Congress's petition "with contempt"—and the Lords and Commons had even rejected petitions from Londoners who supported the Americans. Now, British soldiers "have butchered our countrymen; have burned Charlestown"—a reference to the destruction caused by British bombardment during the Battle of Bunker Hill—and were "exerting [their] utmost power to spread destruction and devastation." Americans had to decide: "unconditional submission to the tyranny of irritated ministers or resistance by force. The latter is our choice."

Dickinson's reluctance to formally separate from Britain would continue to plague Jefferson, Adams, and other independence-minded delegates. Yet he had penned one of the boldest statements of the imperial crisis, and the experience of working alongside him taught Jefferson important lessons about political rhetoric. *A Summary View* had been impressive in its scholarship and eloquence, but Jefferson had not yet learned to express himself as smoothly as the "Pennsylvania farmer." An attentive and quick study, he learned much from Dickinson, and within a year he was able to bring the same concentrated simplicity to his own Declaration.

Jefferson found his next writing assignment easier. Two months before, he had written Virginia's reply to Lord North's conciliatory proposal. Now, the Congress asked him to write another reply, this time on behalf of the Congress.[105] The draft Jefferson prepared was firm. North's idea of commanding the colonies to "make provision" for "the support" of their own governments was an insulting attempt to "intermeddle" with the decisions of American legislatures. "The provisions we have made are such as please ourselves," Jefferson now wrote, and there was no reason Americans should be forced to "provide sinecures" for every "idle or wicked" bureaucrat London might choose to send west. Also, Jefferson repeated, North had not mentioned repealing the Declaratory Act, the Quebec Act, the laws expanding the vice-admiralty courts, or the laws "exempting by mock-trial the murderers of colonists from punishment." And, again returning to his insistence on free trade, Jefferson wrote that it was "not just" that Americans should be taxed by Parliament while at the same time being subjected to the Navigation Acts. "If we are to contribute equally with the other parts of the empire, let us equally with them enjoy free commerce with the whole world."

In short, North's offer was mere propaganda, designed to fool European countries and British subjects into thinking "that there was no matter of dispute between us but the single circumstance of the mode of levying taxes." That was a lie. The true source of the dispute was Parliament's claim of "a right of demanding *ad libitum*"—that is, its power to legislate in all cases whatsoever.[106] By closing down the Massachusetts fisheries and choking off colonial trade, Parliament had proven "unequivocally" that it meant to persist in "indiscriminate legislation over us" regardless of anything Americans might do. In fact, Parliament was not truly interested in maintaining peace. One MP had even spoken "the dreadful sentence '*delenda est Carthago*'" in reference to Boston. Was that the language of conciliation? North's proposal was a sham, "addressed to our fears rather than to our freedom," and Americans would not be fooled.

TO SINK THE WHOLE ISLAND IN THE OCEAN

This time, the Congress made only minimal changes to Jefferson's draft before sending it to London on July 31. It adjourned the next day, and Jefferson headed for Richmond to attend the Virginia Convention, which began setting taxes, arranging recruitment for the colonial militia, and choosing delegates for the next meeting of the Philadelphia Congress. That took a week, and then he was off again, this time to Monticello.

Along the way, he learned that his Tory cousin John Randolph, the colony's attorney general, had decided to abandon Virginia and move to England. Randolph's brother Peyton was then serving as president of the Continental Congress, and another brother, Edmund, was also a prominent rebel, soon to join Washington's military staff. John, however, could not bring himself to support the revolutionary cause. When the *Virginia Gazette* published an article on July 27 calling him "incorrigible" and recommending that he "push for some remote corner of the globe," a chill must have run down his spine.[107] It was all too likely that a mob would follow up the *Gazette*'s veiled threat with violence. John decided it was prudent to leave.

Remembering that he had once expressed interest in buying John Randolph's fine violin, Jefferson saw an excuse to write him a letter for circulation in London. Enclosing a check for the instrument, Jefferson crafted a message that expressed affection for Randolph personally, but asked him to tell people in England that the Americans were prepared to "sink the whole island [of Great Britain] in the ocean" before they would "submit to the rights of legislating for us."[108]

It was harsh language, but it was appropriate to the times. Two days earlier, the king had officially pronounced the Americans in "open and avowed rebellion," which meant that not only the military but also all loyal subjects were legally obligated to "exert their utmost endeavors to suppress such rebellion, and to bring the traitors to justice."[109] A week after that, on September 1, 1775, colonial agents in London handed Lord Dartmouth a copy of the Olive Branch Petition. They had already mailed him one a week earlier and received no reply. This time, they told the colonial secretary that they would like an answer. Dartmouth replied candidly: "No answer," he said, "would be given."[110]

Yet, in one sense, the king did answer the petition. When Parliament's next meeting began in October, George delivered an opening address proclaiming that the Americans "openly avow their revolt, hostility, and rebellion," and that he was determined to crush the uprising. Colonial leaders had been secretly planning this all along, he claimed, conspiring to establish "an independent empire." All the petitions and remonstrances they had sent to London over the past decade had merely been intended "to amuse"—that is, to distract the imperial government from their scheme. And, although London had so far acted in a "spirit of moderation and forbearance" in an attempt "to prevent, if possible, the effusion of blood," the catastrophe had come at last, and it was "the better part of wisdom" to put down the revolt with overwhelming force. To that end, he was dispatching further reinforcements, including foreign soldiers hired by the Crown.[111]

Parliament naturally agreed.[112] In December, it adopted the Prohibitory Act, which forbade the colonies from "all manner of trade and commerce."[113] Any colonial vessels violating that ban would be seized by the government "as if the same were the ships and effects of open enemies," and their crews would be impressed into the Royal Navy. Even more revealingly, Section 24 of the act borrowed language from a law adopted three decades earlier, which governed the capture of foreign ships during wartime.[114] That section allowed the seizure of foreign vessels, but not ships belonging to "territories remaining and continuing in their allegiance to the king, *and under his Majesty's protection*." In other words, Parliament had explicitly declared that Americans were not "under his Majesty's protection" anymore.

To American eyes, that put a climactic end to the question of allegiance. According to ancient legal principles, monarchy was a relationship in which subjects gave the king loyalty in exchange for security. Now, George's government was revoking that guarantee and placing Americans in the same category as "open enemies." During the Stamp Act crisis, John Adams had wondered whether the closure of courts meant Americans had been cast out of royal protection. Now, it had literally happened. The king saw them not as wronged subjects who deserved negotiation and conciliation, but as rebellious servants who should be beaten into submission. "America must be a colony of England or treated as an enemy," the king told Dartmouth. "[England] will be able to make her rebellious children rue the hour that they cast off obedience."[115]

— CHAPTER 10 —

RECURRING TO FIRST PRINCIPLES

I should be very happy if the constitution could carry us safely through all our difficulties without having recourse to higher powers.
—*John Adams*[1]

Thomas Jefferson and John Adams both suffered severe personal blows that autumn. First, Jefferson's 17-month-old baby Jane died in September. While his habitual privacy has shielded all details of the event from biographers, it was surely devastating to both parents. Twenty-six-year-old Martha had already lost one child, the three-year-old son from her first marriage, and her own health was also poor. Jefferson left little record of the anxiety he experienced as he left her and the couple's three-year-old daughter behind to resume his duties in the Continental Congress. But he was distracted enough that after arriving in Philadelphia he complained to an in-law that he had "never received the scrip of a pen from any mortal in Virginia since I left. . . . The suspense under which I am is too terrible to be endured."[2] Then in October, while he was sitting down to dinner with his cousin Peyton Randolph, president of the Continental Congress, the older man suddenly collapsed with a fatal stroke.

Adams, too, was suffering terrible losses. His brother, who had joined the Continental Army, died of illness in camp in August, and in September, an outbreak of dysentery decimated his hometown, killing Abigail's mother and infecting their three-year-old son Thomas. "At first I suddenly thought of setting off immediately for Braintree," he wrote his wife when he heard the news. "Yet the state

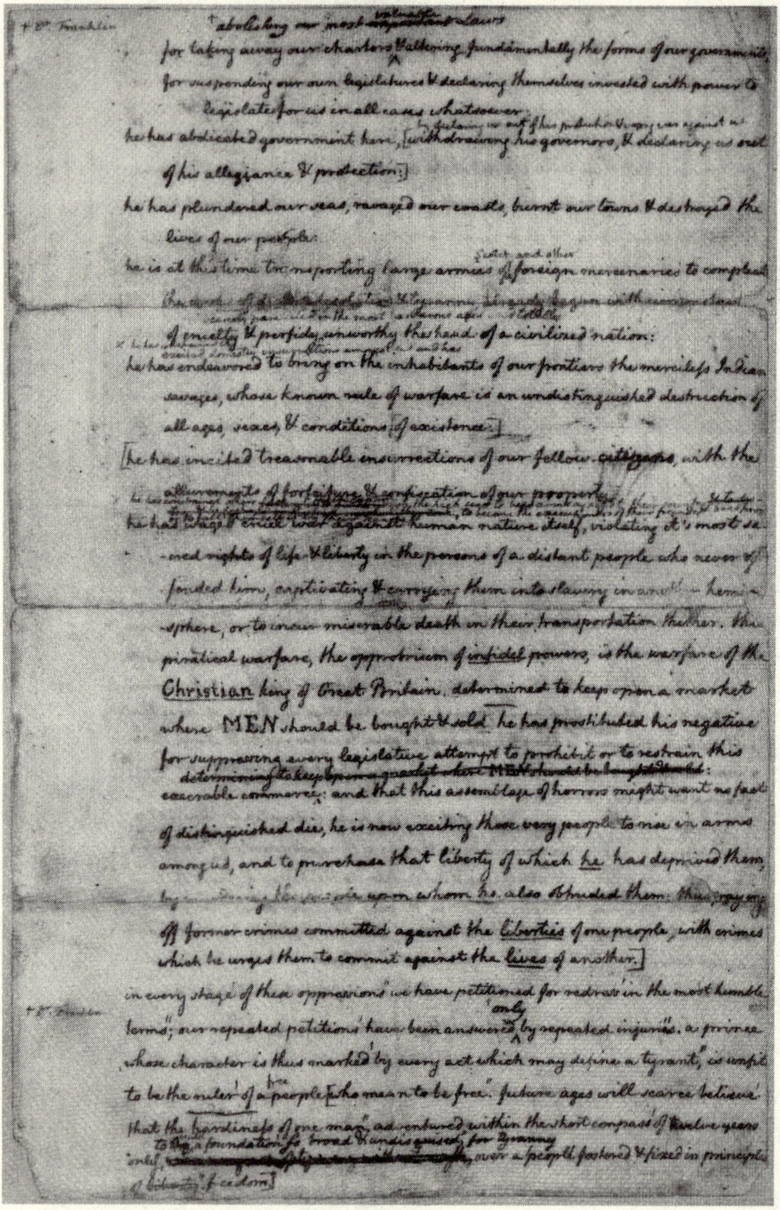
for taking away our charters & altering fundamentally the forms of our governments
for suspending our own legislatures & declaring themselves invested with power to
legislate for us in all cases whatsoever.
he has abdicated government here, [withdrawing his governors, & declaring us out
of his allegiance & protection.]
he has plundered our seas, ravaged our coasts, burnt our towns & destroyed the
lives of our people:
he is at this time transporting large armies of foreign mercenaries to compleat
of cruelty & perfidy unworthy the head of a civilized nation:
he has endeavored to bring on the inhabitants of our frontiers the merciless Indian
savages, whose known rule of warfare is an undistinguished destruction of
all ages, sexes, & conditions [of existence.]
[he has incited treasonable insurrections of our fellow-citizens, with the
allurements of forfeiture & confiscation of our property.
he has waged cruel war against human nature itself, violating it's most sa-
-cred rights of life & liberty in the persons of a distant people who never of-
fended him, captivating & carrying them into slavery in another hemi-
sphere, or to incur miserable death in their transportation thither. this
piratical warfare, the opprobrium of infidel powers, is the warfare of the
Christian king of Great Britain. determined to keep open a market
where MEN should be bought & sold, he has prostituted his negative
for suppressing every legislative attempt to prohibit or to restrain this
execrable commerce: and that this assemblage of horrors might want no fact
of distinguished die, he is now exciting those very people to rise in arms
among us, and to purchase that liberty of which he has deprived them,
by murdering the people upon whom he also obtruded them: thus paying
off former crimes committed against the liberties of one people, with crimes
which he urges them to commit against the lives of another.]
in every stage of these oppressions we have petitioned for redress in the most humble
terms; our repeated petitions have been answered only by repeated injuries. a prince
whose character is thus marked by every act which may define a tyrant, is unfit
to be the ruler of a free people [who mean to be free. future ages will scarce believe
that the hardiness of one man, adventured within the short compass of twelve years
only, to lay a foundation so broad & undisguised, for tyranny over a people fostered & fixed in principles
of freedom.]

Thomas Jefferson's draft of the Declaration of Independence reveals much careful editing and (literal) cut-and-paste.

of public affairs is so critical that I am half afraid to leave my station."[3] He began complaining of mysterious sicknesses of his own, probably psychosomatic. He even imagined himself going blind.

Congressional committees were straining to supply the army—and that raised the question of whether there was any point in sticking to the Continental Association, which was rapidly changing from a tool into an obstacle. It did not seem to be bringing Parliament around, but it was certainly preventing Americans from obtaining necessary supplies. Throughout the summer, there had been talk of opening colonial ports to ships from other countries, so that Americans could get the weapons and matériel they needed, but John Dickinson, still hoping for reconciliation with London, opposed that, and the proposal was defeated in July. The issue would not go away, however, and the idea was raised again in the autumn. Day after day, Adams transcribed into his diary the lengthy, sometimes angry arguments in the Congress. "We can't do without trade," insisted Pennsylvania delegate John Zubly in October.[4] Virginia's George Wythe agreed. "We had better open our trade altogether," he argued. Imports would mean "cash, powder, or foreign manufactures." The alleged virtue of going hungry for virtue's sake might be "a fine subject for philosophers and orators," but Americans needed clothing, food, and weapons. And there were broader benefits, too. "Commerce, whether we consider it in an economical, a moral, or a political light, appears to be a great good. Civility and charity, as well as knowledge are promoted by it."[5]

Other representatives, however, argued that the Continental Association was working, if only Americans would be patient. There was little likelihood that Americans *could* trade anyway, even if they did open the ports. Britain's navy was far too powerful for colonial merchantmen to get past the blockade. Anyway, argued South Carolina's Edward Rutledge, the boycott would help Americans defend themselves. By ensuring that "our people will go into manufactures," it would encourage them to make their own weapons and supplies.[6] Impatient as always, Adams groaned at the interminable arguing. "These refined geniuses, these learned lawyers, these wise statesmen, are so fond of showing their parts and powers as to make their consultations very tedious," he told Abigail.[7] As the end of 1775 approached, the debate remained unresolved. And when word finally arrived in November that the king had indeed refused the Olive Branch Petition, a distracted Congress passed over that information without official comment.

There were more urgent problems to worry about.[8] Virginia's governor, Lord Dunmore, had ordered the Royal Navy to attack the town of Hampton, and on November 7, he declared martial law throughout the colony. More shockingly, he announced that he would free "all indented servants, Negroes, or others (appertaining to rebels) . . . that are able and willing to bear arms, they joining his Majesty's troops, as soon as may be, for the more speedily reducing this colony to a proper sense of their duty."[9]

THE DUNMORE PROCLAMATION

Dunmore intended this proclamation as a weapon of terror. It was an ancient tactic—one used in Greek and Roman times—and it worked.[10] Plantation owners were all too familiar with the numerous slave revolts in the Roman Republic, including three "servile wars" between 135 and 71 BCE, and they feared similar violence in North America. Among the most frightening precedents was the Second Servile War, sparked by the Roman Senate's decision to free 800 Bithynians who had been enslaved for debt.

The Senate did this in hopes that they would join the Roman military, but it sparked a bloody uprising instead. Word of the possibility of freedom excited the enslaved population so much that when one military commander decided to halt the manumissions, the enraged slaves rose up, murdered their masters in their beds, and gathered into an army that swelled to perhaps 12,000 members. "Calamities overspread all Sicily," wrote historian Diodorus Siculus. Slaves "committed all sorts of rapines and acts of wickedness; for they shamefully killed all before them, whether bond or free, that none might be left to tell tales."[11] Virginians also knew that the people they held in chains were *justified* in fighting for their freedom—and that embarrassing fact made the specter of rebellion all the more chilling. "I tremble for my country when I reflect that God is just," wrote Jefferson, when contemplating the possibility. "The Almighty has no attribute which can take side with [whites] in such a contest."[12]

John Murray, the Earl of Dunmore, served as governor of Virginia from September 1771 until June 1775, when he fled to a Royal Navy warship for safety. He later issued a proclamation promising freedom to enslaved Virginians who fought for the Loyalist cause.

In recent years, some writers have pointed to Dunmore's proclamation as proof that Virginians joined the revolutionary cause out of a desire to perpetuate slavery. In his 2021 book *Liberty Is Sweet*, for example, professor Woody Holton likened Dunmore's announcement to Abraham Lincoln's Emancipation Proclamation, a characterization magnified by the authors of *The New York Times Magazine*'s notorious "1619 Project" when they claimed that colonists embraced independence "to ensure that the institution [of slavery] would continue unmolested."[13] But Dunmore was no abolitionist, and neither he nor his superiors had any plan to "molest" the institution of slavery.[14] As an anonymous letter to the *Virginia Gazette* observed at the time, Britain's government "always encouraged and upheld" the practice, blocking efforts by Virginia's legislature to limit slave importation. Dunmore "does not even pretend" to offer freedom "out of any tenderness," the writer noted; his action was only intended to scare white Virginians with the real prospect of race war.[15] And considering how the British government had broken so many promises already, it seemed likely that any slave fleeing to the British would eventually be betrayed—perhaps by being taken to the West Indies and resold. That did end up happening in at least some cases. "After being drawn from their masters by promises of freedom and the king's protection," Dunmore confessed a decade later, they were "every day stolen away from [the Caribbean] islands, shipped, and disposed of."[16]

British troops returned Virginia runaways to masters who remained loyal.[17] And most of the enslaved who joined Dunmore's army were made ditchdiggers, not soldiers. They were given few supplies and no training, and they died of smallpox and other diseases at a monstrous rate.[18] "Almost every thicket affords you the disagreeable prospect of a wretched Negro's carcass brought to the earth by disease and famine," wrote one witness.[19] Dunmore and other British leaders—including General Charles Cornwallis, who took charge of British forces in the southern colonies in 1776 and also encouraged slaves to run to his lines—routinely abandoned them when they became ill. "During the siege [of Yorktown]," wrote an American soldier, "we saw in the woods herds of Negroes which Lord Cornwallis (after he had inveigled them from their proprietors) in love and pity to them, had turned adrift, with no other recompense for their confidence in his humanity than the smallpox for their bounty and starvation and death for their wages."[20] Meanwhile, British generals announced that any black person caught helping the rebels would be sold to a loyal master.[21]

The British were "never genuinely committed to a policy of liberation," explained historian Sylvia Frey.[22] They certainly gave no thought to any plan to help the freedmen establish a self-ruling community in North America. Instead, as one member of Parliament approvingly put it, their goal was only to encourage the enslaved to "rise and imbrue their hands in the blood of their masters."[23] Where Lincoln's Emancipation Proclamation was intended to force slaveholders to respect a constitutional system whereby slavery could gradually be eliminated, Dunmore's sole purpose was to terrorize rebels into returning to an imperial system in which slavery would be preserved. Meanwhile, in what another scholar calls a "conjunction of pragmatism and principle," George Washington on December 30 ordered his own enlistment officers to begin accepting black recruits.[24] Ultimately, as many as 8,000 black soldiers served in integrated units under his command.

None of this absolves slaveholders of their crimes, and indeed some Patriots resorted to savage punishments for slaves who tried to flee to the British, even hanging some to send a message.[25] But the reality is that although the desire for freedom among those who responded to Dunmore's invitation is understandable, and the condemnation of his order by slaveholding Patriots manifested the same hypocrisy that tainted everyone who fought for freedom while keeping others in chains, the Dunmore episode cannot substantiate the 1619 Project's assertion that "one of the primary reasons" for American independence was "to protect the institution of slavery."[26]

On the contrary, more than six months earlier, the world's first anti-slavery organization convened its inaugural meeting in Philadelphia. The Society for the Relief of Free Negroes Unlawfully Held in Bondage began its work in April 1775. It eventually made Benjamin Franklin its president. His anti-slavery views were already well-known. Although he had owned slaves himself early in life, he considered slavery an "atrocious debasement of human nature," and when a Southern delegate to the Continental Congress likened enslaved people to livestock, he spoke up: There was "some difference between them," he said. "Sheep will never make any insurrections."[27] In retirement, Franklin urged Congress to "devise means for removing [this] inconsistency from the character of the American people."[28]

But it was hardly news to the revolutionaries that the cause of freedom they proclaimed was inconsistent with the practice of slavery. In 1773, Patrick Henry wrote that slavery was "as repugnant to humanity, as it is inconsistent with the Bible and destructive to liberty"—and yet, he admitted, "I am master of slaves of my own purchase . . . drawn along by the general inconvenience of living without them. I will not, I cannot justify it."[29] But while white Americans chose to postpone their reckoning with slavery at this time, they knew and openly acknowledged that their principles required emancipation. As far back as 1764, James Otis Jr. had declared that "all men" are "by the law of nature free," whether "white or black."[30] What was extraordinary about the American Revolution—indeed, utterly unprecedented—was the degree of candor with which the colonists admitted that it was, in the words of one Patriot, "incompatible with the glorious struggle America is making for her own liberty to hold in absolute slavery a number of wretches in defiance of all we claim for ourselves[.]"[31]

BEGINNING THE WORLD OVER AGAIN

Throughout the last half of 1775, the Congress strained to make ends meet and to oversee an invasion of Canada, which the members viewed as a grave military threat.[32] That proved a costly failure, and in the meantime, the British began laying waste to American towns. In October, Vice-Admiral Samuel Graves, commanding the Royal Navy's North Atlantic fleet, tried to provision his undersupplied vessels by seizing property from colonists along the Massachusetts coast. When locals resisted, he ordered his subordinate, Lieutenant Henry Mowat, to "chastise" the towns of Marblehead, Salem, Newburyport, Gloucester, Portsmouth (now in New Hampshire), and Falmouth (today's Portland, Maine). Graves told Mowat to "make the most vigorous efforts to burn the towns and destroy the shipping in the harbors," but Mowat only managed to destroy Falmouth—leaving 1,000 people homeless—before being reassigned to other duties.[33]

Then, on New Year's Day, Governor Dunmore ordered ships to bombard Norfolk, Virginia.[34] Ironically, that century-old city was well-known as a Loyalist community, but it was surrounded by rebel militia, and when Dunmore demanded that the residents reprovision his naval vessels, the militia barred the way. The governor flew into a rage and ordered his flotilla to open fire. Loyalists aboard the ships—who had fled to Dunmore for protection—watched in horror, first as British cannonballs set fire to the town, and then as undisciplined Americans gleefully joined in the destruction. In the end, 1,500 homes were left in ruins.

To John Adams, these incidents proved that he had been right all along: There was "no prospect, no probability, no possibility" of reconciliation.[35] Jefferson agreed. "We are told and everything proves it to be true that [George III] is the bitterest enemy we have," he wrote to his Tory cousin John Randolph. "By the god that made me I will cease to exist before I yield to a connection on such terms as the British Parliament propose. . . . We want neither inducement nor power to declare and assert a separation."[36]

Learning of Dunmore's proclamation of martial law, the Continental Congress declared that he had "[torn] up the foundations of civil authority," and that it was time for Virginians to "establish such form of government as in their judgment will best produce the happiness of the people."[37] It issued identical recommendations to New Hampshire and South Carolina.[38] Naturally, creating new governments without royal permission would be tantamount to independence.

Then, a week after the burning of Norfolk, Thomas Paine's pamphlet *Common Sense* appeared in Philadelphia's bookstores. Discarding all talk of compromise, Paine openly urged separation from the mother country. "Men of passive tempers look somewhat lightly over the offenses of Britain, and, still hoping for the best, are apt to call out, 'Come, come, we shall be friends again,'" he wrote. "But examine the passions and feelings of mankind, bring the doctrine of reconciliation to the touchstone of nature, and then tell me, whether you can hereafter love, honor, and faithfully serve the power that has carried fire and sword into your land?"[39] The pamphlet became a phenomenon.

Paine was the emigrant son of a Quaker corset maker whose name was actually Pain. His life in England was miserably poor and stagnant, but he wrote well, and in 1774, after managing to get a letter of recommendation from Benjamin Franklin, he traveled to America to start over. Like Franklin, he arrived penniless and took up the printing trade, immediately publishing revolutionary articles. "It was once the glory of an Englishman to draw the sword only in defense of liberty," he wrote in one of his earliest publications, but Britain was now pursuing a "system of despotism . . . big with destruction to the whole British empire."[40]

Now, setting aside technical arguments about the constitution, charters, or precedent—indeed, he derided the "so much boasted constitution of England" as an "overly complex" mixture of "the base remains of two ancient tyrannies"—Paine offered a thoroughly Lockean argument about the nature of government and individual freedom. Government is neither a transcendent enterprise nor some form of historical force, he wrote. It is a man-made tool for preserving "freedom and security." Monarchy was an "exceedingly ridiculous" way to accomplish those goals; in fact, it was a perverse form of government because it made the ruler's mere will into law. And Parliament's actions now proved that Britain's boasted constitutionalism was a sham. The country's celebrated legal guarantees for freedom actually resulted from "the constitution of the *people*, and not [from] the constitution of the *government*."[41] And King George had "shown himself such an inveterate enemy to liberty, and discovered such a thirst for arbitrary power," that even this modest protection had now been lost. In any event, things had now reached a point that made reconciliation impossible. Even if America and Britain did reach some agreement, George would certainly exert "the whole power of the crown" to retaliate against Americans and keep them "as low and humble as possible." There was no going back—nor should Americans wish it.

Paine's writing offered the perfect combination of simplicity and depth to resonate with ordinary Americans. But *Common Sense* also appealed to an idealistic sense of destiny. "Should an independency be brought about . . . we have every opportunity and every encouragement before us to form the noblest, purest constitution on the face of the earth," he wrote. "We have it in our power to begin the world over again." With that in mind, he ended with a crude sketch of a new government for what he called—apparently for the first time—"the United States of America."[42]

After reading *Common Sense*, John Adams told his wife that he admired Paine's "manly and striking" style but was unpersuaded by the Englishman's suggestions about how the colonies might unite under a new constitution.[43] That was a far more complicated task than the newcomer seemed to recognize. Thus, Adams decided to respond with an anonymous pamphlet of his own, titled *Thoughts on Government*, which appeared in April 1776.[44]

Like Paine, he started not with arcane legal disputes, but with basic principles of natural law. "The happiness of society is the end of government," Adams wrote, just as "the happiness of the individual is the end of man." "Happiness," of course, meant not transient or trivial pleasures, but "virtue"—that is, active and productive engagement in the business of life. Different types of governments, he continued (in an argument borrowed from Montesquieu), have different animating principles—fear or honor can govern people, for example—but the noblest governments operate on the noblest principles. And the best was one that aimed to preserve the people's ability to pursue happiness in peace and safety, without interfering in their lives. That meant a republic, in which the rulers are subordinate to law, with their powers divided into executive, legislative, and judicial, and where the legislature is "in miniature, an exact portrait of the people at large." By implementing such checks and balances, Americans could establish a framework that would be "productive of [society's] ease, its safety, its freedom, or in one word, its happiness." But as long as Americans thought of themselves as displaced Britons rather than at-home Americans, they would be unable to take that step.

THE MOST IMPORTANT RESOLUTION EVER TAKEN IN AMERICA

George III had consistently ignored the colonists' petitions, and even when residents of London asked him again in the spring of 1776 to address the Americans' concerns, he curtly refused. The colonists only had themselves to blame, he said; he would not "alleviate [their] miseries" until they ceased their "unjustifiable resistance" to Parliamentary Supremacy.[45] The message was clear: The government would never consider colonial grievances worthy of discussion.

Combined with his August 1775 proclamation that the colonies were "preparing, ordering, and levying war against us," his October speech to Parliament pronouncing them traitors, and December's Prohibitory Act, which declared that they were outside of his protection, George's refusal to heed even the Londoners' petitions on their behalf removed all doubt. "We are put out of the royal protection," wrote Adams.[46] Independence was the only option left.

At the beginning of the year, Pennsylvania delegate James Wilson—a protégé of John Dickinson and, like him, an opponent of independence—had moved that the Continental Congress "declare to their constituents and the world their present intentions respecting an independency."[47] Samuel Adams quickly got that motion postponed, fearing that supporters of independence did not yet have enough votes.[48] But it could not be held off forever, and on January 24, the Congress appointed a committee to prepare a public statement on independence. It was staffed by pro-reconciliation delegates, including Wilson and Dickinson. That may have been a clever move by the Adamses, because it meant the remaining moderates would be forced to explain why the colonies should *not* declare independence.[49] In any case, the ensuing discussion revealed how far the Americans had already gone down the path of abandoning their legal and constitutional arguments, toward resting their case on the broader principles of political philosophy, instead.

The Scottish-born Wilson was 34. His devoutly religious father had hoped he would become a minister. But, although Wilson had attended the University of St. Andrews on a scholarship, his father's death forced him to leave school and become a teacher instead. He moved to America in 1765, taught for a while at what is now the University of Pennsylvania, and then read law under Dickinson. Two years later, he started a successful law practice, inaugurating a career that brought him recognition as one of America's greatest legal minds. Like his mentor, he was a skilled writer, but the report he now presented revealed the strains required of anyone still trying to resist a final break with Britain.[50] It read like Wilson was arguing with himself.

He began with the basic principle "that all the powers of government are derived from [the people]." Even the king's power came from the consent of the governed. But Parliament "is not elected by the colonists," and therefore "can derive no authority" from them. Nevertheless, it had passed laws to govern them, including the Declaratory Act, which amounted to a "sentence of universal slavery." This was the "root of bitterness" from which the "branches of oppression" had grown. Americans had repeatedly tried to petition Parliament and the king; all such efforts had been rejected on the grounds that the Congress was "an illegal body"—yet, Wilson noted, the same could have been said of the barons at Runnymede, who extracted the Magna Carta from King John, or the Convention Parliament that placed William and Mary on the throne. To be accused of treason was shocking. How could it be "disloyal" to petition the king?

As for the accusation that the Patriots had been conspiring to separate from Britain all along, "we disavow that intention." Their true aim was "the reestablishment of the constitutional rights of the colonies." It was hard to believe this could be accomplished now, however. Much as they cherished their connection with Britain, "the nature of this connection" was "misunderstood or disregarded" in London. Parliament's "arbitrary exertions of power" and the "servile submission" it demanded were a form of slavery, not freedom, and if implemented they would "rend every generous bond asunder." Thus, while "an independent empire is not our *wish,* it may—let [our] oppressors attend—it may be the fate of our countrymen and ourselves." Americans longed for peace, but would not "subscribe to our own slavery." They were "*desirous* to continue subjects" but "*determined* to continue freemen."

Wilson's report came off as a threat to do what everybody already knew had to be done. The Congress silently laid it aside; the committee had accomplished its real job of showing even reluctant members that there was no point in further appeals to the Crown. Not only had civil war broken out—battles had by now taken place in Massachusetts, New York, Virginia, the Carolinas, and even the Bahamas—but governors had fled their posts, courts were closed, and legislatures had been replaced with makeshift "conventions" struggling to maintain law and order. There was no time to be wasted on fantasies of reconciliation. It was time for real business.

In mid-March, George Washington's troops chased the British out of Boston, and weeks later, the Congress announced—after long and grueling debate—that all colonial ports would be opened to trade with "the people of all countries as are not subject to the King of Great Britain" (except that "no slaves [may] be imported into any of the thirteen United Colonies").[51] Opening the ports was tantamount to declaring independence, and weeks after that, the Congress prepared to take the next step: advising the colonies to organize new official governments in place of the jerry-rigged "conventions" and "committees" that had been operating in the place of shuttered legislatures and runaway governors. The Congress had already recommended that step to Virginia, New Hampshire, and South Carolina, but now it urged all the colonies to do likewise.

The delegates knew that organizing new governments on the ruins of monarchical rule meant disavowing royal authority, and John Adams proposed to hammer that point home in a preamble that he moved be added to the Congress's recommendation:

> Whereas his Britannic Majesty, in conjunction with the lords and commons of Great Britain, has, by a late act of Parliament, excluded the inhabitants of these United Colonies from the protection of his crown;
>
> And whereas no answer whatever to the humble petitions of the colonies for redress of grievances and reconciliation with Great Britain has been or is likely to be given, but the whole force of that kingdom, aided by foreign mercenaries, is to be exerted for the destruction of the good people of these colonies;
>
> And whereas, it appears absolutely irreconcilable to reason and good conscience, for the people of these colonies now to take the oaths and affirmations necessary for the support of any government under the crown of Great Britain, and it is necessary that the exercise of every kind of authority under the said crown should be totally suppressed, and all the powers of government exerted, under the authority of the people of the colonies, for the preservation of internal peace, virtue, and good order, as well as for the defense of their lives, liberties, and properties,

> against the hostile invasions and cruel depredations of their enemies; therefore, resolved, &c.[52]

Adams started with the king's refusal even to hear the colonists' petitions and his deeming Americans the equivalent of foreign enemies. These acts "excluded" Americans "from the protection of his crown" and dissolved any colonial obligations toward the king.

Adams's preamble marked the first time the Congress had officially named the king as a cause of America's woes. According to historian Pauline Maier, this reflected a shift in the "form" of the Patriots' argument. "To attack the king," she wrote, "was the way Englishmen announced revolution."[53] But while that's true, Adams's preamble was not employing a merely rhetorical device. Criticizing George directly reflected a genuinely new stage in political developments. Until now, the Patriots had argued that Americans were *not* subject to Parliament's authority, but *were* subject to the king's.[54] That was why they studiously refused even to mention Parliament in such documents as the Olive Branch Petition—a silence that one scholar calls "a renunciation of Parliamentary Supremacy more bold than many of Congress' other measures"[55]—even while they professed loyalty to the king and begged him to intercede on their behalf. Now, however, George had foresworn that duty by refusing to receive their petitions and declaring them outlaws. If he would not stand by the colonial charters, if he would deny his American subjects protection, then their obligation of allegiance was dissolved. Directly attacking the king was therefore not merely symbolic; it was a substantive constitutional argument.

George III's biographer Andrew Roberts claims the king never actually "declared the colonists out of his protection or allegiance: indeed, he was trying to compel them back into both."[56] But the Prohibitory Act expressly used that phrase, which was a well-known legal formula, instantly recognizable by Adams and other attorneys.[57] And even if it had not, there was no way to square any notion of royal "protection" with George's refusal to receive the Americans' petitions, his insistence on their total subjection to Parliament's absolute power, and his belligerent goading of Lord North toward war. More importantly, trying to "compel" people into "allegiance" is an oxymoron. A king who "compels" "allegiance" is not a constitutional monarch, but a despot. "All the British fleet and army cannot change men's opinions," wrote Adams. "An attempt to cram a form of government down the throats of a people, to impose a constitution upon a united and determined people by force, is not within the omnipotence of an English parliament."[58]

Adams's proposed preamble indicated that all the debates between the theories of Parliamentary Supremacy and Prescriptive Right were becoming moot. Americans no longer hoped that London would take their constitutional arguments seriously. From now on, they would rest their case on deeper principles of justice and political legitimacy, instead—that is, on natural law. That, in turn, would require rebuilding American governments from the ground up. "If [Adams's] preamble passes," warned James Wilson, "the people will be instantly in a state of nature."[59] Every legal and political institution would have to be justified anew, not on historical or traditional grounds, but on the grounds of consent and human rights.

On May 15, the Congress took precisely that path. It approved the resolution, including Adams's preamble, and Americans began the task of replacing their delegitimized colonial governments with institutions built by themselves. Adams was therefore well within his rights when he boasted to a friend that his preamble was "the most important resolution that ever was taken in America."[60]

THE APPEAL TO HEAVEN

Yet even after all that had happened, some delegates still clung to hope that King George would resolve their grievances after all. "Why all this haste?" demanded New York's James Duane, in opposing Adams's preamble.[61] True, the king had refused the Olive Branch Petition, British forces had burned Falmouth and Norfolk, and Parliament had declared the colonists to be hostile foreigners, but newspapers kept reporting that London was forming a peace commission to resolve the dispute, and Duane thought Americans should wait to see what the commissioners had to say. To Adams, however, that was all the more reason to hurry. Any such mission would surely be as disingenuous as Lord North's so-called proposal had been—nothing but a ploy to delay, distract, and divide the colonies. "It was one of those delusive contrivances," he wrote afterward, for "lulling the people with idle hopes."[62] And if the Congress failed to act before the commission arrived, moderates like Duane would likely drag the colonies into another limbo, bargaining and quibbling and receiving no redress while Britain built up its military force still more.

In the end, the king did not even choose the commission's members until May 3, and then only empowered them to make peace if the colonists "declare[d] their obedience to the authority of the British Legislature"—which was surrender, not compromise.[63] Its members did not arrive in America until July 14, 1776—10 days too late—and only in September did its leader, Admiral Richard Howe, meet with American representatives.

Howe found himself in an odd position, simultaneously given command of the fleet dispatched to conquer America and charged with making peace. The Congress sent three members to meet with him: Benjamin Franklin, John Rutledge, and John Adams, who seems to have been in an especially sour mood. When Howe said he was not authorized to negotiate with members of the Congress on an official basis, but could converse with them in their private capacities, Adams hotly replied "that he had no objection to Lord Howe's considering him, on the present occasion, merely as a private gentleman, or in any character *except* that of a British Subject."[64] "Mr. Adams," Howe muttered, "is a decided character."[65] The discussion went nowhere.

It hardly mattered. By the summer of 1776, most Americans had become comfortable with the idea of independence. Communities across the land were flooding the Congress with petitions urging separation from Britain. In April, the people of Halifax, North Carolina, announced their support for independence.[66] On May 27, the residents of Malden, Massachusetts, declared that they had once "felt ourselves happy in connection with" Britain but now that "the king and his minions" were trying to "awe us into submission and erect a system of despotism," it was "the ardent wish of our souls that America may become a free and happy state."[67] Two days later, New York's Mechanics Union resolved that although "sorrow fills our hearts" at the idea of breaking with the mother country, the fact that George III had lifted his "iron hand" against them now persuaded them "to separate from, [rather] than to continue any longer in connection with such oppressors."[68] By then, Rhode Island, probably the most democratic colony, had adopted a declaration of independence of its own.

Such expressions of public opinion conflict with the oft-heard claim that the revolutionary leaders were an "elite" who manipulated the lower classes into supporting separation from Britain. On the contrary, from the mobs who terrorized the Stamp Act agents, to the Sons of Liberty who destroyed consignments of tea, to the militiamen who menaced Governor Dunmore for confiscating gunpowder, to the farmers and merchants who signed petitions at community meetings, independence was plainly supported by a large segment of the people—probably between 40 and 45 percent, with only about 15 to 20 percent opposed, and the rest neutral.[69] The colonial elite, if anything, resisted the independence movement. In May 1775, Thomas Jefferson had written that American legislators were exerting their "utmost efforts" to restrain the people's anger toward Britain.[70] Now, it was clear that the Congress was following, not leading, on the question of separation.

The importance of Paine's *Common Sense* in changing public opinion has likely been exaggerated. Adams thought so, at least. He wrote in his memoirs that the pamphlet "probably converted some," but also "excited many writers against" independence. To be sure, Adams was biased by the time he wrote this, having come to hate Paine for political and religious reasons. But while some who endorsed separation did rely on Paine's arguments, even quoting *Common Sense* in their resolutions, the evidence suggests that Americans changed their minds less as a consequence of his pamphlet than as a reaction to King George's refusal of the Olive Branch Petition and his decision to pronounce Americans beyond the pale.[71]

What was happening was what today's political scientists call a realignment. Up to now, Patriots had been divided over whether to view the crisis as a dispute over the constitution and the meaning of colonial charters—in which case they might persuade London to back down—or as a more profound clash over principles of government's legitimacy, which would lead to permanent division. Essentially, all Americans believed in the Lockean natural law theory; that government is charged with protecting the people's rights, rather than molding them into an ideal society or acquiring glory for the nation. But many viewed these principles as abstractions that only took meaningful form when embodied in English legal and political institutions. In other words, although everybody may enjoy a natural right to freedom in the abstract, only the common law and the colonial charters implemented and secured that liberty in real-world terms. That was what Pennsylvania representative Joseph Galloway meant when he said two years earlier that he had "looked for our rights in the laws of nature" but only found them "in a state of political society."[72] It was best to focus on the down-to-earth business of daily politics than to pursue the dangerously idealistic notions of political theory.

To that way of thinking, separation from Britain represented a worse fate than any of Parliament's abuses, because it would strip Americans of the civic identity and political institutions that safeguarded their natural liberty. Yet it was now becoming clear that those things were being taken away whether they liked it or not. King George agreed with the Parliamentary Supremacists that Westminster could revoke charters and override the common law at will. And that choice transformed the imperial crisis from an argument over constitutional law and the traditional rights of Englishmen into a deeper conflict over what kind of political rule was justifiable in the first place. That was a question of political philosophy. And that meant there was no longer any point in arguing about law and history. Alexander Hamilton, then a 20-year-old student at the university later named Columbia, put the point well. When a Tory writer pointed out that New York had no charter to begin with, Hamilton replied, "It is true that New York has no charter. But . . . the sacred rights of mankind are not to be rummaged for among old parchments or musty records. They are written as with a sunbeam in the whole volume of human nature by the hand of the divinity itself, and can never be erased or obscured by mortal power."[73] London had cast Americans adrift. It was futile to assert their Britishness yet again. It was time to appeal to heaven.

John Locke coined the phrase "appeal to heaven" in his *Second Treatise*, as a way of explaining revolution. When "the hands appointed to administer justice" instead engage in injustice, he wrote—"however colored with the name, pretenses, or forms of law"—and when the people have exhausted every legal means of obtaining redress, they may find themselves left with "no appeal on earth." In that case, they are "left to the only remedy . . . an appeal to heaven."[74] Locke meant "appeal" in a lawyerly, as well as a philosophical, sense: The dispute between rulers and the ruled having reached an impasse, the people could seek justice only by moving up to a higher authority—which could include violent resistance. Americans were now preparing to do just that.

The revolutionary consensus did not form overnight, of course. The opposition's strength was proved by the angry debate over Adams's preamble. A third of the entire Continental Congress voted no, and Maryland's delegates even walked out in protest when it was approved on May 15. Independence may have become popular, but many political leaders still held back. Nevertheless, the tide had decisively turned. By recognizing that the bond of royal allegiance had been severed, that royal authority was no longer recognized, and that "all the powers of government" should be based on "the authority of the people" instead of London's permission, the Congress's recommendation that the colonies form new governments effectively meant the end of British rule. That was what Adams meant when he later told his colleagues that declaring independence would merely be "declar[ing] a fact which already exists."[75] By June, Americans had made clear that they would not be governed by Parliament, and if the king took Parliament's side, they would not be ruled by him either.

VIRGINIA CALLS FOR INDEPENDENCE

In the weeks after Adams's preamble was adopted, colonial conventions began preparing new constitutions and new instructions for their representatives. Some even began adopting their own declarations of independence, often in the form of preambles to their new constitutions. Probably the most important of these was Virginia's—and much to his frustration, Thomas Jefferson was largely left out of that process.

He had gone home at the end of 1775, fearing for his wife's health. It seems she had not fully recovered from the death of baby Jane. She had been staying at her family's home, The Forest, which was about 20 miles southeast of Richmond, while her husband was in Philadelphia. But when fighting erupted near Norfolk in December, Thomas, fearing that The Forest was exposed to British naval invasion, gathered the family to the safety of Monticello. He probably planned to return to Philadelphia when the winter snows melted, but he suffered another blow in March, when his mother, Jane Randolph Jefferson, died of a stroke at the age of 56. As usual, he left no record of his feelings at this loss, but despite the long-standing speculation that the two were not close, he suffered one of the migraine attacks that regularly paralyzed him during moments of strain. That lasted five weeks, and not until May did he feel able to return to the Congress.[76] By then, his colony had already effectively decided for independence.

The Congress had urged Virginia on December 4 to create a new government in light of Governor Dunmore's martial law proclamation. The following week, the Convention, now meeting in Richmond, pronounced Dunmore's actions unconstitutional.[77] If "by his single fiat" he could "annul the laws of the land," the Virginians declared, then he had "broken the bonds of society."[78] Then, on May 15—only days after the Congress recommended that all the other colonies create new governments—the Convention endorsed independence. Given the king's decision to answer their petitions for redress with "increased insult, oppression, and a vigorous attempt to effect our total destruction," and the fact that (in words copied verbatim from Adams's preamble) "by a late act, all these colonies are declared to be in rebellion, and out of the protection of the British crown," Virginia found herself forced to choose between "an abject submission to the will of those overbearing tyrants, or a total separation from the crown and government of Great Britain." The Virginians therefore instructed their representatives in Philadelphia to propose a resolution "declar[ing] the United Colonies free and independent states, absolved from all allegiance to, or dependence upon, the crown or parliament of Great Britain."[79]

That resolution was largely the work of Patrick Henry in Richmond and Richard Henry Lee, the tall, well-educated lawyer with the wounded hand whom Adams had befriended at the First Continental Congress, and who was now in Philadelphia serving in the Second. Lee had long supported independence, and he admired Adams's *Thoughts on Government* so much that he oversaw its publication. In April, on the anniversary of the first gunshots at Lexington, Lee sent a copy of Adams's pamphlet to Henry, along with a letter explaining that the time had come for Virginia to "rouse America" and break with Britain. Laws such as the Prohibitory Act had "to every legal intent and purpose dissolved our government," he wrote, in words he plainly expected Henry to share with others. Dunmore's flight and the resulting collapse of the House of Burgesses had left the colony "in the high road to anarchy" for a year. With courts closed, there was not even a "magistrate lawfully qualified to hang a murderer." Americans could not stay in this purgatory forever, being "rebels excluded from the king's protection and magistrates acting under his authority at the same time." Foreign nations would not trade with Americans, let alone provide military support as long as the colonies remained technically connected to Britain.

Lee also warned of the risk that Britain might try to subdue the colonies by carving them up and giving them to other countries. This was not an unrealistic fear. European monarchs routinely partitioned vast areas, such as Canada or Poland, and sold or bartered them to other empires, "disposing of men and countries like livestock on a farm." Only four years earlier, the rulers of Russia, Prussia, and Austria had dismembered Poland and swallowed up the pieces. What was to stop George III from doing something similar in North America? In fact, Westminster had already given large portions of the western frontier to Quebec. It was "certain," Lee thought, "that the present court of London would rather rule despotically a single rod of earth, than govern the world under legal limitations."

Lee closed by encouraging Henry to read Adams's pamphlet—which "proved the business of framing government not to be so difficult a thing as most people imagine"—and to push for independence as quickly as possible.[80] Henry agreed, and moved that the convention order Lee to submit an official independence motion in Philadelphia. After nine days of political wrangling, that motion was unanimously approved, using language modeled on the House of Commons' resolution blessing the Glorious Revolution in 1689.

Back then, the Commons had declared that King James II, "having endeavored to subvert the constitution of the kingdom by breaking the original contract between the king and people and by the advice of Jesuits and other wicked persons having violated the fundamental laws, and having withdrawn himself out of the kingdom," had "abdicated the government."[81] In other words, the English had not arbitrarily replaced their monarch; he had effectively abandoned the throne by reneging on the agreement whereby subjects exchanged loyalty for protection. The fact that he had fled the country because of the arrival of an invading Dutch army was immaterial; he had broken the law and left his subjects to fend for themselves. They were therefore within their rights to establish a new government that would respect the limits of justice.

Now, the Virginians formulated a similar argument. Parliament was made up of wicked men who had conspired to subvert the constitution, and George III had endorsed their efforts. His subordinates—particularly the royal governors—had fled their capitals or, in Massachusetts's case, had been replaced by a military dictator. Thus, the colonists had not overthrown their governments; they had simply vanished. The Burgesses had even tried to convene their regular session in March, as Governor Dunmore had instructed—only to find him still absent.[82] These things added up to abdication by King George and his subordinates more than rebellion on Virginia's part. The colonists had "no alternative left but an abject submission to the will of those over-bearing tyrants, or a total separation from the crown and government of Great Britain."[83]

Thomas Jefferson had returned to Philadelphia by the time the Richmond Convention adopted this resolution, but his thoughts remained at home. On May 16, he told a friend that if Virginia was going to create a new government, he hoped he would be allowed to help. "It is a work of the most interesting nature and such as every individual would wish to have his voice in."[84] After all, there was so much in the colony's laws that needed improvement. In the room he was now renting on Market Street at Seventh, he began sketching thoughts for a new constitution, starting with a preamble that declared the colony independent of British control.[85] That preamble would become, in effect, a rough draft of the Declaration of Independence.

Like other revolutionary leaders, Jefferson started by consulting the precedents of the Glorious Revolution. The Bill of Rights Parliament had adopted when replacing James II opened with a list of grievances making clear how James had subverted the constitution—for example, he had "lev[ied] money [i.e., taxes] for and to the use of the crown" without lawful authority; "[kept] a standing army within this kingdom in time of peace . . . and quarter[ed] soldiers contrary to law"; required "excessive bail" and imposed "illegal and cruel punishments." So Jefferson used the same form in the preamble of his draft Virginia Constitution. He began by asserting that George III—whom Jefferson called by his family name, George Guelph, to underscore that he was a mere mortal, unworthy of the pompous mystique of royal ceremony—had been "heretofore entrusted with the exercise of the kingly office" but had "endeavored to pervert the same into a detestable and insupportable tyranny." He had vetoed "laws the most wholesome and necessary for the public good," "dissolv[ed] legislative assemblies repeatedly and continually for opposing with manly firmness his invasions on the rights of the people," and "combined with others to subject us to a foreign jurisdiction [i.e., Parliament's authority] giving his assent to their pretended acts of legislation." All of this meant he had "abandon[ed]" the colonists and "declar[ed] us out of his allegiance and protection." Jefferson—who tinkered with this document through mid-June—would borrow from it in the Declaration of Independence, in some instances word for word.

He also prepared a bill of rights, which protected freedom of the press, forbade standing armies, secured the right to possess firearms, and guaranteed the right to trial by jury, even in vice-admiralty courts. It pledged "full and free liberty of religious opinion" (a far broader protection than the mere "toleration" provided by British law) and ensured extraordinarily liberal rights to immigrants, making them voting citizens if they proved that they intended to reside in the state for seven years. It also overturned primogeniture and entail, providing that "females shall have equal rights with males" when inheriting property, and, most remarkably, asserted that "no person hereafter coming into this county shall be held within the same in slavery under any pretext whatever."[86]

But Jefferson was not recalled to Virginia to work on a new constitution. Things were moving too swiftly, and by the time he mailed his draft to Richmond, the Convention was already putting its finishing touches on a constitution written by George Mason. Still, the Richmond representatives liked Jefferson's preamble, and therefore tacked it on to the front of Mason's proposal, including the list of grievances. The final version declared that "the government of this country, as formerly exercised under the crown of Great Britain" had been "totally dissolved" by King George's "several acts of misrule."[87] The laws Parliament had passed—the source of the constitutional disputes over the previous decade—had not dissolved America's connection to Britain, because those laws had never been valid to begin with. It was George's collusion with Parliament—his refusal to hear colonial pleas and his brutal efforts to enforce unconstitutional laws—that broke the bond of allegiance and rendered it necessary for Virginia to adopt a "regular, adequate mode of civil polity" in place of colonial rule.

The Richmond Convention had also prepared a bill of rights. In the same document that instructed Virginia's congressional delegates to seek independence, it had appointed a committee to draft a declaration that would "secure substantial and equal liberty to the people" of the new state.[88] That committee, again headed by Mason, presented its draft on May 31, and after long debate, the convention approved it on June 12. That Declaration of Rights—the first of its kind in North America—opened with a quick summary of Whig political philosophy:

> That all men are by nature equally free and independent and have certain rights, of which, when they enter into a state of society, they cannot, by any compact, deprive or divest their posterity; namely, the enjoyment of life and liberty, with the means of acquiring and possessing property, and pursuing and obtaining happiness and safety.
>
> That all power is vested in, and consequently derived from, the people; that magistrates are their trustees and servants, and at all times amenable to them.
>
> That government is, or ought to be, instituted for the common benefit, protection, and security of the people, nation, or community; of all the various modes and forms of government, that is best which is capable of producing the greatest degree of happiness and safety . . . and that whenever any government shall be found inadequate or contrary to these purposes, a majority of the community

> has an indubitable, unalienable, and indefeasible right to reform, alter, or abolish it, in such manner as shall be judged most conducive to the public weal.[89]

These principles were plain enough. To say that all people are naturally free and independent, with the right to pursue happiness, means every person is inherently and inescapably self-responsible—meaning people cannot give away either their capacity to act or their liability for the actions they take. If someone is to be held accountable for his actions, he must be free to choose those actions to begin with. Liberty and responsibility are therefore inextricably connected. Moreover, people are responsible not only to others, but also to themselves: They must discharge the obligation of surviving, thriving, and maximizing their own potential, or suffer the consequences. As the 20th-century philosopher Henry Veatch put it, the process of living well is "first, last, and always a do-it-yourself job"—a self-owed duty.[90] And just as people must be free to fulfill their responsibilities to others, so they must be free to fulfill their *self*-responsibilities. That is an inescapable fact of human life: People literally cannot sell or abandon their personalities, and they cannot escape their duties to themselves. A marathoner cannot delegate to another person the obligation to run as best she can, and a poet cannot hire another person to write poems for him—because even if they tried, the accomplishments and rewards would not actually belong to them. In the same way, the individual's essential *obligation/freedom* to accomplish his human purposes cannot be bargained away or surrendered.

In other words, the inherent individuality of human life makes people's rights "inalienable." Mature human beings cannot avoid being held responsible for their actions—and therefore cannot avoid being free to take those actions. (Children are the obvious exception that proves the rule; lacking full self-responsibility, they also don't enjoy the same freedom as adults.) Freedom is not a privilege given to the individual by others, but a basic fact of human life.

These propositions are called "natural law" because they are not "social constructs"—meaning that they are rooted not in tradition or in social convention but in nature, the same way that it is naturally true that poison will kill or that nourishing food will make one healthy. Human beings are *just built that way.* Not only can they not escape their self-responsibility, or the need for freedom that comes with it, but nobody else may justly take away one's freedom, because no person is inherently superior enough to others to entitle him to control another person's choices.

This is what the term "life" refers to in the classic trinity of "life, liberty, and property." As C. Bradley Thompson explains in his philosophical analysis of the Declaration of Independence, the right to life "means the right of each and every individual to take the actions necessary for the support, development, and well-being of his or her own life."[91] A corollary to this is the right to liberty, which "means to be free of physical constraint or force"—that is, the freedom to work toward self-preservation and self-improvement without interference from others.[92] Another corollary is the right to acquire and possess property, because people can only use their liberty to achieve self-preservation and happiness by transforming the external world into the tools and sustenance they need.

The capstone of these rights is the right to pursue and obtain happiness and safety. These terms, which are synonymous with "flourishing," mean the right to be safe in the *enjoyment* of living, enjoyment being not merely a passive sense of relishing one's acquisitions and achievements (although that is sometimes worthwhile), but the *activity* of being the best one can be. A modern cliché holds that life is a journey, not a destination—and people have the right to make that journey without being attacked by highway robbers or obstructed by arbitrary government roadblocks.

It is sometimes claimed that the classical liberalism of the Virginia Declaration of Rights and the Declaration of Independence is rooted in an "optimistic" or even unrealistic notion of human nature.[93] But on the contrary, classical liberalism recognizes that people can be mistaken, foolish, and corrupt—and holds that for that very reason, they cannot be trusted with power over other people's lives. As Jefferson later put it, "Sometimes it is said that man cannot be trusted with the government of himself. Can he, then, be trusted with the government of others?"[94] The most government can or should attempt is to shield individuals from outside harms, so they can make their own decisions. It exists not to ensure that people live "the good life," but to establish the legal framework in which they can figure out how to attain the good life for themselves—not to make them happy, but to let them *pursue* happiness.[95]

This conception is rooted in the ideas of ancient philosophers such as Aristotle, Epicurus, and Cicero, who held that the goal of life is "tranquility of mind."[96] But it also differs in an important way from the world those philosophers knew. While the ancients tended to celebrate the aristocratic values of martial valor and personal glory, the Enlightenment principle of the pursuit of happiness is a fundamentally *bourgeois* notion—one rooted in the peaceful and productive values of equality and reciprocity.[97] Its finest expression, in fact, is to be found in an image from the Old Testament that George Washington was fond of invoking: "They shall sit every man under his vine and under his fig tree, and none shall make them afraid."[98] Government's role is not to give the people abundance, or to improve their souls, or to achieve the greatest good for the race, the *volk*, or the ruler. It exists "for the common benefit, protection, and security of the people, nation, or community," meaning it will ensure against violence and nuisances whereby one person's poor choices might harm another.

Clear as this framework was, however, the framers of the Virginia Declaration of Rights were immediately confronted by the glaring contradiction of slavery. If all people are entitled to freedom, because none are the natural masters of others, did this not mean that enslaved Virginians should be immediately liberated? The Declaration's principal author, George Mason, was himself a slave owner, yet he acknowledged the hypocrisy of demanding freedom for himself while denying it to the people on his plantation. A decade later, he even refused to sign the Constitution because of its compromises with slavery, which he called "detestable," "diabolical," and "disgraceful."[99] Yet Virginians were terrified of the threat of violence if the people they held in bondage were freed, and it was quite clear that the colony's wealthiest slave owners would reject any effort to emancipate them. During the summer of independence, the framers of the Declaration of Rights were stumped by this problem.

Richard Henry Lee's older brother Thomas, then serving as a member of the Richmond Convention, was repulsed by the debate that ensued. "A certain set of aristocrats, for we have such monsters here, finding that their execrable system [of slavery] cannot be reared on such foundations [as equal liberty], have to this time kept us at bay on the first line [of the declaration], which declares all men to be born equally free and independent," he told his brother. "A number of absurd or unmeaning alterations have been proposed . . . [and] the business has been so delayed."[100]

At last, they settled on a legalistic ambiguity, adding the phrase "when they enter into a state of society" to the declaration's assertion of equal freedom. This meant that the Declaration of Rights viewed Africans and their descendants as standing outside of the "state of society," and therefore not entitled to liberty.[101] Yet this weird caveat made no sense in Lockean terms. For one thing, black Virginians *had* entered into a state of society—most spoke English, professed Christianity, and followed the practices of colonial culture. But even if they had not, this wording would still have meant they were entitled to liberty. It said people could not "deprive or divest their posterity" of freedom "by any compact" when they enter into society. Yet if slaves had not entered into society, then they had joined no compact in the first place, and that logically meant that they still possessed *all* their natural rights, undiluted by any agreement. That only made slavery all the worse.

Nevertheless, the Virginians adopted this bizarre compromise language. In doing so, they knew they were only postponing the issue. The final version of the Declaration of Rights was "not without inconsistency," admitted Jefferson's cousin Edmund Randolph. Its twisted wording revealed that the framers had "an indifference to futurity"—that is, little appreciation for how later generations would decipher their wording.[102] But the clause's ambiguity was enough to satisfy the slaveholders for the moment. Virginia would leave the problem of slavery to be resolved later—someday, somehow.

THE MOTION

With his new instructions in hand, Richard Henry Lee rose in Independence Hall on Friday, June 7, 1776, to officially move that the Congress declare the colonies independent. It was already clear that most colonists favored breaking with Britain. It was also clear, however, that unanimity was more necessary on this point than on any previous matter, and several delegates, including those from Pennsylvania and New York, were still governed by official instructions that prohibited them from voting for independence. Some of those instructions were quite stale—New York's legislature, for example, had not issued new instructions to its representatives since April 1775. Yet those directives still limited what delegates could do.

Debate over Lee's motion began the next day and, after a break for Sunday, resumed on Monday, June 10. The only records of these deliberations are Jefferson's own fragmentary notes, which do not identify who said what, although they do indicate the substance of the momentous argument. Opponents of the motion "saw the impossibility that we should ever again be united with Great Britain," but they still resisted independence because some colonies, especially Pennsylvania and New York, "were not yet ripe."[103] Another concern was worldwide opinion: Advocates of separation hoped it would encourage France or other European powers to come to America's aid, but no definite word had been received from Paris or other capitals. Perhaps it would be wiser to wait until after an alliance was formed before making independence official.

Lee, Adams, and George Wythe made easy work of these arguments. "No gentleman," they pointed out, "argued *against* the policy or the right of separation," and those who questioned the timing were viewing things backward: "The people wait for *us* to lead the way."[104] Declaring independence, they added, was not really such a drastic step, anyhow. "We [have] always been independent of them, their restraints on our trade deriving from our acquiescence only, and not from any rights they possessed of imposing them." Thus, the question was "not whether . . . we should make ourselves what we are not; but whether we should declare a fact which already exists."[105] The only political connection between the colonies and the mother country was through the king, and the king had now "dissolved" that bond by "declar[ing] us out of his protection, and by his levying war on us, a fact which had long ago proved us out of his protection."[106] It was clear that London would "accept nothing less than a carte blanche"—that is, total surrender to Parliament's unlimited power.[107] That would never be acceptable.

After two days of debate, five colonies that had opposed independence—New York, New Jersey, Pennsylvania, Delaware, and Maryland—were wavering. The Congress therefore decided on a strategic delay, postponing a vote to let those delegates seek new instructions. That was a critical move, because in some colonies, especially Pennsylvania, the public favored independence far more than the political leadership did. This brief pause offered a chance for some bare-knuckled politics that would dramatically advance the cause of separation.

The process had actually started a month earlier, during arguments over the resolution calling on the colonies to establish new governments—the resolution to which John Adams added his preamble. When the Congress resolved that "the exercise of every kind of authority under the [British] crown should be totally suppressed," everyone knew its primary target was Pennsylvania, which, unlike many colonies, was still operating under its original legislature instead of a convention. That was problematic because the colony's government was highly undemocratic, so that even after elections were held on May 1, the anti-independence minority remained firmly in charge, led by the stubborn John Dickinson. That left Adams and his allies with little alternative but to force the Keystone Colony's hand by directly calling on its people to create a new government—effectively overthrowing the official Pennsylvania assembly. That had been one of the primary goals of Adams's preamble. When Dickinson's New York ally James Duane complained that the new-governments resolution was "a machine for the fabrication of independence," Adams had replied with a devious smile: "It was independence itself."[108]

It was an extreme form of political hardball, but one warranted by the circumstances. By the summer of 1776, the emergency had reached such proportions that for Pennsylvania to hold out made that colony a pressing danger to the emerging nation's security. A decade afterward, when a similar question arose (what would happen if a handful of states refused to ratify the Constitution?), James Madison answered that "the great principle of self-preservation" and "the transcendent law of nature and of nature's God" provided that "all such institutions are to be sacrificed" for the people's "safety and happiness."[109] Circumstances were even more dire in 1776. Overturning the few remaining obstacles to independence was justified.

On May 20, 10 days after the new-governments resolution passed, a crowd of perhaps 4,000 people met in the park in front of Independence Hall, shouting their demands for separation from Britain and disavowing the Pennsylvania assembly as being "bound by oath and allegiance to our enemy."[110] Yet Dickinson and his allies remained unmoved. Although they drafted new instructions for Pennsylvania's congressional representatives in early June, those instructions—written by Dickinson himself—still managed to avoid mentioning independence. Angry Patriots responded by pasting up signs around Philadelphia that denounced the assembly for effectively seceding from the intercolonial union. Then they convened their own "Provincial Conference"—essentially an unauthorized rival legislature. That conference announced a constitutional convention for July and released a public statement on June 24 "declar[ing] our willingness to concur in a vote of the Congress declaring the United Colonies free and independent" and urging the citizens to "endeavor to remove the prejudice of the weak and ignorant respecting the proposed change in our government."[111]

None of this was authorized by Pennsylvania's official legislature, but public allegiance had shifted so drastically that the colony's official assembly was being delegitimized. Its members stopped attending meetings and it faded into nonexistence. By the time the Congress resumed the independence debate, Dickinson had been humiliated: He remained the official representative of a legislature that had vanished into thin air—representing a colony now governed by a "conference" far more favorable to independence than he. Actually, Dickinson was lucky to get off so easily. Similar miniature revolutions broke out in other colonies, sometimes doling out worse fates to those who resisted independence. New Jersey Patriots even arrested their governor—Benjamin Franklin's estranged son William—and threw him in jail for two years.

THE COMMITTEE

Because most colonies supported Lee's independence motion from the outset, the Congress appointed a committee to spend the hiatus preparing a public statement to accompany the resolution, in case it was approved when the Congress reconvened. Along with

Adams—by now the most notorious advocate of independence—the committee included Benjamin Franklin, Connecticut's Roger Sherman, New York's Robert Livingston, and, of course, Thomas Jefferson.

Decades later, Adams related how he had picked Jefferson to take the first crack at writing the Declaration. "Jefferson proposed to me to make the draft," he recalled.

> I said, "I will not." "You should do it." "Oh! no." "Why will you not? You ought do it." "I will not." "Why?" "Reasons enough." "What can be your reasons?" "Reason first—You are a Virginian, and a Virginian ought to appear at the head of this business. Reason second—I am obnoxious, suspected, and unpopular. You are much otherwise. Reason third—You can write ten times better than I can." "Well," said Jefferson, "if you are decided, I will do as well as I can."[112]

Jefferson remembered things differently. In his recollection, the committee of five asked him to prepare the initial draft, and after doing so, he showed it to Adams and Franklin, then presented it to the others. They made changes before passing the final draft to the Congress for another round of edits.[113] This scenario seems more likely, in part because Adams was not "obnoxious" or "unpopular" in the summer of 1776. By the time he wrote down his memories, almost 50 years after the fact, he felt he had become so, but during the independence summer, he had actually been viewed as one of the Congress's leading lights. Still, there were good reasons for a Virginian to appear at the head of the business. As with Washington's appointment as general, it was wise to ensure that independence not be seen as another reckless Massachusetts notion. Unlike the hotheaded Yankees, Virginians had a reputation for calm statesmanship. A pronouncement by one of them would likely carry more gravity.

It's unclear how much Livingston or Sherman contributed. Sherman had long supported independence; he had told Adams in 1775 that Parliament "had authority to make laws for America in *no case whatsoever*."[114] But like Adams, he and Livingston were extraordinarily busy on committees responsible for organizing the

Continental Army and devising a confederation to unify the colonies under one government. Livingston's presence on the committee is notable, by contrast, because he opposed independence. Given the New York delegates' uncertainty regarding their authority—the new instructions that finally arrived from their colonial convention were so confusingly written that New York's delegates ultimately abstained from the independence vote—Livingston may have been chosen to help influence that colony. As for Franklin, he was stricken with an illness that kept him home during most of the writing process. Thus, the primary responsibility for the initial draft fell to the 33-year-old Jefferson.

He wrote with remarkable speed—taking perhaps just two days. His swiftness was partly due to the fact that he could rely on many previous writings: the Boston Pamphlet, the resolutions of the Stamp Act Congress and the First Continental Congress, his own *Summary View*, and the preamble he had written for the Virginia Constitution. But this was not merely for convenience's sake. His task was not to set forth new ideas, but the opposite: to summarize things on which the American people already agreed and that justified their long-delayed separation from Britain.

A mere list of complaints against the imperial government would not be enough. Americans had recited those grievances many times already. Nor would this be a catalog of Parliament's abuses—after all, what was new this time was the Americans' break with the king. Thus, like the English Bill of Rights, the Declaration would have to take the syllogistic form of a criminal indictment—a style familiar to lawyers such as Adams and Jefferson. It would begin with the rules of law, then list King George's offending actions, and conclude that the two nations must separate. That meant Jefferson had to start at the beginning: with the law of nature.

— PART FOUR —

ONE PEOPLE

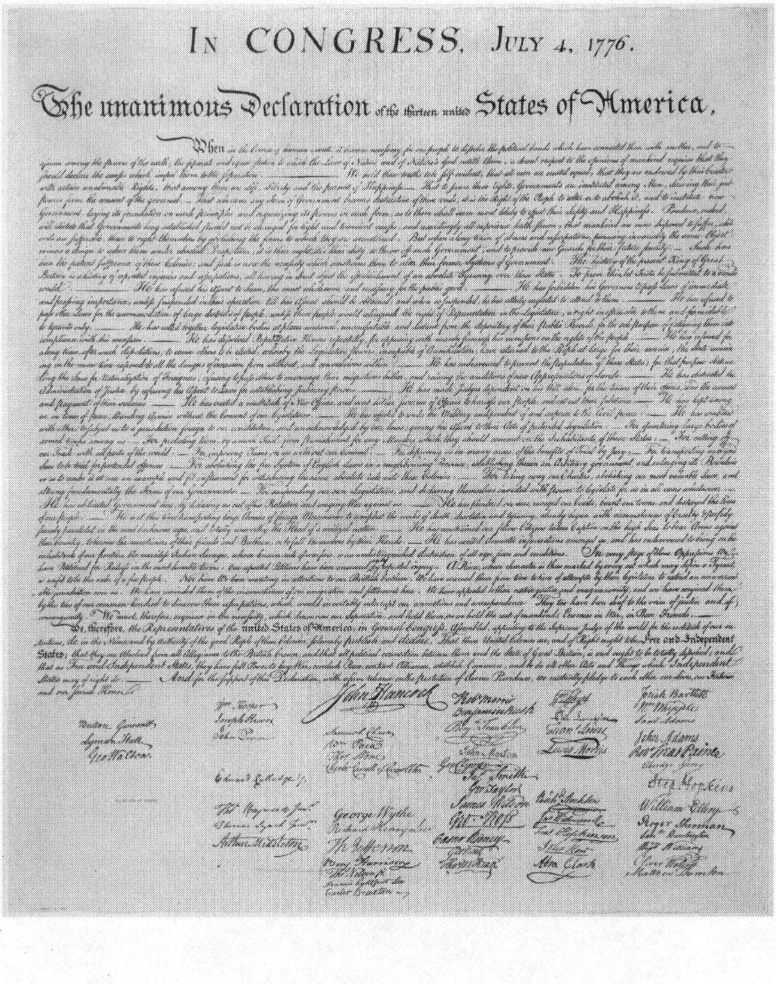
IN CONGRESS, JULY 4, 1776.

The unanimous Declaration of the thirteen united States of America,

— CHAPTER 11 —

UNDERSTANDING THE DECLARATION OF INDEPENDENCE

To place before mankind the common sense of the subject; in terms so plain and firm, as to command their assent, and to justify ourselves in the independent stand we were compelled to take.
—Thomas Jefferson[1]

Thomas Jefferson's draft revealed how much he had learned working with John Dickinson on the Declaration of the Causes and Necessity of Taking Up Arms. The Virginian had started that document with an explanation of why the Continental Congress felt it necessary to make such a statement ("as it behooves those who are called to this great decision to be assured that their cause is approved"), only to have Dickinson replace that with his sketch of the basic premises of classical liberalism. Now, Jefferson did both, opening with an explanation of why Americans were issuing the address and then setting forth the revolutionaries' basic beliefs, before proceeding to a list of specific grievances against King George.

This time, the Americans were not petitioning the monarch, let alone Parliament. Nor were they asking for approval or permission. Instead, this would be a political testament addressed to the world by a nation that had attained its political maturity. "When in the course of human events," it began, "it becomes necessary for a people to advance from that subordination in which they have hitherto remained, and to assume among the powers of the earth . . ."

William Walcutt's 1854 painting Pulling Down the Statue of George III *depicts New Yorkers celebrating independence by destroying a symbol of British rule.*

THE PREMISES

Jefferson's opening lines struck John Adams as close, but not quite right. For one thing, referring to Americans as having "remained" in "subordination" seemed unduly meek. It was wrong to concede that the colonies had ever been "subordinate." As for the word "independent," while noble enough, it was less striking than the more forthright "separate." Adams, Franklin, Sherman, and Livingston made several changes of this sort before they submitted the completed draft to the entire Congress for further editing on June 28. Since then, many scholars have examined each word of the Declaration trying to decipher just who changed what—with notably little success.[2] However the committee of five made its decisions, the version it turned over to the Congress began:

WHEN in the Course of human Events, it becomes necessary for one People to dissolve the Political Bands which have connected them with another, and to assume among the Powers of the Earth the separate and equal Station to which the Laws of Nature and of Nature's God entitle them, a decent Respect to the Opinions of Mankind requires that they should declare the causes which impel them to the Separation.

In the centuries since independence, many intellectuals have quarreled with Jefferson's invocation of the "Laws of Nature and of Nature's God." Some have even argued that classical liberal natural law theory was not really an animating factor in the revolution at all. In his 2025 book, *The Great Contradiction*, historian Joseph Ellis even claimed that the Continental Congress's members were so "fixated" on "their rights as Englishmen" that they "ignored altogether" the Declaration's references to natural law, thereby enabling Jefferson "to smuggle in plain sight, the core principles of the natural rights philosophy into the seminal document of the American founding."[3] Others, such as the 20th-century conservative writer Russell Kirk, have argued that that "the Francophile Jefferson" included this passage as a ploy to persuade Parisian philosophes to ally with the Americans.[4] According to Kirk, natural law played no real role in the revolution; the Patriots were actually seeking to preserve the colonies' traditional autonomy, not to vindicate the radical doctrines of equality and freedom. These assertions echoed the views of South Carolina Senator John C. Calhoun, who in an 1850 speech defending slavery tried to brush off the Declaration's language about equal rights by claiming it was "inserted in our Declaration of Independence without any necessity." The revolution really centered on the "breach of our chartered privileges," he claimed. Classical liberalism had "[no] weight in constructing the governments which were substituted in the place of the colonial."[5]

Such claims are nonsense. Far from being "fixated" on their "English" rights, the Americans had by the spring of 1776 given up on their 12-year effort to lay claim to such rights. Having vainly pleaded with Parliament and King George to respect those rights, they now ceased to assert their Englishness entirely and in the Declaration announced that they were asserting their *human* rights instead. Certainly no "smuggling" was necessary; the natural rights philosophy was ubiquitous in the colonies and had played an important role in the Patriot cause since at least the Boston Pamphlet of 1772. Two years later, the First Continental Congress had debated at length whether to base its arguments on natural law and decided in the affirmative. Nor was any "smuggling" possible, considering that the Declaration was one of the most meticulously edited documents in American history—reviewed by a Congress made up of more than 50 of the country's leading intellectuals. As for seeking to influence France, that country was then governed by an absolute monarch who ruled over his people with a degree of absolutism that exceeded the pretensions of George III by an order of magnitude. Nothing would be less likely to attract Louis XVI's admiration than to announce that every person has inherent rights that no just government may contradict, or that kings are servants rather than masters of the people. Nor was the Continental Congress particularly careful to ensure that he even saw the Declaration. Although the delegates certainly hoped for foreign support, they were so negligent in sending an official copy to Paris that it only arrived in November, well after newspapers had already reported it—hardly an oversight they would have made if their foremost concern had been impressing the French.[6]

As for Calhoun's assertion that natural law principles played no role in the state governments created in 1776, the first line of

Virginia's Bill of Rights is enough to disprove that. Virginians pronounced in the opening sentences of their first state constitution "that all men are by nature equally free and independent and have certain inherent rights," et cetera—language that preceded the Declaration itself by a month. Parliament's "breach of our chartered privileges" may have *initiated* the imperial crisis, but by the summer of independence, both Westminster and Whitehall had proven that those charters were not worth the parchment they were inscribed upon. That forced Americans to take the drastic step of abandoning their chartered privileges and asserting their human rights, instead.

In any case, as Thomas Paine later observed, the distinction between natural rights and the rights of English tradition is to some degree illusory. "The error of those who reason by precedents drawn from antiquity, respecting the rights of man, is that they do not go far enough into antiquity," he wrote. The Patriots may have appealed to precedents of their 17th-century ancestors, but those ancestors had appealed to the precedents of the 15th or 14th centuries, and so on back in time. "If we travel still farther into antiquity," argued Paine, "we shall come to the time when man came from the hand of his Maker. What was he then? *Man*."[7] Arguments based on precedent must eventually "come to the divine origin of the rights of man at the creation," and those inherent human rights must always underlie all political institutions if those institutions are to be legitimate. In short, traditional rights were only arbitrary fictions unless grounded in human nature. And now that Britain had declared colonists ineligible for the protections of British law, the Americans had little choice: They must lay claim to universal principles and natural rights, instead.

But while there was nothing new about Americans asserting their natural rights in 1776, there was a novel phrase in the Declaration's opening paragraph: its reference to "one people." This described what is now called "the American people," a term seldom used before the imperial crisis. Before the adoption of the Sugar and Stamp Acts, colonists rarely even called themselves "American" and would hardly have considered themselves the same "one people" as the residents of other colonies. Now, however, the Declaration announced that they had forged a new *national* identity as a separate people.

That bothered Thomas Hutchinson. The disgruntled former governor of Massachusetts, who had moved to London after being relieved of his governorship two years earlier, published a pamphlet in November 1776 in which he responded to the Declaration point by point. He began by attacking the idea "that the colonies are one distinct people." That was a "false hypothesis," even an "absurd notion," because Americans were and always had been Britons.[8]

That was an ironic assertion from a man who had once said it was "impossible the rights of English subjects should be the same, in every respect, in all parts of the dominions."[9] But in any event, he was wrong. Americans truly had become a distinct people by 1776. Over the century and a half since colonization started, they had developed unique characteristics and mores, as well as special systems of government and even religion. J. Hector St. John de Crèvecoeur, who arrived from France in 1755, wrote that Americans were "western pilgrims" who had escaped the "involuntary idleness, servile dependence, penury, and useless labor" of Europe and had become "a new race . . . whose labors and posterity will one day cause great changes in the world."[10] London's abuses of power in the years since 1764 had now forced them to admit that they comprised a "new race." They honored their English heritage, but they harbored different moral, political, and cultural attitudes. They had grown apart. They had even given up tea.

We hold these Truths to be self-evident, that all Men are created equal, that they are endowed by their Creator with certain unalienable Rights,

Jefferson originally wrote "sacred and undeniable," but changed this to the more succinct "self-evident," possibly at Franklin's suggestion.[11] Ever since, scholars have disputed whether equality and liberty actually are self-evident truths. Much of this quarrel results from confusing "self-evident" with "obvious"—terms that do not mean the same thing. "Self-evident" refers, in the words of philosopher Thomas Reid, to "propositions . . . which appear evident to every man of sound understanding who apprehends the meaning of them distinctly and attends to them without prejudice."[12] The fact that throwing a lit match into water will extinguish it is self-evident, for instance, because anyone with enough experience to know what these words mean will need no demonstration to prove it. Self-evidence also differs from what philosophers call "analytic truths"—a phrase that refers to conclusions that are logically implicit in the premises of a syllogism—because recognizing a self-evident truth may require familiarity with the actual (or "contingent") world. Yet "self-evident" is also not synonymous with the experimental demonstrations of the physical sciences. The fact that gravity is proportional to mass is not a self-evident truth. The fact that rocks fall to the ground when dropped is.

Not only can *facts* be self-evident, but so can *rules*. The rule "two wrongs don't make a right" is self-evident. So is "innocent until proven guilty." The former means that justice cannot be achieved through injustice, and the latter that a person who accuses another of a crime bears the burden of proving his guilt, which is an implicit rule of logic.

The Golden Rule is also a self-evident truth; it requires no investigation to justify it beyond an ordinary acquaintance with human nature. Because we know that every person is an essentially self-directed, self-responsible, self-interested being seeking to survive and thrive, we expect others to resent being harmed and to appreciate being helped, just as we would. Consequently, the basic principle of interpersonal morality—to treat others as one wishes to be treated—is self-evident to anyone sufficiently acquainted with human beings to form a mature judgment. Although it might be illustrated, rephrased, or elaborated on, it need not be *proven* beyond ordinary experience. The principle that "all men are created equal" is equally self-evident; indeed, it is implicit in the Golden Rule. No ordinary adult is marked out as so far superior that he is entitled to run the life of another in the same way that a parent is (self-evidently) responsible for his child's welfare. And because each person is responsible to both himself and others, each is equally entitled to freedom.

One persistent myth about the Declaration is that Jefferson and his colleagues meant not that all *individuals* have equal rights, but only that the colonies, as government entities, were the *political* equal of other sovereign nations.[13] No evidence supports this interpretation. Instead, the Declaration clearly speaks the language of Lockean natural rights theory, which holds that every *person* enjoys the same autonomy and responsibility as all others.[14] Americans surely thought their governments were entitled to respect, but that was because those governments represented *individuals* who, according to Lockean theory, have equal rights.

The Declaration's individualism also explains one of its most striking features: its lack of any reference to racial, religious, or cultural ties as the foundation of political union.[15] The "one people" to which it refers are bound together not by shared ancestry, religion, or even language, but by their recognition of the self-evident truths it pronounces. Equally striking is that the Declaration sets forth *truths* as the foundation stone of the American polity—not noble lies as in Plato's *Republic* or religious dogma as in the Mayflower Compact. Rooted in reason and deliberation, rather than accident and force, the Declaration even acknowledges that "mankind" have a variety of "opinions" and that these deserve "respect." Where the Mayflower Compact began "We, whose names are underwritten . . . having undertaken for the glory of God and advancement of the Christian faith, and the honor of our king and country," the Declaration pronounces an inherently universal doctrine, comprehensible by unassisted reason.[16]

Another common misunderstanding is the idea that the equality principle only applies in the state of nature, and therefore that the Declaration's authors did not mean it to refer to actual people in contemporaneous times.[17] This charge makes no sense because, according to Lockean liberalism, the equality of people in the state of nature has crucial implications for the governments people form when establishing civil society. Equality is, for example, what justifies—indeed, mandates—government by consent. It also forbids rulers from arbitrarily favoring some citizens over others when exercising authority. The equality of which the Declaration speaks is the equality of individual rights—not a merely abstract notion but a standard by which all actual governments must abide.

By "created equal," the Declaration obviously does not mean that people are equal in terms of talents, skills, or character or that they should be made equal through the redistribution of wealth or by compelling some to labor for others. It just means that nobody is entitled to dictate how others may live. Put another way, the natural equality that characterizes human nature *is* the possession of the same basic freedom.[18] People are born into unequal circumstances—some rich and others poor. They may use their rights in ways that make them unequal—some may work hard and prosper, while others invest their resources foolishly and suffer. None of this is relevant, however, to the Declaration's contention that they are equally entitled, indeed *required by nature*, to manage their own lives.

Jefferson modeled the equality clause on the Virginia Declaration of Rights, which observed in its first section that "all men are by nature equally free and independent and have certain inherent rights." Striving for Tacitus-like concision, he realized that George Mason's phrasing ("equally free and independent") could be collapsed into "created equal" and that "by nature" and "inherent" are technically redundant. He also moved the term "inalienable," which occurs elsewhere in the Virginia Declaration, into the opening sentence. Mason had declared that the right to alter or abolish government is "indubitable, inalienable, and indefeasible"—a triple redundancy Jefferson streamlined by calling these rights "inalienable."

As noted in chapter 3, "inalienability" was crucial to refute Thomas Hobbes's argument that when people establish government, they surrender all their rights to it. Hobbes concluded from this premise that rebellion against government is never justifiable, even if rulers abuse their power. Although few in America or Britain openly embraced Hobbes's philosophy in the 1770s, some did contend that rebellion against government was never acceptable. Many Quakers and Anglicans in particular argued that Christianity required passive obedience in all circumstances. Others claimed that the colonists had surrendered their claims to self-government when they accepted royal charters in the 17th century and acquiesced in Parliament's legislation in the years after that. Americans raised no ruckus against the Declaratory Act and failed to declare the Navigation Acts unconstitutional. Did that not amount to waiving their rights? By asserting *inalienability*, Jefferson replied that the colonists could not be bound by any previous agreement that intruded too deeply into the liberty to which everyone is entitled.

There's another revealing divergence between Jefferson's language and that used in the Virginia Declaration. Where the Virginians, in an effort not to offend slaveholders, inserted the weird qualifier "when they enter into a state of society," Jefferson declined to follow their lead. Instead, his wording asserts unequivocally that the equality of rights is inherent in human beings, whose rights may never be justly taken away.

That among these are Life, Liberty, and the Pursuit of Happiness;

Jefferson's decision to modify Locke's traditional trio of rights—life, liberty, and property (or "estate")—has led to confusion over the years.[19] Some have asserted that substituting "pursuit of happiness" for "property" signaled that property is less important than other rights. But Jefferson and his colleagues viewed the right to buy, sell, own, and use property as indispensable to personal freedom. The real reason Jefferson used "pursuit of happiness" is more subtle.

In writing the Virginia Declaration, George Mason had identified the basic rights as "the enjoyment of life and liberty, with the means of acquiring and possessing property, and pursuing and obtaining happiness and safety," a phrase that was more comprehensive but also wordier. Steeped in the ideas of such philosophers as Aristotle, Epicurus, and Cicero, who held that "happiness" or "flourishing" is the purpose of existence, Mason, like Jefferson and Adams, thought the ultimate good of human activity is the well-lived individual life. The reason to acquire and possess property is that it helps one flourish. Thus, in simplifying Mason's philosophical assertions, Jefferson was saying that people have specific rights *because* they have the more general right to pursue happiness.

One aspect of this right that scholars too often neglect is its foundational connection to economic freedom. Many Americans in 1776 owned few or no tangible assets—especially immigrants, who often reached American cities penniless, as Franklin had in Philadelphia more than 50 years before. Immigration to America surged in the mid-18th century, with perhaps 400,000 Europeans arriving between 1740 and 1770, many owning nothing but their labor.[20]

Locke considered labor a kind of property, and the Scottish moral philosopher Adam Smith agreed in *Wealth of Nations*, published just four months before the Declaration. "The property which every man has in his own labor, as it is the original foundation of all other property, so it is the most sacred and inviolable," Smith wrote. "The patrimony of a poor man lies in the strength and dexterity of his hands." To deprive someone of the right to use his labor to earn a living "in what manner he thinks proper" is therefore "a manifest encroachment upon the just liberty both of the workman, and of those who might be disposed to employ him."[21]

Jefferson had been among the most outspoken critics of British trade restrictions, arguing in *A Summary View* and his responses to Lord North that mercantilism unjustly deprived workingmen of their right to earn a living. In short, the phrase "pursuit of happiness" refers to *freedom of opportunity*. It encompasses the principle that people have the right to use their liberty to obtain property and thereby enjoy happiness in peace.

Considering that in the American cultural tradition, opportunity has always been closely associated with the West, it was fitting that this phrase would originate with Jefferson, who was essentially a Westerner. He was conscious of the fact himself. A year earlier, in his draft of the Declaration of the Causes and Necessity of Taking Up Arms, he had written that "the political institutions of America, its various soils and climates, opened a certain resource to the unfortunate and to the enterprising of every country, and ensured to them the acquisition and free possession of property."[22] Aware that immigrants typically came in hopes of using their labor to acquire land and build a future on the frontier, he now articulated a distinctively American political vision, rooted in European classical liberalism, but with a special emphasis on the freedom to grow, improve, and prosper.

Another subtle but important innovation in the Declaration's phrasing is its use of the word "liberty" in the singular, rather than the plural form. In ancient legal documents such as the Magna Carta, kings gave the people lists of specific "liberties"—using the plural because the monarch was granting only a finite number of rights. Reversing that idea, the Declaration asserts that people naturally enjoy "liberty"—a word that literally means an infinite number of freedoms—and that government's powers, not individual rights, are finite and limited.[23] Jefferson himself later defined "liberty" as "unobstructed action according to our will, within the limits drawn around us by the equal rights of others," with the caveat, "I do not add 'within the limits of the law'; because law is often but the tyrant's will, and always so when it violates the right of an individual."[24]

Whereas ancient legal documents presumed that the king owned all rights and could parcel them out as he chose, the Declaration views the individual as presumptively free, with the people giving the government its powers piecemeal. As James Madison put it, in an essay contrasting the Magna Carta with the Declaration: "In Europe, charters of liberty have been granted by power. America has set the example . . . of charters of power granted by liberty."[25]

That to secure these Rights, Governments are instituted among Men, deriving their just Powers from the Consent of the Governed, that whenever any Form of Government becomes destructive of these Ends, it is the Right of the People to alter or to abolish it, and to institute new Government, laying its Foundation on such Principles, and organizing its Powers in such Form, as to them shall seem most likely to effect their Safety and Happiness.

The Declaration holds that government's purpose is to preserve—to secure—the rights that belong to people both by nature and by acquisition. This principle traced its origin not only to 17th-century classical liberals such as Locke but to ancient thinkers as well. "The chief purpose in the establishment of the constitutional state," wrote Cicero, was that "individual property rights might be secured."[26]

By the time of the revolution, the idea that government is an essentially contractual relationship, in which the authorities derive their powers from the consent of the governed, was commonplace. Even Loyalists generally agreed with it; they simply argued that Americans *were* represented in Parliament, in an abstract sense, or that by emigrating to America, their forebears had surrendered the right to vote.[27] But the Declaration sets that debate aside entirely. Instead, it invokes consent as justifying the right of *revolution*. Because government officials are servants, not masters, the people may alter or abolish unsatisfactory governments and create whatever alternative they think will better serve their needs.

There's an important limit, however. Only "*just* powers" derive from the consent of the governed; the people have no right to give their government *un*just powers. Just as they cannot rightly commit robbery or murder, so they cannot deputize the government to do so. That explains why the Declaration's closing lines assert that the new states may only do "acts and things which independent states may *of right* do." The principle that government's powers are cabined by the universal principles of justice runs throughout the Declaration's text, which refers to justice more than to any other value except liberty.[28] Because government exists to secure individual rights, the people are justified in changing or overthrowing it if it fails in that task.

Consent therefore plays a dual role, both justifying and limiting government power. As Jefferson later said, the people "are inherently independent of all *but moral* law."[29] The people cannot consent to tyrannical or despotic governments, even if they were so deluded as to try. Nor can they excuse evil government actions by "consenting" to them. Implicitly recognizing the risk of the "tyranny of the majority," the Declaration sees democracy as an *instrumental* good—not as an end, but as a means to achieving a higher political value: the preservation of individual freedom. As Jefferson put it, while "the will of the majority is in all cases to prevail, that will to be rightful must be reasonable" and must recognize that "the minority possess their equal rights, which equal law must protect."[30]

This implicit prioritization of rights over democracy has proven to be one of the Declaration's most controversial features, as critics claim that its individualist vision elevates "selfishness" over "community" or "the common good." But the Declaration recognizes that the preservation of each individual's freedom *is* the common good, at least as far as the political realm is concerned. It is the only political ambition that, when achieved, imposes no injustice upon some people for the gratification of others. Nothing about this fact is inconsistent with acknowledging the importance of community, the value of helping the less fortunate, or the need to work together to address social ills such as poverty or pollution. In fact, working to remedy such problems can sometimes bring one more personal "happiness" than the acquisitive and productive activities of the marketplace. But the Declaration recognizes that most of these issues are better addressed through "civil society"—the realm of private charitable and social organizations, which operate on the basis of personal choice and voluntary cooperation—than in the political realm, which is governed by compulsion.

The Declaration's recognition that preserving individual freedom is the highest political good—the only truly *common* political good—does not, as communitarians sometimes charge, make it a manifesto for so-called atomistic individualism.[31] Rather, it recognizes that social problems are often too complicated to be solved by government and that efforts to impose political solutions for social problems usually backfire, worsening the original problem and violating the rights of the innocent. Thus, the best way to address them is typically through private institutions—charities, churches, trade organizations, and the like—for the same reason that the best kinds of interpersonal relationships are those we freely choose.[32] In short, the Declaration prioritizes the individual's right to pursue his or her own happiness, while recognizing that this pursuit is often most fruitful in the company of others. That explains why it ends with one of the strongest forms of community bond imaginable: a mutual pledge of life, fortune, and sacred honor.

Prudence, indeed, will dictate that Governments long established should not be changed for light and transient Causes; and accordingly all Experience hath shewn, that Mankind are more disposed to suffer, while Evils are sufferable, than to right themselves by abolishing the Forms to which they are accustomed. But when a long Train of Abuses and Usurpations, pursuing invariably the same Object, evinces a Design to reduce them under absolute Despotism, it is their Right, it is their Duty, to throw off such Government, and to provide new Guards for their future Security.

Jefferson said that he consulted no books or pamphlets when writing the Declaration but that when Richard Henry Lee saw it, he "charged it as copied from Locke."[33] If so, Lee had a keen eye. In 1689, Locke phrased his rationale for revolution in quite similar terms. It was "evident in itself," he wrote, that "all mankind" are created "equal and independent," and that although they "are more disposed to suffer, than [to] right themselves by resistance," the people have the right "whenever the legislators endeavor to take away, and destroy [their] property," or "endeavor to grasp themselves, or put into the hands of any other, an absolute power over [their] lives, liberties, and estates," to "resume their original liberty, and, by the establishment of a new legislative, such as they shall think fit, provide for their own safety and security."[34] In the *Second Treatise*'s closing chapters, Locke responded to those who feared that this principle would lead to frequent rebellions. Revolutions, he explained, are not justified by "every little mismanagement in public affairs" or even "great mistakes" by rulers. Instead, the people have a right to rebel only when "a long train of abuses, prevarications, and artifices, all tending the same way," prove that the authorities are seeking "to reduce them to slavery under arbitrary power."[35]

Jefferson had used markedly similar wording in *A Summary View*—written only five years after his intense, self-directed crash course on political theory—and now he used it in the Declaration.[36] Of course, these parallels are no surprise; by the summer of 1776, Locke's wording had been quoted and paraphrased so often in declarations, petitions, and newspaper debates that most Patriot leaders could recite it by heart.

Although Locke's arguments for revolution were well-known on both sides of the Atlantic, they remained controversial in the 1770s, despite the Glorious Revolution having vindicated them almost a century earlier. William Blackstone, for example, thought they could justify rebelling against a king but not against Parliament, which "has absolute, sovereign, and uncontrollable authority." Acknowledging that "Mr. Locke and other theoretical writers" had reasoned to the contrary, Blackstone concluded that their views, "however just . . . in theory," could never be accepted in practice. On the contrary, "as [long as] the English constitution lasts . . . the power of Parliament is absolute and without control."[37]

Jefferson took the opposite view. No government that claims "absolute" power can ever be legitimate, because the people can no more surrender their rights to a legislature than they can to a king. Their rights are "inalienable," meaning that the people en masse always retain the power to change their government and even overthrow it if it becomes abusive enough. In fact, the Declaration calls this not just a right, but a "duty"—a duty the people owe to themselves and their children (whose rights they have no authority to abandon). This duty was so essential that Franklin even incorporated it into a proposed national motto. In the weeks following independence, when the Continental Congress considered adopting a new set of symbols for use in official documents, Franklin designed a national seal depicting Moses parting the Red Sea, surrounded by the words "Rebellion to tyrants is obedience to God."[38] His proposal was rejected, but Jefferson liked the slogan so much he had it painted on his dishes. He gave one of the bowls to John Adams as a present.[39]

Such has been the patient Sufferance of these Colonies; and such is now the Necessity which constrains them to alter their former Systems of Government. The History of the present King of Great Britain is a History of repeated Injuries and Usurpations, all having in direct Object the Establishment of an absolute Tyranny over these States. To prove this, let Facts be submitted to a candid World.

This passage marks the first mention of the king—against whom the entire Declaration was addressed. The document never refers to Parliament by name, calling it only "a jurisdiction foreign to our constitution"—which was consistent with the Patriots' view that Westminster never had legislative authority over the colonies in the first place. They thought Americans were bound to the British political system only by sharing the same monarch, which was why they had consistently professed loyalty to George III, even if they sometimes did so through clenched teeth. They thought the king's job was to stand above the political system, adjudicating disputes among subjects. Yet George had now declared himself unwilling to do that, thus breaking the reciprocal bond of allegiance and protection. Because that was the sole thread connecting America with Britain, severing it rendered the colonies independent.

Fifty years later, Adams claimed that he had disliked Jefferson's reference to George as a "tyrant." He remembered thinking the charge "too personal," adding that he "never believed George to be a tyrant in disposition and in nature." Calling the king tyrannical was "too passionate and too much like scolding."[40] But by the time he wrote this, Adams's memory was influenced by memories of the French Revolution and the Napoleonic Wars, which had drawn his sympathies toward England. During the independence summer, by contrast, he offered no objection to the word "tyrant."[41]

In fact, it was appropriate. Tyrants rule by fear and intimidation rather than consent, and by 1776, George had made clear that he intended to subdue the Americans by violence and terror. What's more, he approved Parliament's claim to total authority over the colonies—a degree of absolutism that included the power to override fundamental constitutional guarantees. His support for parliamentary absolutism was not inevitable; he could have chosen otherwise. Yet he insisted on backing up Westminster's assertions with overwhelming force, proving much more belligerent than even most of his subordinates. As historian Andrew O'Shaughnessy observes, George was "the main driving force of the British war for America," regularly urging violence even when his advisers recommended against it.[42]

Still, Adams was right to detect a "personal" tone in Jefferson's initial draft. Some passages even struck a melodramatic note, complaining that America's "unfeeling" British "brethren" had ignored their complaints and that by reelecting Lord North's government in the 1774 parliamentary elections, the British people had "given the last" to the Americans' "agonizing affection." The Congress removed these lachrymose phrases, making the Declaration more dignified and timeless.

But Jefferson was not finished with George III. He never could view the king's policies as the product of a decent human character, and that low opinion was confirmed a decade later when he met the king in person. In March 1786, Adams, serving as American ambassador in London, had the opportunity to introduce the Virginian to Britain's ruler. The meeting went badly. "It was impossible for anything to be more ungracious," Jefferson recalled. Whether the king turned his back on the Americans, as legend has it, or showed them some other rudeness, Jefferson said afterward: "I saw at once that the ulcerations in the narrow mind of that mulish being left nothing to be expected on the subject of my attendance."[43] He could not resist pointing out that George had literally ended up in a straitjacket.

Jefferson had the same contempt for other kings. Louis XVI was "a fool, of my own knowledge." The kings of Spain, Portugal, and other countries were "fools" and "idiot[s]." The king of Prussia was "a mere hog." He thought their mental infirmities were due to inbreeding and debilitating luxury. "Take any race of animals, confine them in idleness and inaction, whether in a sty, a stable, or a stateroom, pamper them with high diet, gratify all their sexual appetites, immerse them in sensualities, nourish their passions, let everything bend before them, and banish whatever might lead them to think, and in a few generations they become all body and no mind."[44] Jefferson, in fact, detested the British empire, viewing it as a corrupting influence in the world. Adams, however, never shook his belief that, as warped as Britain's political system might be, its art, culture, and law were invaluable inheritances, and that Americans and Britons must always enjoy—to use the diplomatic language of a later age—a "special relationship."

THE GRIEVANCES

Having set out the major premise—that any ruler who violates the principles of justice and seeks to destroy individual liberty is unworthy of allegiance—Jefferson proceeded to the minor premise: the list of incidents that proved George III had violated his subjects' trust. In framing this list, Jefferson used the wording he had prepared for the new Virginia Constitution, as well as the list of complaints from his *Summary View*. To these were added grievances from the Boston Pamphlet, probably at Adams's recommendation, as well as other items. After the committee of five submitted its draft to the Congress for editing, the delegates spent two days revising the list. As finally adopted on July 4, the list began:

He has refused his Assent to Laws, the most wholesome and necessary for the public Good.

As soon as the Declaration was made public, critics began complaining that the grievances were so broadly worded that it was hard to determine which exact actions the colonists were referring to. But the Congress had good reason for avoiding specifics. Countless other resolutions had already listed the laws to which Americans objected; the First Continental Congress had even provided citations so people could look them up. To do that again would bog down the Declaration and invite critics to dispute every jot and tittle. The time for such quibbling had passed. The English Bill of Rights in 1689 used general terms to indict James II, and the Declaration's Framers followed that lead.

Still, today's readers are sometimes puzzled about which "wholesome" laws the Crown blocked. To begin with, colonists objected to the very fact that their legislation was always subject to a London veto. In some cases, the king ordered governors to reject whole categories of laws. The colonies were not allowed to grant divorces, for example, without royal approval.[45] Colonial governors were commanded to block bills to tax European imports or to pay colonial lobbyists in London.[46] Worse, the home government had for decades barred the colonies from printing their own money. This created a chronic cash shortage, which forced Americans to barter or use complicated accounting devices to pay their bills, often at a financial loss. This policy of starving the colonists of cash could have cruel consequences in an age when debt was punishable by imprisonment. A borrower forced to settle up by selling his belongings might receive only half or a quarter of their value, effectively forcing him to pay double. Not only did London repeatedly bar the colonies from issuing currency—first by royal decree, then by statute in 1751 and 1764[47]—but also it blocked colonial attempts to adopt bankruptcy legislation.[48] Colonists might easily die in debtors' prison as a result of such policies.

Jefferson, however, had another, more important class of legislation in mind: The king forbade the colonists from adopting laws restricting the importation of slaves. The colonies—especially Virginia—had repeatedly tried to ban or restrict slave imports, only to be overridden by London. To Jefferson and other anti-slavery Patriots, restricting the slave trade offered a potential first step toward eliminating slavery itself. But the imperial government made clear that it would not allow Americans to hurt the Royal African Company's bottom line. Thus, as Jefferson complained in *A Summary View*, King George preferred "the immediate advantages of a few African corsairs"—that is, British slave catchers—"to the lasting interests of the American states, and to the rights of human nature, [which were] deeply wounded by this infamous practice."[49]

HE has forbidden his Governors to pass Laws of immediate and pressing Importance, unless suspended in their Operation till his Assent should be obtained; and when so suspended, he has utterly neglected to attend to them.

The royal veto meant that bills passed by American legislatures had to be shipped to England for review and, if approved, sent back before going into effect. This process took months even if the king's officers acted quickly. In practice, however, the Colonial Office and the king's Privy Council often took much longer. In 1770, for example, Virginia lawmakers passed a bill to prevent horse stealing; the Board of Trade in London did not get around to approving it until March 1773.[50] One New Jersey bill went eight years before being reviewed by the board. A South Carolina law adopted in 1696 was blocked in 1734.[51] A New Hampshire statute passed in 1718 was not reviewed until 1769—and then it was vetoed.[52] London also required colonial bills to contain "suspending clauses," postponing implementation until royal approval could be obtained.[53] The delays and disruptions caused by this protracted process and the potential of after-the-fact vetoes rendered colonial lawmaking a frustrating, insulting, and often futile process.

He has refused to pass other Laws for the Accommodation of large Districts of People, unless those People would relinquish the Right of Representation in the Legislature, a Right inestimable to them, and formidable to Tyrants only.

After the French and Indian War, the British government grew increasingly uncomfortable with the rapid expansion of the American colonies. Westward movement in particular seemed to threaten London's hegemony, because the larger the population and the more distant from the imperial capital, the more independent-minded Americans would become. One London intellectual urged Parliament "to obstruct than encourage" American westward movement, because otherwise "an army of an hundred thousand" would "not be able to control" the colonists, "whose hearts glow with the flame of liberty."[54] The government accordingly began discouraging emigration to America—for example, nullifying colonial offers to pay travel costs for immigrants or to give them free land.[55] It also sought to prevent the colonies from reapportioning their legislatures to accommodate people who moved west.

Population growth radically distorted the apportionment of these legislatures. In Pennsylvania, for example, the ratio went from one representative for every 336 adult white males in 1730 to one representative for every 1,301 in 1770.[56] Yet the colonies—especially Virginia, Massachusetts, New York, New Jersey, and New Hampshire—were forbidden to take steps to give frontier towns their own representatives.[57] In North Carolina alone, the Colonial Office vetoed 13 bills providing for the creation of new townships to prevent additional representatives from being added to the colony's legislature.[58]

He has called together Legislative Bodies at Places unusual, uncomfortable, and distant from the Depository of their public Records, for the sole Purpose of fatiguing them into Compliance with his Measures.

This grievance did not appear in Jefferson's initial draft and was probably added at Adams's urging. He had participated in the months-long dispute with Governor Hutchinson over moving the Massachusetts legislature from Boston to Cambridge, and he knew of General Gage's order moving the legislature to Salem in 1774. The worst abuse had occurred not in Massachusetts but in South Carolina, where the governor ordered the legislature to meet in Beaufort instead of Charleston for the express purpose of preventing his political opponents from attending. These ploys—which doubtless brought to mind the schemes of the Stuart monarchs (especially Charles II, who in 1681 moved Parliament from London to Oxford because its residents were more supportive of the monarchy)—had no other purpose than to subvert the constitution by silencing the people's representatives.

He has dissolved Representative Houses repeatedly, for opposing with manly Firmness his Invasions on the Rights of the People.

Practically all the colonies had their legislatures closed, at least temporarily, by royal governors seeking to silence opposition to Parliament's authority. Representatives in Virginia and Massachusetts were repeatedly sent home for passing resolutions against unconstitutional taxes and regulations, and Parliament had adopted laws permanently closing the legislatures of Massachusetts and New York.

Westminster viewed such actions as unremarkable, because it saw colonial assemblies as subordinate institutions. But to the colonists, who thought their legislatures were miniature parliaments, these were outrageous violations of political autonomy.

He has refused for a long Time, after such Dissolutions, to cause others to be elected; whereby the Legislative Powers, incapable of Annihilation, have returned to the People at large for their exercise; the State remaining in the meantime exposed to all the Dangers of Invasion from without, and Convulsions within.

This accusation drew another subtle but suggestive parallel between George III and the Stuart kings. Attempting to rule without Parliament was widely viewed as among the Stuart dynasty's worst offenses; one that justified the civil war and the Glorious Revolution. Now, America's governors—the king's representatives—had repeatedly shut down colonial legislatures, then delayed reopening them for so long as to render it impossible for the representatives to conduct business. The Massachusetts legislature was closed indefinitely. Governor Dunmore had prorogued Virginia's legislature in August 1774 and only called them back into session when forced to, nearly a year later. North Carolina's governor dissolved the legislature then fled the colony. In South Carolina, a furious dispute between the governor and the assembly led to four prorogations in the space of 18 months, with the result that the colony adopted no legislation *at all* after February 1771.[59]

Colonists had responded to these closures by establishing "conventions" to operate in place of their legislatures, but British authorities refused to acknowledge the conventions' legitimacy. The Declaration justified them by invoking Lockean natural law theory: The lawmaking power is "incapable of annihilation" because it belongs inherently to the people. If Parliament closed their legislatures, "the people at large" were free to establish new ones and even entirely new state governments.

He has endeavored to prevent the Population of these States; for that Purpose obstructing the Laws for Naturalization of Foreigners; refusing to pass others to encourage their Migrations hither, and raising the Conditions of new Appropriations of Lands.

Americans knew immigration was key to economic and social growth. "In Europe," wrote Jefferson, "the object is to make the most of their land, labor being abundant," whereas in America, the goal was "to make the most of our labor, land being abundant."[60] The same logic, however, made Britain increasingly suspicious of immigrants. The 1660 Navigation Act expressly barred anyone not English-born from working as a merchant or from commanding a trading vessel.[61] Even ships purchased in the colonies from foreigners were subjected to heavy tariffs.[62] Meanwhile, the lack of a uniform naturalization policy led to frustrating inconsistencies. Naturalization in one colony was invalid in other colonies.[63] Colonies resorted to naturalizing people on a case-by-case basis, but London barred Virginia from doing so, allowing only the governor personally to naturalize immigrants.[64] Then, the Colonial Office instructed America's royal governors not to sign any naturalization laws.[65]

The empire cracked down still further in the mid-1770s. Fearing that America's growth threatened its hegemony and was draining talent from the Old World to the New, London banned colonial governors from approving naturalizations "upon any pretense whatsoever."[66] It also barred nonnaturalized foreigners from owning land in the colonies. This tended to reinforce London's autocratic rule, since voting rights depended on property ownership. The government followed that up by prohibiting colonies from giving away land to newcomers, as they had done for years in hopes of attracting immigrants. From now on, Parliament said, colonial governments had to sell land to the highest bidder—and sell it with a quitrent attached.[67]

Even banning land grants wasn't enough for some. In May 1774, Governor Dunmore urged the Colonial Office to make sure only "men of credit and ability" bought property on the frontier, because the West was "becoming the asylum" of "disorderly and unruly people . . . who, carrying with them an abhorrence of all authority and control, establish themselves in defiance of both and become the continual plague and embarrassment of every government."[68] Parliament, in short, was using its control over land titles as a choke chain on America's rapidly growing population.

HE has obstructed the Administration of Justice, by refusing his Assent to Laws for establishing Judiciary Powers.

HE has made Judges dependent on his Will alone, for the Tenure of their Offices, and the Amount and Payment of their Salaries.

In his first draft, Jefferson accused the king of "suffer[ing] the administration of justice totally to cease in some of these colonies" by "refusing his assent to laws for establishing judiciary powers," but the Congress moderated his language.[69] The courts had indeed ceased to operate in Virginia and Massachusetts—in Virginia because Dunmore dissolved the legislature before it adopted a "fee bill" and in Massachusetts because jurymen refused to proceed under a system in which judges were paid directly by the king.

North Carolina courts were also closed, thanks to a years-long dispute regarding laws that enabled American lenders to "attach" the assets of English borrowers who failed to pay their bills. The right to seize assets from British debtors was crucial to American businessmen, who had no other practical way to recover from defaulting borrowers located across the sea. But in 1772, London officials forbade the colony's legislature from authorizing this practice. Thus, when lawmakers defiantly included a foreign attachments provision in a bill to reform their legal system, Royal Governor Josiah Martin blocked it. The legislators responded by refusing to establish a court system unless he backed down. It was unfair, they argued, that imperial officials let New York and Pennsylvania adopt foreign attachment laws, but not North Carolina. An impasse ensued. Martin tried organizing a separate judicial system on his own prerogative, but Patriots argued that this was unconstitutional. Courts, argued James Iredell—a Patriot who later served on the US Supreme Court—could only be established "with the consent of the inhabitants, signified either by themselves or their deputies in some public act."[70] North Carolina's judiciary therefore closed in 1773 and remained closed when the war broke out.[71]

These were just some of the many clashes between Britain and the colonies over the organization of their judicial systems. The king had also disallowed the creation of a Pennsylvania Supreme Court unless the legislature narrowed its jurisdiction, blocked New York from empowering justices of the peace to decide cases involving less than £5 in damages, and vetoed a Virginia law that would have barred appeals of lawsuits involving fewer than £10.[72] He barred efforts by Pennsylvania, New York, and both Carolinas to provide judges with lifetime terms and in 1761 instructed colonial governors to veto all such bills in the future.[73] The empire wanted judges to answer to London, not to Americans.

In editing this clause, the Congress removed Jefferson's claim that the administration of justice had *totally* ceased, probably because by mid-1776 the colonists were beginning to establish their own alternatives. Nevertheless, former Massachusetts Governor Thomas Hutchinson objected even to the more moderate assertion that the administration of justice had been "obstructed." In his pamphlet criticizing the Declaration, he claimed that the only example he could think of was the North Carolina foreign attachment dispute, which he considered trivial.[74] He ignored the closure of courts in Virginia, the disputes in Pennsylvania and other colonies, and the long history of fights between London and the colonies regarding the independence of judges.

Judicial independence was crucial to the Americans, however, and especially to John Adams, who thought it essential to constitutional government. When London announced plans to pay judges' salaries directly, he had maintained that this would make it impossible for Americans to obtain justice when challenging the government in court. Judges would inevitably fall prey to a "base servility of spirit" toward their paymasters and engage in "sordid, nauseous, and impious adulations to [their] superiors" rather than deciding cases neutrally.[75] Adams would have had little patience for those who today claim that judicial review (the power of a court to declare a law unconstitutional) was an invention of the 19th century, or who assert that this practice is undemocratic and that courts should be "restrained" instead of "active."[76] Courts had always held the power to declare laws unconstitutional, and in Adams' view, a vigilant and independent judiciary was indispensable to the rule of law and the preservation of liberty.

HE has erected a Multitude of new Offices, and sent hither Swarms of Officers to harass our People, and eat out their Substance.

Here Jefferson employed the "swarms" metaphor that had already become a staple of American Patriot rhetoric.[77] It was an apt image indeed to describe the plight of a people who were being governed like conquered foreigners doomed to labor for London's enrichment, rather than for themselves. Such a life was the opposite of the American ideal of personal independence. But in his pamphlet answering the Declaration, Thomas Hutchinson ridiculed the "swarms" complaint, arguing that there were no more than 30 or 40 such "officers"—that is, members of the American Customs Board and their subordinates—and that this was hardly enough to seriously burden the taxpayers of the 13 colonies.

What Hutchinson was ignoring was that by "officers," the Declaration's authors were referring to the entire cadre of enforcers dispatched by England, which included thousands of sailors, soldiers, and inspectors, all of whom stood to profit from taxes and forfeitures. The Mutiny and Quartering Acts, too, forced colonists to house and supply these troops, who were stationed in America to surveil the locals. Parliament's plan to pay governors, judges, and other bureaucrats with taxes taken from colonists—instead of leaving such decisions to local representatives—also meant that virtually every bureaucrat, clerk, deputy, and hanger-on would be paid with substance eaten out of the unconsenting people of America. If Parliament's next step was to create a new class of nobles to control the continent, as Governor Bernard had recommended in 1764, there was every reason to expect the swarms of "pensioners" and "parasites" to grow.

He has kept among us, in Times of Peace, Standing Armies without the consent of our Legislatures.

Jefferson obviously had in mind the military occupation of Boston that began in 1768, but Whitehall had determined to maintain a permanent military presence in North America long before that. Following the French and Indian War, it stationed thousands of troops in the West (supplied and quartered at the colonists' expense), ostensibly to protect Americans from French incursions or Native uprisings, but also to block westward migration. Americans were not initially alarmed at these developments, because most troops were posted far from major population centers. But in the years surrounding the Stamp Act, London had sent thousands more soldiers to Massachusetts, New York, and other colonies, and there they remained. This army—answerable exclusively to London—first served to menace the Americans. Then, with Thomas Gage's selection as military governor, it became the official government, transforming the colony into a military autocracy.

Any Englishman would immediately have recognized the parallel with the Stuart monarchy. In the 1680s, James II had maintained some 20,000 troops in England, despite there being no threat of war, because they enabled him to intimidate the people into obeying his commands. When he was overthrown at last, Parliament denounced him for "raising and keeping a standing army within this kingdom in time of peace without consent of Parliament, and quartering soldiers contrary to law."[78] Now Jefferson consciously imitated that wording to draw another parallel between George and the despised Stuarts.

He has affected to render the Military independent of and superior to the Civil Power.

General Gage's appointment as governor of Massachusetts, with instructions empowering him to force civilian officials to assist him, meant all government in that colony was effectively run by the army. He had dissolved the legislature and implemented martial law, and Governor Dunmore had proclaimed martial law in Virginia too, as did the governors of Quebec and Nova Scotia. They claimed the Mutiny Acts justified their actions, but as Adams's friend Josiah Quincy pointed out, that only made things worse, because those statutes contained "no provision for securing the obedience of the military to the civil power, on which the preservation of our constitution depends." That was dangerous because "wherever an effectual provision is not made to secure the obedience of soldiers to the laws of their country, the military has constantly subverted and swallowed up the civil power."[79]

The legality of these martial law proclamations was doubtful. At the time, it was unclear whether British jurisprudence even recognized the principle of martial law.[80] Blackstone and others said it did, but only when civilian institutions were incapable of operating, which was not the case in Virginia or Massachusetts.[81] Although

Dunmore and Gage claimed that civilian rule had collapsed there, that wasn't true; after the gunpowder dispute in Virginia was peacefully resolved, there had been no further disruptions, and the House of Burgesses had even convened and held an orderly session. It was Dunmore's own refusal to return to Williamsburg that obstructed the government. As for Boston, Gage's presence was the *source* of disorder; he was even holding the city's disarmed populace hostage.

Once again, these actions resembled the oppressions of the Stuarts, who had exploited declarations of martial law to expand their power. The 1628 Petition of Right condemned Charles I for empowering his deputies to enforce the law through "such summary course and order as is agreeable to martial law." Sixty years later, James II not only declared martial law in many English cities, but also granted commissions to the East India Company authorizing it to employ martial law in countries where it operated.[82] That made it clear that London viewed the colonies as equivalent to conquered territories, to be governed by military decree rather than representation and the rule of law. And just as such actions had justified the overthrow of James II, now they justified independence from George III.

THE KING AND PARLIAMENT

The list of grievances Jefferson prepared for the Virginia Constitution weeks earlier had separated the abuses of the king's *executive* powers—which included the actions of his governors and military officers—from his wrongful approval of Parliament's unconstitutional *legislation*. Now, he used that format again, setting complaints against George himself apart from those concerning the laws he should have vetoed. Structuring the Declaration this way enabled Jefferson to mention the Intolerable Acts and other statutes without acknowledging that Parliament had any authority to pass them in the first place.

He has combined with others to subject us to a Jurisdiction foreign to our Constitution, and unacknowledged by our Laws, giving his Assent to their Acts of pretended Legislation:

The "jurisdiction foreign to our constitution" was Parliament, whose powers were "foreign" to, and "unacknowledged" by, the colonists.

The Lords and Commons had no more authority to legislate for America than today's California legislature has to adopt laws for Florida. Their acts were therefore "pretended." In fact, Westminster's purported authority was so "pretended" that the Declaration never bothers to mention Parliament by name.

According to the Patriots' constitutional theory, the monarch was an umpire, standing apart from the partisan arguments of daily politics and responsible for resolving disputes between factions in society. This meant he should veto Parliament's unconstitutional legislation. Yet by the 1770s, the king's veto power had fallen into disuse. While kings had no compunctions about vetoing *colonial* laws, they had not rejected a bill from the Lords and Commons since 1708.[83] In *A Summary View*, Jefferson had urged George III to "resume the exercise of his negative power" to protect the colonists, but the king declined to do so, firmly convinced of Parliamentary Supremacy.[84] He was therefore to blame for the "pretended legislation" that followed.

For quartering large Bodies of Armed Troops among us;

The quartering of troops was a key complaint against James II and one of the reasons for his overthrow. Yet Parliament, ignoring that lesson, had now adopted multiple Quartering Acts, forcing the colonists to provide housing for soldiers, not just for the financial convenience of the military, but to better enable the government to spy on the colonists. That plainly violated the revered common-law maxim that a man's home is his castle.

For protecting them, by a mock Trial, from Punishment for any Murders which they should commit on the Inhabitants of these States;

The 1774 Administration of Justice Act, or "Murder Act," provided that British officials who killed colonists while engaged in official business could be tried in Britain instead of America. Patriots viewed that as a violation of the common-law principle of "vicinage," whereby a defendant should be tried in the general neighborhood where the crime occurred. The consequence was to effectively strip colonial juries of their powers and to guarantee pro-British bias in any case involving a customs officer who killed an American.

Loyalists such as Thomas Hutchinson considered this complaint silly. In their eyes, the act had been designed to protect government agents against the *anti*-British bias of *colonial* juries. The common law, they said, recognizes an exception to the vicinage rule: If there is reason to believe locals are prejudiced against a defendant, a judge can order a change of venue. Hutchinson argued that this was all the act did.[85]

But that was sophistry. The Boston Massacre trial had spectacularly proved that even inflamed American juries could administer impartial justice. And in any event, transferring cases 3,000 miles away—forcing defendants and witnesses to undergo expensive and dangerous months-long sea voyages to testify—was far too burdensome. Prejudiced juries might be a risk, but colonial judges could already deal with that problem by changing the venue to a nearby county. There was no reason to send cases to another continent. On the other hand, if *all* colonial juries were *inherently* biased against British officials, that was all the more reason for the two governments to separate.

For cutting off our Trade with all Parts of the World;

The 1775 Prohibitory Act forbade the colonists from engaging in trade with any country other than Britain. That act—one of the severest punishments Parliament inflicted on the Americans—sought to starve the people into submission, just the latest in a series of such efforts after the Boston Port Act and the Restraining Acts. The Prohibitory Act went further than those laws by authorizing the Royal Navy, and even private subjects acting under letters of marque, to attack American merchant vessels. In short, the act placed American merchants outside the law.

Historian Andrew Roberts, echoing Thomas Hutchinson's critique of the Declaration, faults Jefferson and his colleagues for "[giving] George's acts in suppressing the rebellion as a reason for the rebellion itself."[86] It was fallacious, he claims, to cite Parliament's punitive measures as justifying the revolt. But the Declaration did not purport to give reasons for *rebellion*—it gave reasons for *independence*. That distinction is important. Americans had already issued many statements justifying rebellion, including the Suffolk Resolves, the Boston Pamphlet, and the Declaration of the Causes and Necessity of Taking Up Arms. But by July 1776, the actions London took to penalize American resistance had made clear that the two sides could never reconcile. The fact that George had approved those extreme measures—at the very time Americans were respectfully petitioning him—proved his unwillingness to consider their grievances. That left them no choice but to expand a mere rebellion into a permanent division. It was therefore entirely logical for them to cite London's punishments as reasons for abandoning hopes of reunion and making a permanent break. By way of analogy, it would indeed be illogical for an employee who has been disciplined by the boss for improper behavior to claim that the punishment somehow justified the misconduct—but it would be perfectly reasonable for the employee to cite that punishment as a reason for getting a different job.

FOR imposing Taxes on us without our Consent;

Even as the war progressed, there were those who tried to belittle the American Revolution as nothing but a petty spat over the price of tea. Anglican preacher Jonathan Boucher, the anonymous newspaper writer Massachusettensis, and Governor Hutchinson himself tried ridiculing the Patriots for choosing to "rebel rather than pay a duty of three-pence per pound."[87] But colonists had repeatedly explained that the dispute was not about the financial burden. It was about the legitimacy of Parliament's power. Americans were willing to pay their share toward military protection and other public services—but only through the constitutional method of requisition, not through direct compulsion or confiscation by juryless courts and mercenary informants and bounty hunters. Taxes should be levied by elected representatives, not by residents of an island on the opposite side of the Atlantic.

FOR depriving us, in many Cases, of the Benefits of Trial by Jury;

This grievance referred primarily to the vice-admiralty courts, which Parliament expanded beyond their original maritime jurisdiction in the 1760s. The Sugar, Stamp, and Townshend Acts allowed these courts to try even ordinary cases of tax violations occurring on land, by judges answerable to the Crown instead of local citizens. But other laws also denied colonists the right to trial by jury.

Under the White Pines Acts (adopted in 1711, 1722, and 1729), Parliament restricted the colonists' right to cut down pine trees, in an effort to reserve them for the Royal Navy to use as masts for sailing ships.[88] All white pines located on land "that now belongs or hereafter shall belong to the crown" were declared off-limits, "except only such as are the property of private persons"—and no tree larger than 24 inches in diameter could be cut without a permit, even if it was growing on private property.[89] Anybody accused of felling a tree without permission could be tried by a justice of the peace, presumed guilty until proven innocent, and punished by forfeiture plus court costs. Because white pines are among the most common trees in the American Northeast, these acts imposed a severe constraint on the colonists. As one scholar notes, rigorous enforcement "would have prevented the settler from clearing his land for the planting of crops. If he built his rude cabin out of white pine, or even sold the logs to purchase 'English goods,' the Surveyor-General could bring him to trial."[90] That could easily bankrupt a person.

The White Pines Acts led to violent confrontations between colonists and British officials. In fact, colonial resistance made them so hard to implement that by the 1750s, Parliament had given up. A decade later, however, it strengthened enforcement as part of its effort to generate revenue from the colonies. This led to another round of violence, such as one 1772 incident in which a New Hampshire sheriff was severely beaten when he tried to arrest a gang of lumbermen for cutting white pines. (Adams was familiar with the White Pines Acts; as an attorney, he had served as counsel in at least one vice-admiralty case involving the acts.[91])

For transporting us beyond Seas to be tried for pretended Offences;

Not only did the Murder Act enable government officials who killed colonists while enforcing the customs laws to transfer their cases to Britain, where juries were more likely to acquit them, but the Treason Act of 1543 and the Dockyards Act of 1772 also empowered prosecutors to order colonists to England for trial if accused of either treason or the damaging of Royal Navy facilities.[92] This, too, violated the principle of "vicinage."

The phrase "pretended offenses" hinted at the way British criminal law was sometimes so vague that officials could exploit its ambiguous language for political purposes. The most infamous example was treason, a concept so loosely defined that monarchs had for centuries levied the accusation against political opponents precisely because it meant whatever the king said it meant. (That was why, in 1787, the Framers of the US Constitution would take care to precisely define the term.) British law was full of such hazily defined words and quasi-legal practices. Impressment, for example, was not sanctioned by any law, but was still practiced and deemed legal by British courts based merely on the fact that the abuse had gone on for so long.[93] As a consequence, someone resisting impressment, such as Adams's client Michael Corbet, might defend himself against this quasi-legal kidnapping and find himself accused of the "pretended offense" of murder. He might even be sent to Britain for trial and, as Boston citizens put it, "whether condemned or acquitted, he will probably be ruined by the expense of attending the trial, and his long absence from his family and business."[94]

For abolishing the free System of English Laws in a neighboring Province, establishing therein an arbitrary Government and enlarging its Boundaries, so as to render it at once an Example and fit Instrument for introducing the same absolute Rule into these Colonies;

Jefferson did not write this charge; it was probably added at Franklin's suggestion. It focused on the Quebec Act, which instituted the French civil law system, instead of the English common law, in Britain's newly acquired Canadian province. That act not only denied the Quebecois such long-standing legal protections as trial by jury, the right to counsel, and habeas corpus, but also provided that their laws would be made by a governor and council chosen in London, rather than by an elected legislature. All of this was because British law barred Catholics from holding public office, which meant the act simultaneously violated the Catholics' religious rights and their right to choose their own lawmakers, even while it established the Catholic Church in the province, threatening the freedoms of Protestants. The revolutionaries feared that this set a precedent for future action against them, too—especially if schemes to establish an American bishopric proceeded. It was easy to imagine Parliament and the Anglican Church taking over Massachusetts or other colonies, stripping dissenting sects of their constitutional rights, and imposing a local autocracy—all of which it could do if it enjoyed truly absolute power.

For taking away our Charters, abolishing our most valuable Laws, and altering fundamentally the Forms of our Governments;

The revoking or rewriting of colonial charters was a sore subject with Americans; it brought to mind the Dominion of New England crisis, which had provoked the people of Massachusetts to rebel against Edmund Andros. But all colonies prized their charters, which promised them the rights enjoyed by native-born Britons. Legislation such as the Massachusetts Government Act proved that Parliament had no respect for these written promises.

In his rebuttal of the Declaration, Thomas Hutchinson ridiculed the idea that charters were "*sacred*" and "not to be revoked nor altered by the authority of *Parliament*."[95] Given his adherence to the theory of Parliamentary Supremacy, that was a natural reaction. But to Adams, Jefferson, and their colleagues, such flippancy only proved what they most feared: Parliament had no respect for the British constitution. If it really was all-powerful, it could not only revoke colonial charters, but even repeal the Magna Carta, the Bill of Rights, and every other protection the constitution promised.

For suspending our own Legislatures, and declaring themselves invested with Power to legislate for us in all Cases whatsoever.

This allegation differed from the earlier reference to the king having "dissolved representative houses repeatedly," because in those situations, *governors*, acting under royal authority, exercised their power to close legislatures—whereas this section referred to

Parliament's acts, specifically the New York Restraining Act and the Massachusetts Government Act, which shut down those legislatures by statute.

Then, of course, there was the Declaratory Act, the true source of all other abuses. In the Patriots' view, Parliament's assertion of power to legislate "in all cases whatsoever" radically altered the national constitution, laying claim to authority far beyond anything previously accepted in English law. It was also contrary to natural law, since no legitimate government could ever claim power to legislate in all cases whatsoever. Such authority would make Parliament the judge in its own case—the quintessential violation of natural law[96]—and would transform the Lords and Commons into a many-headed tyrant, unlimited in power or principle. Such an unreasonable proposition justified the Americans defending themselves with violence.

He has abdicated Government here, by declaring us out of his Protection and waging War against us.

Adams had been arguing since the Stamp Act shutdowns of 1765 that the imperial government's failure to provide Americans with law and order amounted to dissolving their bond of allegiance. But the Prohibitory Act went far beyond the abuses of those days. By expressly declaring that the "rebellious colonies" were no longer "under his Majesty's protection,"[97] London had ruptured the contract of allegiance and nullified royal authority over America. This again paralleled the experiences of the Stuart age. In 1689, the English Bill of Rights asserted that James II's attempts to "subvert" the "laws and liberties of this kingdom," combined with his fleeing the country, were equivalent to abdicating the throne. Now, the Americans asserted that George III's abuses entitled them to seek new safeguards for their rights.

He has plundered our Seas, ravaged our Coasts, burnt our Towns, and destroyed the Lives of our People.

Nowhere is Jefferson's debt to Tacitus clearer than in this powerful sentence. In his *Agricola*, the Roman writer told of a Scottish chief named Calgacus who in 84 CE delivered an impassioned speech to rally his men against the empire's troops. The Romans were "plunderers of the earth" who robbed the land and ravaged the sea, he declared, before concluding with the famous lines, *auferre, trucidare, rapere, falsis nominibus imperium, atque ubi solitudinem faciunt, pacem appellant*—"to spoil, to butcher, and to commit every kind of violence they style by a lying name, *Government*, and when they have spread a general desolation, they call it *Peace*."[98] Now, Jefferson borrowed the Latin author's rhythmic phrases and haunting vocabulary both to allude to London's policy of rule by force and to liken it to the tactics employed by the ancient empire all Christians regarded as the archetypical tyranny.

It was a fitting analogy. British forces burned Charlestown, Massachusetts, in June 1775, Falmouth, Massachusetts, in October, and Norfolk, Virginia, in January. By then, the Royal Navy had burned or tried to burn more than a dozen other seaside towns. It also forced a score of coastal cities to provide supplies, seizing cargo ships in Savannah, Georgia; raiding communities in places like Noodle's Island, Massachusetts, and Narragansett Bay, Rhode Island; and firing on towns that refused to comply, including Stonington in Connecticut, Brunswick Town in North Carolina, Newport and Bristol in Rhode Island, and even lower Manhattan.[99] Like the imperial Romans, the British might boast of their advanced civilization, but their actual policies were built on arrogance, greed, and brute force.

He is, at this Time, transporting large Armies of foreign Mercenaries to complete the Works of Death, Desolation, and Tyranny, already begun with circumstances of Cruelty and Perfidy, scarcely paralleled in the most barbarous Ages, and totally unworthy the Head of a civilized Nation.

King George informed Parliament in October 1775 that he had received "friendly offers of foreign assistance" in putting down the American rebellion and he alluded to the possibility of using "my Electoral troops" for that purpose, as well.[100] This was a reference to the Electorate of Hanover, the region of what is now Germany over which George also reigned. The king had decided to employ German soldiers—the so-called Hessians—after Empress Catherine the Great rejected his request for Russian troops.

Using non-British forces against British subjects was something Americans, and even many in England, viewed with horror. Blackstone wrote in the 1760s that if the government found it necessary to employ soldiers to put down an insurrection, English law required that "the armies with which [this task] is entrusted" be "composed of natural subjects" who "have the same spirit with the people."[101] Otherwise, the king could abuse his power for his own purposes, because foreign soldiers were less likely to know the language, to care about harming civilians, to understand the country's political dynamics, or to be familiar with local customs—all of which increased the risk of "collateral damage" and even civil war. Yet London ignored these risks in 1776. British General Henry Clinton, who took over for Thomas Gage in September, even said it was advantageous that Hessians spoke no English, because they would be less likely to be swayed by American talk of liberty: "They have no language but their own," he wrote. "They cannot desert."[102] The king's decision to enlist some 30,000 Hessians to subdue the colonists proved once more that he saw Americans not as subjects to be protected, but as servants to be whipped.[103]

Clinton's concerns about desertion were well-grounded. Whereas today the word "mercenaries" refers to military men who choose to fight for money, King George's mercenaries were more akin to slaves. They had little say in their own fate; their services were bought and sold by European monarchs. Desertion rates were therefore quite high, and in the months after independence, Jefferson helped devise a plan to encourage desertions by offering citizenship, religious toleration, and 50 acres of land to "all such foreigners who shall leave the armies of his Brittanic Majesty."[104] As the war proceeded, he even invited some German prisoners of war to dine at Monticello and befriended several of their officers in hopes of encouraging high-level defections.

He has constrained our fellow Citizens taken Captive on the high Seas to bear Arms against their Country, to become the Executioners of their Friends and Brethren, or to fall themselves by their Hands.

Not only had the Royal Navy engaged in impressment for decades—ignoring laws that promised colonists immunity from the practice—but also the Prohibitory Act specified that American sailors captured aboard merchant vessels would be "considered . . . to be as much in the service of his Majesty" as if they "had entered themselves voluntarily to serve on board his Majesty's . . . vessels."[105] In other words, they would be conscripted into the British military and forced to fight their fellow Americans in battle. (Today, such practices are prohibited by the Geneva Convention.[106])

Colonists had long hated impressment. Adams was especially outspoken about its evils. It was "a kind of civil war," he wrote, "upon innocent, unoffending subjects."[107] Jefferson and Franklin agreed; in 1781, Franklin published a withering review of a book by a lawyer who defended the practice. "If impressing seamen is of right by common law in Britain," Franklin wrote, "slavery is then of right by common law," since there was "no slavery worse than that sailors are subjected to."[108] And 30 years after the revolution, then-President Jefferson made Britain's continuing use of impressment one of the reasons for his embargo against that country, in the lead-up to the War of 1812.[109]

He has excited domestic Insurrections amongst us, and has endeavoured to bring on the Inhabitants of our Frontiers, the merciless Indian Savages, whose known Rule of Warfare, is an undistinguished Destruction, of all Ages, Sexes, and Conditions.

Lord Dunmore's threat to free the slaves of rebels if they joined his army terrified Virginians, with their nightmares of "servile war." But the colonists were even more afraid of Native American warriors, especially in Virginia, where memories of such incidents as the 1622 assault by the Powhatan—who killed a third of the colony's entire white population—were undiminished. Superbly skilled Cherokee, Iroquois, and Mohawk fighters knew the North American geography well, could travel silently, and had a reputation for brutality. The Huron, Miami, and other tribes even practiced cannibalism, mutilation, and the ritual torture of captives.[110] When Delaware tribesmen captured some American soldiers in Ohio in July 1782, they stripped the commanding officer naked, beat him with sticks, tied him to a stake, cut off his ears, scalped him, and scalded him to death over the course of several hours by covering him with hot coals and burning gunpowder.[111]

Jefferson sympathized in principle with Native victims of white aggression. In *Notes on the State of Virginia*, he denounced the thuggish Indian killers Michael Cresap and Daniel Greathouse for their roles in the 1774 massacre of the family of a Mingo chief in what is now Ohio. That incident had given Governor Dunmore an excuse to raise an army to fight the Native Americans near Pittsburgh, a five-month conflict called "Lord Dunmore's War" that was waged without approval from Virginia's legislature.[112] (Another example of imperial authorities making the military superior to the civilian power, it alarmed Virginians so much that the soldiers felt it necessary to issue a statement reassuring the public that they would not take up arms against the Patriots.[113])

Idealists like Jefferson and Franklin liked to think colonists and Native Americans would get along peacefully were it not for foolhardy British interference.[114] That was naive, but it indicates that the Declaration's complaint regarding British "endeavors" to incite the tribes against "the inhabitants of our frontiers" was more a critique of imperial meddling than of the Native Americans themselves, whom Jefferson, Franklin, and others knew were often engaging in the natural right of self-defense.

Historian Gary Nash nevertheless called the Declaration's "blanket indictment" of Native Americans "dishonest" and "duplicitous."[115] The Indigenous peoples were the victims of white hostility, Nash wrote, and Jefferson's description of them as "merciless savages" ignored their "morality, generosity, bravery," and "Christian virtues."[116] But this was itself a distortion. Although many colonists, including Jefferson, admired the Native Americans' virtue, they combined that admiration with abject dread of their practice of total war. In their eyes, indigenous Americans were "savages"—a term with less pejorative force then it has now—who could be "inoffensive" but also astoundingly violent. In September 1780, for example, Cherokee tribesmen under the command of British General Banastre "the Butcher" Tarleton scalped and burned alive 17 captured American soldiers in Augusta, South Carolina.[117] Of course, white soldiers were sometimes equally cruel—as when George Rogers Clark tomahawked a group of Native prisoners to death in 1779 to intimidate the British.[118] But Anglo-Americans considered their own rules of warfare civilized, because these required avoiding civilian casualties and unnecessary destruction, which Native warriors never professed to do.

As Rutgers history professor Peter Silver observes, tribal tactics were "in the most literal sense, terroristic . . . carefully planned and carried out . . . to induce the greatest fright possible." Eyewitnesses reported that Native warriors "[fell] on exactly those people—children, women, farm folk obliviously going about their housework and harvesting, sleeping people 'surprised and murdered in their beds'—who could make no resistance."[119] On July 1, 1776—while the Congress was editing the Declaration—the Cherokee began a series of assaults on Southwestern settlements, killing and capturing men, women, and children, whom they scalped, mutilated, and burned at the stake.[120] Whites who committed similar atrocities were more blameworthy, precisely because they professed to be civilized. But that does not lessen the terror Native brutalities evoked.

Many Americans blamed irresponsible whites for stirring up violence between the two groups, either by attacking tribes without provocation—which led to endless reprisals, as with the Cresap episode—or by literally hiring tribes to attack other whites. British officials were among the worst offenders. In 1775, after the Congress negotiated a neutrality agreement with the Six Nations (later called the Iroquois Confederacy), the Patriots were shocked to discover that his Majesty's army bribed several tribes into reneging on the agreement.[121] Quebec Governor Henry Hamilton was plausibly alleged to have paid Native warriors bounties for American scalps—but not for prisoners.[122] Given that Parliament had often claimed that its taxes would provide military protection against Native attacks, it seemed especially perfidious for London to connive to provoke those attacks now.

Some historians have given the impression that colonists were embittered by London's philanthropic effort to protect Native Americans against white depredations. Nash, for example, repeated the hoary claim that King George's October 1763 proclamation forbidding colonists from settling west of the Appalachian Mountains represented an "attempt to forge a long-range enlightened Indian policy," and that Americans rebelled in part because they were "determined to seize western lands."[123] But that proclamation was not an act of royal benevolence toward indigenous Americans. It was part of a self-serving policy designed to keep colonists close to the Atlantic and dependent on British imports, as opposed to becoming self-sufficient farmers in the West.[124] Worse, the proclamation's consequences for Native Americans were devastating in practice. It forbade colonists from "mak[ing] any purchase from the said Indians of any lands" and asserted that the territory belonged to the Crown, instead.[125] In other words, it stripped Natives of their property rights. As legal scholar Stuart Banner explains, this meant settlers "had no reason to care whether the Indians had once owned the land."[126] After 1763, frontiersmen could not acquire ownership through negotiation, but only through political favoritism in London—or violence.[127] Far from being an "Indians' 'Bill of Rights,'" as another writer calls it, the proclamation deprived them of any say in the disposition of the frontier, thus ultimately worsening their bargaining position vis-à-vis the settlers.[128]

True, some Britons were shocked by colonial attacks on Native Americans, as were many colonists. But the imperial government never actually interceded to help tribes resist white encroachment.[129] Its actions were wholly opportunistic—as was its recruitment of warriors. "The dread the people of New England, etc., have of a war with the savages," the colonial secretary told General John Burgoyne in 1775, "proves the expediency of our holding that scourge over them."[130]

As for the enslaved, the Declaration's reference to "domestic insurrections" strikes readers today as hypocritical, because it appears to condemn Governor Dunmore's grant of freedom to slaves even while proclaiming the rights of humanity. But this accusation of hypocrisy is nothing new. In 1776, Tory writer John Lind—who, like Thomas Hutchinson, published a pamphlet responding line by line to the Declaration—ridiculed the Patriots for just that: "Is it for *them* to complain *of the offer of freedom* held out to these wretched beings? of the offer of reinstating them in that *equality* which, in this very paper, is declared to be the *gift of God to all*?"[131] What Lind overlooked was that Americans did not deny that it was self-contradictory for them to hold slaves while proclaiming liberty to be every person's birthright. On the contrary, their embarrassment over that inconsistency had been particularly glaring when Virginians drafted their

Declaration of Rights. Jefferson went even further, admitting that slaves were justified in violently rebelling against their oppressors. The thought that God's "justice cannot sleep forever" made him "tremble," he wrote.[132] And when, in 1800, enslaved Virginian Gabriel Prosser was arrested for planning an uprising, Jefferson counseled then-Governor James Monroe to deport Prosser and his allies instead of executing them, as state law called for, because they had been justifiably fighting for their liberty.[133]

The real story of the "domestic insurrections" passage is more complicated than today's readers often realize. In his initial sketch of the list of grievances, Jefferson wrote that the king and his deputies were "inciting insurrections of our fellow ~~subjects~~ citizens with the allurements of forfeiture and confiscation."[134] This did not refer to slavery at all, but to efforts by British leaders to encourage American Loyalists or neutrals ("subjects," which Jefferson changed to "citizens") to help suppress the rebellion. Under Britain's laws of attainder and forfeiture, Patriots were liable to having their property confiscated for treason—and likely bestowed on informants as a reward. Jefferson was saying that this "allurement" was designed to encourage infighting among colonists. There were, indeed, sections of America dominated by Loyalist opinion, which served as a "fifth column" during the revolution.[135] As the war progressed, it turned out to be the Patriots who confiscated Loyalists' estates and sold them to raise funds for the war effort; Jefferson himself drafted at least one bill of attainder for this purpose.[136] But at the time he wrote the Declaration, the fear that Loyalists would sabotage the revolution was a realistic one.

Jefferson had then followed that allegation with a separate clause accusing the king of "prompting our negroes to rise in arms among us; those very negroes whom by an inhuman use of his negative he hath from time to time refused us permission to exclude by law."[137] Coupling the complaint of inciting insurrection with a complaint about the monarchy's refusal to let colonists ban the slave trade cushioned the charge of hypocrisy by acknowledging slavery to be "inhuman"—again implicitly admitting that slaves who "rose in arms" were justified in doing so—while also saying that the violence and civilian casualties that would likely result from a servile war were things no worthy monarch would intentionally provoke.

In his next draft, Jefferson expanded on this point. Retaining the "treasonable insurrections" clause (regarding Loyalists), he deleted the "rise in arms" clause and replaced it with a paragraph-long accusation against the king, into which he poured more vitriol than anywhere else in the document. This indignant passage, longer than any other in the Declaration, condemned the king for fostering and maintaining slavery, using words that made the entire list of grievances seem to rise to this climax:

> He has waged cruel war against human nature itself, violating its most sacred rights of life and liberty in the persons of a distant people who never offended him, captivating and carrying them into slavery in another hemisphere, or to incur miserable death in their transportation thither. This piratical warfare, the opprobrium of <u>infidel</u> powers, is the warfare of the *Christian* king of Great Britain. Determined to keep open a market where MEN should be bought and sold, he has prostituted his negative for suppressing every legislative attempt to prohibit or to restrain this execrable commerce. And that this assemblage of horrors might want no fact of distinguished die, he is now exciting those very people to rise in arms among us, and to purchase that liberty of which <u>he</u> has deprived them, by murdering the people upon whom <u>he</u> also obtruded them; thus paying off former crimes committed against the <u>liberties</u> of one people, with crimes which he urges them to commit against the <u>lives</u> of another.[138]

This paragraph reiterated the complaint in *A Summary View* that while the king refused to veto Parliament's bills, he did veto colonial bills, including those that aimed to restrain the slave trade—which George then followed with a complete ban on laws limiting slave importation. The bottom line was clear: The king and his deputies were creating a tragically explosive situation by enslaving people to increase imperial wealth, then unleashing the victims of slavery on white Virginians to increase imperial power.

Jefferson had come to hate slavery at an early age, thanks largely to the influence of George Wythe, who was now in Philadelphia, ready to add his signature to his protégé's Declaration. But Jefferson's wording in this passage indicates how far he had come in his antipathy toward the "peculiar institution." Even John Locke had considered slavery legitimate in some circumstances; for example, he defended the enslavement of enemies captured in war on the theory that if killing a soldier on the battlefield was acceptable, enslaving him for life—which was less cruel—was also acceptable. But Jefferson rejected that logic. During his student days, he wrote in the margin of one of his books (something the bibliophile Jefferson rarely did) that Locke's theory was obsolete. Modern "civilized" warfare, he noted, made it clear that "we have no right to take the life of an enemy unless our own preservation renders it necessary." And to allow a captured enemy soldier to remain alive "admits that there was no necessity to take it."[140] It logically followed that enslaving him was morally forbidden. These remarks indicate Jefferson's belief—premature, as it turned out—that European civilization was coming to its senses about slavery. Yet the imperial government was obstructing that progress out of greed. Thus, Jefferson now accused the king of making "cruel war" on Africans by sending British ships to that continent to kidnap its inhabitants or buy them from native slave traders—a "war" in which Britain was the aggressor, and in which the king *himself* was the "merciless savage" attacking people of all ages, sexes, and conditions.

Jefferson was proud of this passage, and Adams admired it, too. Five decades later, Adams recalled that he was "delighted with its high tone, and the flights of oratory with which it abounded, especially that concerning Negro slavery."[139] The Declaration's rhetorical momentum rose from relatively minor accusations of failing to approve "wholesome" legislation to a denunciation of the king as a false Christian, a pirate who would embarrass even "infidels," and a man willing to trick slaves into murdering his subjects.

Bizarrely, recent historians have viewed this paragraph not as proof of Jefferson's anti-slavery views, but as evidence of his mendacity. They contend that blaming the monarchy for slavery's presence in America was so implausible that it proves Jefferson was engaging in a rhetorical sleight of hand. Joseph Ellis, for example, accused Jefferson of "juggling two incompatible formulations: One is to blame the king for slavery; the other is to blame him for emancipating the slaves."[141] Garry Wills, too, claimed that Jefferson was "twist[ing] language and logic in an unfortunate way," and that the Virginian actually thought "the king's real crime [was] his attempt to *free* Virginia's slaves."[142]

These accusations are off base. For one thing, the Dunmore proclamation did *not* free Virginia's slaves. It only promised freedom to slaves "appertaining to rebels" who were "able and willing to bear arms" for the king—not to anyone enslaved by a Loyalist, or to women, children, the infirm, the elderly, or anyone else unable to fight in the British military.

More importantly, although Jefferson was, indeed, engaged in rhetorical legerdemain, it was essentially the opposite of what Ellis, Wills, and others asserted. The political maneuver Jefferson was attempting aimed not to excuse slavery, but to damn it. Convinced that the revolution offered a rare chance to wipe away the inherited evils of English tradition, he hoped to place Americans irrevocably *on the record* about slavery's evil, in a way that would force them to work toward its eventual eradication. His goal was to tie Americans to the mast of their revolutionary principles.

Jefferson, Adams, and their colleagues knew the revolution presented a truly special opportunity. "I wish with you that the genius of this country may expand itself, now [that] the shackles are knocked off," Adams wrote a friend in the weeks after independence. "But there is not a little danger of its becoming still more contracted. If a sufficient scope is not allowed for the human mind to exert itself, if genius and learning are not sufficiently encouraged, instead of improving by this resolution, we shall become more despicably narrow, timid, selfish, base and barbarous."[143]

Jefferson, too, saw that the moment "for fixing every essential right on a legal basis" was *now*. With royal government swept away, there was nothing "to restrain us from doing right" and reforming colonial law "with a single eye to reason." He feared that "from the conclusion of this war we shall be going downhill"; once independence was achieved, politicians would lose "the general pulse of reformation," and citizens would "forget themselves, but in the sole faculty of making money." Therefore, "the shackles . . . which shall not be knocked off at the conclusion of this war will remain on us long, will be made heavier and heavier, till our rights shall revive or expire in a convulsion."[144] The moment must be seized to embed an anti-slavery element into the new nation's soul.

Jefferson was already planning an ambitious set of legal reforms for his home state—everything from abolishing the established church and providing for the manumission of slaves to establishing a public school system and reforming the criminal code. Now, in drafting the Declaration, he saw an opportunity. Knowing that people are typically less willing to admit their own faults than to blame others, he hoped that by asserting the injustice of slavery in unmistakable terms while simultaneously scapegoating the king, the Declaration would make it easier for his countrymen to view the practice as *un-American*. They might come to believe that slavery, like an established religion or the cruel punishments of English common law, was an outworn European notion, forced on Americans more or less against their will. Later historians might quibble about this, but the creation of a social narrative is part of a statesman's job during the act of founding—that is, of consecrating. When done right, it can draw the people toward what Abraham Lincoln later called their "better angels."[145]

There were good reasons to think this gambit would succeed. Public consciousness did seem to be awakening to slavery's evils. In 1785, Jefferson told a British abolitionist that Americans living north of the Chesapeake were becoming hostile to slavery, because the younger generation had "sucked in the principles of liberty as it were with their mother's milk."[146] Adams agreed. Slavery, he wrote in 1801, was "fast diminishing."[147] Vermont banned it in 1777. Other states passed gradual anti-slavery laws, which did not liberate those already in chains but forbade new enslavement, thereby slowly closing down the practice. Pennsylvania did so in 1780, Rhode Island and Connecticut in 1784, New York in 1799, and New Jersey in 1804. Massachusetts's Supreme Court declared slavery unconstitutional in 1783, on the grounds that it violated the principle "that all men are born free and equal."[148] These reforms all went one way: No state chose to implement slavery where it had not existed before. Meanwhile, economists, notably including Adam Smith, were explaining that slavery is economically counterproductive.[149] It therefore seemed plausible that with the right incentives, Americans might eliminate it entirely.

Of course, that was not to be. On Tuesday, July 1, the drafting committee presented the Declaration to the Continental Congress for clause-by-clause discussion and debate, and Jefferson watched as his fellow delegates whittled away much of its latter half—entirely removing his attack on slavery. No records remain of who said what during these debates, although Jefferson recalled that Adams tirelessly defended every word in the draft, while he remained silent, as always. The "cruel war on human nature" passage was eliminated "in complaisance [*sic*] to South Carolina and Georgia, who had never attempted to restrain the importation of slaves, and who, on the contrary, still wished to continue it," Jefferson wrote, as well as some Northerners, who, although holding "few slaves themselves," were "pretty considerable carriers of them to others."[150] After deleting the paragraph, the Congress also changed the preceding clause, so that instead of denouncing the king and his governors for inciting "insurrections" by "our fellow citizens"—that is, white Loyalists—the final wording condemned him for "excit[ing] domestic insurrections," lumping together all types of internal sabotage that the British were provoking.

Watching his Declaration being edited was a maddening experience for Jefferson. Franklin noticed him squirming in his chair and tried to soothe him with an anecdote. It reminded him of a hatmaker, he said, who designed a sign to advertise his store. It bore the phrase "John Thomson—makes and sells hats for ready money" and a picture of a hat. But when he showed it to friends, they suggested removing "for ready money": Obviously if he *sold* hats, it was for money. Another said "makes" was unnecessary, too. He sold them whether he made them or not. Others suggested painting over the word "hats," and so on—until eventually the sign simply read "John Thomson" with a picture of a hat. It wasn't a particularly funny story, but it stuck in Jefferson's memory.[151]

When he returned to his apartment, the still-frustrated author wrote out several painstaking copies of his original version, with marks to indicate the changes the Congress had made, and sent them to friends, asking them to agree that his initial draft was better. Fifty years later, he did the same in his memoirs. His disappointment at the failure of his effort to embed a denunciation of slavery into the Declaration remained with him for the rest of his life.

THEREFORE . . .

In every stage of these Oppressions we have petitioned for Redress in the most humble Terms. Our repeated Petitions have been answered only by repeated Injury. A Prince whose Character is thus marked by every act which may define a Tyrant, is unfit to be the Ruler of a free People.

Nor have we been wanting in Attentions to our British Brethren. We have warned them from Time to Time of Attempts by their Legislature to extend an unwarrantable Jurisdiction over us. We have reminded them of the Circumstances of our Emigration and Settlement here. We have appealed to their native Justice and Magnanimity, and we have conjured them by the Ties of our common Kindred to disavow these Usurpations, which would inevitably interrupt our Connections and Correspondence. They, too, have been deaf to the Voice of Justice and of Consanguinity. We must, therefore, acquiesce in the Necessity which denounces our Separation, and hold them, as we hold the rest of Mankind, Enemies in War, in Peace Friends.

Jefferson had included a longer, more emotional reproach directed at the British public for failing to rally to America's cause. "We must endeavor to forget our former love for them," he wrote. "The road to glory and happiness is open to us, too; we will climb it in a separate state."[152] All of this was wisely removed during the debates on July 2 and 3. The result was more concise and mature in tone.

We, therefore, the Representatives of the UNITED STATES OF AMERICA, in General Congress, Assembled, appealing to the Supreme Judge of the World for the Rectitude of our Intentions, do, in the Name, and by Authority of the good People of these Colonies, solemnly Publish and Declare, That these United Colonies are, and of Right ought to be, Free and Independent States; that they are absolved from all Allegiance to the British Crown, and that all political Connection between them and the State of Great-Britain, is and ought to be totally dissolved; and that as Free and Independent States, they have full Power to levy War, conclude Peace, contract Alliances, establish Commerce, and to do all other Acts and Things which Independent States may of right do. And for the support of this Declaration, with a firm Reliance on the Protection of divine Providence, we mutually pledge to each other our Lives, our Fortunes, and our sacred Honor.

This final paragraph incorporated the language of Richard Henry Lee's original resolution but added three noteworthy elements. The first was some additional references to God—as "Supreme Judge of the World" and as the source of "protection"—so that, along with Jefferson's original reference to the author of "nature's laws," the Almighty is described in legislative, executive, and judicial capacities, a combination that in the hands of any fallible mortal would be "the very definition of tyranny."[153]

These religious references play an important role in the Declaration's overall argument, making it clear that the Americans were no longer looking to Britain for any of these things. They were ceasing to ask the king to fairly "judge" their intentions—something they *had* asked in the Olive Branch Petition—or to provide them "protection," which he explicitly refused.[154] Least of all would they ask him to play any role in legislating for them. They would now make law for themselves.[155]

Yet the people's legislative power is limited by a second important phrase: "of right." Repeated twice in the final paragraph, this phrase connects the moral principles of natural law with the legal principles of constitutional law. Again reflecting its Lockean roots, the Declaration acknowledges that nature's laws constrain government legitimacy—that is, that all legislatures are subject to moral limits drawn by the rights that all people inherently enjoy. The newly independent states may only do things that states may do "of right."

It was a long-standing English tradition to use the phrase "of right" or "of right ought to be" in declarations of authority or other laws addressing questions of legitimacy. Because rights or powers could be acquired by long-established custom, the authorities could bless a custom—officially recognizing it as lawful—by acknowledging it to be "of right." Thus, for example, Parliament declared in 1547 that it was treason to deny that Edward VI and his heirs "of right ought to be kings" of England.[156] It later declared it treason to assert that Queen Mary I "is not or of right ought not to be Queen."[157] And in 1719, it declared that Ireland "is and of right ought to be subordinate" to Britain.[158]

The most prominent use of the phrase, however—the one the Declaration's readers would have immediately thought of—had been in the 1766 Declaratory Act. That law asserted that the colonies "have been, are, and of right ought to be, subordinate unto and dependent upon the imperial crown and Parliament," and that Parliament "had, has, and of right ought to have, full power and authority" to legislate for "the colonies and people of America . . . in all cases whatsoever."[159] Now, the Declaration threw this language back in Westminster's face. It made clear that, as Roger Sherman told John Adams at the First Continental Congress, "The reverse of the Declaratory Act was true."[160] "Of right," Parliament had *no* authority over America.

The third remarkable feature of the final paragraph is its concluding acknowledgment of the unity of the "good people" in whose name the Declaration is promulgated. The opening reference to "*one* people" and the closing reference to the "good people" of "these *united* colonies" cement America's national unity. The former colonies are free and independent not separately, but unitedly. When, 50 years later, Jefferson called the Declaration "the fundamental act of union of these states," he meant it literally: the document announced that the American people were a single nation.[161] That proposition proved controversial in the 19th century, when Southerners began arguing that state "sovereignty" entitled them to secede from the union. But when the Congress voted to approve the Declaration, its members knew that they were standing not as Englishmen asserting the traditional rights of a race whose home was 3,000 miles away, but as members of a new, single national entity, whose rights were those of all mankind.

— CHAPTER 12 —

INDEPENDENCE FOREVER

Posterity! You will never know how much it cost the present generation, to preserve your freedom! I hope you will make a good use of it. If you do not, I shall repent in Heaven that I ever took half the pains to preserve it.
—John Adams[1]

Even before the debate over Richard Henry Lee's independence motion began on July 1, it was clear that most colonies supported the proposal. That support did not guarantee passage, however, because congressional rules required nine yes votes for a motion to prevail, and only eight colonies were firmly in the affirmative camp by the time debates began. John Dickinson now led the opposition, and although he was a lame duck—his own colonial government having been effectively replaced by one that supported independence—he nevertheless delivered a powerful speech against the motion. Mustering an array of rational objections, he emphasized the daunting practical problems independence would cause: Americans were inadequately armed and supplied; they had no foreign allies; they had not yet formed a central government.

But Adams, Jefferson, and their allies knew they could not wait forever. Years afterward, Jefferson, in a romantic mood, composed an imaginary dialogue between his heart and his head and reflected that independence had been declared despite seemingly logical arguments like Dickinson's: "If our country, when pressed with wrongs at the point of the bayonet, had been governed by its heads instead of its hearts, where should we have been now?" his emotions ask

In June 2020, rioters at Thomas Jefferson High School in Portland, Oregon, tore a statute of Thomas Jefferson off its pedestal.

his reason. "You began to calculate and to compare wealth and numbers. We threw up a few pulsations of our warmest blood; we supplied enthusiasm against wealth and numbers; we put our existence to the hazard, when the hazard seemed against us, and we saved our country."[2] When Dickinson argued that the colonies were so unprepared that separating from Britain now would be like putting to sea "in a skiff made of paper," he may have been right.[3] But the others knew the only alternative was to drown.

When Dickinson was done, the delegates ran an informal tally and found that South Carolina planned to vote yes, crossing the nine-vote threshold. Respecting the need for unanimity, Dickinson and another anti-independence delegate stayed home the next day, which allowed James Wilson—who had changed his mind to support independence—to cast a decisive "aye" on Pennsylvania's behalf.[4] New York's delegates also lacked authority to approve independence, so they abstained, although New York's legislature adopted resolutions approving separation shortly afterward. That was enough for the Continental Congress to call the vote "unanimous" and to begin editing the Declaration, which it approved on July 4.

The finished document reflected the yin and yang strengths of its principal authors. It spoke with Adams's realism about "acquiescing in the necessity" of independence and Jefferson's idealism about the laws of nature and the sacredness of honor. It combined Adams's East Coast fixation on order—offended by the mother country's arbitrariness, its disruption of common-law rights, and its withdrawal of royal protection—with Jefferson's Western-minded focus on opportunity, outraged by Britain's restrictions on economic freedom, its limits on territorial expansion, and its wartime terror tactics.

Many years later, Pennsylvania delegate Benjamin Rush vividly recalled the "solemnity" of the day when the members put their signatures to the Declaration. "Do you recollect the pensive and awful silence which pervaded the house when we were called up, one after another, to the table of the President of Congress, to [sign] what was believed by many at that time to be our own death warrants?" he asked Adams.[5] Rush's memory was faulty, however; the signing took place over the course of many days. As for solemnity, although the Patriots understood the gravity of their act, Adams expressed only glee at the time. It was a "day of deliverance," he told his wife.

Its anniversary should be marked "with shows, games, sports, guns, bells, bonfires and illuminations from one end of this continent to the other from this time forward forever."[6] Abigail agreed. "Though your letters never fail to give me pleasure, be the subject what it will, yet it was greatly heightened by the prospect of the future happiness and glory of our country," she told him. "May the foundation of our new constitution be justice, truth, and righteousness."[7]

For his part, Jefferson was ready to go home. Anxious about his wife's health (Martha was likely pregnant and risked miscarriage), he urged his replacement "for Godsake" to hurry.[8] He spent the afternoon of July 4, 1776, at the London Book-Store at the corner of Market and Second Streets. He loved book shopping, but the store's owner, John Sparhawk, sold many other things, too, including medicine, musical instruments, and cutlery. Jefferson picked up several pairs of gloves for Martha and a new thermometer for himself, as he had decided to start recording the temperature every day to help the progress of science. (It was 76 degrees.) But if he had hoped to see her soon, he was disappointed. Not until September was he given permission to go home. A month later, he took his family with him to Williamsburg, where he began his long-anticipated project of rewriting Virginia's legal code.

It's likely, therefore, that he and Adams stood together on July 8, as the Declaration was read in public for the first time, in front of Philadelphia's Independence Hall. Citizens had been summoned for the announcement by the ringing of the bells, one of which, originally cast in London in 1751, bore the Biblical motto, "Proclaim liberty throughout all the land unto all the inhabitants thereof." In New York, General George Washington ordered the Declaration read to the troops. He reported to the Congress that it "seemed to have their most hearty assent."[9] Local citizens immediately toppled the statue of George III that the city had erected in gratitude for the repeal of the Stamp Act and melted it down to make bullets.

John Adams had little time for celebrations. Now chairman of the Board of War and Ordnance, the Congress's most powerful committee, he was responsible for managing the entire military. He would not see Abigail again until October, nearly a year after leaving home. After that, the war dragged on for another seven years, before he and Benjamin Franklin traveled to England to negotiate the treaty ending the war and bringing recognition of American independence. Adams would then serve as ambassador to Great Britain, vice president, and president. Not until 1801 was he again able to make Braintree his permanent residence.

NONSENSE UPON STILTS

Critiques of the Declaration began to appear almost the moment it was published. Thomas Hutchinson released his pamphlet, *Strictures upon the Declaration of the Congress*, criticizing it clause by clause, and Parliament paid London writer John Lind to publish his book-length *Answer to the Declaration of the American Congress*, condemning its authors for treachery and disloyalty.

The most interesting critique, however, came from philosopher Jeremy Bentham, who helped Lind write his pamphlet, and who, at the age of 28, was still years away from formulating his theory of utilitarianism. Bentham had nothing but contempt for the idea of individual rights, which he later dismissed as "rhetorical nonsense—nonsense upon stilts." Rights, he believed, are nothing more than permissions given to people by the state whenever doing so is "advantageous to the society in question." That meant "there is no right which, when the abolition of it is advantageous to society, should not be abolished."[10] He never paused to ask why, if rights should be spurned as nonsensical fictions, the entire notion of legitimate authority is not also a sham. If rights are nonsense because they are invisible and can be violated, then laws, promises, and logic must also be nonsense, since they, too, are invisible and can be violated. On Bentham's premises, the only thing that can be "real" is the arbitrary use of coercion.

Bentham's contempt for abstract principles—which he mistook for down-to-earth realism—led him to reject even the proposition that a person has a right to his own life. If that were true, he argued, no military could ever engage in warfare. In fact, "nothing which can be called government ever was, or ever could be . . . exercised by but at the expense of one or other of those rights." But denying the possibility that government can operate while respecting individual rights means that government is inevitably arbitrary—limited by no higher principles—and therefore that it can never act justly.

According to Bentham's logic, might literally makes right—because nothing else can.

Yet even while discarding the Declaration's principles, Bentham complained that American rebels were violating the rights of others. He did not mean slaves—he never attempted a principled attack on slavery—he meant Loyalists.[11] Observing that the newly independent states had begun adopting bills of attainder, confiscation acts, and laws banishing Loyalists from the newly independent states, he accused the Americans of hypocrisy. If people have an "inalienable" right to pursue happiness, how could the Patriots deprive their political opponents of that right?

Bentham wasn't wrong that confiscations and attainders violated individual rights on a massive scale—about £1 billion was seized from Loyalists and disputes over compensating them continued into the next century.[12] But he was the one committing hypocrisy by criticizing Americans for violating rights whose existence he himself denied. If there is no right that should not be abolished when doing so is to society's advantage, he had no grounds to complain.[13] Under his theory, Patriots such as Alexander Hamilton and John Jay, who spent the postwar years in protracted efforts to obtain compensation for the victimized Loyalists, were simply wasting their time. Nor should the Constitution of 1787 have forbidden bills of attainder if, as he thought, principles such as rights or justice are only "a cloud of words."[14] In Bentham's theory, individuals implicitly belong to the state, unless and until it chooses to give them some temporary permission to live, own, think, love, speak, pray, or be. "All men are born free?" he scoffed. "Absurd and miserable nonsense!"[15]

Bentham's hostility to the principles of natural law was amplified in the following decade by revulsion toward the French Revolution, which horrified many in Britain and America because of what they saw as its fanatical rationalism. According to these critics, the Reign of Terror was not the betrayal of a once-idealistic revolutionary movement; it was the inevitable consequence of Enlightenment political philosophy. Its fundamental error lay in prioritizing logic and reason over faith, habit, and reverence for antiquity. This view gave rise to a reactionary movement that condemned *reason itself* as the source of anarchy, greed, atheism, race mixing, and the destruction of traditional family and ethnic ties. The classic statement of this anti-ideological ideology was Edmund Burke's *Reflections on the Revolution in France*, published in 1790.

According to Burke, politics is about time-honored hierarchies, long-standing customs, and mysticism—or, more precisely, mystique—rather than principled individualism or rational cost-benefit analysis. Burke derided the "sophisters, economists, and calculators" who failed to see that government is a matter of "sentiment" or intuition and what he called "the unbought grace of life." In other words, the state is a kind of collective illusion, and the only way to maintain that illusion is through ceremony and glamour—as well as coercion—which will lull the populace into practicing the "submission," "obedience," "subordination," and "loyalty to rank" that mark healthy societies.[16] John Adams thought that "government [is] a plain, simple, intelligible thing founded in nature and reason and quite comprehensible by common sense."[17] Burke would have called that Jacobinism.

Burke was a bellwether of the Romantic movement, which prioritized cultural, emotional, or even instinctual considerations over reason, logic, and material progress, and which came to reject the principles of the Declaration of Independence. Romanticism viewed the state more as a tribe than a contract, and because tribal connections are based on "dark traditional forces . . . which we cannot identify and cannot analyze," the Romantics execrated individualism, reason, and economics. These, after all, tend to encourage the overthrow of ancient hierarchies and obsolete social traditions.[18] Romanticism represented a new age of faith, with the state as a spiritual, rather than rational, institution. That attitude was plainly incompatible with the reason-based philosophy of the Declaration, which carried the seeds of destruction for such time-honored institutions as slavery.

Romanticism did not become a considerable force in America until the 1830s, but a precursor appeared among members of the Federalist Party soon after independence.[19] Mortified by the French Revolution and the seeming mob rule of some states, Federalists embraced an authoritarian creed that scorned change, extolled religious hierarchy, and even censored dissenting opinions, as in the Sedition Act of 1798. In 1805, Jefferson labeled them "anti-philosophers" who "dread reformation, and exert all their faculties to maintain the ascendency of habit over the duty of improving our reason, and obeying its mandates."[20] But although he viewed his own election in 1800 as a victory over this "reign of witches," he despaired toward the end of his life that Romanticism was gaining the upper hand.[21] Its notions of government by sentiment and hierarchy instead of reason and equality seemed like a throwback to the ideas that the revolution rejected. John Adams shared this fear. He never subscribed to Burke's sentimental theory of government and was shocked by the authoritarianism of some of his fellow Federalists.[22] His desire, he told Jefferson in 1823, had always been to see "rational principles, and rational systems of government . . . prevail and be established."[23]

A SON OF THE REVOLUTION

In retirement, Jefferson was distressed to see the rising generation of law students embrace the ideas of William Blackstone, that arch-champion of Parliamentary Supremacy.[24] They even began applying Blackstone's theory to their state governments, arguing that when independence was declared, Parliament's "irresistible, absolute, uncontrolled authority" had simply transferred over to the states, which now enjoyed the same total power that the Lords and Commons once claimed.[25] That, in turn, meant states could inflict slavery on whomever they pleased, and even secede from the union.[26]

In 1823, the 80-year-old Jefferson told James Madison that he feared the Declaration's principles might be "buried in utter oblivion."[27] And indeed, within a decade, Southern leaders were explicitly rejecting the Declaration or offering clever reinterpretations of it that obscured its principles. A quarter century after Jefferson's death, South Carolina's John C. Calhoun announced that there was "not a word of truth" in the proposition that all men are created equal. People "are not born free," he said. "Nor is it less false that they are born 'equal.'" Such assertions were "inserted" in the Declaration "without any necessity." The real reason for independence had been Britain's "lawless encroachment on our acknowledged and well-established rights by the parent country," not the principles of equal freedom.[28] Calhoun uttered these denials, of course, because the Declaration's language was plainly incompatible with slavery. Preserving the "peculiar institution" required jettisoning its principles.

Slavery was not the only reason reactionaries turned against the Declaration; as Gordon Wood has shown, its doctrines rapidly dissolved traditions of rank and hierarchy, unleashing an unprecedented wave of entrepreneurialism that totally changed how Americans lived, to the astonishment of all and the horror of many.[29] Washington Irving's famous story "Rip Van Winkle" was a hit in 1819 because it captured the dizzying speed with which America had transformed from a congeries of sleepy provincial towns into a bustling capitalist society—on its way to becoming an industrial powerhouse. Nothing could be more apt than the fact that the Declaration's last surviving signer, Maryland's Charles Carroll, laid the cornerstone of the Baltimore and Ohio Railroad on July 4, 1828.

Yet slavery was the focal point of the cultural battle regarding the emergence of capitalism, with its transformative ideas of individual liberty and equal rights.[30] South Carolina Governor James Hammond claimed in 1845 that the peculiar institution was "sacred and natural" because it was governed by "the sentiments and sympathies of humanity," as opposed to the "modern, artificial *money-power* system" of capitalism.[31] The Romantic notion that government is a matter of habit, sentiment, and "loyalty to rank" was much more amenable to slave owners than was the mutual bargaining and rational calculation associated with capitalism. In an 1853 speech denouncing abolitionists, the English Romantic Thomas Carlyle condemned the whole discipline of economics—nicknaming it "the dismal science"—because it "finds the secret of this universe in 'supply and demand,' and reduces the duty of human governors to that of letting men alone." Carlyle thought society should instead be based on stability, sentiment, "obedience," and the "reveren[t]" "relation of master to servant and of superior to inferior."[32] Pro-slavery ideology, in short, became America's first anti-capitalist doctrine.

When the Civil War began, Confederate Vice President Alexander Stephens proudly announced that his new slaveholding country was based "upon the great truth that the negro is not equal to the white man." The Declaration was obsolete, he announced. It was premised on the "fundamentally wrong" idea "of the equality of races," which the Confederacy would now correct.[33] Other defenders of slavery offered a more nuanced argument. Illinois Senator

Stephen A. Douglas said in his debates with Abraham Lincoln that the Declaration did not actually mean what it said. "The words, 'all men are created equal,'" he claimed, "allude only . . . to men of European birth or descent, being white men. . . . The Declaration of Independence only included the white people of the United States."[34] The Supreme Court endorsed that view in the 1857 *Dred Scott* decision. The Declaration's actual wording "would seem to embrace the whole human family," Chief Justice Roger Taney admitted, but the revolutionary fathers could not *possibly* have meant that, because otherwise it "would have been utterly and flagrantly inconsistent with the principles they asserted" for them not to immediately free the slaves.[35]

Anti-slavery thinkers had the better argument. Cheerfully embracing the Declaration, they insisted that its principles did, indeed, apply to "all"—and required emancipation. In a speech responding to *Dred Scott*, Lincoln pointed out that despite the opinion's extraordinary length—over 100 pages—the only evidence Taney offered to support his bizarre reading of the Declaration was the fact that its authors did not immediately abolish slavery. Yet there were many reasons they failed to do so, ranging from political unfeasibility to personal hypocrisy, none of which proved that the revolutionaries had not meant what they said. They *did* mean it, Lincoln concluded. "The assertion that 'all men are created equal' was of no *practical* use in effecting our separation from Great Britain," but was "placed in the Declaration . . . for future use . . . [as] a stumbling block to those who in after times might seek to turn a free people back into the hateful paths of despotism."[36] Patriots had admitted in 1776 that slavery was incompatible with the Declaration; they knew the nation must end it somehow.

Thus, from the anarchist William Lloyd Garrison to the constitutionalist Frederick Douglass, abolitionists of all stripes rightly embraced the Declaration as the premiere exposition of the national creed. Of course, Jefferson himself was to blame for some of the slave masters' distortions of its legacy. Less than a decade after independence was declared, he published *Notes on the State of Virginia*, in which he combined condemnations of slavery with his "suspicion" that "blacks . . . are inferior to the whites in the endowments both of body and mind."[37] He did not think this alleged inferiority justified slavery, but he did think it proved that emancipation should be gradual and that the freedmen would have to leave North America. When Adams read the book, he said the passages attacking slavery were "worth diamonds"—but its racist sections unfortunately gave champions of slavery plenty of material to support their claims that black Americans did not deserve freedom.[38]

As it turned out, the most important person to emphasize the Declaration's relevance for the slavery question—as well as all other matters of American constitutional law—was John Adams's son John Quincy Adams. Literally a child of the revolution, he was 59 and serving as president when his father and Jefferson died simultaneously on July 4, 1826. John Quincy had witnessed the Battle of Bunker Hill, was superbly educated at Harvard and Leiden Universities, and began working in government at the age of 15. George Washington appointed him ambassador to the Netherlands, and he also served as ambassador to Portugal, Prussia, Russia, and Britain. He became a senator, was appointed to the Supreme Court (but declined to serve), and became secretary of state before assuming the presidency.

His four years in the White House were undistinguished, but his reputation grew when he returned to Washington as a congressman in 1830. There, he became one of a tiny handful of anti-slavery representatives and a scourge to the new generation of pro-slavery politicians. On one occasion in 1842, when a Virginia legislator condemned him for his opposition to slavery, he defended himself by pointing out that he had known Washington, Jefferson, Madison, and Monroe personally and could testify from firsthand knowledge that "they all abhorred slavery." In fact, "there was not an abolitionist of the wildest character in the Northern States but might find in the writings of Jefferson, at the time of the Declaration of Independence and during his whole life down to its very last year, a justification for everything they say."[39]

John Quincy Adams mentored such anti-slavery figures as Charles Sumner and William Seward, and Abraham Lincoln served with him in Congress. But nobody more emphatically tied the Declaration of Independence to the anti-slavery cause than he did. For almost a decade, he led a lonely crusade against the "gag rule," which barred abolitionist petitions from being introduced in Congress. In 1842, Southern representatives tried to censure him for seeking to introduce a petition from radical abolitionists who wanted the

Northern states to secede from the Union so as to have no further connection with slavery. When pro-slavery congressmen professed to be shocked by the idea of secession, Adams replied by having the clerk of the House of Representatives read the Declaration aloud. When the man grew tired, Adams spurred him on, shouting "Proceed, proceed, proceed! Down to the 'right and duty'!"—whereupon the clerk recited the language justifying rebellion against oppressive government.[40]

Adams published two long pamphlets, in 1831 and 1839, explaining the relationship between the Declaration and the Constitution and helping to set the intellectual framework for the rising anti-slavery movement. The Union's true foundation, he argued, lay in the Declaration's self-evident truths. That document was as much a marriage as a divorce; it had not only announced the country's separation from Britain but also bound the colonies together. This bond arose from certain shared principles—vows, so to speak—which the Declaration pronounced "in terms so clear, so explicit, so unequivocal" that they formed the very fiber of American national identity.[41] According to the Declaration, "The natural rights of man, and the constituent power of the people [are] the *only* sources of legitimate government."[42] The United States was only a nation—could only *be* a nation—on account of the people's commitment to these propositions:

> The colonies were transformed into States. Their inhabitants were proclaimed to be *one people*, renouncing all allegiance to the British crown; all co-patriotism with the British nation; all claims to chartered rights as Englishmen. Thenceforth their charter was the Declaration of Independence. Their rights the natural rights of mankind. Their government, such as should be instituted by themselves, under the solemn pledges of perpetual union, founded on the self-evident truths proclaimed in the Declaration.[43]

Americanness itself was defined by the Declaration's premises. That document was not merely a rhetorical statement, but a basic law—a *constitution*, in fact. Not only did it create the "union" that the 1787 Constitution later made "more perfect," but also it limited the states' power: They could only do those things states may do "of right." That meant anyone who, "adopting the doctrine of Blackstone," argued that states have "uncontrollable, unlimited, despotic power" was deluded. "Sovereignty, thus defined, is in direct contradiction to the Declaration of Independence," wrote Adams, "and incompatible with the nature of our institutions."[44] Since the Declaration and the Constitution "are parts of one consistent whole, founded upon one and the same theory of government," states did not and could not possess the kind of power Parliament had once wrongly claimed over the colonies.[45]

FREEDOM NATIONAL

On these premises, John Quincy Adams and other anti-slavery thinkers built a theory known as "Freedom National," which held that because the Declaration creates American nationhood, its principle of equal liberty forms the baseline of all federal law. That meant slavery was a political aberration that could only exist if "positively" established by state law.[46]

The implications of this theory were important because as Americans moved west—out of established states and into territories owned and managed by the federal government—debates over slavery's spread became more intense. The 1820 Missouri crisis, the Compromise of 1850, the Kansas–Nebraska Act of 1854, and the *Dred Scott* case in 1857 all revolved around the question of whether, and how, Congress could bar slavery from expanding toward the Pacific. According to the Freedom National theory, not only *could* the federal government ban slavery from western lands, but it *must* do so.

Congress and the courts, dominated by pro-slavery politicians, generally rejected this theory, of course. But it served as a crucial rallying point for abolitionist lawyers. Its most important implication concerned the connection between federal and state *citizenship*. The Constitution refers to federal citizenship (requiring, for example, that members of Congress be "citizen[s] of the United States"), but it never defined that word until after the Civil War. Instead, federal citizenship was treated as a function of state citizenship—and states could impose whatever limits they pleased. That set the stage for horrendous conflict, given that some states, such as Massachusetts, allowed free black people to be citizens, whereas others, such as South Carolina, did not. A black sailor from Boston, whose Massachusetts citizenship made him an American citizen, might find himself deprived of rights if his ship sailed to Charleston, where South Carolina's Negro Seamen Act forbade him stepping ashore. This blatantly violated the Constitution's promise that "the citizens of each state shall be entitled to all privileges and immunities of citizens in the several states."[47] Likewise, Congress let Missouri join the Union with a constitution that prohibited free black people—who could be US citizens—from even entering the state. When that happened, John Quincy Adams wrote in his diary that he considered it essentially the end of the federal Union.[48] Indeed, such conflicts eventually led to America's deadliest war.

Some anti-slavery intellectuals, such as Frederick Douglass, took the Freedom National theory even further, arguing that slavery was actually unconstitutional. Years before the Thirteenth Amendment was adopted, they pointed out that the Constitution never mentions slavery but does say that "the people" cannot be deprived of liberty without due process of law. This "people" must be the same "one people" who pronounced their independence in the Declaration—a document that also makes no mention of slavery or race. Therefore, Douglass argued, enslaved black Americans must be *citizens of the United States*. That meant their captivity violated several constitutional provisions.[49]

Although the Supreme Court rejected these arguments in *Dred Scott*—ruling that slavery, not freedom, was the constitutional baseline—the Union's victory in the Civil War gave anti-slavery leaders the chance to rescue the Constitution from what they viewed as the Court's pro-slavery misinterpretations. They did not view the Thirteenth, Fourteenth, and Fifteenth Amendments as *changing* the Constitution, so much as brushing away the misreadings foisted upon it by judges and politicians who had been determined to ignore or to twist its words in the service of slavery.

Those amendments paralleled the Declaration's self-evident truths, making clear that the Constitution is to be interpreted within its principles.[50] The Thirteenth, by abolishing slavery, reiterated that all men are created equal. The Fourteenth, by defining federal citizenship and clarifying that there are "privileges or immunities" attendant to that citizenship, which states may not abridge, echoed the principle that people have inalienable rights.[51] Also, by requiring states to provide people with equal protection and barring them from taking away lives, liberty, or property except by due process of law, the amendment made clear that governments are instituted to preserve rights and should be changed if they fail to do so. The Fifteenth Amendment, by guaranteeing the freedmen's right to vote, vindicated the principle that government derives its just powers from the consent of the governed. Together, the Reconstruction Amendments vindicated the Declaration's classical liberal vision.[52]

Anti-slavery leaders did not stop there. They also reinforced the Declaration's constitutional significance at the state level.[53] In 1864, Nevada applied for admission to the Union, the first state to do so after Southern congressmen resigned to join the Confederacy. Anti-slavery leaders therefore recognized a unique opportunity. Before then, new states were deemed fit for admission if their proposed constitutions did not contradict the federal Constitution; when Congress invited Missouri to apply for statehood in 1820, it was only required to draft a constitution that was "republican and not repugnant to the constitution of the United States."[54] But when Nevada sought admission, Congress—now controlled by anti-slavery Republicans—required it to submit a proposed constitution that "shall be republican, and not repugnant to the constitution of the United States, *and the principles of the Declaration of Independence*."[55] That requirement has applied to every state since.[56]

DISCARDING THE DECLARATION

In the 20th century, however, intellectuals affiliated with the Progressive movement revived the argument that the Declaration is only a rhetorical or political statement with no constitutional significance. Combining the arguments of Jeremy Bentham and the theories of German philosophers such as Georg Hegel and Johann Fichte, they dismissed natural rights as obsolete superstitions and claimed that morality and justice are not real things rooted in an unchanging human nature, but social constructs that can be altered to suit collective needs.[57] That meant every form of human liberty is actually an allowance the state can alter or revoke. "Rights of property and the liberty of the individual," declared Progressive Supreme Court Justice Louis Brandeis, "must be remolded, from time to time, to meet the changing needs of society."[58] His colleague Oliver Wendell Holmes was even more frank: "All my life I have sneered at the natural rights of man."[59]

Progressives thought that by creating, destroying, or rearranging these permission-style "rights," government experts could fashion a more efficient and productive society. They pursued ambitious schemes for "remolding" people, including everything from racial segregation and eugenics to the prohibition of alcohol and the compulsory flag salute. Their political program replicated many of the policies the American revolutionaries had despised, from taxes far more intrusive than the Stamp Act and conscription that replicated the evils of impressment to administrative agencies more autocratic than anything the American Board of Customs could have imagined. Progressive political scientist Charles Edward Merriam wrote in 1903 that the "exigencies" of modern life required government control over economic and personal choices, and "it is [now] fully conceded that there are no 'natural rights' which bar the way. The question is now one of expediency rather than of principle."[60] The Founders' view "that men possess inherent and inalienable rights," he concluded, "has been generally given up."[61]

That was a recipe for totalitarianism, and those who supported it saw the Declaration as a stumbling block, just as Lincoln predicted. President Calvin Coolidge, who opposed such ideas, remarked that although Progressives claimed to represent a new, cutting-edge form of political thought, they were really just resurrecting the worn-out notion of Parliamentary Supremacy that the Patriots rejected. "It is often asserted that the world has made a great deal of progress since 1776," he said on the Declaration's 150th anniversary, but "if all men are created equal, that is final. If they are endowed with inalienable rights, that is final." Anyone who denies those propositions is going backward, not forward. "Their ideas are not more modern, but more ancient, than those of the revolutionary fathers."[62]

Progressives, however, believed that history gradually unveils ever more perfect social institutions to people through their collective action.[63] Thus, they claimed that the Declaration was not necessarily *untrue*, just *imperfect*. Its authors had a shortsighted or corrupt notion of their own words' meaning. Yet history, as manifested by government administration, would slowly improve it as modern America reconceptualized its national faith. "I do not for a moment believe that the Americanism of today should be a mere submission to the American ideals of the period of the Declaration of Independence," wrote Progressive Republican Theodore Roosevelt.[64] Progressive Democrat Woodrow Wilson agreed. "We are not bound to adhere to the doctrines held by the signers of the Declaration," he said. "We have come to a new age and a new attitude towards questions of government."[65] The Founders' ideas were outdated. Ideas like separation of powers or checks and balances had become too confining.

Labeling the Declaration a relic played an important role in the Progressive effort to change the nation's understanding of the Constitution. If the Declaration's propositions about inherent human rights and the necessary limits on government power are true, then government intrusions into private life—through wealth redistribution, the control of property, the restriction of speech, and so forth—are morally inadmissible. If the Fourteenth Amendment's provision barring states from depriving people of "liberty" without due process of "law" were interpreted in light of the Declaration's principles, which explain what government actions qualify as "law" in the first place, then government's capacity to interfere with liberty would be significantly constrained.[66] On the other hand, discarding those principles would lend credence to the notion that voters and politicians may revoke or "remold" individual rights whenever they think doing so will serve pragmatic purposes. Progressive intellectuals consequently sought to downplay the Declaration or twist its meaning. In 1904, one scholar of the Declaration acknowledged that "[in] recent times . . . the judiciary is beginning to free itself from [the Declaration's] concepts"—and that was proved a year later, when Justice Oliver Wendell Holmes wrote a dissenting opinion in *Lochner v. New York*—an opinion that took on the status of scripture for 20th-century Progressives.[67]

Lochner concerned a New York law prohibiting bakers from working more than 10 hours a day or 60 hours per week. The restriction was not intended to protect the public, or the workers themselves; laboring in bakeries for long hours was no doubt exhausting, but it presented no particular threat to the health of employees or consumers.[68] Instead, the law was adopted at the behest of union leaders who hoped that limiting the workday's length would induce bakeries to hire more.[69] Yet by forbidding employees from working extra hours and thereby earning additional income, the law sacrificed their freedom of choice.

When a German immigrant named Aman Schmitter agreed with his employer, Joseph Lochner, to work longer than the law allowed, Lochner was charged with a crime. His lawyers argued in the Supreme Court that the law violated the Fourteenth Amendment by depriving both employer and employee of "liberty" without "due process of law"—a phrase well understood as prohibiting arbitrary or senseless government restrictions. They pointed to a centuries-old body of precedent affirming the individual's right to make whatever contracts one wishes, as long as one harms no other person.

The Court agreed. In a five-to-four decision, it said states may regulate businesses to protect the public from dangerous food, to shield employees from hazardous working conditions, or to prevent the exploitation of children or the mentally infirm—but could not otherwise interfere with individual economic decisions. Because none of those circumstances were present in the *Lochner* case, the bakeshop law could only be regarded as a "meddlesome interference[] with the rights of the individual"—specifically the right of "grown and intelligent men [to] labor to earn their living."[70] If the government could dictate what jobs they could take or what contracts they could make by legislative ipse dixit, "no trade, no occupation, no mode of earning one's living, could escape [its] all-pervading power," and the state could "cripple the ability of the laborer to support himself and his family."[71]

That ruling was an unremarkable application of the classical liberal principles articulated in the Declaration and secured by the Constitution: People are presumptively free to pursue happiness by whatever means they choose, as long as it is consistent with the rights of others.[72] Government's role is to protect their freedom to make their own decisions and to secure the fruits of their labor—not to dictate how many hours they ought to work.

Justice Holmes took a far more extraordinary position in his dissent. He began with a direct assault on the very idea of constitutional principles. "A constitution," he asserted, "is made for people of fundamentally differing views."[73] The notion that legal protections for "liberty" include a person's right "to do as he likes so long as he does not interfere with the liberty of others to do the same" was only a "shibboleth"—a mere "theory" that "a large part of the country does not entertain."[74] Courts had no place blocking the majority's will, because "the word 'liberty,' in the 14th Amendment is perverted when it is held to prevent the natural outcome of a dominant opinion."[75]

This was a direct repudiation of the classical liberal tradition. The idea that a constitution can be made for people "of fundamentally differing views" would have struck the Declaration's authors as absurd; constitutions can be made only among people who *agree* on fundamental issues, even if they disagree about details. The First Continental Congress's lengthy debate over whether to rest the American case on natural law or only on English tradition demonstrated the lengths to which the Founders went to form a consensus about fundamental principles—and the Declaration's purpose had been to set forth those *shared* views, ideals the Constitution aimed to preserve and promote.

Among those principles was the individual's right to pursue happiness without arbitrary interference, whether from other people or the state itself. For Holmes to deride this as a meaningless slogan meant rejecting the most fundamental elements of the constitutional system—a rejection reinforced by Holmes's bizarre statement that the word "liberty" is "perverted" when it is used to protect individuals against "dominant opinion." That, of course, is precisely what "liberty" means: No majority, no matter how "dominant," may justly intrude on individual autonomy.

Holmes did not actually consider himself a Progressive, but Progressives lionized him because his belief that the individual is effectively the creature of the state served their political goals. His *Lochner* dissent became a rallying cry for those who sought to eliminate long-standing legal guarantees for economic freedom and thereby expand government's control over private life, especially beginning with the Great Depression. Their efforts paid off in 1934, when the Supreme Court brushed aside centuries of legal precedent to establish the "rational basis test," a legal theory still used today, which effectively made Holmes's dissent into law. Under that test, the right to pursue happiness, or to acquire, possess, and enjoy private property exists largely at the government's mercy—to a degree that would have been considered extreme even in the days of British colonial rule.[76]

THE MODERN REJECTION

Although Progressivism is typically associated with the political left, 20th-century conservatives proved every bit as hostile toward the Declaration of Independence. Russell Kirk and other post–New Deal traditionalists viewed its propositions about equality, liberty, and revolution as abhorrent because they were incompatible with the reverence for tradition and authority that Kirk thought essential to social stability. In his books on American history, Kirk downplayed the significance of natural law and promoted the arguments of Edmund Burke and John C. Calhoun. "If we seek to understand the motives of the men who accomplished the American Revolution," he wrote, we should "not [look] to the Declaration."[77] Instead, the revolution's *true* impetus was the restoration of traditional English rights, rooted in sentiment and habit, not abstract principle.

Even today, some writers still maintain this position. British politician Daniel Hannan wrote in his 2013 book *Inventing Freedom* that "the Patriots believed they were fighting for . . . their rights as Britons" and that "the American Revolution was an internal argument followed by a civil war."[78] But this is silly. The reason the Patriots wrote the Declaration was to announce that they were *no longer British*, were renouncing the protections of English law, and had ceased to consider their dispute with the imperial government as an "internal argument." That explains why the Declaration makes no reference at all to the "rights of Britons."

As we've seen, there's a sense in which the distinction between "the rights of Englishmen" and natural rights is a false one. Political thinkers of Jefferson and Adams's day admired English law, not because it purported to vest one particular ethnic group with special legal privileges, but because it protected the rights all human beings have by nature, albeit in distinctively English ways. Freedom of speech and private property are natural rights that English law guaranteed, or purported to. Trial by jury is not a Lockean natural right, but a practice that evolved through English history; yet it is praiseworthy because it helps secure the natural right not to be falsely punished. Even such peculiarly English principles as "no taxation without representation" or the "vicinage" rule reflected the underlying natural law idea that government depends on the consent of the governed—derived from the precept that a true political society reflects a community of interests rather than a patrimonial hierarchy or a predatory despotism.[79] The appeal to natural law in 1776 can be regarded as "conservative" in the sense that the natural law tradition stretches back to the days of ancient Greece and even the Hebrews. But America's Founders were in no sense fighting for "their rights as Britons" after announcing their separation from Britain.

Far from being dispassionate descriptions of American history, Kirk's (and Hannan's) claims reflected a politically motivated effort to downplay the role of philosophical principles in American political history.[80] Kirk thought the evils of modernity, from Soviet communism to the breakdown of the traditional family, were traceable to the rise of ideology, as opposed to "custom, convention, and continuity."[81] And because the Declaration sets forth an ideology rooted in abstract principles rather than custom and convention, it appeared fundamentally anti-conservative. Thus, 20th-century conservative intellectuals often treated the Declaration as irrelevant, false, or even insidious.

On the eve of the nation's bicentennial, Irving Kristol, a journalist long affiliated with the American Enterprise Institute, echoed Kirk by encouraging students to "ignore" the Patriots' "grandiloquent declamations."[82] The revolution, he insisted, was aimed not at vindicating natural rights, but at "bring[ing] our political institutions into a more perfect correspondence with an actual 'American way of life.'"[83] Another conservative intellectual, Georgetown professor Martin Diamond, claimed the Declaration expressed admirable "feelings and sentiments" but was "neutral on the question of forms of government" and "offer[ed] no guidance whatsoever" for the creation of "American democratic institutions."[84] And William Rehnquist, chief justice of the Supreme Court, went even further.

In a 1975 speech at the University of Texas, he denied the validity of moral law entirely, claiming instead that if a nation "adopts a constitution and incorporates in that constitution safeguards for individual liberty," those safeguards "take on a generalized moral rightness or goodness . . . simply because they have been incorporated in a constitution" and *not* "because of any intrinsic worth nor because of any unique origins in someone's idea of natural justice."[85] In other words, there are no natural laws—there's only the all-encompassing, all-legitimating power of the majority.[86]

None of this was true. Far from aligning "political institutions" with "an actual 'American way of life,'" the revolution utterly transformed that way of life.[87] Americans in the 1760s lived in grudging subservience to British overlords. By the end of the century, their society had been entirely refashioned into a dynamic, self-governing nation that had no hereditary aristocracy, that was abolishing slavery, and that embraced a culture of equality and freedom so pervasive that, as Alexis de Tocqueville observed, even the rich felt obliged to at least pretend to work for a living. Diamond's notion that the Declaration "offer[ed] no guidance" for "American democratic institutions" was even stranger. The Declaration sets forth truths (not "feelings and sentiments") that establish standards of political legitimacy. Americans aimed at those standards when replacing their colonial governments with new, constitutional ones—and they continue to aim at those standards today.[88] As for Rehnquist's idea that constitutional principles are made legitimate solely because they are "incorporated in a constitution by a people," the political philosopher Harry Jaffa offered the fittest response. It was "discouraging," Jaffa wrote, that the country's chief justice "does not, in the least, believe in the principles of the Declaration."[89] Nazi and Bolshevik principles were adopted into German and Soviet constitutions, too. Did that make them legitimate?

The most explicit conservative attack on the Declaration came, however, from another judge: Robert Bork, whose 1997 book *Slouching Towards Gomorrah* condemned the document as the source of an entire menu of modern evils.[90] Mocking people who "grow misty-eyed" at its references to liberty and the pursuit of happiness, Bork argued that those principles actually lead to "personal license and social disorder."[91] Equality and liberty are the "twin thrusts" that "free the individual from all moral and legal constraints," he wrote, and their ultimate consequence is to create "the autonomous individual who [stands] in an adversarial relationship to any institution or group that attempt[s] to set limits to acceptable thought and behavior."[92] The fruits of the Declaration's principles are actually "rot and decadence," because only religious dogma and rigid social hierarchies can ensure a stable social order.[93]

These criticisms would have struck Jefferson as nothing new. Bork and his allies were merely echoing the words of those he called "anti-philosophers," who believed in "the ascendency of habit over the duty of improving our reason, and obeying its mandates."[94] In 1823, he acknowledged that his political opponents thought people "cannot be restrained within the limits of order and justice [except] by forces physical and moral wielded over them by authorities independent of their will." Since they thought the people could not govern themselves by reason, these would-be despots instead sought to prop up "kings, hereditary nobles, and priests" to "fascinate the eyes of the people and excite in them a humble adoration and submission as to an order of superior beings." But Jefferson believed

> that man [is] a rational animal, endowed by nature with rights, and with an innate sense of justice, and that he [can] be restrained from wrong, and protected in right, by moderate powers, confided to persons of his own choice, and held to their duties by dependence on his own will. . . . We [believe] that men, enjoying in ease and security the full fruits of their own industry, enlisted by all their interests on the side of law and order, habituated to think for themselves and to follow their reason as their guide, [will] be more easily and safely governed than with minds nourished in error, and vitiated and debased, as in Europe, by ignorance, indigence and oppression.[95]

The question is not whether liberty and equality automatically make people good—they certainly do not—but whether oppression and inequality will make them better. Nobody denies that some people use their liberty in unwise or immoral ways, or squander life's opportunities by acting thoughtlessly or even criminally.

But government's role is to ensure that those who use their freedom wisely, productively, peacefully—or even in harmlessly foolish ways—are protected against interference by others, whether robbers or bureaucrats. Bork's words reflected an extreme form of authoritarianism that holds that for ordinary people to be good, they must *obey*—while some autocrat issues dictates from on high that "set limits" on what behaviors are "acceptable."

THE DECLARATION AS LAW

By the end of the 20th century, and into the 21st, both left and right had united in rejecting the Declaration's propositions about liberty and equality. That was for two related reasons: the growth of cultural relativism and the belief that ethics is essentially a function of subjective emotion. Beginning in the 1930s, philosophers advancing theories of "emotivism" or "noncognitivism" claimed that morality rests not on verifiable truths about human nature but on mere personal or emotional disapproval. The renowned logician A. J. Ayer, for example, wrote that a moral assertion "expresses no proposition that can be either true or false."[96] Many were drawn to this idea because it seemed "scientific," due to the prevalent taboo against deriving "ought" statements from "is" statements.[97]

Philosophers today largely reject that taboo, thanks to the revival of interest in Aristotelian thought, but it remains a powerful force within the legal profession.[98] As a consequence, it was late 20th-century lawyers who first claimed that the Declaration of Independence is not law. Prominent law professor Douglas Laycock published an article in 1991 entitled "The Declaration Is Not Law."[99] Justice Antonin Scalia repeatedly asserted that it "is not part of our law" and "not a legal prescription."[100] During her 2020 confirmation hearings, Justice Amy Coney Barrett was directly asked about the legal status of the Declaration. "It's not law," she replied. "It isn't binding law."[101] But that's not true.

The Declaration is a statute adopted by the Continental Congress, which was the nation's legislature at the time.[102] It had the *effect* of law: It severed the United States from Great Britain and authorized the country to make war, conclude peace, and contract alliances, all of which the Congress proceeded to do. It has always appeared in collections of federal statutes and still does—on page 1 of Volume 1 of the *Statutes at Large*, and at the beginning of the first volume of the *United States Code*.[103] It's even implicitly referenced in the Constitution itself, which concludes with the line "done in convention by the unanimous consent of the states present the seventeenth day of September in the year of our Lord one thousand seven hundred and eighty-seven *and of the independence of the United States of America the twelfth*."[104] It has also been implicitly incorporated into every state constitution since 1864. It obviously continues to have legal force every day that the United States operates as an independent country. It's hard to imagine what else would be necessary to make it law.

The belief that the Declaration is not "law" rests on a crabbed conception of what counts as "law." Under the influence of Jeremy Bentham and Oliver Wendell Holmes, many modern lawyers think legal pronouncements must *command* or be backed by *penalties* to qualify. But statutes often lack these elements and are nevertheless laws. Those specifying how to make a will, for example, or declaring what types of marriages are considered valid, cannot be plausibly described as "commands" enforced by "penalties."[105] Other laws are "aspirational," meaning they specify goals in general terms; these may not be enforceable by a court order, but they're still laws. For instance, 42 U.S.C. § 18351(a)—which governs American participation in the International Space Station (ISS) program—declares, "It shall be the policy of the United States, in consultation with its international partners in the ISS program, to support full and complete utilization of the ISS." If that's a law, the Declaration must be, too.

Setting forth aspirations is one of law's most important roles. Laws often enunciate principles to explain how to interpret other laws or to guide officials in discharging their duties. The Constitution itself does this. Nobody denies that the Ninth and Tenth Amendments are "law"—yet they don't command anyone to do anything or impose punishments for noncompliance. Instead, they tell future generations how to interpret the Constitution. Lawyers sometimes speak of decisions such as *New York v. United States* "applying" the Tenth Amendment, but that's just a shorthand way of saying the Supreme Court followed the principles articulated in the amendment when deciding those cases.[106] In the same sense, we can speak of courts "applying" the Declaration of Independence when they rely on its principles of liberty and equality.

Courts often do just that. As legal historian R. H. Helmholz explains, American lawyers routinely invoked the Declaration's principles in legal arguments throughout the 19th century, even in cases involving "mundane questions related to family law and the law of inheritance."[107] John Quincy Adams cited the Declaration in his famous argument before the Supreme Court in the *Amistad* case to support his contention that enslaved Africans had the right to kill their enslavers in self-defense.[108] More recently, Justice Clarence Thomas has repeatedly relied on it to decide cases involving racial discrimination. "The Constitution's colorblind rule reflects one of the core principles upon which our Nation was founded: that 'all men are created equal,'" he wrote in 2023.[109]

State courts also frequently apply the Declaration. In 2025 alone, the Tennessee Supreme Court cited it when interpreting the state constitution's rules governing the right to petition; the Ohio Court of Appeals cited it to interpret its constitutional protection for jury trial rights; an Iowa Supreme Court justice cited it when applying the rule of "vicinage"; and two justices on the Arizona Supreme Court cited it in discussing the powers of administrative agencies during emergencies.[110] In 2006, Justice James Johnson of the Washington Supreme Court wrote that the principle of "no taxation without representation" should be constitutionally binding in that state because Washington was required, like all states since 1864, to ensure that its constitution was consistent with the Declaration.[111] In 1946, Virginia's highest court ruled that "a person's business, occupation, or calling is . . . included in the right to liberty and the pursuit of happiness," and consequently that the state could not force professional photographers to get a government license to practice their business.[112] Almost six decades later, the Pennsylvania Supreme Court agreed, striking down a licensing law with this observation: "Included within the right to possess property and pursue happiness is the right to pursue a chosen occupation."[113]

More complicated are recent legal controversies concerning abortion rights. These frequently involve constitutional language deliberately modeled on the Declaration.[114] In *Hodes & Nauser v. Schmidt*, the Kansas Supreme Court was asked to interpret a clause in that state's constitution that protects "equal and inalienable natural rights, among which are life, liberty, and the pursuit of happiness." The justices said this includes the right to "personal autonomy and decision-making about issues that affect one's physical health, family formation, and family life." That, they concluded, means the state "cannot intrude on a person's control of his or her own body when doing so will cause harm to the individual."[115]

Since 2020, judges in at least nine other states have consulted the Declaration's natural rights principles when applying their own state constitutional guarantees to the abortion question.[116] Whether the reference to "life" in these clauses allows (or even mandates) that the state punish abortion, or whether, on the contrary, the right to "liberty" forbids states from—as one Georgia judge put it—forcing women to "serve as human incubators" against their will is beyond the scope of this book, but such questions clearly cannot be answered without employing natural law arguments.[117]

The bottom line is that the Declaration *is* law, but a particular *kind* of law. Its broad wording does not prescribe what side of the road to drive on, or define medical malpractice, or specify the punishment for petty theft, or declare whether a construction crew owes pedestrians only a "reasonable" degree of care or something more stringent. Instead, it sets forth principles of legitimacy that serve as guideposts for constitutional interpretation and enforcement. "The values of innate rights and self-government mandated by the Declaration," concludes legal scholar Alexander Tsesis, "are constitutionally binding . . . and should be used as deciding values in cases involving human dignity."[118]

Most importantly, the Declaration provides an ethical-political compass to guide government. Legal scholars in recent years have stressed that constitutions are not morally neutral mechanisms for accomplishing whatever political leaders or voting majorities want to do. Instead, a constitution must fit within a broader ethical-political framework if it is to operate legitimately, if officials are to know how to distinguish proper from improper acts, and if the government that the constitution erects is to wield authority instead of mere power.[119] The Declaration of Independence sets forth that framework.

— AFTERWORD —

1776 VERSUS 1619

Is it a dream?
Nay, but the lack of it the dream,
And, failing it, life's lore and wealth a dream,
And all the world a dream.
—Walt Whitman[1]

When the *New York Times*'s 1619 Project was unveiled, it began with an audacious claim: "The moment [America] began," it said, was on an August day four centuries earlier, when about 20 enslaved Africans were brought ashore in Virginia and sold. This incident, the *Times* writers claimed, "is the country's very origin." Although the nation's "official birthdate" came long after, it is really "out of slavery—and the anti-black racism it required" that "nearly everything that has truly made America exceptional" grew.[2]

These opening sentences—and subsequent statements by project organizer Nikole Hannah-Jones—later generated even more controversy when it was revealed that *Times* editors altered the online version of the project's text after being criticized for calling 1619 the nation's "true founding." Scholars such as economic historian Phil Magness justly viewed these unacknowledged edits as violations of journalistic standards, but the project's editors responded by saying they were immaterial, because the idea that 1619 was the "true founding" was never meant to be taken *literally*. "We know this nation marks its founding at 1776," wrote Hannah-Jones.[3] The phrase "true founding" was "always a metaphoric argument." *New York Times Magazine* editor in chief Jake Silverstein repeated this defense in an article days afterward: The year 1619 was always meant

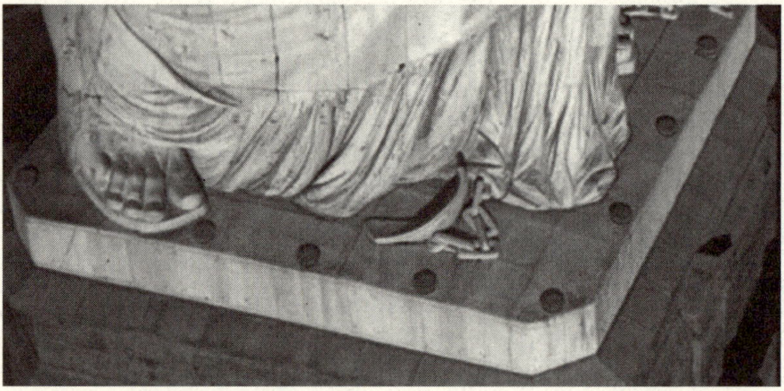

Sculptor Frédéric-Auguste Bartholdi depicted broken shackles by the feet of the Statue of Liberty to honor the abolition of slavery 21 years before the statue was erected.

as "a metaphor." Whatever errors the editors may have committed, the project's "'core premises' remain unshaken."[4]

But this defense missed the point. *Obviously* the "true founding" claim was always a metaphor, because all foundings are metaphors. Like a corporation, an athletic team, or a social club, a nation is a theoretical or imaginative institution—a legal fiction—which means its origin is necessarily spoken of in metaphor, ritual, and symbolism. Philosopher Hannah Arendt, whose book *On Revolution* is almost entirely devoted to this question, wrote that foundings are fundamentally about "binding and promising, combining and covenanting," because "the human faculty of making and keeping promises" is the essential "world-building capacity of man"—indeed, it is "the highest human faculty."[5] We typically speak of promises in metaphorical terms for the same reason we use poetic terms to speak of love: because these things are made of words. Only the language of reverence can give those words any power to compel. Thus, to speak of America's "founding" *at all* is necessarily to speak of what makes Americans a "people," and that is necessarily to speak in metaphorical language.

When Abraham Lincoln said that the nation was "conceived in liberty" four score and seven years before the dedication of Gettysburg Cemetery—that is, in 1776—and when, a century later, Martin Luther King Jr. referred to the Declaration as America's "promissory note," they were speaking in metaphors. And when the *Times* writers insisted to the contrary that America was conceived not in liberty but in slavery, they, too, were obviously speaking in metaphor. For Hannah-Jones and Silverstein to accuse their critics of being excessively literal is therefore to set up a straw man. Their choice to use one metaphor over another was always the essence of the controversy over the 1619 Project. The question the project posed was whether the American nation should be viewed as having its genesis not in the Declaration of Independence, with its covenants of equality and liberty, but in a commercial transaction for human flesh.

ERASING

For one metaphor to be more fruitful than another requires that it provide a better explanation for the subject in question. And the 1619 metaphor failed that test, not because it got the dates wrong, but because its effort to frame the question in (literally) black-and-white terms essentially requires ignoring large swaths of American history. America is not, and never has been, a simple dichotomy of black versus white any more than the nation's story falls into the tidy dichotomy of exploiter and exploited, oppressor and oppressed. Instead, its conceiving principle—that each individual is of infinite value and has a right to pursue his or her own happiness in peace—has manifested itself in far more complicated ways, resulting in far more interesting human stories of triumph, treachery, loss, and victory, than is dreamed of in any effort to portray American history as "us" versus "them."

Take California, for example. The nation's most productive state accounts today for 13 percent of the United States' entire agricultural output, 5 percent of its mineral production, and 11 percent of its manufacturing. If the enslavement of Africans and their descendants was the source of American prosperity, as the 1619 Project's authors claimed, it should be most evident here. Yet black slavery was never a major factor in California, which was always a free state. Instead, it was the cruel experience of Chinese "coolie" labor that shaped California's early years. Anywhere between 20,000 and 100,000 Chinese immigrants arrived in the 1850s and 1860s to mine for gold and build the railroads.[6] The Chinese and Japanese populations (few whites bothered to differentiate between the two) farmed, fished, mined, and worked as domestic labor throughout the century even while enduring brutal mistreatment and discrimination by Americans and European immigrants. "In many districts of the vast Pacific coast, so strong is the wild, free love of justice in the hearts of the people," wrote Mark Twain in a bitter 1870 article, "that whenever any secret and mysterious crime is committed, they say, 'Let justice be done, though the heavens fall,' and go straightway and [lynch] a Chinaman."[7]

Chinese laborers—who were basically purchased wholesale from labor companies in China—were assigned the most perilous tasks in building the transcontinental railroad. Nobody knows exactly how many died, because nobody bothered to write it down. "On average," writes Iris Chang in *The Chinese in America*, "three laborers perished for every two miles of track laid. . . . Twenty thousand pounds of their bones [were] shipped [back] to China."[8]

In 1878, the state held a constitutional convention for the express purpose of throwing the Chinese and Japanese out of the state, and the decades that followed witnessed scores of race riots in which Chinatowns and Japantowns were incinerated and Asians slaughtered. In 1906, when San Francisco was leveled by earthquake and fire, many locals saw it as an opportunity to evict the Chinese and looted the city's wrecked Chinatown. The federal government did its best to prevent rebuilding, and only the personal intercession of China's empress ensured that it was restored.

Soon afterward, the federal government turned Angel Island in San Francisco Bay into a holding pen—a reverse Ellis Island—where 175,000 Asian immigrants were detained, sometimes for years, before being considered for admission.[9] Those allowed in faced various kinds of bigotry, not the least of which was internment in prison camps and the confiscation of their property during World War II. Not until 1952 did it become legal for Asian immigrants to own land in California. Even today, the state discriminates against Asian Americans by illegally practicing racial preferences in college admissions that exclude many of them from public universities.

The Asian American story is distinctive but not unique. Many other minority groups have faced mistreatment, including the indigenous population, who, centuries before the Chinese arrived, were enslaved by the conquistadores or used in ways tantamount to enslavement. But none of this was mentioned in the 1619 Project articles, and when pressed on the question, Hannah-Jones responded on Twitter, "Most Asian Americans arrived in this country after the end of legal segregation and discrimination, thanks to the Black resistance struggle"—which apparently means their history can be ignored.

LIONIZING AND DISPARAGING

The fashionable term for this is "erasing," and it's easy to see why she did it: The "reframing" that the 1619 Project attempted is rooted in an ideology that views America's political-economic foundation—that is, capitalism—as not just tainted by racism, but also designed to immiserate minorities and enrich those on top. According to this worldview, racism is not a bug, but a feature of

American institutions. But that narrative collapses in light of the struggles, and especially the successes, of countless Americans of all races who have found this country to be a refuge and a land of opportunity.

The *Times*'s proposed metaphor of a 1619 founding omitted not only the Chinese who built the railroads and the Native Americans who built the missions, but also the Irish of Boston, the Italians of New York, the Cubans of Florida, the Germans of Wisconsin, the Cherokee of Georgia, the Mexicans of Texas, and the Hawaiians of, well, Hawaii, many of whom have taken advantage of liberty to realize the nation's founding promise. To accept the 1619 metaphor requires ignoring such heroic triumphs as Madam C. J. Walker, Quanah Parker, Irving Berlin, A. P. Giannini, Arnold Schwarzenegger, Ellison Onizuka, Maria Contreras-Sweet, and countless others.

More generally, that metaphor ignored the fact that the racial conflicts that have plagued American history are far from unique to the United States. On the contrary, every square inch of the planet, from Rwanda to Nanking, from Poland to Colombia, has known such bigotry. Slavery, too, is ubiquitous in mankind's past. It may, in fact, be the oldest human institution after the family—and it is still practiced today in parts of Africa and the Middle East, to say nothing of forced labor camps in communist countries. What was unique about America was that its Founding marked the very first time a nation was expressly created on principles incompatible with slavery.[10] Little wonder that the world's first anti-slavery society was established in Philadelphia in 1775. And little wonder that—for all its awful shortfalls—America has served as a refuge for the oppressed, from the Huguenots to the Hmong.

Had the *Times* set out to tell that story—to celebrate the struggles of Americans whose ancestors were once excluded and exploited, and whose victories are still too little known—things might have turned out differently. At first, there was some hope that it might. As *Times* correspondent Bret Stephens observed in one column, Hannah-Jones expressed in her opening essay the "unabashedly patriotic thought" that black Americans have more than earned the right to celebrate their Americanness.[11] But that idea clashed with the 1619 Project's larger thesis that capitalism is inherently exploitative, and that "anti-black racism" is the real nucleus of American nationhood.

This implicit conflict of visions plagued the project from the outset. Although Jake Silverstein later claimed that the point of the project was "to think of the 244 years of effort to live up to our founding ideals as part of a larger freedom story," that only makes sense if those "founding ideals" are, indeed, our Founding ideals—which is just what the 1619 Project articles denied.[12] Hannah-Jones, for example, declared in the opening essay that "one of the primary reasons the colonists decided to declare their independence from Britain was because they wanted to protect the institution of slavery" and that the "white men" who wrote "all men are created equal" really "did not believe [those words] to be true."[13] But if the nation's Founding principles are actually racism and oppression, then it's senseless to celebrate any effort to realize its ideals.

Rather than resolve this contradiction, the project's authors, especially Hannah-Jones, took refuge in it, alternately affirming and denying the Declaration's self-evident truths to suit the convenience of the moment. In Progressive circles, they claimed that America is a fundamentally racist nation, and then when criticized as anti-American, insisted that the project was merely a patriotic testament to the way black Americans have vindicated the nation's noble creed. So which is it?

In a 2017 interview, *Atlantic* editor in chief Jeffrey Goldberg tried in vain to pin Hannah-Jones down on this question. "Is at the bottom what we're talking about a lack of understanding on the part of white America about the actual lived lives of African Americans?" he asked. "I would say we're not grappling [with] what this country is about," she replied. Goldberg persisted: "You're not one of these people who says, '[racism] is not who we are'[?]" "No," she answered, "this is clearly who we are. . . . [Racism] is embedded in the DNA of this country."[14] But if that's true, it makes no sense to celebrate, as Hannah-Jones did in a later interview, the way that "black people have been willing to put their bodies on the line . . . to make our *founding ideals* true."[15] If the 1619 metaphor were truly compelling, it would not be necessary to dodge back and forth between lionizing the nation's soul and disparaging it.

Even more lamentable was the way the 1619 Project omitted entire stages of history that are crucial to understanding how that soul developed. A reader could easily come away from the

1619 essays with the impression that American attitudes toward slavery smoothly transitioned from the (allegedly) pro-slavery views of the country's Founders to the days of the Civil War. (In fact, the essays nowhere mentioned secession or its causes, and they skipped from the 1857 *Dred Scott* decision to Lincoln's attempt five years later to persuade black Americans to emigrate.) But the reality is that attitudes toward slavery shifted significantly after 1800, as a reactionary movement opposed to the principles of the American Revolution gained followers. Southern politicians began describing slavery as a "positive good" and overtly denouncing the Declaration as either legally insignificant or an outright lie.

That movement appalled many of those who remained steadfast in their American faith—people such as John Quincy Adams, William Jay, Joshua Giddings, Charles Sumner, Frederick Douglass, and Salmon P. Chase. Their efforts to resist the pro-slavery perversions of the Constitution went unmentioned in the 1619 Project essays, however. So did the origin of the Fourteenth Amendment, adopted in 1868, whose proponents viewed it as a re-Founding, as a rededication to the principles of American nationhood. To use the Christian metaphor natural to the era, they set forth a New Covenant for the American people, which was meant not to abolish, but to fulfill the law. That makes no sense if racism is built into the country's metaphorical DNA.

All of this matters beyond the history classrooms, because the metaphors we find persuasive about the nation's identity say something not just about the nation's past, but also about ourselves in the present. As Arendt was keen to emphasize, the "binding and promising, combining and covenanting" that marks a nation's founding is reenacted with every new generation.[16] That's why we teach history to kids and require new citizens to take classes about civic institutions. To adopt the 1619 metaphor instead of 1776 or 1868 means to accept a particular understanding of the nature of Americanness—one profoundly contrary to that expressed in both the nation's Founding and re-Founding documents.

A NEW BIRTH OF FREEDOM

For some, in fact, it means a commitment to the proposition that commitments are meaningless in any event. Such nihilism has become a distressing trend in recent years, thanks to intellectuals who contend that the American character is not only infected with, but actually constructed out of, racism. Foremost among these is Ta-Nehisi Coates, celebrity author of the National Book Award–winning *Between the World and Me,* who claims that "America is literally unimaginable without plundered labor shackled to plundered land, without the organizing principle of whiteness as citizenship" and that racism "remains, as it has since 1776, at the heart of this country's political life."[17]

Coates's cynicism is so extreme that, toward the end of his book, he relates how unmoved he was by the September 11 attacks and the outpouring of national grief that followed—which he calls "ridiculous" and "overwrought." The bravery of firefighters and police officers (many of them black), who rushed to rescue the innocent as the Twin Towers collapsed only to be chopped to pieces by razor-sharp fragments of burning steel, he regards with detachment, if not disgust. "Hell upon [them]," he writes. "They were not human to me."[18]

Such nihilism is the logical consequence of a certain conception of what America stands for—one that regards the country as pledged to oppression, instead of liberation. And the real-world consequences of that nihilism were starkly revealed when Hannah-Jones celebrated the riots that broke out across the nation in the summer of 2020, saying that she would be "honor[ed]" if the violence, arson, vandalism, and destruction of monuments that marked those months came to be known as the "1619 Riots."[19]

Whatever else America might be, it is a land of idealism. Ideals are not just a part of our tradition, but also the source of the country's legal being. The Declaration of Independence, after all, announced not only that the nation was independent, but that it "*of right ought to be*," meaning that the country's institutional legitimacy is premised on the validity of the "self-evident truths" to which the Founders pledged their "sacred honor." The Constitution continued in this vein, proclaiming that among its purposes was the preservation of liberty (an abstract principle) for "our posterity." That was why Lincoln said that the Declaration's truths are "the definitions and axioms" of American nationhood and warned that anyone who sneers at them or denies their validity is "supplanting the principles of free government." The country can only survive, he said—and will only deserve to survive—if the efforts of such detractors are "repulse[d]."[20]

To the extent that the 1619 Project caused Americans to learn more about black history and to view the civil rights struggles of past generations in light of the American covenants of liberty, it served an honorable purpose. But it accomplished this only to the degree that readers "repulsed" the larger metaphor that the project offered. Everything, in fact, that makes America great originates in the fact that Americans *do not* take the sale of human property in August 1619 as the source of their nationhood—that, on the contrary, they are disgusted by what accepting that metaphor would say about their nation. In seeking to debunk American principles, the project's authors were led to ignore history, to disregard some of the nation's most moving and revealing qualities, and, most importantly, to distort the metaphors whereby we became, and continue to become, "one people."

NOTES

ABBREVIATIONS:

ARW = Gordon S. Wood, ed., *John Adams: Revolutionary Writings 1755–1775*, 2 vols. (Library of America, 2011).

Cappon = Lester Cappon, ed., *The Adams-Jefferson Letters* (University of North Carolina Press, 1959).

Cobbett = William Cobbett, *Parliamentary History of England*, 36 vols. (London, 1812–1820).

D&A = L. H. Butterfield, ed., *Diary and Autobiography of John Adams*, 4 vols. (Atheneum, 1964).

Force = Peter Force, ed., *American Archives*, Series 4, 6 vols. (Washington, 1837–1846).

JCC = Worthington C. Ford, ed., *Journals of the Continental Congress*, 34 vols. (Government Printing Office, 1904–1937).

JHBV = *Journals of the House of Burgesses of Virginia*, 13 vols. (Virginia State Library, 1915).

JHRM = *Journals of the House of Representatives of Massachusetts, 1715–1779*, 65 vols. (Massachusetts Historical Society, 1919–1990).

JW = Merrill Peterson, ed., *Thomas Jefferson: Writings* (Library of America, 1984).

Pamphlets = Gordon Wood, ed., *The American Revolution: Writings from the Pamphlet Debate*, 2 vols. (Library of America, 2015).

PTJ = Julian P. Boyd et al., eds., *The Papers of Thomas Jefferson*, 48 vols. (Princeton University Press, 1950– present).

SaL = Danby Pickering, ed., *Statutes at Large*, 46 vols. (Cambridge, 1762–1807).

PROLOGUE

1. *JW*, p. 1259.

2. Cappon, p. 614.

3. Charles Francis Adams, *The Life of John Adams*, rev. ed. (Philadelphia, 1871), vol. 2, p. 403 (emphasis added).

4. *JW*, p. 1517.

5. For example, in his book *English Liberties*, first published in 1680 and reprinted countless times over the following century, Henry Care wrote, "The constitution of our *English* government (the best in the world) is no arbitrary *tyranny*, like the *Turkish* grand seigneurs, or the *French* kings, whose wills (or rather *lusts*) dispose of the lives and fortunes of their unhappy subjects; nor an *oligarchy*, where the great ones . . . prey upon and live by devouring the *lesser* at their pleasure; nor yet a *democracy* or popular state, much less an *anarchy* [but a state where people are] so guarded in their persons and properties by the fence of law as renders them *free-men*, not slaves." Henry Care, *English Liberties, or, The Free-Born Subject's Inheritance* (London, 1691), p. 1.

6. *Semayne's Case*, 77 Eng. Rep. 194 (K.B. 1604).

7. *Pennsylvania Gazette*, June 8, 1774, p. 1.

8. William Blackstone, *Commentaries on the Laws of England* (London, 1809), vol. 1, p. 161.

9. A particularly fine statement of the case for Parliamentary Supremacy is H. T. Dickinson, ed., *Britain and the American Revolution* (Longman, 1998), chap. 3. It deserves to be read alongside John Phillip Reid's *Constitutional History of the American Revolution*.

10. *JCC*, vol. 5, p. 425.

11. Leland G. Stauber, *The American Revolution: A Grand Mistake* (Prometheus Books, 2010), pp. 155, 258–60.

12. Conrad Black, *Flight of the Eagle: A Strategic History of the United States* (Encounter, 2013), p. 62.

13. Bryan Caplan, "Independence Day: Any Reason to Celebrate?," *EconLog* (blog), July 4, 2007.

14. Robert Middlekauff, *The Glorious Cause: The American Revolution, 1763–1789* (Oxford University Press, 1982), p. vii.

15. Eric Foner, ed., *Thomas Paine: Writings* (Library of America, 1995), p. 91 (emphasis altered).

16. *JW*, p. 875.

17. Gordon S. Wood, ed., *John Adams: Writings from the New Nation 1784–1826* (Library of America, 2016), p. 466.

18. *JW*, p. 1501. The charge that Jefferson "plagiarized" the Declaration (see, for example, Kevin Phillips, *1775: A Good Year for Revolution* [Penguin, 2012], p. 436) has always been a silly one. The Declaration is a legal, not literary or scholarly, document, and the concept of plagiarism simply does not apply to legal documents, where questions of priority are not a concern and where writers necessarily rely on time-tested formulas and phrases. In fact, originality is typically a detriment in legal documents. Nor is it reasonable to expect the authors of the Declaration to have added attributory footnotes. Moreover, many of the arguments Locke advanced in his *Treatises* were not original to *him*; similar wording can be found in the writings of John Milton and other 17th-century thinkers.

Akhil Reed Amar's assertion (in *Born Equal* [Basic Books, 2025], p. 621), that Jefferson "den[ied]" he had "borrowed liberally from Locke"—which Amar says was "not fine"—rests on a misrepresentation. Jefferson never denied that he borrowed liberally from Locke; on the contrary, he openly admitted that the Declaration was based in part on the writings of "Aristotle, Cicero, Locke, [and] Sidney." *JW*, p. 1501. What he denied was that he "turned to [either] book or pamphlet while writing [the Declaration]." James Norton Smith, ed., *The Republic of Letters* (Norton, 1995), vol. 3, p. 1876. As we have seen, he hardly needed to, because Lockean phrases were common parlance at the time.

19. In reality, the last signer of the Declaration, Maryland's Charles Carroll, died in 1832 at the age of 95.

20. Irving Kristol, "The American Revolution as a Successful Revolution" in Irving Kristol et al., *America's Continuing Revolution* (American Enterprise Institute, 1975), p. 15; and Carl Becker, *The Declaration of Independence: A Study in the History of Political Ideas* (Vintage, 1942), p. 277.

21. John Phillip Reid, "The Irrelevance of the Declaration," in *Law and the American Revolution and the Revolution in the Law*, ed. Hendrik Hartog (New York University Press, 1981), pp. 46–89.

22. Kevin Phillips, *1775: A Good Year for Revolution* (Penguin, 2012), p. 212.

23. Michael Zuckert, *Natural Rights and the New Republicanism* (Princeton University Press, 1994); and C. Bradley Thompson, *America's Revolutionary Mind: A Moral History of the American Revolution and the Declaration That Defined It* (Encounter, 2019).

24. Michael Zuckert, "Natural Rights and Imperial Constitutionalism: The American Revolution and the Development of the American Amalgam," in *Natural Rights Liberalism from Locke to Nozick*, ed. Ellen Frankel Paul, Fred D. Miller Jr., and Jeffrey Paul (Cambridge University Press, 2005), p. 33.

25. Hannah Arendt, *On Revolution* (Penguin, 1990), p. 149.

26. Don E. Fehrenbacher, ed., *Abraham Lincoln: Speeches and Writings 1859–1865* (Library of America, 1989), p. 19. Pauline Maier (*American Scripture: Making the Declaration of Independence* [Knopf, 1997], p. 192) contends that the Declaration was "not [intended] to lay down principles to guide and limit [the] successor [to British government]." As we will see later, this is false. The Declaration specifies the limits on *all* legitimate government, and as Maier's own book demonstrates, those principles were recited throughout the new state constitutions adopted at the time of independence. Her effort to distinguish those constitutions from the Declaration on the grounds that the former but not the latter "could . . . be enforced in the courts" is irrelevant, since the same principles appeared in state constitutions, which could be—and, at least in the Quock Walker case, were—enforced by courts.

27. Craig Nelson, *Thomas Paine: Enlightenment, Revolution, and the Birth of Modern Nations* (Penguin, 2006), p. xi.

CHAPTER 1

1. *D&A*, vol. 3, p. 257.

2. R. B. Bernstein, *The Education of John Adams* (Oxford University Press, 2020), p. 17. Adams told different versions of this story; I have assumed they worked two days.

3. L. H. Butterfield, ed., *Adams Family Correspondence* (Massachusetts Historical Society, 1963), vol. 2, p. 239.

4. C. D. Yonge, trans., *Cicero's Tusculan Disputations* (New York, 1877), p. 441.

5. John Trenchard and Thomas Gordon, *Cato's Letters*, ed. Ronald Hamowy (Liberty Fund, 1995), vol. 1, p. 405 (No. 59).

6. T. Meyler-Warlow, trans., *Cicero's Pro Cluentio* (London, 1889), p. 56.

7. Walter Miller, trans., *De Officiis* (Heinemann, 1928), pp. 253–55.

8. Clinton Walker Keyes, trans., *The Laws* (Heinemann, 1928), p. 329.

9. Keyes, *Laws*, pp. 332–33.

10. Keyes, *Laws*, p. 333.

11. Miller, *De Officiis*, p. 259.

12. Jonathan Mayhew, *A Discourse Concerning Unlimited Submission and Non-Resistance to the Higher Powers* (Boston, 1750).

13. Mayhew, *Discourse*, pp. 10–11.

14. Mayhew, *Discourse*, pp. 23, 27.

15. Mayhew, *Discourse*, pp. 12, 13.

16. Mayhew, *Discourse*, pp. 49–50.

17. Mayhew, *Discourse*, p. 52.

18. Mayhew, *Discourse*, p. 54.

19. Cappon, p. 527.

20. Edward Holyoke, *Integrity and Religion to Be Principally Regarded by Such as Design Others to Stations of Public Trust* (Boston, 1736), p. 9.

21. Holyoke, *Integrity*, p. 13.

22. *The Works of the Reverend George Whitefield* (London, 1771), vol. 4, p. 213.

23. *D&A*, vol. 3, pp. 261–62.

24. Cappon, p. 509.

25. *D&A*, vol. 3, p. 262.

26. Charles R. Kesler and Clinton Rossiter, eds., *The Federalist Papers* (Signet, 2003), p. 436.

27. Robert J. Taylor, Mary-Jo Kline, and Gregg L. Lint, eds., *Papers of John Adams* (Belknap, 1977), vol. 1, p. 3.

28. *JW*, p. 739.

29. *JW*, p. 735.

30. *D&A*, vol. 3, p. 274.

31. *D&A*, vol. 1, p. 63.

32. *D&A*, vol. 1, p. 55.

33. *D&A*, vol. 3, p. 272.

34. *D&A*, vol. 3, p. 273.

35. *D&A*, vol. 1, p. 64.

36. *Order in Government: The British Plan* (London, 1741), p. 13.

37. John Phillip Reid, *In a Defiant Stance* (Penn State University Press, 1977), chap. 4.

38. Edward Channing and Archibald Cary Coolidge, eds., *The Barrington-Bernard Correspondence* (Harvard University, 1912), p. 53.

39. Charles Andrews, "The Acts of Trade," in *The Old Empire: From the Beginnings to 1783*, ed. J. Holland Rose (Macmillan, 1929), vol. 1, p. 274.

40. Thomas Hutchinson, *History of the Province of Massachusetts Bay from 1749 to 1774* (London, 1828), p. 89.

41. Thomas C. Barrow, *Trade and Empire: The British Customs Service in Colonial America, 1660–1775* (Harvard University Press, 1967).

42. Ken Shumate, *The Sugar Act and the American Revolution* (Westholme, 2023), p. 167n8.

43. See, for example, Peter Andreas, *Smuggler Nation: How Illicit Trade Made America* (Oxford University Press, 2013); Larry Sawers, "The Navigation Acts Revisited," *Economic History Review* 45, no. 2 (1992): 262–84; and Peter McClelland, "The New Economic History and the Burdens of the Navigation Acts: A Comment," *Economic History Review* 26, no. 4 (1973): 679–86.

44. George III also suffered from periodic mental disturbances that modern scholars believe to be bipolar disorder. Beginning in 1765, he occasionally lapsed into psychotic episodes—babbling incoherently, striking out violently, brooding silently—that left courtiers baffled. The condition appears not to have become too serious until the 1780s, however. Andrew Roberts, *The Last King of America: The Misunderstood Reign of George III* (Viking, 2021), p. 135.

45. Roberts, *Last King*, p. 27.

46. William Blackstone, *Commentaries on the Laws of England* (London, 1809), vol. 1, p. 161.

47. M. H. Smith, *The Writs of Assistance Case* (University of California Press, 1978), p. 128.

48. Charles Francis Adams, ed., *The Works of John Adams* (Boston, 1856), vol. 1, p. 247.

49. Matthew Hale, *History of Pleas of the Crown* (Lawbook Exchange, 2003), vol. 1, p. 580; vol. 2, p. 114.

50. L. Kinvin Wroth and Hiller B. Zobel, eds., *Legal Papers of John Adams* (Belknap, 1965), vol. 2, p. 142.

51. C. Adams, *Works of John Adams*, vol. 10, p. 248.

52. Thomas Hutchinson, *History of the Colony of Massachusetts Bay* (London, 1828), vol. 4, p. 92.

53. Although Otis's lawsuit was the most famous of the colonial efforts to resist the writs of assistance, it was not the last or even the most bitter. In 1769, the Virginia Supreme Court refused to comply with the prescribed rules for issuing such writs. "Of all the colonies," wrote historian Oliver Dickerson, "Virginia appears to be the one where the issue over writs of assistance was most stubbornly fought." "Writs of Assistance as a Cause of the American Revolution," in *The Era of the American Revolution*, ed. Richard B. Morris (Columbia University Press, 1939), p. 72.

54. C. Adams, *Works of John Adams*, vol. 10, p. 245.

55. Francis Bernard, *Select Letters on the Trade and Government of America*, 2nd ed. (London, 1774), p. 68.

56. Bernard, *Select Letters*, p. 79.

57. Bernard, *Select Letters*, pp. 71–75.

58. Colin Nicholson, *The "Infamas Govener": Francis Bernard and the Origins of the American Revolution* (Northeastern University Press, 2001), pp. 86–99.

59. 4 Geo. 3 c. 15, *SaL*, vol. 26, pp. 33–51.

60. *SaL*, vol. 26, p. 19.

61. Carl Ubbelohde, *The Vice-Admiralty Courts and the American Revolution* (University Press of North Carolina, 1960), pp. 50–51.

62. 3 Geo. 3 c. 22, *SaL*, vol. 25 (part 1), pp. 345–51; Joseph R. Frese, "Smuggling, the Navy, and the Customs Service 1763–1772," in *Seafaring in Colonial Massachusetts* (Colonial Society of Massachusetts, 1980), pp. 199–212; and Theodore Draper, *A Struggle for Power: The American Revolution* (Knopf, 1997), p. 208.

63. Leonard W. Labaree, ed., *The Papers of Benjamin Franklin* (Yale University Press, 1967), vol. 11, pp. 215–16.

64. *Pamphlets*, vol. 1, pp. 43–142 (emphasis added).

65. Harry Alonzo Cushing, ed., *Writings of Samuel Adams* (G. P. Putnam's Sons, 1904), vol. 1, pp. 8–9.

66. Cushing, *Writings of Samuel Adams*, vol. 1, p. 5.

67. Michael Derderian, "This Licentious Republic: Maritime Skirmishes in Narragansett Bay 1763–1769," *Journal of the American Revolution*, October 2017.

68. William R. Nester, *The Struggle for Power in Colonial America, 1607–1776* (Lexington Books, 2017), p. 265.

69. Edmund S. Morgan, ed., *Prologue to Revolution: Sources and Documents on the Stamp Act Crisis 1764–1766* (University of North Carolina Press, 1959), pp. 8–14.

70. Edmund S. Morgan, *Benjamin Franklin* (Yale University Press, 2002), p. 150. See also John L. Bullion, *A Great and Necessary Measure: George Grenville and the Genesis of the Stamp Act* (University of Missouri Press, 1982), pp. 121–22, 269n28.

71. Edmund S. Morgan and Helen M. Morgan, *The Stamp Act Crisis: Prologue to Revolution* (University of North Carolina Press, 1962), pp. 56–64.

72. For American readers: "England" refers to the country of England itself (and "English" to its language, law, and customs), whereas "Britain" refers to the nation after the 1707 Act of Union united it with Scotland—which until then was an independent country.

CHAPTER 2

1. *ARW*, vol. 1, p. 390.

2. Thomas Rutherforth, *Institutes of Natural Law* (Cambridge, 1756), vol. 2, p. 292.

3. Mary Beth Norton (*1774: The Long Year of Revolution* [Vintage, 2020], pp. 125–26) claims that the word "unconstitutional" was a "neologism" in the revolutionary era, and that it had "appeared only rarely in American newspapers before 1765." That, however, was because before the Sugar Act of 1764, Parliament had rarely engaged in unconstitutional actions in America. The *Oxford English Dictionary* reports that the first recorded use of the word was in 1734. Of course, phrases such as "repugnant to the constitution" can be found in much older literature. See, for example, *The Eighth Collection of Papers Relating to the Present Juncture of Affairs in England* (London, 1689), p. 25.

4. J. P. Steffes, quoted in Henrich A. Rommen, *The Natural Law*, trans. Thomas R. Hanley (Liberty Fund, 1998), p. 159.

5. Edward Coke, *Institutes of the Laws of England*, vol. 1 (London, 1823), p. 97b.

6. *Calvin's Case*, 77 Eng. Rep. 377, 382 (Exch. Ch. 1608).

7. Charles Kesler and Clinton Rossiter, eds., *The Federalist Papers* (Signet, 2003), p. 467.

8. Kesler and Rossiter, *The Federalist Papers*, p. 27.

9. J. A. Leo Lemay, ed., *Franklin: Writings* (Library of America, 1987), p. 608 ("*imagining* that they recommended themselves to their sovereign by the liberality of their voluntary grants . . .") (emphasis added).

10. Richard Pipes (*Property and Freedom* [Knopf, 1999]) offers a thorough contrast between the czar's "patrimonial" ownership of all property and the English principle of private ownership.

11. Cobbett, vol. 18, p. 260.

12. William Blackstone, *Commentaries on the Laws of England* (London, 1809), vol. 1, p. 161. As Edward Fischel later observed, "The Americans . . . had taken up arms against the application of Blackstone's theory of the unrestricted legislative authority of the Parliament." Richard Jenery Shee, trans., *The English Constitution* (London, 1863), p. 485.

13. William Paley, *Principles of Moral and Political Philosophy* (Dublin, 1785), vol. 2, p. 204.

14. Howard Zinn, *A People's History of the United States* (Harper Perennial, 1980), pp. 59, 66.

15. Andrew Roberts, *The Last King of America: The Misunderstood Reign of George III* (Viking, 2021), p. 133.

16. *ARW*, vol. 1, p. 499.

17. Charles Howard McIlwain, *The Political Works of James I* (Harvard University Press, 1918), vol. 1, p. 62.

18. Jeffrey Denys Goldsworthy, *The Sovereignty of Parliament: History and Philosophy* (Clarendon Press, 1999), p. 53.

19. The MP appears to have been framed. Kira von Ostenfeld-Suske, "Secret Outlawries: The Case Against Sir Francis Goodwin and Its Impact on the House of Commons' Right to Review Electoral Returns," *The Mirror—Undergraduate History Journal* 21, no. 1 (2001): 165–66.

20. J. P. Kenyon, ed., *The Stuart Constitution*, 2nd ed. (Cambridge University Press, 1986), p. 31.

21. Kenyon, *The Stuart Constitution*, p. 37.

22. Peter Ackroyd, *Rebellion: The History of England from James I to the Glorious Revolution* (St. Martin's Press, 2015), p. 12.

23. J. G. White, *History of the Ward of Walbrook* (London, 1904), pp. 227–28.

24. Harry Hallam, *The Constitutional History of England* (London, 1846), vol. 1, pp. 456–57.

25. Catherine Drinker Bowen, *The Lion and the Throne: The Life of Sir Edward Coke* (Little, Brown, 1957), pp. 304–6.

26. Bowen, *Lion and the Throne*, p. 305.

27. Timothy Sandefur, *The Right to Earn a Living: Economic Freedom and the Law* (Cato Institute, 2010), chap. 2.

28. *The Ipswich Tailors Case*, 77 Eng. Rep. 1218, 1219 (1615).

29. 21 Jac. 1 c. 3, *SaL*, vol. 7, pp. 255–60.

30. *JHBV*, vol. 1, p. 3.

31. *The Charters and General Laws of the Colony and Province of Massachusetts Bay* (Boston, 1814), p. 9.

32. James F. Larkin, ed., *Stuart Royal Proclamations* (Clarendon Press, 1983), vol. 2, pp. 27–29.

33. "Letter from Privy Council, July 22, 1634," *Virginia Magazine of History and Biography* 17, no. 2 (1909): 113.

34. Warren M. Billings and Maria E. Kimberly, eds., *The Papers of Sir William Berkeley, 1605–1677* (Library of Virginia, 2007), pp. 29–30; and Warren M. Billings, *A Little Parliament* (Library of Virginia, 2004), p. 16.

35. Charles S. Hyenman and Donald S. Lutz, eds., *American Political Writings During the Founding Era* (Liberty Press, 1983), vol. 1, p. 78.

36. Ackroyd, *Rebellion*, p. 144.

37. Kevin Sharpe, *The Personal Rule of Charles I* (Yale University Press, 1992), p. 581.

38. "*Rex v. Hampden* (The Ship-Money Case)," in *State Trials*, ed. T. B. Howell (London, 1816), vol. 3, p. 1129; and Mark A. Graber, "Ship-Money: The Case That Time and Whittington Forgot," *Constitutional Commentary* 35 (2020): 54.

39. Ackroyd, *Rebellion*, pp. 152–53. It's easy to laugh at this quaint and bizarre story, until one recalls that tyrannical governments have frequently asserted control over soap. It was rationed in the Soviet Union until the fall of the Berlin Wall.

40. Samuel Rawson Gardiner, *The Constitutional Documents of the Puritan Revolution, 1625–1660* (Clarendon Press, 1906), pp. 212–13.

41. Ackroyd, *Rebellion*, p. 235.

42. Kenyon, *Stuart Constitution*, p. 15.

43. J. A. St. John, *Prose Works of John Milton* (London, 1848), vol. 2, pp. 17–18.

44. Selma R. Williams, *Kings, Commoners, and Colonists: Puritan Politics in Old and New England 1603–1660* (Atheneum, 1974), pp. 169–70.

45. The best account of the effect of the war on the colonies is Carla Gardina Pestana, *The English Atlantic in an Age of Revolution 1640–1661* (Harvard University Press, 2004).

46. Richard L. Perry and John C. Cooper, eds., *Sources of Our Liberties* (American Bar Foundation, 1952), pp. 148–61.

47. Warren M. Billings, *Sir William Berkeley and the Forging of Colonial Virginia* (Louisiana State University Press, 2004), p. 107.

48. Kenyon, *Stuart Constitution*, p. 292.

49. Pestana, *The English Atlantic*, p. 92.

50. Albert Bushnell Hart, ed., *American History Told by Contemporaries* (Macmillan, 1900), vol. 1, p. 233.

51. William Waller Hening, ed., *Statutes at Large [of Virginia]* (Richmond, 1809), vol. 1, pp. 363–65.

52. *Charters and General Laws of the Colony and Province of Massachusetts Bay* (Boston, 1814), p. 713.

53. Augustine Jones, *The Life and Work of Thomas Dudley, The Second Governor of Massachusetts* (Boston, 1899), pp. 402–3.

54. Thomas Hutchinson, *History of the Colony of Massachusetts Bay*, 3rd ed. (Salem, 1795), vol. 1, pp. 452–53 (emphasis added).

55. C. H. Firth and R. S. Rait, *Acts and Ordinances of the Interregnum* (His Majesty's Stationery Office, 1911), vol. 2, pp. 559–62.

56. Pestana, *The English Atlantic*, p. 175.

57. Viola Florence Barnes, *The Dominion of New England* (Yale University Press, 1923), 152–53.

58. Wim Klooster, "Inter-Imperial Smuggling in the Americas, 1600–1800," in *Soundings in Atlantic History*, ed. Bernard Bailyn and Patricia L. Denault (Harvard University Press, 2009), p. 161.

59. Carl A. Herzog, "Sailing Illicit Voyages: Colonial Smuggling Operations Between North America and the West Indies, 1714–1776" (PhD diss., University of Massachusetts Amherst, 2020), p. 63.

60. Andrew Clark, ed., *The Life and Times of Anthony Wood* (Oxford, 1891), vol. 1, pp. 465–66.

61. The terms of the treaty remained secret until 1830. Antonia Fraser, *Charles II* (Contact, 1979), pp. 275–76.

62. "The True Condition of Things in the Plantation of Virginia from 1665 to 1676," *Magazine of Western History* 13, no. 3 (1891): 282.

63. 12 Car. 2. c. 18, *SaL*, vol. 7, pp. 452–60.

64. David S. Lovejoy, *The Glorious Revolution in America* (Wesleyan University Press, 1972), p. 17.

65. Michael G. Hall, Lawrence H. Leder, and Michael G. Kammen, eds., *The Glorious Revolution in America: Documents on the Colonial Crisis of 1689* (University of North Carolina Press, 1964), pp. 12–13.

66. John Burk, *The History of Virginia from Its First Settlement to the Present Day* (Petersburg, VA, 1805), vol. 2 App., pp. lxi–lxii.

67. *A Collection of Original Papers Relative to the History of the Colony of Massachusetts-Bay* (Boston, 1769), p. 506.

68. Nathaniel B. Shurtleff, ed., *Records of Massachusetts* (Boston, 1854), vol. 5, p. 200.

69. Shurtleff, *Records of Massachusetts*, vol. 5, p. 201.

70. Ackroyd, *Rebellion*, p. 428.

71. *JHBV*, vol. 2, p. 228.

72. Brian Weiser, *Charles II and the Politics of Access* (Boydell Press, 2003), pp. 162–65.

73. Murray Rothbard, *Conceived in Liberty* (Mises Institute, 1999), vol. 1, p. 56.

74. Beverley Bond Jr., *The Quit-Rent System in the American Colonies* (Yale University Press, 1919), p. 48.

75. Barnes, *Dominion*, p. 196.

76. Alvin Rabushka, *Taxation in Colonial America* (Princeton University Press, 2008), pp. 328–30.

77. J. H. Crooker, "John Wise, the Forgotten American," *Magazine of Western History* 8, no. 5 (1888): 399; and Jack M. Sosin, *English America and the Revolution of 1688* (University of Nebraska Press, 1982), p. 73.

78. Charles J. Hoadley, ed., *The Public Records of the Colony of Connecticut* (Hartford, 1881), p. 656.

79. Rothbard, *Conceived in Liberty*, vol. 1, p. 384.

80. John Phillip Reid, *Constitutional History of the American Revolution*, vol. 2, *The Authority to Tax* (University of Wisconsin Press, 1987), p. 143.

81. *The Colonial Laws of New York* (Albany, 1894), vol. 1, p. 111.

82. Stephen Saunders Webb, *The Governors-General: The English Army and the Definition of Empire 1569–1681* (University of North Carolina Press, 1979), p. 379.

83. Sean Gailmard, *Agents of Empire: English Imperial Governance and the Making of American Institutions* (Harvard University Press, 2024), pp. 182–83.

84. Henry M. Baird, *The Huguenots and the Revocation of the Edict of Nantes* (New York, 1895), vol. 2, p. 28.

85. Lovejoy, *Glorious Revolution*, p. 286.

86. Scott John Hammond, Kevin R. Hardwick, and Howard L. Lubert, eds., *Classics of American Political and Constitutional Thought* (Hackett, 2007), vol. 1, p. 73.

87. Robert Noxon Toppan, *Edward Randolph* (Boston, 1899), vol. 5, p. 262.

88. Nathaniel Byfield, *An Account of the Late Revolution in New England* (London, 1689), pp. 7–19.

89. *An Address Presented to the King, August 7th, 1689* (London, 1689), p. 1.

90. *JHBV*, vol. 2, pp. 316, 328.

91. Gailmard, *Agents of Empire*, p. 190.

92. *D&A*, vol. 1, p. 341.

93. *D&A*, vol. 1, p. 358.

94. John Phillip Reid, *Constitutional History of the American Revolution*, vol. 3, *The Authority to Legislate* (University of Wisconsin Press, 1991), p. 212.

CHAPTER 3

1. Margaret A. Hogan et al., eds., *Adams Family Correspondence* (Massachusetts Historical Society, 2011), vol. 10, p. 23.

2. Cesare Cuttica, *Sir Robert Filmer (1588–1653) and the Patriotic Monarch* (Manchester University Press, 2012).

3. Johann P. Sommerville, ed., *Sir Robert Filmer: Patriarcha and Other Writings* (Cambridge University Press, 1991), pp. 16, 44.

4. Algernon Sidney, "Of Love," in *A Collection of Scarce and Valuable Tracts on the Most Interesting and Entertaining Subjects* (London, 1743), vol. 2, p. 402.

5. Gilbert Burnet, *Burnet's History of My Own Time*, ed. Osmond Airy (Clarendon Press, 1900), vol. 2, p. 352.

6. *An Exact Account of the Trial of Algernon Sidney* (London, 1683), p. 2.

7. William Scott, ed., *The Essence of Algernon Sidney's Work on Government* (London, 1795), p. 37.

8. *An Exact Account*, p. 3.

9. Algernon Sidney, *Discourses Concerning Government*, ed. Thomas G. West (Liberty Fund, 1990), p. 34.

10. Sidney, *Discourses*, pp. 191, 510–11.

11. Sidney, *Discourses*, p. 510.

12. Sidney, *Discourses*, p. 31.

13. Sommerville, *Sir Robert Filmer*, p. 2 (Filmer: "The desire of liberty was the cause of the fall of Adam").

14. Sidney, *Discourses*, pp. 31, 510.

15. Alan Cromartie, "The God of Thomas Hobbes," *The Historical Journal* 5, no. 4 (2008): 857–79.

16. Richard Tuck, ed., *Thomas Hobbes: Leviathan*, rev. student ed. (Cambridge University Press, 1999), p. 90.

17. Tuck, *Thomas Hobbes: Leviathan*, p. 90.

18. Tuck, *Thomas Hobbes: Leviathan*, p. 89.

19. Sidney, *Discourses*, p. 417.

20. Sidney, *Discourses*, p. 416.

21. H. R. Fox Bourne, *The Life of John Locke* (New York, 1876), vol. 1, p. 200n2.

22. Peter Laslett, ed., *John Locke: Two Treatises of Government*, rev. ed. (Mento, 1963), p. 311.

23. Laslett, *Two Treatises*, p. 309; and Richard Hooker, *Of the Laws of Ecclesiastical Polity*, ed. Arthur Stephen McGrade (Cambridge University Press, 2002), p. 80.

24. While it's clear that Locke is seeking to refute Hobbes as well as Filmer in *Two Treatises*, "it is a most remarkable fact that it has not been possible to find a single referenced extract from the works of Hobbes in the whole Lockean corpus." Laslett, *Two Treatises*, p. 87.

25. For an insightful critique of this argument, see Eric Mack, *John Locke* (Bloomsbury, 2013).

26. Laslett, *Two Treatises*, p. 176.

27. 10 & 11 Will. 3 c. 10, *SaL*, vol. 10, pp. 249–57.

28. 5 Geo. 2 c. 22, *SaL*, vol. 16, pp. 304–8.

29. 6 Geo. 2 c. 13, *SaL*, vol. 16, pp. 374–79.

30. 23 Geo. 2 c. 29, *SaL*, vol. 20, pp. 97–102.

31. David Ramsay, "The Advantages of American Independence," in *American Eloquence: A Collection of Speeches and Addresses*, ed. Frank Moore (New York, 1871), vol. 1, p. 314.

32. Richard Bland, *A Fragment on the Pistole Fee, Claimed by the Governor of Virginia, 1753* (Brooklyn, 1891), pp. 37–38.

33. *Manuscripts of the Marquess of Townshend* (London, 1887), p. 263.

34. "A Quaker Imperialist's View of the British Colonies in America: 1732," *Pennsylvania Magazine of History and Biography* 60, no. 2 (1936): 114.

35. Jack P. Greene, *Peripheries and Center: Constitutional Development in the Extended Polities of the British Empire and the United States, 1607–1788* (Norton, 1986), pp. 47–48.

36. H. T. Dickinson, "The Eighteenth-Century Debate on the Sovereignty of Parliament," *Transactions of the Royal Historical Society* 26 (1976): 189–210. The theory was not new; the scope of parliamentary power had been debated throughout the 17th century. Philip Hamburger, *Law and Judicial Duty* (Harvard University Press, 2008), pp. 243–54; and Jeffrey Goldsworthy, *The Sovereignty of Parliament: History and Philosophy* (Clarendon Press, 1999).

37. This contract should not be confused with the Lockean "social compact," which is supposed to be the source of society, not just of the state.

38. *Pamphlets*, vol. 1, pp. 470–71 (emphasis removed).

39. Scott J. Hammond, Kevin R. Hardwick, and Howard L. Lubert, eds., *Classics of American Political and Constitutional Thought* (Hackett, 2007), vol. 1, p. 176.

40. R. C. Simmons and P. D. G. Thomas, eds., *Proceedings and Debates of the British Parliaments Respecting North America, 1754–1783* (Kraus International, 1984), vol. 3, p. 32.

41. *ARW*, vol. 1, p. 518.

42. 77 Eng. Rep. 377 (Exch. Ch. 1608).

43. Henry Horwitz, *Parliamentary Policy and Politics in the Reign of William III* (Manchester University Press, 1977), pp. 161–62, 164–66.

44. Kermit L. Hall and Mark David Hall, eds., *Collected Works of James Wilson* (Liberty Fund, 2007), vol. 1, p. 20.

45. John Phillip Reid, *Constitutional History of the American Revolution*, vol. 2, *The Authority to Tax* (University of Wisconsin Press, 1987), pp. 116–17.

46. 6 Geo. 2. c. 13, *SaL*, vol. 16, pp. 374–79. Also called the Sugar Act of 1733, officially titled "An Act for the Better Securing and Encouraging the Trade of His Majesty's Sugar Colonies in America."

47. Alvin Rabushka, *Taxation in Colonial America* (Princeton University Press, 2008), p. 735.

48. Ken Shumate, *1764: The First Year of the American Revolution* (Westholme, 2021), p. xv.

49. Cobbett, vol. 8, p. 1262.

50. Cobbett, vol. 8, p. 1262.

51. J. A. Leo Lemay, ed., *Benjamin Franklin: Writings* (Library of America, 1984), p. 405.

52. Peter Jupp, *Lord Grenville* (Clarendon Press, 1985).

53. 4 Geo. 3. c. 15, *SaL*, vol. 26, pp. 33–51.

54. Shumate, *1764*, p. 42.

55. Edward Hughes, "The English Stamp Duties, 1664–1764," *English Historical Review* 56, no. 222 (1941): 234–64.

56. *Pamphlets*, vol. 1, p. 223.

57. *Pamphlets*, vol. 1, pp. 135–36.

58. Henry Alonzo Cushing, ed., *Writings of Samuel Adams* (G. P. Putnam's Sons, 1904), vol. 1, p. 5.

59. *Speeches of the Governors of Massachusetts from 1765 to 1775* (Boston, 1818), p. 22.

60. Shumate, *1764*, pp. 71–174.

61. Shumate, *1764,* p. 42.

62. Robert Middlekauff, *The Glorious Cause: The American Revolution, 1763–1789* (Oxford University Press, 2007), pp. 65–66.

63. Reid, *Authority to Tax*, p. 199.

64. Edmund S. Morgan and Helen M. Morgan, *The Stamp Act Crisis: Prologue to Revolution* (University of North Carolina Press, 1962), p. 55.

65. Shumate, *1764*, pp. 178–79.

66. Edmund S. Morgan, ed., *Prologue to Revolution: Sources and Documents on the Stamp Act Crisis 1764–1766* (University of North Carolina Press, 1959), p. 30.

67. Cobbett, vol. 16, pp. 38–39 (emphasis added).

68. "During the war the colonies annually contributed to the charge of it," wrote Thomas Hutchinson, "some of them so largely that the Parliament was convinced that the burden would be insupportable and from year to year made them compensations." John W. Tyler, *The Correspondence of Thomas Hutchinson* (Colonial Society of Massachusetts, 2014), vol. 1, p. 214.

69. *Pamphlets*, vol. 1, p. 354.

70. Francis Bernard, *Select Letters on the Trade and Government of America*, 2nd ed. (London, 1774), p. 36.

71. *Pamphlets*, vol. 1, p. 135.

72. *Collections of the Massachusetts Historical Society*, Series 6 (Boston, 1897), vol. 9, p. 49.

CHAPTER 4

1. *ARW*, vol. 2, p. 302.

2. Edmund S. Morgan, ed., *Prologue to Revolution: Sources and Documents on the Stamp Act Crisis, 1764–1766* (University of North Carolina Press, 1959), p. 48.

3. Morgan, *Prologue to Revolution*, p. 14.

4. William Wirt, *The Life of Patrick Henry*, rev. ed. (Philadelphia, 1836), p. 84. Later historians doubted whether Henry used these words, which were first recorded by the Virginia lawyer and scholar William Wirt in 1836. But Wirt, who knew Jefferson, asked the elder man for confirmation. Jefferson replied that he "well remember[ed] the cry of treason, the pause of Mr. Henry at the name of George III, and the presence of mind with which he closed his sentence, and baffled the charge vociferated."

5. *JW*, p. 6.

6. Bernard Bailyn, *The Ordeal of Thomas Hutchinson* (Belknap, 1974), p. 26.

7. John W. Tyler, *The Correspondence of Thomas Hutchinson* (Colonial Society of Massachusetts, 2020), vol. 2, pp. 495–512.

8. *D&A*, vol. 1, p. 307.

9. *D&A*, vol. 1, p. 260.

10. *D&A*, vol. 2, p. 81.

11. *D&A*, vol. 1, p. 324.

12. Tyler, *Correspondence of Thomas Hutchinson*, vol. 1, p. 212.

13. Thomas Hutchinson, *History of the Province of Massachusetts Bay from 1749 to 1774* (London, 1828), vol. 3, p. 114.

14. *Speeches of the Governors of Massachusetts from 1765 to 1775* (Boston, 1818), pp. 22–23 (emphasis added).

15. Hutchinson, *History*, vol. 3, p. 114.

16. *Speeches of the Governors*, p. 24.

17. *D&A*, vol. 2, p. 119.

18. *D&A*, vol. 3, p. 284.

19. *ARW*, vol. 2, p. 120.

20. *ARW*, vol. 2, p. 123.

21. Deirdre McCloskey, "Bourgeois Virtue," *American Scholar* 63, no. 2 (1994): 179. In *The Radicalism of the American Revolution* (Knopf, 1993), Gordon Wood describes this as the rise of the ideal of the "gentleman," but I take these as synonymous.

22. Friedrich Knapp, *The Life of Frederick William von Steuben* (New York, 1859), p. 699.

23. *ARW*, vol. 1, p. 132.

24. *ARW*, vol. 1, p. 133.

25. A. J. Langguth, *Patriots: The Men Who Started the American Revolution* (Simon & Schuster, 1988), p. 53.

26. Peter Linebaugh and Marcus Rediker, *The Many-Headed Hydra* (Beacon Press, 2000), p. 151.

27. Denver Brunsman, *The Evil Necessity: British Naval Impressment in the Eighteenth-Century Atlantic World* (University of Virginia Press, 2013), p. 6.

28. 6 Anne c. 37 § 9, *SaL*, vol. 11, p. 438.

29. 19 Geo. 2 c. 30, *SaL*, vol. 18, pp. 472–75. Section 7 of the statute contained an exception "in case of any threatened or actual invasion of any of His Majesty's said colonies in America, or in case of any other unforeseen and emergent necessity or occasion requiring [impressment]," so long as such impressment was done "with the concurrence, approbation, and consent of the governor . . . and of the council for the time being of the said colonies . . . but not otherwise."

30. Brunsman, *Evil Necessity*, pp. 227–33.

31. *Address to the Inhabitants of Massachusetts-Bay and Especially of Boston, by a Lover of His Country* (Boston, 1747).

32. William V. Wells, *The Life and Public Services of Samuel Adams* (Boston, 1856), vol. 1, p. 14.

33. Brunsman, *Evil Necessity*, p. 13.

34. Margaret A. Hogan et al., eds., *Adams Family Correspondence* (Massachusetts Historical Society, 2011), vol. 10, p. 56.

35. Charles Francis Adams, ed., *The Works of John Adams* (Boston, 1856), vol. 10, p. 364.

36. George Pomeroy Anderson, "Ebenezer Mackintosh: Stamp Act Rioter and Patriot," *Transactions of the Colonial Society of Massachusetts, 1924–1926* (Colonial Society of Massachusetts, 1927), vol. 26, pp. 15–64.

37. Franklin Bowditch Dexter, ed., *Extracts from the Itineraries and Other Miscellanies of Ezra Stiles* (Yale University Press, 1916), p. 436.

38. Galatians 5:12–13.

39. Harry S. Stout, *The New England Soul: Preaching and Religious Culture in Colonial New England* (Oxford University Press, 1986), pp. 262–63.

40. Patrick J. Mullins, *Father of Liberty: Jonathan Mayhew and the Principles of the American Revolution* (University Press of Kansas, 2017), pp. 160–61.

41. Daniel Coquillette and Neil Longly York, eds., *Portrait of a Patriot: The Major Political and Legal Papers of Josiah Quincy, Jr.* (University Press of Virginia, 2010), vol. 5, pp. 452–54.

42. *D&A*, vol. 1, p. 260.

43. "The Stamp Act Riots of 1765," St. Kitts National Archives.

44. Molly Perry, "Buried Liberties and Hanging Effigies," in *Community Without Consent: New Perspectives on the Stamp Act*, ed. Zachary McLeod Hutchins (Dartmouth College Press, 2016), p. 55. There is reason to doubt the truth of this unconfirmed report. Dinna Spindel, "The Stamp Act Crisis in the British West Indies," *Journal of American Studies* 11, no. 2 (1977): 220–21.

45. *Speeches of the Governors*, pp. 40–41.

46. *Journal of the First Congress of the American Colonies in Opposition to the Tyrannical Acts of the British Parliament* (New York, 1845), p. 28.

47. *ARW*, vol. 2, p. 126.

48. *Speeches of the Governors*, pp. 43–47.

49. *Speeches of the Governors*, pp. 50–51.

50. Arthur M. Schlesinger, *The Colonial Merchants and the American Revolution* (Beard Books, 1939), pp. 76–82.

51. Edmund S. Morgan and Helen M. Morgan, *The Stamp Act Crisis: Prologue to Revolution* (University of North Carolina Press, 1962), p. 168.

52. Oliver M. Dickerson, *The Navigation Acts and the American Revolution* (University of Pennsylvania Press, 1951), p. 206n8.

53. *D&A*, vol. 1, p. 263.

54. *D&A*, vol. 1, p. 270.

55. William Shakespeare, *Henry VIII*, ed. Jonathan Crewe (Penguin, 2001), p. 84.

56. In a commentary on the Book of Joshua, the Puritan theologian Matthew Poole had explained a passage in which God, angered by the Israelites' failure to abide by their covenant with Him, tells Joshua, "Neither will I be with you anymore." This, Poole wrote, meant the Israelites had "put themselves out of [God's] protection and blessing, and therefore are liable to the same destruction which belongs to [an] accursed people." Matthew Poole, *Annotations upon the Holy Bible*, 3rd ed. (London, 1696), vol. 1, p. 289.

57. William Wake, *The State of the Church and Clergy of England* (London, 1703), p. 251.

58. 25 Edw. 3 c. 2, *SaL*, vol. 2, pp. 50–53.

59. 16 R. 2 c. 5, *SaL*, vol. 2, pp. 350–54.

60. Cobbett, vol. 3, p. 55. Blackstone discussed the penalty in William Blackstone, *Commentaries on the Laws of England* (London, 1809), vol. 2, pp. 112–13.

61. *D&A*, vol. 1, p. 266.

62. John Hampden to William Pym, *Boston Gazette*, January 6, 1766.

63. *D&A*, vol. 1, pp. 286–87.

64. *ARW*, vol. 2, p. 106.

65. *ARW*, vol. 2, p. 149.

66. *D&A*, vol. 1, p. 305.

67. *D&A*, vol. 1, p. 308.

68. Francis Thackeray, *History of the Right Honorable William Pitt* (London, 1827), vol. 2, pp. 83–84.

69. 6 Geo 3. c. 12 (emphasis added), *SaL*, vol. 27, pp. 19–20. See also Lawrence Henry Gipson, "The Great Debate in the Committee of the Whole House of Commons on the Stamp Act 1766, as Reported by Nathaniel Ryder," *Pennsylvania Magazine of History and Biography* 81, no. 1 (1962): 10–41; and Timothy Pitkin, *A Political and Civil History of the United States of America* (New Haven, 1828), vol. 1, pp. 196–212.

CHAPTER 5

1. *JW*, p. 1321.

2. Mary Newton Standard, *Colonial Virginia: Its People and Customs* (Lippincott, 1917), p. 140.

3. Psalms 124:7.

4. Ellis Sandoz, ed., *Political Sermons of the American Founding Era: 1730–1805*, 2nd ed. (Liberty Fund, 1998), vol. 1, p. 251.

5. John Thomas Scharf, *History of Maryland* (Baltimore, 1879), vol. 1, p. 552.

6. George P. Donehoo, ed., *Pennsylvania: A History* (Lewis Historical Publishing Co., 1926), vol. 2, p. 1034.

7. David Thomas Konig and Michael P. Zuckert, eds., *Jefferson's Legal Commonplace Book* (Princeton University Press, 2019), pp. 41–44.

8. *JW*, p. 3.

9. *JW*, p. 1194.

10. Cappon, p. 467.

11. *JW*, p. 1072.

12. Alfred John Church and William Jackson Brodribb, trans., *The Annals of Tacitus* (London, 1895), p. 91.

13. Alfred John Church and William Jackson Brodribb, trans., *The Agricola and Germany of Tacitus* (London, 1868), p. 37.

14. Church and Brodribb, *Agricola and Germany*, p. 19.

15. John Alvis, ed., *Areopagitica and Other Political Writings of John Milton* (Liberty Fund, 1999), p. 221.

16. W. R. Paton, trans., *Polybius: The Histories* (William Heinemann, 1923), vol. 3, pp. 287–89.

17. Henry St. John, Viscount Bolingbroke, *On Patriotism, Parties and the Idea of a Patriot King* (New Direction, 2020), p. 91 (emphasis altered).

18. Alexander Hamilton encapsulated the lessons of the classical authors well in *Federalist* no. 1. "History will teach us," he wrote, "that . . . of those men who have overturned the liberties of republics, the greatest number have begun their career by paying an obsequious court to the people; commencing demagogues, and ending tyrants." Charles Kesler and Clinton Rossiter, eds., *The Federalist Papers* (Signet, 2003), p. 29.

19. Jonathan Swift, *The Works of Jonathan Swift* (London, 1843), vol. 1, p. 293.

20. John Milton, *Paradise Lost* (Oxford University Press, 2005), p. 354.

21. Sarah N. Randolph, *The Domestic Life of Thomas Jefferson* (New York, 1871), p. 23.

22. *JW*, pp. 1466–67.

23. *JW*, p. 1342.

24. *JW*, p. 1431.

25. *JW*, p. 1122.

26. W. E. Leonard, trans., *T. Lucretius Carus on the Nature of Things* (J. M. Dent, 1921), p. 6.

27. *JW*, p. 1432.

28. John Locke, *An Essay Concerning Human Understanding*, ed. Kenneth P. Winkler (Hackett, 1996), p. 108.

29. Jeffrey Rosen, *The Pursuit of Happiness* (Simon & Schuster, 2024), chap. 9; and Timothy Sandefur, "The Greeks and America's Founding Fathers, Part 1: Greek Frame," *Objective Standard*, Summer 2016.

30. *JW*, p. 1431.

31. Matthew 19:21.

32. Cappon, p. 467.

33. Whitney J. Oates, ed., *The Stoic and Epicurean Philosophers* (Modern Library, 1940), p. 298. Note the parallel with 1 Corinthians 12:15–21.

34. Oates, *Stoic and Epicurean*, p. 332.

35. Oates, *Stoic and Epicurean*, p. 334.
36. *JW*, p. 779.
37. Cappon, p. 358.
38. Cappon, p. 467.
39. *JW*, p. 761.
40. Cappon, p. 443.
41. *JW*, p. 1249.
42. Margaret Bayard Smith, *The First Forty Years of Washington Society*, ed. Gaillard Hunt (Charles Scribner's Sons, 1906), p. 12.
43. Jack N. Rakove, ed., *James Madison: Writings* (Library of America, 1999), p. 860.
44. *JW*, p. 4.
45. Desmond King-Hele, ed., *The Essential Writings of Erasmus Darwin* (MacGibbon & Kee, 1968), p. 31.
46. *JW*, p. 939.
47. Peter Laslett, ed., *John Locke: Two Treatises of Government*, rev. ed. (Mento, 1963), pp. 328–29.
48. Locke, *Essay Concerning Human Understanding*, p. 108.
49. Although Bacon never literally used this phrase, a similar phrase, *ipsa scientia potestas est*, appeared in his famous 1597 *Meditationes Sacrae.* Bacon's secretary, Thomas Hobbes, did use the precise phrase *scientia potentia est* in his book *Leviathan*. Jefferson often used the slogan. Monticello.org, "Knowledge Is Power (Quotation)."
50. Daniel R. Coquillette, *Francis Bacon* (Stanford University Press, 1992), pp. 257–76.
51. Benjamin Farrington, trans., *The Philosophy of Francis Bacon* (Liverpool University Press, 1964), p. 131.
52. John M. Robertson, ed., *The Philosophical Works of Francis Bacon* (Routledge, 1905), p. 731.
53. Francis Bacon, *The Advancement of Learning*, 4th ed., ed. William Aldis Wright (Oxford, 1891), pp. 42–43 (emphasis added).
54. Robertson, *Philosophical Works of Francis Bacon*, p. 755.
55. *JW*, p. 902.
56. Robertson, *Philosophical Works of Francis Bacon*, p. 756.
57. *JW*, p. 904.
58. Coquillette, *Francis Bacon*, pp. 100–101.
59. *JW*, p. 1416.
60. *PTJ* (Retirement Series), vol. 14, p. 434.
61. *JW*, p. 734.
62. *JW*, p. 1557.
63. Dumas Malone, *Jefferson the Virginian* (St. Martin's Press, 1948), p. 73.
64. *JW*, p. 4; and Bruce Chadwick, *I Am Murdered: George Wythe, Thomas Jefferson, and the Killing That Shocked a New Nation* (John Wiley & Sons, 2009).

65. *JW*, p. 735.

66. *JW*, p. 1513.

67. Montesquieu, *The Spirit of the Laws*, trans. Thomas Nugent (Cincinnati, 1873), vol. 2, p. 41.

68. Jerry Z. Muller, *Capitalism and the Jews* (Princeton University Press, 2010).

69. Montesquieu, *Spirit of the Laws*, vol. 1, pp. 365–66.

70. Voltaire, *The Works of Voltaire: A Contemporary Version* (E. R. DuMont, 1901), vol. 12, pp. 294–95.

71. Barbara Tuchman, *A Distant Mirror* (Ballantine Books, 1978), p. 37.

72. Montesquieu, *Spirit of the Laws*, vol. 1, pp. 365–66.

73. Biographers have often depicted Jefferson as suspicious of, or even hostile to, capitalism. Yet he shared the view that the freedom to exchange goods and services was both a consequence and a cause of a healthy society. His beliefs in this respect were so strong that in retirement, he even translated and published a book by the laissez-faire French economist Antoine Destutt de Tracy—a commentary on Montesquieu's *Spirit of the Laws*—in which Tracy wrote that (in Jefferson's translation) it is "ridiculous to doubt of commerce being a good . . . or only . . . useful to one of the parties concerned in it." Commerce, said Tracy, "should be free." Antoine Louis Claude Destutt de Tracy, *A Commentary and Review of Montesquieu's Spirit of the Laws*, trans. Thomas Jefferson (Philadelphia, 1811), pp. 206, 278.

74. I omit here any discussion of the theory of "virtual representation," which was put forward by such figures as Thomas Whately to justify the exclusion of Americans from Parliament, because it was never taken seriously by the colonists. See Gordon S. Wood, *Power and Liberty: Constitutionalism in the American Revolution* (Oxford University Press, 2021), chap. 1.

75. Mansfield is today highly regarded as the author of *Somerset v. Stewart*, 98 Eng. Rep. 499 (K.B. 1772), among the most prominent legal cases against slavery. Contrary to popular impression, however, Mansfield—who struggled mightily to avoid rendering any decision in the case—did not hold that slavery violated English law. He held only that a master could not transport a slave out of England for sale elsewhere. The narrowness of this ruling accounts for the relatively small effect it had on slavery in both Britain and America at the time. Anthony Lester and Geoffrey Bindman, *Race and Law in Great Britain* (Harvard University Press, 1972), pp. 32–33.

76. Cobbett, vol. 16, pp. 172–77.

77. H. W. V. Temperley, "Debates on the Declaratory Act and the Repeal of the Stamp Act, 1766," *American Historical Review* 17, no. 3 (1912): 585.

78. Cobbett, vol. 16, pp. 172–77.

79. J. A. Leo Lemay, ed., *Benjamin Franklin: Writings* (Library of America, 1987), p. 407.

80. *Pamphlets*, vol. 1, p. 341.

81. *Pamphlets*, vol. 1, p. 347.

82. *Pamphlets*, vol. 1, p. 341 (emphasis added).

83. *Pamphlets*, vol. 1, p. 361.

84. *Pamphlets*, vol. 1, p. 351.

85. *Pamphlets*, vol. 1, p. 345.

86. *Pamphlets*, vol. 1, p. 352.

87. 5 Geo. 3 c. 11, *SaL*, vol. 26, pp. 176–79.

88. 6 Geo. 1 c. 5, *SaL*, vol. 14, pp. 204–5.

89. 6 Geo. 3 c. 12, *SaL*, vol. 27, pp. 19–20.

90. Archives of Maryland, *Proceedings and Acts of the General Assembly of Maryland May 9, 1766 to June 22, 1768* (Maryland Historical Society, 1944), vol. 61, p. 182.

91. Jack P. Greene, *Peripheries and Center: Constitutional Development in the Extended Polities of the British Empire and the United States, 1607–1788* (Norton, 1986), pp. 61–62.

92. *D&A*, vol. 3, p. 285.

93. *Pamphlets*, vol. 1, p. 350.

94. *Pamphlets*, vol. 1, p. 346 (emphasis added).

CHAPTER 6

1. *PTJ*, vol. 10, p. 378.

2. *Acts and Resolves Private and Public of the Province of Massachusetts Bay* (Boston, 1861), vol. 4, pp. 944–45. By the time Massachusetts learned of this repeal, it had already paid the compensation. Lawrence Henry Gipson, *The British Empire Before the American Revolution* (Knopf, 1965), vol. 11, pp. 25–26.

3. Mutiny Act of 1765, 6 Geo. 3 c. 8, *SaL*, vol. 27, pp. 12–14; Mutiny in America Act of 1765, 6 Geo. 3 c. 18, *SaL*, vol. 27, pp. 34–35; and Quartering Act of 1765, 5 Geo. 3 c. 33, *SaL*, vol. 26, pp. 305–18.

4. John Phillip Reid, *Constitutional History of the American Revolution*, vol. 3, *The Authority to Legislate* (University of Wisconsin Press, 1991), p. 275.

5. 7 Geo. 3 c. 59, *SaL*, vol. 27, pp. 607–10.

6. Nicholas Varga, "The New York Restraining Act: Its Passage and Some Effects, 1766–1768," *New York History* 37, no. 3 (1956): 233–58.

7. William James Smith, ed., *The Grenville Papers* (London, 1853), vol. 4, p. 266.

8. Revenue Act of 1767, 7 Geo. 3 c. 46, *SaL*, vol. 27, pp. 505–12.

9. 7 Geo. 3 c. 46 §§ 4–5, *SaL*, vol. 27, pp. 250–55 (emphasis added).

10. *Pamphlets*, vol. 1, p. 453 (emphasis altered).

11. 7 Geo. 3 c. 41, *SaL*, vol. 27, pp. 447–49.

12. 7 Geo. 3 c. 56, *SaL*, vol. 27, pp. 600–605.

13. 8 Geo. 3 c. 22, *SaL*, vol. 28, pp. 70–71.

14. Ralph Volney Harlow, *Samuel Adams: Promoter of the American Revolution* (Henry Holt, 1923), pp. 103–6.

15. *JHRM*, vol. 44, pp. 236–39.

16. William Griffith, Letter May 9, 1768, *Historical Notes of the American Colonies and Revolution, from 1754 to 1776* (Burlington, NJ, 1836), pp. 33–36; and *Petition, Memorial, and Remonstrance from the House of Burgesses* (Williamsburg, VA, 1769), p. 9.

17. Peter Laslett, ed., *John Locke: Two Treatises of Government*, rev. ed. (Mento, 1963), p. 407.

18. *Petition, Memorial, and Remonstrance*, p. 9.

19. *Petition, Memorial, and Remonstrance*, p. 11.

20. *Records of the Colony of Rhode Island and Providence Plantations* (Providence, 1861), vol. 6, p. 561.

21. *JW*, p. 5.

22. *Pamphlets*, vol. 1, pp. 457, 480 (emphasis removed).

23. *Pamphlets*, vol. 1, p. 470 (emphasis removed).

24. Vicary Gibbs, ed., *The Complete Peerage*, rev. ed. (St. Catherine Press, 1916), vol. 4, p. 458.

25. *The Manuscripts of the Marquis of Ormonde* (London, 1885), p. 15.

26. Peter D. G. Thomas, *The Townshend Duties Crisis: The Second Phase of the American Revolution, 1767–1773* (Clarendon Press, 1987), p. 81.

27. Oliver M. Dickerson, *The Navigation Acts and the American Revolution* (Octagon Books, 1974), p. 242. For some important corrections to Dickerson's characterization of the case, see Carl Ubbelohde, *The Vice-Admiralty Courts and the American Revolution* (University Press of North Carolina, 1960).

28. *D&A*, vol. 3, p. 306.

29. *ARW*, vol. 2, p. 126.

30. L. Kinvin Wroth and Hiller B. Zobel, eds., *Legal Papers of John Adams* (Harvard University Press, 1965), vol. 2, pp. 194–210.

31. Henry Alonzo Cushing, ed., *The Writings of Samuel Adams* (G. P. Putnam's Sons, 1904), vol. 1, p. 222.

32. Paul Leicester Ford, ed., *The Writings of John Dickinson* (Philadelphia, 1895), vol. 1, p. 431.

33. *ARW*, vol. 1, p. 176.

34. Thomas Hutchinson, *Strictures upon the Declaration of the Congress at Philadelphia* (London, 1776), p. 19.

35. *Letters to the Ministry from Governor Bernard, General Gage, and Commodore Hood* (Boston, 1769), p. 34.

36. *Journal of the House of Lords Volume 32, 1768–1770* (London, 1767–1830), British History Online, accessed November 13, 2024.

37. 35 Hen. 8 c. 2, *SaL*, vol. 5, p. 199.

38. Eric Hinderaker, *Boston's Massacre* (Harvard University Press, 2017), pp. 112–13.

39. *D&A*, vol. 3, pp. 289–90.

40. *D&A*, vol. 3, p. 291.

41. Willard Sterne Randall, *Thomas Jefferson: A Life* (Holt, 1993), pp. 102–9.

42. Allen D. Chandler, ed., *Colonial Records of the State of Georgia* (Franklin-Turner Co., 1907), vol. 14, p. 656. New York's petitions to the king and Parliament, adopted in December 1768, were only placed in the journals on April 9, 1769. *Journal of the Votes and Proceedings of the General Assembly of the Colony of New York from 1766 to 1776, Inclusive* (New York: J. Buel, 1820), pp. 11–17. See also *Documents Relative to the Colonial History of the State of New York* (Albany, 1857), vol. 8, 143–44; and Don Cook, *The Long Fuse: How England Lost the American Colonies* (Atlantic Monthly Press, 1995), p. 131.

43. *Journals of the House of Commons* (London, 1803), vol. 32, pp. 185–86, 194.

44. Patrick Henderson, "Smallpox and Patriotism: The Norfolk Riots, 1768–1769," *Virginia Magazine of History and Biography* 73, no. 4 (1965): 413–24. The doctors later hired Jefferson to sue the rioters.

45. Thomas, *Townshend Duties Crisis*, p. 87.

46. Taylor Stoermer, "Will the Real Lord Botetourt Please Stand?," *Journal of the American Revolution*, February 26, 2013.

47. *JHBV*, vol. 11, pp. 215–16.

48. *JHBV*, vol. 11, p. 218.

49. *JW*, p. 6.

50. *PTJ* (Retirement Series), vol. 16, p. 229.

51. Clinton Rossiter, *Six Characters in Search of a Republic* (Harcourt, Brace & World, 1964), p. 157.

52. *Pamphlets*, vol. 1, pp. 307–29.

53. *PTJ* (Retirement Series), vol. 8, p. 643.

54. *JW*, p. 110.

55. *JW*, p. 9.

56. Charles Francis Adams, ed., *The Works of John Adams* (Boston, 1854), vol. 9, p. 318.

57. C. Adams, *Works of John Adams*, vol. 2, p. 224.

58. Pauline Maier, *Resistance to Revolution* (Norton, 1991), pp. 16–26.

59. C. Adams, *Works of John Adams*, vol. 2, p. 226.

60. *A Report of the Record Commissioners of the City of Boston, Containing the Boston Town Records, 1758–1769* (Boston, 1886), p. 324.

61. Robert Allison, *The Boston Massacre* (Commonwealth Editions, 2006), pp. 4–5.

62. Allison, *Boston Massacre*, p. 7.

63. A. J. Langguth, *Patriots: The Men Who Started the American Revolution* (Simon & Schuster, 1988). This book offers a particularly vivid account of the massacre.

64. John W. Tyler, ed., *The Correspondence of Thomas Hutchinson* (Colonial Society of Massachusetts, 2021), vol. 3, p. 120.

65. The record is unclear whether Samuel was involved in arranging for John to take up Preston's defense. John wrote nothing to this effect in his diaries or letters. Yet it is extremely difficult to doubt that Samuel saw the potential for using the trial to establish the colony's capacity to ensure justice, and many historians have concluded that he must have been involved. John K. Alexander, *Samuel Adams: The Life of an American Revolutionary* (Rowman & Littlefield, 2011), p. 109; and Hiller B. Zobel, *The Boston Massacre* (Norton, 1970), pp. 220–21. Others, however, maintain that Samuel hoped the soldiers would be convicted. Stacy Schiff, *The Revolutionary Samuel Adams* (Back Bay Books, 2022), p. 200.

66. *ARW*, vol. 1, p. 306.

67. *D&A*, vol. 3, p. 293.

68. *D&A*, vol. 3, p. 294.

69. Thomas Hutchinson, *History of the Province of Massachusetts Bay from 1749 to 1774* (London, 1828), vol. 3, p. 233.

70. *JHRM*, vol. 47, p. 20.

71. Thomas Hutchinson, *Strictures upon the Declaration of the Congress at Philadelphia* (London, 1776), p. 13.

72. *JHRM*, vol. 47, p. 27. For a fuller account of the "secret" instructions, see Bernard Bailyn, *The Ordeal of Thomas Hutchinson* (Belknap, 1974), pp. 170–75.

73. *JHRM*, vol. 47, p. 27.

74. *JHRM*, vol. 47, p. 43.

75. *JHRM*, vol. 47, p. 27.

76. Stanley Kenneth Deaton, *Revolutionary Charleston, 1765–1800* (PhD diss., University of Florida, 1997), pp. 81–83; and Alan D. Watson, "The Beaufort Removal and the Revolutionary Impulse in South Carolina," *South Carolina Historical Magazine* 84 (1983): 121–35.

77. Curiously, no mention of the South Carolina episode appears in Pauline Maier's *American Scripture* (Knopf, 1997), in which she treats the removal of colonial legislatures as a triviality. See especially pp. 110–11.

78. *JHRM*, vol. 47, p. 30.

79. *JHRM*, vol. 47, p. 88.

80. *JHRM*, vol. 47, p. 98.

81. Merrill Jensen, ed., *English Historical Documents: American Colonial Documents to 1776* (Eyre & Spottiswoode, 1969), vol. 9, p. 787; *Speeches of the Governors of Massachusetts from 1765 to 1775* (Boston, 1818), p. 413; and *JHRM*, vol. 50, p. 262.

82. *JHRM*, vol. 50, p. 291.

83. In the summer of 1774, when Governor Lord Dunmore of Virginia fled Williamsburg for a warship near Yorktown, the House of Burgesses asked him to return to the capital, to which he replied that for his own safety, it would be better for them to convene in Yorktown. This the Burgesses refused to do. Declaring that "[Williamsburg] and [Williamsburg] alone, is established by law for holding our General Assemblies," the Burgesses resolved that requiring them to carry their messages to Yorktown to communicate with the governor was "a high breach of the rights and privileges of this House." *JHBV*, vol. 13, pp. 262, 281.

84. *JHRM*, vol. 47, pp. 68–69.

85. *PTJ*, vol. 1, p. 34.

86. *JW*, p. 285.

87. *JW*, p. 494.

88. *JW*, p. 245.

89. *JW*, p. 245.

90. Laslett, *Two Treatises*, pp. 402–3.

91. Robert R. Rea, *The English Press in Politics, 1760–1774* (University of Nebraska Press, 1963), pp. 201–11.

92. As James Madison was to explain years later, the British believed that "the danger of encroachments on the rights of the people" was "confined to the executive magistrate," so that "the representatives of the people in the legislature" were "exempt . . . from distrust"—whereas in what became the United States, "encroachments [on the rights of the people] are regarded as possible from the [legislative branch] as well as from [the executive branch]." Jack N. Rakove, ed., *James Madison: Writings* (Library of America, 1999), p. 645.

93. John Phillip Reid, *Constitutional History of the American Revolution*, vol. 4, *The Authority of Law* (University of Wisconsin Press, 1993), p. 55.

94. *PTJ*, vol. 1, p. 34.

95. Aaron Schwabach, "Thomas Jefferson as an Unsuccessful Advocate for Freedom in *Howell v. Netherland*," *Thomas Jefferson Law Review* 20 (1998): 129–38.

96. *PTJ*, vol. 8, p. 357.

97. Cara Rogers Stevens, *Thomas Jefferson and the Fight Against Slavery* (University Press of Kansas, 2024), p. 38.

98. Schwabach, "Unsuccessful Advocate," p. 135.

99. Schwabach, "Unsuccessful Advocate," p. 137 (emphasis added).

100. Randall, *Jefferson: A Life*, pp. 147–48.

101. Keith R. Bradley, "Roman Slavery and Roman Law," *Historical Reflections* 15, no. 3 (1988): 481.

102. Samuel Johnson, *Taxation No Tyranny: An Answer to the Resolutions and Address of the American Congress* (London, 1775), p. 89. It is

worth noting that Johnson was not in this passage accusing Americans of injustice for practicing slavery. Quoting Johnson out of context can give that impression, but read in context, Johnson's point is clear: He made this comment as part of an argument that one *can*—contrary to the Americans' claims—practice compulsory servitude without placing oneself at risk of tyranny. In other words, Johnson was not seeking to vindicate the rights of Africans but to denigrate those of white colonists.

103. As Edmund Burke said, "In Virginia and the Carolinas, they have a vast multitude of slaves. Where this is the case in any part of the world, those who are free, are by far the most proud and jealous of their freedom. Freedom is to them not only an enjoyment, but a kind of rank and privilege. Not seeing there, that freedom, as in countries where it is a common blessing . . . may be united with much abject toil [and] great misery . . . liberty looks, amongst them, like something that is more noble and liberal. I do not mean . . . to commend the superior morality of this sentiment . . . but I cannot alter the nature of man." *Speeches of the Right Honorable Edmund Burke* (London, 1816), vol. 1, p. 290.

104. J. A. Leo Lemay, ed., *Benjamin Franklin: Writings* (Library of America, 1987), pp. 646–53.

105. Sean M. Kelley, *American Slavers: Merchants, Mariners, and the Transatlantic Commerce in Captives, 1644–1865* (Yale University Press, 2023), p. 155.

106. Leonard Woods Labaree, ed., *Royal Instructions to British Colonial Governors, 1670–1776* (Appleton-Century, 1935), vol. 2, p. 679.

107. Labaree, *Royal Instructions*, vol. 2, pp. 673–74.

108. The specifics of the bill are unclear; no copy of it survives. And the House of Burgesses' records are silent on the matter, because it was the practice of the time not to record details of motions the House rejected.

109. *JW*, p. 1344.

110. *JW*, p. 1344.

111. *JW*, p. 270.

112. *JW*, p. 1202.

113. Gordon S. Wood, ed., *John Adams: Writings from the New Nation, 1784–1826* (Library of America, 2016), p. 406.

114. *JW*, p. 264. On this point, too, Adams agreed. "I shudder when I think of the calamities which slavery is likely to produce in this country," he told his daughter-in-law in 1820. "If the gangrene is not stopped, I can see nothing but insurrections of the blacks against the whites and massacres by the whites in their turn of the blacks . . . till at last the whites exasperated to madness shall be wicked enough to exterminate the negroes." Wood, *John Adams*, pp. 406, 654–55.

115. *JW*, p. 1434.
116. *JW*, p. 1345.
117. Cobbett, vol. 23, p. 1027.
118. *JW*, p. 44.

CHAPTER 7

1. *JW*, p. 112.
2. *D&A*, vol. 1, p. 351.
3. Peter D. G. Thomas, *The Townshend Duties Crisis* (Clarendon Press, 1987), p. 135.
4. *The Trumbull Papers: Collections of the Massachusetts Historical Society* (Boston, 1885), vol. 9, p. 305.
5. Robert B. Tucker and David C. Hendrickson, *The Fall of the First British Empire* (Johns Hopkins University Press, 1982), p. 283.
6. Thomas, *Townshend Duties Crisis*, p. 137.
7. Cobbett, vol. 16, pp. 852–54.
8. 10 Geo. 3 c. 17, *SaL*, vol. 28 (part 1), p. 294.
9. *JW*, p. 6.
10. Stacy Schiff, *The Revolutionary Samuel Adams* (Back Bay Books, 2022), p. 208.
11. *D&A* vol. 2, p. 15.
12. *D&A*, vol. 2, p. 7.
13. John Russell Bartlett, ed., *Records of the Colony of Rhode Island and Providence Plantations* (Providence, 1862), vol. 7, p. 42.
14. J. A. Leo Lemay, ed., *Benjamin Franklin: Writings* (Library of America, 1987), p. 660.
15. *Pamphlets*, vol. 2, p. 901.
16. William Willcox, ed., *The Papers of Benjamin Franklin* (Yale University Press, 1975), vol. 20, p. 308.
17. Peter Rushton and Gwenda Morgan, *Treason and Rebellion in the British Atlantic, 1685–1800* (Bloomsbury, 2020), p. 141.
18. Neil L. York, "The Uses of Law and the Gaspee Affair," *Rhode Island History* 51, no. 1 (1992): 3–21; and Thomas, *Townshend Duties Crisis*, pp. 226–31.
19. Bartlett, *Records of the Colony of Rhode Island*, vol. 7, pp. 112–13.
20. *JW*, p. 6.
21. *JHBV*, vol. 13, p. 28.
22. John Mercer Garnett, "The Committee of Correspondence and the Call for the First Congress," *Collections of the Virginia Historical Society* (Richmond, 1892), vol. 11 (n.s.), p. 16.
23. *Acts and Resolves of the Province of Massachusetts Bay* (Boston, 1869), vol. 1, p. 16; and *JHRM*, vol. 49, p. 105.
24. *JHRM*, vol. 49, p. 122.

25. *JHRM*, vol. 49, p. 128.

26. John W. Tyler, *The Correspondence of Thomas Hutchinson* (Colonial Society of Massachusetts, 2020), vol. 5, p. 97.

27. Harry Alonzo Cushing, ed., *Writings of Samuel Adams* (G. P. Putnam's Sons, 1906), vol. 2, pp. 369–70.

28. *D&A*, vol. 2, p. 78.

29. *D&A*, vol. 3, p. 298.

30. *D&A*, vol. 3, p. 299.

31. Tyler, *Correspondence of Thomas Hutchinson*, vol. 5, p. 437.

32. *D&A*, vol. 3, p. 302.

33. *Pamphlets*, vol. 1, pp. 759–88. Unless otherwise noted, quotations in this paragraph and the next seven paragraphs are from this publication.

34. Leonard Woods Labaree, *Royal Instructions to British Colonial Governors, 1670–1776* (Appleton-Century, 1935), pp. 48–49.

35. Nancy L. Rhoden, *Revolutionary Anglicanism: The Colonial Church of England During the American Revolution* (Macmillan, 1999), p. 42.

36. Gordon S. Wood, *The Radicalism of the American Revolution* (Knopf, 1991), p. 112.

37. Bruce Frohnen, ed., *The American Republic* (Liberty Fund, 2010), p. 173. Boucher's speech outraged parishioners so much that within months, he fled to England, where he was awarded a pension. Anne Y. Zimmer, *Jonathan Boucher, Loyalist in Exile* (Wayne State University Press, 1978), p. 200.

38. Arthur Lyon Cross, *The Anglican Episcopate and the American Colonies* (Longmans, Green & Co., 1902). The Boston Pamphlet also objected to the unilateral changes London had made to the boundaries of several colonies. In 1764, for example, the Board of Trade had reset the border between New York and New Hampshire at the Connecticut River, whereupon New York declared New Hampshire property deeds invalid and forced owners to take out expensive new paperwork. Three years later, the Privy Council reversed that order, throwing into confusion titles to almost two million acres of land. Residents of these "Hampshire Grants" resented this so much that it sparked what one historian calls "small-scale border warfare" between the two colonies. Kevin Phillips, *1775: A Good Year for Revolution* (Penguin, 2012), p. 176.

39. Tyler, *Correspondence of Thomas Hutchinson*, vol. 5, p. 76.

40. "To the King," *Massachusetts Spy*, September 10, 1772.

41. Leonard W. Levy, *Legacy of Suppression* (Harvard University Press, 1960), pp. 67–75.

42. Tyler, *Correspondence of Thomas Hutchinson*, vol. 5, p. 119.

43. Tyler, *Correspondence of Thomas Hutchinson*, vol. 5, p. 120.

44. Tyler, *Correspondence of Thomas Hutchinson*, vol. 5, p. 125.

45. *JHRM*, vol. 49, pp. 137–43.

46. *JHRM*, vol. 49, pp. 178–90.

47. *JHRM*, vol. 49, pp. 229–41.

48. *JHRM*, vol. 49, pp. 268–80 (emphasis added).

49. Tyler, *Correspondence of Thomas Hutchinson*, vol. 5, p. 209.

50. Tyler, *Correspondence of Thomas Hutchinson*, vol. 5, p. 196.

51. Bernard Bailyn, *The Ordeal of Thomas Hutchinson* (Belknap, 1974), p. 235.

52. *D&A*, vol. 2, p. 80.

53. *Copy of Letters Sent to Great-Britain by His Excellency Thomas Hutchinson* (Boston, 1773).

54. *D&A*, vol. 2, pp. 84–85.

55. *JHRM*, vol. 50, pp. 58–61.

56. Albert Henry Smyth, ed., *The Writings of Benjamin Franklin* (Macmillan, 1906), vol. 6, p. 266.

57. Bailyn, *Ordeal*, p. 376.

58. Bailyn, *Ordeal*, p. xii.

59. Cobbett, vol. 21, p. 771.

60. 13 Geo. 3 c. 44, *SaL*, vol. 30 (part 1), pp. 74–77.

61. Scaevola, "To the Commissioners Appointed by the East India Company" (1773); and Wesley S. Griswold, *The Boston Tea Party, 16 December 1773: The Night the Revolution Began* (Abacus Press, 1973), pp. 17–18.

62. L. F. S. Upton, "Proceedings of the Body Respecting the Tea," *William & Mary Quarterly* 22, no. 2 (1965): 299.

63. See, for example, Mary Beth Norton, *1774: The Long Year of Revolution* (Knopf, 2020), p. 45.

64. Benjamin Woods Labaree, *The Boston Tea Party* (Oxford University Press, 1964), p. 132.

65. Schiff, *Revolutionary Samuel Adams*, p. 241.

66. B. Labaree, *Tea Party*, pp. 174–76.

67. This incident is richly described in Norton, *1774*, pp. 203–6.

68. Joseph Cummins, *Ten Tea Parties: Patriotic Protests That History Forgot* (Quirk Books, 2012).

69. *D&A*, vol. 2, p. 86.

70. John Greenough to Thomas Greenough, March 1, 1774, Greenough Papers, Massachusetts Historical Society.

71. Quoted in Norton, *1774,* p. 56.

72. *D&A*, vol. 2, p. 86.

73. *ARW*, vol. 1, p. 289.

CHAPTER 8

1. *D&A*, vol. 2, p. 93.

2. W. Bodham Donne, ed., *The Correspondence of King George the Third with Lord North* (London, 1867), p. 164.

3. William B. Willcox, ed., *The Papers of Benjamin Franklin* (Yale University Press, 1978), vol. 21, pp. 37–70.

4. Willcox, *Papers of Benjamin Franklin*, vol. 21, p. 110.

5. 14 Geo. 3 c. 19, *SaL*, vol. 30 (part 1), pp. 336–41.

6. Peter D. G. Thomas, *Lord North* (Allen Lane, 1976), p. 76.

7. Ross J. S. Hoffman, *Edmund Burke, New York Agent* (American Philosophical Society, 1956), p. 246.

8. *Journals of the House of Commons* (London, 1804), vol. 34, p. 541.

9. John W. Tyler, *The Correspondence of Thomas Hutchinson* (Colonial Society of Massachusetts, 2020), vol. 5, p. 456.

10. Force, vol. 1, p. 46.

11. 24 Geo. 3 c. 19 § 2, *SaL*, vol. 30 (part 1), p. 337.

12. Force, vol. 2, p. 666.

13. Bob Ruppert, "The Winter of 1774–1775 in Boston," *Journal of the American Revolution*, October 17, 2023, https://allthingsliberty.com/2023/10/the-winter-of-1774-1775-in-boston/.

14. *ARW*, vol. 1, p. 294.

15. Clarence Edwin Carter, ed., *The Correspondence of General Thomas Gage with the Secretaries of State, 1763–1775* (Yale University Press, 1931), vol. 1, p. 85.

16. Merrill Jensen, ed., *English Historical Documents: American Colonial Documents to 1776* (Eyre & Spottiswoode, 1969), vol. 9, p. 787.

17. *Massachusetts Royal Commissions, 1681–1774* (Colonial Society of Massachusetts, 1913), pp. 174–83.

18. The Continental Congress responded by declaring that the Massachusetts Government Act was unconstitutional, that citizens owed it "no obedience," and that the offices of governor and lieutenant governor should be considered empty. *JCC*, vol. 2, p. 83.

19. 14 Geo. 3 c. 39, *SaL*, vol. 30 (part 1), pp. 367–71.

20. William Blackstone, *Commentaries on the Laws of England* (London, 1809), vol. 1, p. 359. See also Edward Coke, *Institutes of the Laws of England* (London, 1823), vol. 1, p. 125a.

21. *Candid Observations on Two Pamphlets Lately Published* (Barbados, 1766), pp. 21–22.

22. 14 Geo. 3 c. 45, *SaL*, vol. 30 (part 1), pp. 381–90.

23. Quartering Act, 14 Geo. 3 c. 54, *SaL*, vol. 30 (part 1), pp. 410–11; and Quebec Act, 14 Geo. 3 c. 83, *SaL*, vol. 30 (part 1), pp. 549–54.

24. John Henry Merryman and Rogelio Pérez-Perdomo, *The Civil Law Tradition*, 3rd ed. (Stanford University Press, 2007), p. 129.

25. At nearly the same time Jefferson's *A Summary View* was published, Lord Mansfield ruled in *Campbell v. Hall*, 98 Eng. Rep. 1045 (K.B. 1774), that even if the king conquered a new country, or proclaimed new laws for it, that power was "subordinate to . . . the supreme legislature and Parliament. . . . He cannot exempt an inhabitant from the laws of trade, or the authority of Parliament." That meant that even if he promised colonists in writing that they could have their own legislature, that, too, was always "subordinate" to the Lords and Commons. Colonial charters held no weight against Parliament's commands. Norman S. Poser, *Lord Mansfield: Justice in the Age of Reason* (McGill-Queen's University Press, 2013), pp. 309–10.

26. Clarence S. Brigham, ed., *British Royal Proclamations Relating to America, 1603–1783* (Burt Franklin, 1911), p. 214.

27. John Phillip Reid, *Constitutional History of the American Revolution*, vol. 4, *The Authority of Law* (University of Wisconsin Press, 1993), pp. 23–26.

28. Richad R. Beeman, *Our Lives, Our Fortunes, and Our Sacred Honor: The Forging of American Independence, 1774–1776* (Basic Books, 2013), p. 164. Beeman claimed the Quebec Act "was aimed at protecting the liberties of the French Catholic residents of that province" (p. 402), ignoring the fact that it deprived the Quebecois of criminal procedure protections as well as their right to vote, and, for non-Catholics, their religious freedom.

29. *Pamphlets*, vol. 2, p. 369 (emphasis eliminated).

30. Harry Alonzo Cushing, ed., *The Writings of Samuel Adams* (G. P. Putnam's Sons, 1907), vol. 3, pp. 107–8.

31. Albert Edmond Hogan, *Pacific Blockade* (Clarendon Press, 1908).

32. Cushing, *Writings of Samuel Adams*, vol. 3, p. 110.

33. *JW*, p. 46.

34. Although often presented as established fact, the relationship between John Wayles and Betty Hemings remains unsubstantiated. William G. Hyland Jr., *Martha Jefferson: An Intimate Life with Thomas Jefferson* (Rowman & Littlefield, 2015), pp. 225–29.

35. Gaye Wilson, "Elizabeth Jefferson," Monticello.org, February 1999, https://www.monticello.org/research-education/thomas-jefferson-encyclopedia/elizabeth-jefferson/.

36. Willard Sterne Randall, *Thomas Jefferson: A Life* (Holt, 1993), p. 181.

37. *JW*, p. 896.

38. *JW*, p. 8.

39. *JHBV*, vol. 13, p. 124.

40. Nicholas B. Wainwright, "Turmoil at Pittsburgh: Diary of Augustine Prevost, 1774," *Pennsylvania Magazine of History and Biography* 85, no. 2 (1961): 143.

41. James Corbett David, *Dunmore's New World* (University of Virginia Press, 2013), p. 21.

42. *JHBV*, vol. 13, p. 132.

43. *JW*, p. 9.

44. *Virginia Gazette*, August 4, 1774, https://research.colonialwilliamsburg.org/DigitalLibrary/va-gazettes/VGSinglePage.cfm?issueIDNo=74.R.30.

45. *PTJ*, vol. 1, pp. 119–20.

46. *JW*, p. 9.

47. *JW*, pp. 105–22. Unless otherwise noted, all quotations in this section are from this publication.

48. *PTJ*, vol. 9, p. 71.

49. Cobbett, vol. 16, p. 175.

50. *Rex v. Cowle*, 97 Eng. Rep. 587, 597 (K.B. 1759).

51. Christopher Michael Curtis, *Jefferson's Freeholders and the Politics of Ownership in the Old Dominion* (Cambridge University Press, 2012), p. 63.

52. Specifically on the writings of legal historians Henry Spelman and John Dalrymple. H. Trevor Colbourn, *The Lamp of Experience: Whig History and the Intellectual Origins of the American Revolution* (Norton, 1965), p. 162.

53. *PTJ*, vol. 1, p. 492.

54. Thus, Jefferson would go on to champion the elimination of "primogeniture" and "entail," feudal property rules that governed the inheritance of land upon an owner's death. Overturning these rules, he told Adams when they were both living in retirement, "laid the axe to the root of pseudo-aristocracy." *JW*, pp. 1307–8.

55. Kermit L. Hall and Mark David Hall, eds., *Collected Works of James Wilson* (Liberty Fund, 2007), vol. 1, pp. 3–31.

56. Joseph Ellis, *American Sphinx: The Character of Thomas Jefferson* (Random House, 1996), p. 38.

57. Ronald Dworkin, *Law's Empire* (Belknap, 1986), p. 229.

58. "The British Empire," wrote Randolph Adams in 1922, "has survived by doing in practice what the Americans asked Parliament to do openly in the period [of the revolution], that is, it has quietly dropped overboard the theory of Parliamentary [Supremacy] as far as the empire is concerned." *Political Ideas of the American Revolution* (Trinity College Press, 1922), p. 126.

59. William Waller Hening, ed., *Statutes at Large [of Virginia]* (New York, 1823), vol. 1, p. 364. Unless otherwise noted, quotations in this paragraph and the next six paragraphs are from this publication.

60. Elmer Beecher Russell, *The Review of American Colonial Legislation by the King in Council* (Columbia University, 1915), p. 188.

61. Russell, *Review of American Colonial Legislation*, p. 184.

62. J. Wright, ed., *Sir Henry Cavendish's Debates of the House of Commons During the Thirteenth Parliament of Great Britain* (London, 1841), vol. 1, p. 517.

63. Jeff Broadwater and Troy L. Kickler, eds., *North Carolina's Revolutionary Founders* (University of North Carolina Press, 2019), pp. 7–9; Jack P. Greene, "Bridge to Revolution: The Wilkes Fund Controversy in South Carolina, 1769–1775," *Journal of Southern History* 29, no. 1 (1963): 19–52; and Andrew O'Shaughnessy and Kenneth Coleman, *The American Revolution in Georgia, 1763–1789* (University of Georgia Press 2021), pp. 16–38.

64. Brendan McConville, *The King's Three Faces* (University of North Carolina Press, 2006), pp. 11, 106.

65. J. A. Leo Lemay, ed., *Benjamin Franklin: Writings* (Library of America, 1987), pp. 607–15. Unless otherwise noted, quotations in this paragraph and the next two paragraphs are from this publication.

66. Huw V. Bowen, "The 'Little Parliament': The General Court of the East India Company, 1750–1784," *Historical Journal* 34, no. 4 (1991): 865.

67. Lemay, *Franklin: Writings*, p. 615.

68. *ARW*, vol. 1, p. 301.

69. *ARW*, vol. 1, p. 310. Georgia was the only colony not to send a delegation.

70. *D&A*, vol. 2, p. 117.

71. *D&A*, vol. 2, p. 120.

72. J. L. Bell, "He Would Raise a Thousand Men at His Own Expence?," *Boston 1775* (blog), March 16, 2019.

73. *D&A*, vol. 2, p. 121.

74. *D&A*, vol. 2, pp. 124–25.

75. *D&A*, vol. 2, p. 126.

76. Douglas Bradburn, *The Citizenship Revolution: Politics and the Creation of the American Union* (University of Virginia Press, 2009), p. 24.

77. Thomas Fleming, *1776: Year of Illusions* (W. W. Norton, 1975), p. 260.

78. *D&A*, vol. 2, p. 173.

79. *D&A*, vol. 2, p. 129.

80. Force, vol. 1, p. 608.

81. *D&A*, vol. 2, p. 129.

82. *D&A*, vol. 2, p. 148.

83. Edith Gelles, ed., *Abigail Adams: Letters* (Library of America, 2016), p. 30.

84. *Journals of Each Provincial Congress of Massachusetts* (Boston, 1838), p. 618.

85. *ARW*, vol. 1, p. 319.

86. L. H. Butterfield, ed., *Adams Family Correspondence* (Belknap, 1963), vol. 1, p. 159.

87. The best account of the Powder Alarm is Mary Beth Norton, *1774: The Long Year of Revolution* (Knopf, 2020), chap. 5.

88. Force, vol. 1, p. 769.

89. *Journals of Each Provincial Congress of Massachusetts*, pp. 601–6. Unless otherwise noted, quotations in this paragraph and the next paragraph are from this publication.

90. *D&A*, vol. 2, p. 134.

91. Butterfield, *Adams Family Correspondence*, vol. 1, p. 158.

92. Kevin Phillips, *1775: A Good Year for Revolution* (Penguin, 2012), p. 227.

93. *JCC*, vol. 1, p. 58.

94. *JCC*, vol. 1, p. 102.

95. The most infamous kind of mob violence was tarring and feathering, a humiliating and potentially deadly form of punishment in which tar—sometimes boiling hot—was poured over the victim, followed by a coat of feathers. Remarkably, although some 70 instances of tarring and feathering occurred between 1766 and 1776, no such cases involved importers of British goods until 1774. Benjamin H. Irvin, "Tar, Feathers, and the Enemies of American Liberties, 1768–1776," *New England Quarterly* 76, no. 2 (2003): 197–238.

96. *Correspondence and Journals of Samuel Blachley Webb* (New York, 1893), vol. 1, pp. 41–42.

97. Phillips, *1775*, p. 269; and Mark Somos, *American States of Nature: The Origins of Independence, 1761–1775* (Oxford University Press, 2019).

98. Robert J. Taylor et al., eds., *Papers of John Adams* (Belknap, 1977), vol. 2, p. 191.

99. Taylor et al., *Papers of John Adams*, vol. 2, p. 191.

100. *JCC*, vol. 1, pp. 63–73. Unless otherwise noted, quotations in this paragraph and the next two paragraphs are from this publication.

101. The three cited statutes were the Sugar Act, the Currency Act—which barred colonists from issuing paper currency—and the Postage Act of 1765, which the colonists viewed as imposing a form of taxation. Tories often pointed to the Postage Act as a precedent for parliamentary taxation in which the colonists had acquiesced; Benjamin Franklin himself had served as postmaster. After trying with little success to argue that the Postage Act was not actually a form of taxation (a view Franklin defended), the colonists gave up and created their own separate postage system in May 1775. They called it the Constitutional Post. Franklin became its first postmaster. Winifred Gallagher, *How the Post Office Created America* (Penguin, 2016), pp. 25–26.

102. *D&A*, vol. 3, pp. 309–10.

103. Edmund C. Burnett, *Letters of Members of the Continental Congress* (Carnegie Institution, 1921), vol. 1, p. 74.

104. *PTJ*, vol. 10, p. 378.

105. *JCC*, vol. 1, p. 83.

106. *JCC*, vol. 1, p. 89.

107. *JCC*, vol. 1, pp. 115–21.

108. *JCC*, vol. 1, pp. 105–13. Unless otherwise noted, quotations in this paragraph and the next six paragraphs are from this publication.

109. *JCC*, vol. 1, p. 98.

110. *JCC*, vol. 1, p. 101.

CHAPTER 9

1. *PTJ*, vol. 1, p. 195.

2. *PTJ*, vol. 1, pp. 154–55.

3. Frank L. Dewey, *Thomas Jefferson, Lawyer* (University Press of Virginia, 1986), pp. 94–106.

4. *PTJ*, vol. 1, pp. 38–40.

5. *ARW*, vol. 1, p. 323.

6. *ARW*, vol. 1, p. 351.

7. Albert Henry Smyth, ed., *The Writings of Benjamin Franklin* (Macmillan, 1907), vol. 6, pp. 303–7.

8. Richard Beeman, *Our Lives, Our Fortunes and Our Sacred Honor: The Forging of American Independence, 1774–1776* (Basic Books, 2013), p. 177.

9. *The Colonial and State Records of North Carolina* (University of North Carolina Library, 2004), vol. 9, p. 1108.

10. W. Bodham Donne, ed., *The Correspondence of King George the Third with Lord North* (London, 1867), p. 215.

11. Andrew Roberts, *The Last King of America* (Viking, 2021), p. 252.

12. Force, vol. 1, pp. 1513–69. See also Merrill Jensen, *The Founding of a Nation* (Hackett Publishing, 1968), p. 576. The king technically did receive the London petition, but declared his "utmost astonishment" at such petitions and said he would "steadily pursue" Parliament's measures. *Addresses, Remonstrances, and Petitions to the Throne* (London, 1865), p. 36.

13. Force, vol. 1, pp. 1819–20.

14. John Phillip Reid, *Constitutional History of the American Revolution*, vol. 1, *The Authority of Rights* (University of Wisconsin Press, 1988), p. 22.

15. *The Parliamentary Register During the First Session of the Fourteenth Parliament* (London, 1802), vol. 1, pp. 1–2.

16. John Fortescue, ed., *The Correspondence of George III* (Macmillan, 1928), vol. 3, p. 156.

17. Their author was a successful attorney named Daniel Leonard, an acquaintance of Adams, although Adams himself thought they were written by the colony's Tory attorney general, Jonathan Sewall.

18. *ARW*, vol. 1, p. 437.

19. *ARW*, vol. 1, p. 441.

20. *ARW*, vol. 1, p. 427.

21. *ARW*, vol. 1, p. 397.

22. *ARW*, vol. 1, p. 387 (emphasis removed); and Gordon S. Wood, "Conspiracy and the Paranoid Style: Causality and Deceit in the Eighteenth Century," *William & Mary Quarterly* 39, no. 3 (1982): 401–41. Modern historians have often dismissed this accusation, labeling it a "conspiracy theory" and characterizing the revolutionaries as downright paranoid. But during Adams's lifetime, the term "conspiracy" did not carry the connotations of delusion it has today; it simply meant an agreement between people to do an unlawful thing. The Patriots contended that Tories knew that what they were doing was contrary to the British constitution—what trained lawyer could not?—and that they were endeavoring to implement their schemes by subverting the colonial charters. This accusation may seem unfair to Tories who sincerely believed in Parliamentary Supremacy, but their sincerity does not prove they were unaware of the consequences of their actions, let alone that those actions were in fact lawful. As Adams put it, "If the Parliament has not a legal authority to overturn [the Massachusetts] constitution, and subject [the colonists] to such acts as are lately passed, every man who accepts of any commission and takes any steps to carry those acts into execution, is guilty of overt acts of treason and rebellion." *ARW*, vol. 1, p. 418. Parliament's leaders were, indeed, engaged in a program of radically altering the American political system, and had gone to such drastic lengths as to send thousands of troops to Boston and dissolve colonial legislatures in an effort to coerce Americans into submission—while refusing even to listen to petitions seeking peaceful resolutions. It is no neurosis to regard that as a conspiracy against the constitution. In the 1860s, Confederates were certainly sincere in their own beliefs that slavery and secession were constitutional, but that does not excuse them from the charge of conspiracy.

23. *ARW*, vol. 1, p. 418.

24. *ARW*, vol. 1, p. 423.

25. *ARW*, vol. 1, p. 442.

26. *ARW*, vol. 1, p. 517.

27. *ARW*, vol. 1, p. 524.

28. *ARW*, vol. 1, p. 582.

29. *ARW*, vol. 1, p. 537.

30. *ARW*, vol. 1, p. 614.

31. *ARW*, vol. 1, p. 525.

32. *ARW*, vol. 1, p. 527.

33. K. G. Davies, *Documents of the American Revolution* (Irish University Press, 1975), vol. 9, p. 39.

34. Allen French, *The Day of Concord and Lexington* (Little, Brown, 1925), p. 41.

35. Force, vol. 2, p. 374. The exact number of weapons surrendered is unknown. One diarist at the time calculated 2,674. Edward Lillie Pierce, ed., *Letters and Diary of John Rowe* (W. B. Clarke, 1903), p. 293; but

recent research has found a number of conflicting inventories. J. L. Bell, "Arms (Deliver'd by the Inhabitants in April 1775)," *Boston 1775* (blog), July 20, 2023.

36. Butterfield, ed., *Adams Family Correspondence* (Belknap, 1963), vol. 1, p. 209.

37. *D&A*, vol. 3, p. 314.

38. Butterfield, *Adams Family Correspondence*, vol. 1, p. 192.

39. *PTJ*, vol. 1, p. 165.

40. *PTJ*, vol. 1, p. 166.

41. *PTJ*, vol. 1, p. 166n1.

42. In fact, no contemporaneous record of Henry's words exists. The wording that has been traditionally accepted was first published in 1816 and is based on the recollections of St. George Tucker, who witnessed the event. William Wirt, *Sketches of the Life and Character of Patrick Henry*, rev. ed. (Philadelphia, 1844), p. 94; and Thomas S. Kidd, *Patrick Henry: First Among Patriots* (Basic Books, 2011), p. 98.

43. Michael Kranish, *Flight from Monticello: Thomas Jefferson at War* (Oxford University Press, 2010), pp. 56–57.

44. Jon Kukla, *Patrick Henry: Champion of Liberty* (Simon & Schuster, 2017), pp. 173–84.

45. Hugh F. Ranklin, *North Carolina in the American Revolution* (State Department of Archives and History, 1965), p. 8.

46. Lawrence Shaw Mayo, *John Wentworth* (Harvard University Press, 1921), p. 156.

47. Beeman, *Our Lives, Our Fortunes*, pp. 284–85; Kevin Phillips, *1775: A Good Year for Revolution* (Penguin, 2012), pp. 4, 541; and John Thomas Scharf, *History of Maryland* (Baltimore, 1879), vol. 2, p. 217.

48. Jensen, *Founding of a Nation*, pp. 577–78.

49. Samuel Eliot Morison, ed., *Sources and Documents Illustrating the American Revolution, 1764–1788*, 2nd ed. (Clarendon Press, 1962), p. 138.

50. Cobbett, vol. 18, p. 297; New England Fisheries Act, 15 Geo. 3 c. 10, *SaL*, vol. 31 (part 1), pp. 4–11; and Trade Act of 1775, 15 Geo. 3 c. 18, *SaL*, vol. 31 (part 1), pp. 37–43.

51. *PTJ*, vol. 1, pp. 170–74. Unless otherwise noted, quotations in this paragraph and the next three paragraphs are from this publication.

52. Richard J. Werther, "The Lord North Conciliatory Proposal: A Case of Too Little Too Late," *Journal of the American Revolution*, October 31, 2023.

53. Morison, *Sources and Documents*, p. 138.

54. The 1774 general election, held between October 5 and November 10, had returned a landslide Tory majority to Parliament.

55. *JHBV*, vol. 13, p. 245.

56. *JHBV*, vol. 13, p. 247.

57. *JHBV*, vol. 13, p. 215.
58. *JHBV*, vol. 13, p. 261.
59. Force, vol. 2, pp. 968–69.
60. Edith Gelles, ed., *Abigail Adams: Letters* (Library of America, 2016), pp. 47–48.
61. Gelles, *Abigail Adams*, p. 50.
62. William Willcox, ed., *The American Rebellion: Sir Henry Clinton's Narrative of His Campaigns, 1775–1782* (Archon Books, 1971), p. 19 (emphasis added).
63. Charles Francis Adams, ed., *The Works of John Adams* (Boston, 1850), vol. 2, p. 514.
64. *D&A*, vol. 2, p. 218.
65. *JW*, p. 1235.
66. Adams, *Works of John Adams*, vol. 2, p. 514.
67. C. Bradley Thompson, *John Adams and the Spirit of Liberty* (University of Kansas Press, 1995), p. 6.
68. James Norton Smith, ed., *The Republic of Letters* (Norton, 1995), vol. 1, pp. 462–63.
69. *JW*, p. 12; and *PTJ*, vol. 10, p. 378.
70. *D&A*, vol. 3, p. 321.
71. L. H. Butterfield, ed., *Adams Family Correspondence* (Athenaeum, 1965), vol. 1, p. 225.
72. *ARW*, vol. 2, p. 12.
73. Adams's memory of the events of 1775 was also frequently faulty, as he confessed to Jefferson when he admitted in 1813 that he could not even remember who had written the petition to the king, and probably had not known at the time. "I was so shallow a politician that I was not [then] aware of the importance of those compositions." Cappon, p. 392.
74. Allen C. Thomas, *The History of the Society of Friends in America* (London, 1854), vol. 2, p. 301.
75. Isaac Sharpless, *A History of Quaker Government in Pennsylvania* (Philadelphia, 1899), vol. 2, p. 128.
76. *D&A*, vol. 1, p. 279.
77. W. B. Allen, ed., *George Washington: A Collection* (Liberty Fund, 1988), p. 534 (emphasis added). See also Arthur Scherr, "John Adams Confronts Quakers and Baptists During the Revolution: A Paradox of the Quest for Liberty," *Journal of Church and State* 59, no. 2 (2017): 256–79.
78. Jane E. Calvert, *Penman of the Founding: A Biography of John Dickinson* (Oxford University Press, 2024), p. 244.
79. Jerrilyn Greene Marston, *King and Congress: The Transfer of Political Legitimacy, 1774–1776* (Princeton University Press, 2014), pp. 210–13.
80. Calvert, *Penman of the Founding*, pp. 270, 446.

81. *Collections of the New York Historical Society for the Year 1878*, vol. 1, *Revolutionary Papers* (New York, 1879), p. 269 (Joseph Reed).

82. Paul H. Smith, ed., *Letters of Delegates to Congress: 1774–1789* (Library of Congress, 1979), vol. 4, p. 338.

83. Edmund C. Burnett, ed., *Letters of Members of the Continental Congress* (Carnegie Institution, 1921), vol. 1, p. 460.

84. Smith, *Letters of the Delegates*, vol. 4, p. 352.

85. *D&A*, vol. 3, p. 365.

86. Burnett, *Letters*, vol. 1, p. 157.

87. *D&A*, vol. 3, p. 318.

88. *ARW*, vol. 2, p. 14.

89. *JW*, p. 12.

90. Albert Ellery Bergh, ed., *Writings of Thomas Jefferson* (Thomas Jefferson Memorial Association, 1904), vol. 5, pp. 445–46.

91. *PTJ*, vol. 1, p. 220.

92. *JW*, p. 12. Although the word "Congress" was not omitted from the petition, its language was carefully written to give the impression that it was sent not in the name of the Congress, but in the members' personal capacities. This gave Adams and his allies good reason to oppose it even aside from questions of time wasting. Had King George *accepted* the petition—unlikely, but not impossible—it certainly would have destroyed the Congress. The colonists would then have abandoned concerted action and resorted to separate or even private negotiation with London. This would almost certainly have proved fruitless—but would have been interminable, would have sparked intercolonial rivalry, and would have destroyed the Congress's political capital, perhaps for a generation. Even if George had merely *pretended* to accept the petition, it would have bought the British time to build up forces in America while stifling the colonists' capacity to develop their own military resources.

93. *Minutes of the Provincial Congress and the Council of Safety of the State of New Jersey* (Trenton, 1879), pp. 88–92.

94. Force, vol. 1, p. 1134.

95. Force, vol. 1, p. 1314.

96. Force, vol. 1, p. 1315.

97. *JCC*, vol. 3, p. 404.

98. Force, vol. 3, p. 1874.

99. Marston, *King and Congress*, pp. 210–13.

100. *PTJ*, vol. 1, pp. 187–222, contain Jefferson's initial draft, his clean draft for the committee, and the version as edited by Dickinson. The surviving text is so heavily interlineated and edited that it is impossible to discern with precision Jefferson's exact original wording. I have therefore quoted with some latitude. Unless otherwise noted, quotations from the Declaration are from this source.

101. *PTJ*, vol. 1, p. 195.

102. *JW*, p. 12.

103. Calvert, *Penman of the Founding*, pp. 246–47.

104. "God only Who confers [freedom] upon us, can deprive us of it . . . and we can no way understand that He does so, unless He had so declared by express revelation, or had set some distinguishing marks of dominion and subjection upon men; and, as an ingenious person not long since said, caused some to be born with crowns upon their heads, and all others with saddles upon their backs." Algernon Sidney, *Discourses Concerning Government*, ed. Thomas G. West (Liberty Fund, 1990), pp. 510–11. Jefferson paraphrased Sidney's words on his deathbed. *JW*, p. 1517.

105. *PTJ*, vol. 1, pp. 225–33.

106. In his diary, Adams put it more frankly. North "rocks the cradle, and sings lullaby, and the innocent children go to sleep, while he prepares the birch to whip the poor babes." *D&A*, vol. 2, p. 181.

107. Willard Sterne Randall, *Thomas Jefferson: A Life* (Holt, 1993), p. 246.

108. *JW*, p. 750.

109. Force, vol. 3, pp. 240–41.

110. Force, vol. 3, p. 627.

111. *The Parliamentary Register, Second Session of the Fourteenth Parliament* (London, 1776), vol. 3, pp. 1–3.

112. *Parliamentary Register*, vol. 3, pp. 74–76.

113. 16 Geo. 3 c. 5, *SaL*, vol. 31 (part 1), pp. 135–54.

114. 13 Geo. 2 c. 4 § 18, *SaL*, vol. 17, p. 368.

115. *The Manuscripts of Rye and Hereford Corporations* (London, 1892), p. 502.

CHAPTER 10

1. *D&A*, vol. 3, p. 301.

2. *PTJ*, vol. 1, p. 252.

3. L. H. Butterfield, ed., *Adams Family Correspondence* (Belknap, 1963), vol. 1, p. 289.

4. *D&A*, vol. 2, p. 193.

5. *D&A*, vol. 2, pp. 211–15.

6. *JCC*, vol. 3, p. 479.

7. *ARW*, vol. 1, p. 326.

8. *JCC*, vol. 3, p. 343.

9. Force, vol. 3, p. 1385.

10. Thucydides reports that when the Spartan general Pausanias sought to overthrow the polis, he promised the Helots freedom if they would support him. This effort was foiled. Charles Forster Smith, trans., *Thucydides: History of the Peloponnesian War* (Harvard University Press, 1951), vol. 1, p. 223. At the battle of Beneventum in 275 BCE, Tiberius Gracchus promised to free slaves who would bring him the heads of

slaughtered enemies. According to the historian Livy (a favorite of Jefferson's), this proved counterproductive, as the bravest enslaved soldiers wasted time decapitating enemy corpses instead of pressing the battle. D. Spillan and Cyrus Edmonds, trans., *History of Rome by Titus Livius* (George Bell & Sons, 1909), vol. 2, pp. 912–13. See also Christopher Leslie Brown and Philip D. Morgan, eds., *Arming Slaves* (Yale University Press, 2006).

11. G. Booth, trans., *The Historical Library of Diodorus the Sicilian* (London, 1700), pp. 730–32.

12. *JW*, p. 289.

13. Woody Holton, *Liberty Is Sweet* (Simon & Schuster, 2021), pp. 202–4; and Nikole Hannah-Jones et al., *The 1619 Project: A New Origin Story* (One World, 2021), p. 16.

14. Phillip P. Magness, *The 1619 Project Myth* (Independent Institute, 2025), pp. 24–28, 120–21, 126–27; Sylvia R. Frey, "Between Slavery and Freedom: Virginia Blacks in the American Revolution," *Journal of Southern History* 49, no. 3 (1983): 387; and Lloyd Dobyns, "Fighting . . . Maybe for Freedom, but Probably Not," *Colonial Williamsburg Journal* 29, no. 4 (2007): 58–64.

15. John Rhodehamel, ed., *The American Revolution: Writings from the War for Independence* (Library of America, 2001), pp. 81–86.

16. Andrew Lawler, *A Perfect Frenzy* (Atlantic Monthly Press, 2025), p. 404. See also Harvey Amani Whitfield, *North to Bondage: Loyalist Slavery in the Maritimes* (UBC Press, 2016).

17. Robert Olwell, *Masters, Slaves, and Subjects* (Cornell University Press, 1998), p. 252.

18. John E. Selby, *The Revolution in Virginia* (Colonial Williamsburg Foundation, 1988), p. 67.

19. Quoted in Gregory J. W. Urwin, "The Yorktown Tragedy: Washington's Slave Roundup," *Journal of the American Revolution*, October 19, 2021.

20. Joseph Plumb Martin, *A Narrative of Some of the Adventures, Dangers and Sufferings of a Revolutionary Soldier*, ed. George F. Scheer (New York Times, 1968), p. 241.

21. Lawler, *Perfect Frenzy*, p. 387.

22. Frey, "Between Slavery and Freedom," p. 387. See also Edward J. Larson, *American Inheritance* (W. W. Norton, 2023), p. 98: "The British . . . fostered or repudiated slavery as best served their imperial purposes."

23. R. C. Simmons and P. D. G. Thomas, eds., *Proceedings and Debates of the British Parliaments Respecting North America* (Kraus International, 1987), vol. 6, p. 96.

24. Alan Gilbert, *Black Patriots and Loyalists* (University of Chicago Press, 2012), pp. 46, 63.

25. Frey, "Between Slavery and Freedom," p. 384.

26. Hannah-Jones et al., *The 1619 Project*, p. 16. See also Magness, *The 1619 Project*, pp. 111–24.

27. J. A. Leo Lemay, ed., *Benjamin Franklin: Writings* (Library of America, 1987), p. 1154; and *D&A*, vol. 2, p. 246.

28. "Benjamin Franklin's Anti-Slavery Petitions to Congress," US National Archives, https://www.archives.gov/legislative/features/franklin.

29. Moses Coit Tyler, *Patrick Henry* (Boston, 1898), p. 388.

30. *Pamphlets*, vol. 1, p. 69.

31. Robert J. Taylor et al., eds., *Papers of John Adams* (Belknap, 1979), vol, 3, p. 19. As historian Gordon Wood concludes, one of the most extraordinary features of the revolution is that it "suddenly and effectively ended the cultural climate that had allowed black slavery. . . . Americans in 1775–76 began attacking it with a vehemence that was inconceivable earlier." *The Radicalism of the American Revolution* (Knopf, 1992), p. 186.

32. Gene Prochnow, "Construing Congress's Hasty, Ill-Fated 1775 Decision to Invade Canada," *Journal of the American Revolution*, May 21, 2024.

33. Louis Arthur Norton, "Henry Mowat: Miscreant of the Maine Coast," *Maine History* 43, no. 1 (2007): 6–7.

34. Although Dunmore initiated the attack on Norfolk, Patriot troops eventually burned most of the town to deny his troops cover. David Lee Russell, *The American Revolution in the Southern Colonies* (McFarland & Co., 2000), pp. 74–75.

35. Butterfield, *Adams Family Correspondence,* vol. 1, p. 348.

36. *PTJ*, vol. 1, p. 269.

37. *JCC*, vol. 3, p. 404.

38. *JCC*, vol. 3, pp. 319, 326–27.

39. Moncure Conway, ed., *Writings of Thomas Paine* (G. P. Putnam's Sons, 1906), vol. 1, p. 90.

40. Conway, *Writings of Thomas Paine*, vol. 1, p. 12.

41. Eric Foner, ed., *Thomas Paine: Collected Writings* (Library of America, 1995), pp. 9–11 (emphasis altered).

42. Foner, *Paine: Collected Writings*, p. 52.

43. *ARW*, vol. 2, p. 45.

44. *ARW*, vol. 2, pp. 49–56.

45. Force, vol. 5, pp. 462–63.

46. Force, vol. 3, p. 240; 16 Geo. 3 c. 5 § 24, *SaL*, vol. 31, p. 145; and *ARW*, vol. 2, p. 53.

47. Edmund C. Burnett, ed., *Letters of Members of the Continental Congress* (Carnegie Institute, 1921), vol. 1, p. 304.

48. Burnett, *Letters of Members of the Continental Congress*, vol. 1, p. 311.

49. *JCC*, vol. 4, p. 87.

50. *JCC*, vol. 4, pp. 134–46. Unless otherwise noted, quotations in this paragraph and the next two paragraphs are from this publication.

51. *JCC*, vol. 4, pp. 257–58.

52. *ARW*, vol. 2, pp. 68–69.

53. Pauline Maier, *American Scripture: Making the Declaration of Independence* (Knopf, 1997), p. 38.

54. Daniel Webster made the point well in a speech delivered on the 50th anniversary of independence. The Declaration makes no reference to Parliament because "the colonies had never admitted themselves subject to Parliament," he said. "That was precisely the point of the original controversy. They had uniformly denied that Parliament had authority to make laws for them. There was, therefore, no subjection to Parliament to be thrown off." Webster noted that there was one objection: Parliament's power to regulate colonial trade had long been conceded. *The Works of Daniel Webster* (Boston, 1851), vol. 1, pp. 127–28.

55. Herbert Friedenwald, *The Declaration of Independence: An Interpretation and An Analysis* (Macmillan, 1904), p. 165.

56. Andrew Roberts, *The Last King of America* (Viking, 2021), p. 303.

57. 16 Geo. 3 c. 5 § 24, *SaL*, vol. 31, p. 145. Even if London had not used those words, the facts spoke for themselves. William Blackstone, who devoted a chapter of his *Commentaries on the Laws of England* to the "duties" of kings, described the "reciprocal" relationship between monarch and subject—a relationship rooted in "reason and the rules of natural law"—as one in which the people rendered allegiance in exchange for protection. James II had broken that contract in 1689 by "subvert[ing] the constitution," Blackstone wrote, and that entitled Parliament to declare that he had abdicated the throne. William Blackstone, *Commentaries on the Laws of England* (London, 1809), vol. 1, p. 211. Now, Adams and his colleagues asserted that George III had done something similar, renouncing his duty to safeguard his American subjects. When one opponent of independence told Adams that George had not explicitly declared colonists out of his protection, Adams had a quick reply: "James II never declared the people of England out of his protection [either]," he said, "yet his actions proved it, and the Parliament declared it." *JCC*, vol. 6, p. 1089. (It is not clear from the records who was speaking, but given the importance Adams attached to this point, he seems most likely.)

58. Robert J. Taylor et al., eds., *Papers of John Adams* (Belknap, 1977), vol. 2, p. 393.

59. *JCC*, vol. 6, p. 1076. Technically speaking, Wilson was wrong. According to Lockean political theory, a true state of nature exists before the *social* compact, which forms civil society. Declaring independence from Britain meant only the dissolution of the *political* compact, but it did not destroy civil society. By 1787, Wilson had changed his mind. He "could not admit the doctrine that when the colonies became independent of Great Britain, they became independent also of each other," he told the Constitutional Convention. "They were independent not

individually but *unitedly*." Max Farrand, ed., *Records of the Federal Convention* (Yale University Press, 1911), vol. 1, p. 324.

60. Burnett, *Letters of Members of the Continental Congress*, vol. 1, p. 445.

61. *JCC*, vol. 6, p. 1075.

62. *D&A*, vol. 3, p. 381.

63. Weldon Amzy Brown, "The Howe Peace Commission of 1776," *North Carolina Historical Review* 13, no. 2 (1936): 125.

64. Rhodehamel, *The American Revolution*, pp. 190–91 (emphasis added).

65. D&A, vol. 3, p. 423.

66. Russell, *The American Revolution in the Southern Colonies*, p. 84.

67. Force, vol. 6, pp. 602–3.

68. Force, vol. 6, p. 615.

69. Robert M. Calhoon, "Loyalism and Neutrality," in *A Companion to the American Revolution*, ed. Jack P. Greene and J. R. Poole (Blackwell, 2000), pp. 235–47. A persistent myth holds that John Adams estimated support for the revolution at about one-third of the populace. In fact, Adams was speaking of American support for the *French* Revolution. William Marina, "The American Revolution and the Minority Myth," *Independent Review*, January 1, 1975; and Michael Schellhammer, "Critical Thinking," *Journal of the American Revolution*, February 11, 2013.

70. *PTJ*, vol. 1, p. 166.

71. *D&A*, vol. 3, pp. 334–35; and Maier, *American Scripture*, p. 91.

72. *D&A*, vol. 2, p. 129.

73. John C. Hamilton, ed., *The Works of Alexander Hamilton* (New York, 1850), vol. 2, p. 80.

74. Peter Laslett, ed., *Locke: Two Treatises of Government*, rev. ed. (Mento, 1963), p. 322. See also John Trenchard and Thomas Gordon, *Cato's Letters*, ed. Ronald Hamowy (Liberty Fund, 1995), vol. 1, p. 408 ("recourse to heaven").

75. *PTJ*, vol. 1, p. 311. These words come from Jefferson's notes on the debates over the Declaration. Jefferson did not attribute them to particular speakers, but it's reasonable to speculate that they were spoken by Adams.

76. Dumas Malone, *Jefferson the Virginian* (St. Martin's Press, 1948), p. 216.

77. *JCC*, vol. 3, p. 404.

78. *The Proceedings of the Convention of Delegates for the Counties and Corporations in the Colony of Virginia* (Richmond, 1816), pp. 63–65.

79. *Proceedings of the Convention*, pp. 15–16.

80. James Curtis Ballagh, ed., *The Letters of Richard Henry Lee* (Macmillan, 1911) vol. 1, pp. 176–80.

81. *Journals of the House of Commons* (London, 1803), vol. 10, p. 14.

82. Willard Sterne Randall, *Thomas Jefferson: A Life* (Holt, 1993), pp. 260–61.

83. *PTJ*, vol. 1, pp. 290–91.

84. *PTJ*, vol. 1, p. 292.

85. *PTJ*, vol. 1, pp. 337–45.

86. *PTJ*, vol. 1, pp. 356–64; and Jane Calvert, *Penman of the Founding: A Biography of John Dickinson* (Oxford University Press, 2024), p. 263. In her biography of John Dickinson, Jane Calvert credits the Pennsylvanian for adding a sex-neutral guarantee of religious freedom to the Articles of Confederation, writing that "nothing like this—explicit protection for the fundamental rights of women—had ever been written into an Anglo-American Constitution." Jefferson's draft constitution, however, which was written days earlier, included not only guarantees for women's equal inheritance of land, but also provisions guaranteeing religious freedom to "all persons," preventing the enslavement of any "person," and naturalizing "all persons" who met certain requirements.

87. William Walter Hening, ed., *Statutes at Large [of Virginia]* (Richmond, 1809), vol. 1, pp. 50–51.

88. *Proceedings of the Convention*, p. 16.

89. *Proceedings of the Convention*, p. 42.

90. Henry B. Veatch, *Human Rights: Fact or Fancy?* (University of Louisiana Press, 1985), p. 167.

91. C. Bradley Thompson, *America's Revolutionary Mind* (Encounter, 2019), p. 186.

92. Thompson, *America's Revolutionary Mind*, p. 188.

93. Allen Jayne, *Jefferson's Declaration of Independence* (University Press of Kentucky, 2014), p. 137.

94. *JW*, p. 493.

95. Douglas Den Uyl and Douglas Rasmussen, *The Realist Turn: Repositioning Liberalism* (Palgrave Macmillan, 2020).

96. Jeffrey Rosen, *The Pursuit of Happiness* (Simon & Schuster, 2024), p. 209.

97. Deirdre McCloskey, "Bourgeois Virtue," *American Scholar* 63, no. 2 (1994): 177–91. Actually, the difference between the ancient and bourgeois conceptions of happiness tends to be exaggerated. See Bernard Yack, *The Problems of a Political Animal* (University of California Press, 1993). Aristotle himself decried those who idealized the autocratic polis of Sparta and its martial political virtues, on the grounds that the Spartans were "not a happy people." The wise legislator, he wrote, should aim at "the provision of leisure and the establishment of peace," which appear much more bourgeois in orientation. Richard McKeon, ed., *The Basic Works of Aristotle* (Random House, 1941), p. 1299.

98. Micah 4:4. The same metaphor is used in 1 Kings 4:25 and Zechariah 3:10.

99. Bernard Bailyn, ed., *Debate on the Constitution* (Library of America, 1993), vol. 2, p. 706.

100. "Thomas Ludwell Lee to Richard Henry Lee, June 1, 1776," *Southern Literary Messenger* (n.s.) 5, no. 21 (1858): 325–26.

101. Jeff Broadwater, *George Mason: Forgotten Founder* (University of North Carolina Press, 2006), pp. 84–85.

102. Moncure Conway, *Omitted Chapters of History Disclosed in the Life and Papers of Edmund Randolph* (New York, 1889), p. 30.

103. *JCC*, vol. 6, pp. 1087–88.

104. *JCC*, vol. 6, p. 1090 (emphasis altered).

105. *JCC*, vol. 6, p. 1090.

106. *JCC*, vol. 6, p. 1090.

107. *JCC*, vol. 6, p. 1090.

108. *D&A*, vol. 3, p. 386.

109. Charles Kesler and Clinton Rossiter, eds., *The Federalist Papers* (Signet, 2003), p. 276.

110. Charles H. Lincoln, *The Revolutionary Movement in Pennsylvania* (Ginn & Co., 1901), p. 255; and James E. Gibson, "The Pennsylvania Provincial Congress of 1776," *Pennsylvania Magazine of History and Biography* 58, no. 4 (1934): 312–41.

111. Gibson, "Provincial Conference of 1776," p. 332.

112. Charles Francis Adams, ed., *Works of John Adams* (Boston, 1850), vol. 2, p. 514.

113. James Norton Smith, ed., *The Republic of Letters* (Norton, 1995), vol. 3, pp. 1875–77; and Maier, *American Scripture*, pp. 99–105.

114. *D&A*, vol. 2, p. 100 (emphasis added).

CHAPTER 11

1. *JW*, p. 1501.

2. See Carl Becker, *The Declaration of Independence: A Study in the History of Political Ideas* (Vintage, 1942); Julian P. Boyd, *The Declaration of Independence: The Evolution of the Text*, rev. ed., ed. Gerard W. Gawalt (Thomas Jefferson Foundation, 1999); and Pauline Maier, *American Scripture: Making the Declaration of Independence* (Knopf, 1997).

3. Joseph J. Ellis, *The Great Contradiction* (Knopf, 2025), pp. 43–44. See also Timothy Sandefur, Review of *The Great Contradiction* by Joseph Ellis, *Objective Standard*, October 28, 2025.

4. Russell Kirk, *Rights and Duties*, ed. Mitchell S. Muncy (Spence Publishing, 1997), p. 57.

5. H. Lee Cheek Jr., ed., *John C. Calhoun: Selected Writings and Speeches* (Regnery, 2003), p. 681.

6. Maier, *American Scripture*, p. 130. What's more, the Congress's Committee of Secret Correspondence, responsible for foreign relations, was staffed by its most moderate members, including Dickinson, who argued that *postponing* the Declaration was more likely to ensure French support. Declaring independence now, he claimed, would look like treating the French with "contempt." J. H. Powell, ed., "Speech of John

Dickinson Opposing the Declaration of Independence, 1 July, 1776," *Pennsylvania Magazine of History and Biography* 65, no. 4 (1941): 472.

7. Eric Foner, ed., *Thomas Paine: Collected Writings* (Library of America, 1995), pp. 461–62 (emphasis added). Unless otherwise noted, quotations in this paragraph are from this publication.

8. Thomas Hutchinson, *Strictures upon the Declaration of the Congress at Philadelphia* (London, 1776), p. 9.

9. *JHRM*, vol. 49, pp. 137–43. In fact, Hutchinson argued that only "one *political* band" connected the colonists with Britain, and that was "the supreme legislative authority" of Parliament, which "has essential right . . . to keep all parts of the empire entire until there may be a separation consistent with the general good of the empire, of which good . . . [Parliament] must be the sole judge." Hutchinson, *Strictures*, p. 9. In other words, all Britons were effectively Parliament's property, to be disposed of solely as it willed.

10. J. Hector St. John de Crèvecoeur, *Letters from an American Farmer* (Dutton, 1957), p. 39.

11. There is no evidence to support the oft-heard claim that this change appears in Franklin's handwriting; on the contrary, it is clearly in Jefferson's. Franklin was fond of the phrase, however, and it appeared frequently in his writings, including his 1774 pamphlet *Principles of Trade*, where he twice used it in much the same way that it is used in this paragraph. Richard E. Amacher, *Benjamin Franklin* (Twayne Publishers, 1962), p. 101. On the other hand, Jefferson also used it occasionally, including in his famous letter to James Madison arguing that "the earth belongs usufruct to the living," a proposition "which I suppose to be self-evident." *JW*, p. 959. A variant of "self-evident" appears in Locke. See Peter Laslett, ed., *John Locke: Two Treatises of Government*, rev. ed. (Mento, 1963), p. 5 ("evident in itself").

12. Thomas Reid, *Essays on the Powers of the Human Mind* (Edinburgh, 1803), vol. 1, p. 242. For helpful discussions of self-evidence, see Harry V. Jaffa, *Equality and Liberty: Theory and Practice in American Politics* (Oxford University Press, 1965), pp. 176–78; and C. Bradley Thompson, *America's Revolutionary Mind* (Encounter, 2019), chap. 3.

13. See, for example, "How the Meaning of the Declaration of Independence Changed Over Time," *Stanford Report*, July 1, 2020. In his debates with Abraham Lincoln, Stephen A. Douglas made the same assertion. Paul M. Angle, ed., *The Complete Lincoln–Douglas Debates of 1858* (University of Chicago Press, 1991), p. 81.

14. Consider the terminology: In passages where the Declaration does speak of the colonies collectively, it uses the term "people," as in "one people"—whereas this sentence uses the plural term "all men." (It also says that "they"—all men—possess rights such as "life" and "the pursuit of happiness," rights that cannot be sensibly ascribed to collective entities.)

15. Ilya Somin, "The Universalist Principles of the Declaration of Independence," *Volokh Conspiracy* (blog), July 4, 2019.

16. Charles W. Eliot, ed., *American Historical Documents 1000–1904* (P. F. Collier & Son, 1910), p. 62.

17. See, for example, Maier, *American Scripture*, p. 192; and Richard A. Posner, *The Problematics of Moral and Legal Theory* (Belknap, 1999), p. 111.

18. As Declaration scholar Harry Jaffa put it: "The equality of all men by nature and the freedom of all men by nature differ as the concavity of a curved line differs from its convexity. They two are distinguishable, but inseparable." *How to Think About the American Revolution* (Carolina Academic Press, 1978), p. 40.

19. One interesting aspect of Locke's triumvirate is that they are effectively the *same* right seen from different angles: They refer to the right of self-ownership in the present tense (life), the future tense (liberty), and the past tense (property). In other words, one's self-possession at *this* instant is synonymous with one's right to exist in the now; one's self-possession in the *future* means one's "liberty" to decide how to act in the next minute, day, or year; and how one has used that "liberty" in the *past* is manifested in the property one has acquired. Thus, "life, liberty, and property," or as Locke phrased it, "life, liberty, and estate," are different ways of viewing the inherent self-responsibility and self-direction that classical liberalism considers the individual's most basic right.

20. Aaron Fogleman, "Migrations to the Thirteen North American Colonies, 1700–1775: New Estimates," *Journal of Interdisciplinary History* 22, no. 4 (1992): 698.

21. Adam Smith, *Wealth of Nations* (Liberty Fund, 1976), vol. 1, p. 138.

22. *PTJ*, vol. 1, p. 193. Jefferson biographer Alf Mapp notes that this was "an early statement of what would come to be known as 'the American dream.'" *Thomas Jefferson: A Strange Case of Mistaken Identity* (Madison Books, 1987), p. 100.

23. John Phillip Reid, *The Concept of Liberty in the Age of the American Revolution* (University of Chicago Press, 1988), p. 120. Or in Locke's words, a person's freedom to "dispose, and order as he lists," his "actions, possessions, and his whole property, within the allowance of those laws under which he is, and therein not to be subject to the arbitrary will of another." Laslett, *Two Treatises*, p. 348.

24. Joyce Appleby and Terence Ball, eds., *Jefferson: Political Writings* (Cambridge University Press, 1999), p. 224.

25. Jack Rakove, ed., *James Madison: Writings* (Library of America, 1999), p. 502.

26. Walter Miller, trans., *Cicero: De Officiis* (William Heinemann, 1913), p. 249.

27. John Phillip Reid, *The Concept of Representation in the Age of the American Revolution* (University of Chicago Press, 1989). This was the

theory of "virtual representation," which was much debated at the time but was never taken seriously by the colonists.

28. The Declaration refers to "safety" or "security" three times; "happiness" twice; "life," "truth," "friendship," and "kinship" once each. It invokes variants of "justice" four times, and variants of "freedom" or "liberty" six times.

29. *JW*, p. 1426 (emphasis added).

30. *JW*, p. 493. James Madison would likewise declare, "Whatever be the hypothesis of the origin of the *lex majoris partis*, it is evident that it operates as a plenary substitute of the will of the majority of the society, for the will of the whole society, and that the sovereignty of the society as vested in and exercisable by the majority, may do anything that could be *rightfully* done, by the unanimous concurrence of the members; the reserved rights of individuals (of conscience for example), in becoming parties to the original compact, being beyond the legitimate reach of sovereignty, wherever vested or however viewed." Gaillard Hunt, ed., *The Writings of James Madison* (G. P. Putnam's Sons, 1910), vol. 9, p. 570.

31. See, for example, John Marsh, *The Liberal Delusion* (Arena Books, 2012), p. 51.

32. The recognition that the state's highest good is the preservation of individual rights has often been characterized as a "modern" notion—that is, traceable to the ideas of Locke and his contemporaries—but it also manifested the point made by Aristotle, Cicero, St. Thomas Aquinas, and other ancient thinkers, that the difference between true government and a mere gang of robbers lies not in the form, but in the substance—not in the means, but the ends. A legitimate government pursues the public good, whereas any political institution that engages in predation, enslavement, or arbitrary rule is a criminal enterprise *even if* the people consent to it. "There is no maxim in my opinion which is more liable to be misapplied," wrote James Madison in 1786, "than the [saying] that 'the interest of the majority is the political standard of right and wrong.' Taking the word 'interest' as synonymous with 'ultimate happiness,' *in which sense it is qualified with every necessary moral ingredient*, the proposition is no doubt true. But taking it in the popular sense, as referring to immediate augmentation of property and wealth, nothing can be more false. In the latter sense it would be the interest of the majority in every community to despoil and enslave the minority of individuals." Ralph Ketcham, ed., *Selected Writings of James Madison* (Hackett, 2006), p. 28 (emphasis added).

33. James Morton Smith, ed., *The Republic of Letters: The Correspondence Between Thomas Jefferson and James Madison, 1776–1826* (W. W. Norton, 1995), vol. 3, p. 1876.

34. Laslett, *Two Treatises*, pp. 310–11, 460–61, 466.

35. Laslett, *Two Treatises*, pp. 460, 463.

36. Boyd, *Evolution*, p. 27. In his initial draft, Jefferson wrote that Parliament's plans revealed a scheme to reduce America under "arbitrary

power," but Adams and Franklin changed this to the more effective "absolute despotism."

37. William Blackstone, *Commentaries on the Laws of England* (London, 1809), vol. 1, p. 162.

38. L. H. Butterfield, ed., *Adams Family Correspondence* (Belknap, 1963), vol. 2, p. 96.

39. Edmund Quincy, *Life of Josiah Quincy* (Boston, 1869), p. 386; and Catherine Drinker Bowen, "John Adams His Bowl," *The Atlantic*, May 1946.

40. Charles Francis Adams, ed., *Works of John Adams* (Boston, 1850), vol. 2, p. 514.

41. Adams himself described the king as a tyrant at the time. See, for example, Butterfield, *Adams Family Correspondence*, vol. 2, p. 24; and Gregg L. Lint et al., eds., *Papers of John Adams* (Belknap, 1989), vol. 8, p. 358.

42. Andrew J. O'Shaughnessy, "Thomas Jefferson and George III," YouTube, September 14, 2004.

43. *JW*, p. 57.

44. *JW*, p. 1221.

45. Elmer Beecher Russell, *The Review of American Colonial Legislation by the King in Council* (Columbia University, 1915), pp. 171–73.

46. Russell, *Review of American Colonial Legislation*, p. 507.

47. 24 Geo. 2 c. 53, *SaL*, vol. 20, pp. 306–9; and 4 Geo. 3 c. 34, *SaL*, vol. 26, pp. 103–5.

48. Kevin Phillips, *1775: A Good Year for Revolution* (Penguin, 2012), chap. 3.

49. *JW*, p. 116.

50. "Journal, March 1773: Volume 80," in *Journals of the Board of Trade and Plantations: Volume 13, January 1768–December 1775*, ed. K. H. Ledward (H. M. Stationery Office, 1937), pp. 342–51.

51. Dudley Odell McGovney, "The British Privy Council's Power to Restrain the Legislatures of Colonial America: Power to Disallow Statutes: Power to Veto," *University of Pennsylvania Law Review* 94, no. 1 (1945): 72.

52. Charles M. Andrews, *The Royal Disallowance* (American Antiquarian Society, 1914), p. 9.

53. Russell, *Review of American Colonial Legislation*, p. 507.

54. Thomas Short, *A Comparative History of the Increase and Decrease of Mankind in England* (London, 1767), pp. 164–65.

55. Marilyn C. Baseler, *Asylum for Mankind: America 1607–1800* (Cornell University Press, 1998), pp. 123–25.

56. Gordon S. Wood, *The Radicalism of the American Revolution* (Knopf, 1992), p. 128.

57. Sydney George Fisher, "The Twenty-Eight Charges Against the King in the Declaration of Independence," *Pennsylvania Magazine of*

History and Biography 31, no. 3 (1907), p. 273; and Russell, *Review of American Colonial Legislation*, pp. 604–6.

58. Russell, *Review of American Colonial Legislation*, p. 606.

59. Jack P. Greene, "Bridge to Revolution: The Wilkes Fund Controversy in South Carolina, 1769–1775," *Journal of Southern History* 29, no. 1 (1963): 52.

60. *JW*, p. 212.

61. 12 Ch. 2 c. 18, *SaL*, vol. 7, pp. 452–60; and George Louis Beer, *The Old Colonial System* (Macmillan, 1912), vol. 1, p. 70.

62. Beer, *Old Colonial System*, vol. 1, p. 67.

63. A. H. Carpenter, "Naturalization in England and the American Colonies," *American Historical Review* 9, no. 2 (1904): 288–303.

64. Russell, *Review of American Colonial Legislation*, p. 169.

65. 14 Geo. 3 c. 84, *SaL*, vol. 30 (part 1), pp. 554–55. This law provided that naturalized subjects must reside in Britain or its dominions for seven years before enjoying "immunities or indulgences in trade which are or may be enjoyed or claimed therein by natural-born British subjects."

66. *Documents Relative to the Colonial History of the State of New York* (Albany, 1857), vol. 8, p. 402.

67. *Documents Relative to New York*, vol. 8, pp. 357–58; and Bernard Bailyn, *Voyagers to the West* (Vintage, 1986), p. 56.

68. K. G. Davies, ed., *Documents of the American Revolution* (Irish University Press, 1975), vol. 8, p. 114.

69. *PTJ*, vol. 1, p. 425.

70. H. Braughn Taylor, "The Foreign Attachment Law and the Coming of the Revolution in North Carolina," *North Carolina Historical Review* 52, no. 1 (1975): 25.

71. In *American Scripture* (pp. 110–11), Pauline Maier ignores the closure of courts in Massachusetts and Virginia and blames North Carolina's Patriots for closing that colony's courts by refusing to compromise. But it is hard to see why they should have conceded to Britain's purported authority on a matter so important to them. And if the matter was a trifling one, as Hutchinson implied, why should London not have conceded it?

72. Russell, *Review of American Colonial Legislation*, pp. 582–85.

73. Russell, *Review of American Colonial Legislation*, p. 608.

74. Hutchinson, *Strictures*, pp. 16–17.

75. Adams, *Works of John Adams*, vol. 3, p. 567.

76. This common myth is repeated, for example, in Erin Chemerinsky, *We the People: A Progressive Reading of the Constitution for the Twenty-First Century* (Macmillan, 2018), p. 15. In fact, judicial review was a familiar feature of jurisprudence long before *Marbury*. William Michael Treanor, "Judicial Review Before *Marbury*," *Stanford Law Review* 58, no. 2 (2005): 455–562.

77. Taken from Job 5:5: "Whose harvest the hungry eateth up, and taketh it even out of the thorns, and the robber swalloweth up their substance."

78. William Smith, *The Constitutional History of England*, rev. ed. (London, 1888), p. 521.

79. Daniel R. Coquillette and Neil Longley York, eds., *Portrait of a Patriot: The Major Political and Legal Papers of Josiah Quincy Jr.* (Colonial Society of Massachusetts, 2014), vol. 6, p. 217.

80. Sir Matthew Hale had declared in 1713 that it was not, but it was generally accepted that a breakdown in civilian order could authorize what we now call martial law. In Hale's day, the distinction between martial law and military law was poorly understood. Abhishek Singhvi and Khagesh Gautam, *The Law of Emergency Powers* (Springer, 2020), pp. 22–23.

81. Blackstone, *Commentaries*, vol. 1, pp. 413–14.

82. David Wooton, ed., *Divine Right and Democracy: An Anthology of Political Writing in Stuart England* (Hackett, 2003), p. 170.

83. Although the King of England today theoretically retains veto power, it has still not been exercised since that bill.

84. *JW*, p. 115.

85. Hutchinson, *Strictures*, p. 22.

86. Andrew Roberts, *The Last King of America* (Viking, 2021), p. 303; and Hutchinson, *Strictures*, p. 22.

87. Hutchinson, *Strictures*, p. 23. See also Bruce Frohnen, ed., *The American Republic* (Liberty Fund, 2010), p. 176 (Boucher); and *ARW*, vol. 1, p. 332 (Massachusettensis).

88. 9 Ann., c. 17, *SaL*, vol. 12, pp. 185–86; 8 Geo. 1 c. 12, *SaL*, vol. 14, pp. 384–88; 2 Geo. 2 c. 35, *SaL*, vol. 16, pp. 102–10; and Joseph J. Malone, *Pine Trees and Politics: The Naval Stores and Forest Policy in Colonial New England, 1691–1775* (University of Washington Press, 1964).

89. 2 Geo. 2 c. 35, §§ 1–2, *SaL*, vol. 5, p. 521.

90. Malone, *Pine Trees*, p. 141.

91. See L. Kinvin Wroth and Hiller B. Zobel, eds., *Legal Papers of John Adams* (University of California Press, 1965), vol. 2, pp. 247–59.

92. 35 Hen. 8 c. 2, *SaL*, vol. 5, p. 199; and 12 Geo. 3 c. 24, *SaL*, vol. 30, p. 30.

93. Blackstone, *Commentaries*, vol. 2, p. 418.

94. *Votes and Proceedings of the Freeholder and Other Inhabitants of the Town of Boston* (Boston, 1772), p. 27.

95. Hutchinson, *Strictures*, p. 27.

96. The principle *nemo iudex in causa sua*—no person may be the judge in his own cause—was invoked long before it was formally stated by the Byzantine emperor and legal reformer Justinian. D. E. C. Yale, "*Iudex in Propria Causa*: An Historical Excursus," *Cambridge Law Journal* 33, no. 1 (1974): 80–96. The rule that no person can be trusted to objectively decide a dispute in which he or she has a significant stake in the outcome is a natural law, not a mere convention, because it is not

a creature of agreement or historical tradition, but of human nature. Modern-day game theorists refer to it as the divide-and-choose principle of fair division. Steven J. Brams and Alan D. Taylor, *Fair Division: From Cake-Cutting to Dispute Resolution* (Cambridge University Press, 1996). For the same reason, no government entity can be trusted to decide the extent of its own powers.

97. 16 Geo. 3 c. 5 § 24, *SaL*, vol. 31 (part 1), p. 145.

98. Thomas Gordon, trans., *The Works of Tacitus* (London, 1731), vol. 2, p. 376. Gordon's translation was Jefferson's favorite.

99. Phillips, *1775*, pp. 346–47, 400; and David Lee Russell, *The American Revolution in the Southern Colonies* (McFarland & Co., 2000), p. 85.

100. William Belsham, *Memoirs of the Reign of George III*, 3rd ed. (Dublin, 1796), vol. 1, p. 329.

101. Blackstone, *Commentaries*, vol. 2, pp. 414–16.

102. In fact, historians estimate that about 15 percent of the Hessians deserted. Rodney Atwood, *The Hessians* (Cambridge University Press, 1980), pp. 24, 204.

103. Atwood, *The Hessians*, p. 153. The exact number of Hessians sent to America is not known, but 30,000 seems the best estimate.

104. Lyman H. Butterfield, "Psychological Warfare in 1776: The Jefferson-Franklin Plan to Cause Hessian Desertions," *Proceedings of the American Philosophical Society* 94, no. 3 (1950): 236.

105. 16 Geo. 3 c. 5 § 4, *SaL*, vol. 31 (part 1), p. 137.

106. Geneva Convention, Art. 130.

107. Adams, *Works of John Adams*, vol. 9, p. 317.

108. Jared Sparks, ed., *Works of Benjmain Franklin* (Boston, 1836), vol. 2, p. 334.

109. Paul A. Gilje, *Free Trade and Sailors' Rights in the War of 1812* (Cambridge University Press, 2013).

110. Thomas S. Abler, "Iroquois Cannibalism: Fact Not Fiction," *Ethnohistory* 27, no. 4 (1980): 309–16; Elizabeth Tooker, *An Ethnography of the Huron Indians, 1615–1649* (Government Printing Office, 1964), pp. 31–39; and Bruce G. Trigger, *The Huron: Farmers of the North* (Holt, Rinehart & Winston, 1969), pp. 44–53.

111. Parker B. Brown, "The Historical Accuracy of the Captivity Narrative of Doctor John Knight," *Western Pennsylvania Historical Magazine* 70, no. 1 (1987): 53–67.

112. Virginia and Pennsylvania disputed the possession of the Pittsburgh area (then called Fort Pitt). Their disagreement remained unresolved when the war with Britain began. For an argument that Dunmore's war was a justified response to unprovoked Native aggression, see Glen F. Williams, *Dunmore's War* (Westholme, 2017).

113. Henry Howe, ed., *Historical Collections of Ohio* (Cincinnati, 1851), p. 408.

114. See, for example, J. A. Leo Lemay, ed., *Benjamin Franklin: Writings* (Library of America, 1987), pp. 540–58. For Jefferson's views regarding Indian matters, see David Bergeron, "Thomas Jefferson and His Thinking About Native Americans," *Science Politique* 67, no. 3 (2017): 457–519. Some writers have characterized Jefferson as wishing to eradicate the Native population, quoting out of context a 1779 letter he wrote to Indian fighter George Rogers Clark in which he said of the Shawnee, Mingo, Munsee, and Wyandot, "The same world will scarcely do for them and us." *PTJ*, vol. 3, pp. 258–59. Context makes clear, however, that Jefferson was referring to hostile tribes that aligned with the British. Jefferson's considered Indian policy was to encourage cultural assimilation, the encouragement of agriculture, and removal of tribes that refused these things.

115. Gary B. Nash, *The Unknown American Revolution* (Penguin, 2005), pp. 212–13.

116. Nash, *Unknown American Revolution*, p. 215.

117. Russell, *American Revolution in the Southern Colonies*, p. 181.

118. William R. Nester, *George Rogers Clark: "I Glory in War"* (University of Oklahoma Press, 2012), pp. 143, 147–51.

119. Peter Silver, *Our Savage Neighbors: How Indian War Transformed Early America* (W. W. Norton, 2008), pp. 41, 58.

120. David Narrett, *The Cherokees in War and at Peace, 1670–1840* (Harvard University Press, 2025), p. 341.

121. Ethan A. Schmidt, *Native Americans in the American Revolution* (Praeger, 2014), pp. 129–30; and Richard Beeman, *Our Lives, Our Fortunes and Our Sacred Honor: The Forging of American Independence, 1774–1776* (Basic Books, 2013), p. 403. Beeman entirely ignored British recruitment of Native warriors, claiming that it was only the Americans' "relentless move westward" that "[caused] most of the inciting."

122. American forces captured Hamilton, and Jefferson—by then governor of Virginia—sentenced him to a year and a half in irons for the crime. He later dropped the charges, however, in part because the chief witness proved to have perjured himself, and in part because Washington thought international law required that Hamilton be paroled. Historians remain uncertain as to whether Hamilton paid bounties for scalps, but he certainly did receive them from allied tribesmen. Bernard W. Sheehan, "'The Famous Hair Buyer General': Henry Hamilton, George Rogers Clark, and the American Indian," *Indiana Magazine of History* 79, no. 1 (1983): 1–28. In any case, scalp-buying was a long-standing practice of British colonial administrators. Henry J. Young, "A Note on Scalp Bounties in Pennsylvania," *Pennsylvania History* 24, no. 3 (1957): 207–18.

123. Nash, *Unknown American Revolution*, pp. 71, 435. Some writers have claimed that if independence had been avoided, Native Americans would have experienced better treatment at the hands of a

British-American government. *Vox* writer Dylan Matthews, for example, asserted in 2015 that "absent the revolution . . . fewer [indigenous] people would have died." "3 Reasons the American Revolution Was a Mistake," *Vox*, July 3, 2015. Yet this seems implausible, given Matthews's concession that in the years after independence, British Canadian authorities "committed horrible, indefensible crimes" against First Nations. True, fewer clashes occurred between Natives and whites in Canada, but that's not surprising, given that its white population in 1776 was less than one-tenth that of the United States—and is still about one-tenth of the United States'. Selena Zhao, "A Progressive Facade: Comparing the U.S. and Canada's Treatment of Indigenous Peoples," *Harvard Policy Review*, January 22, 2021. Yet even today, although Native Americans in the United States suffer from deplorable rates of poverty, addiction, drug abuse, suicide, and other social maladies, they are better off in all these respects than are members of Canadian First Nations. The median income among Canadian First Nation households, for example, is approximately US$30,000, whereas the average income for American Indian households is about US$43,000. Moreover, the British imperial government's horrific treatment of natives in India, Kenya, and Australia in the years after 1776 makes it hard to believe that postponing independence would have resulted in better treatment of indigenous Americans.

124. That was what Lord Hillsborough thought, at least. In 1772, he wrote that the line had been drawn to ensure that American "settlements should lie within the reach of the trade and commerce of this kingdom." Albert Henry Smyth, ed., *Writings of Benjamin Franklin* (Macmillan, 1906), vol. 5, p. 468. The prime minister, Lord Bute, emphasized that it was Britain's "policy" to "set bounds . . . to the extent of the settlement" of the West because otherwise Parliament "could no longer maintain dominion" over the colonists. Thomas C. Barrow, *Trade and Empire: The British Customs Service in Colonial America* (Harvard University Press, 1967), p. 176. A memo prepared for the Earl of Egremont encouraged the establishment of "some line for a western boundary . . . beyond which our people should not at present be permitted to settle, hence as their numbers increased, they should emigrate to Nova Scotia, or to the provinces on the southern frontier, where they would be useful to their mother country, instead of planting themselves in the heart of America, out of the reach of government, and where, from the great difficulty of procuring European commodities, they would be compelled to commence manufactures, to the infinite prejudice of Britain." Verner W. Crane, "Hints Relative to the Division and Government of the Conquered and Newly Acquired Countries in America," *Mississippi Valley Historical Review* 8, no. 4 (1922): 371.

125. Samuel Eliot Morison, ed., *Sources and Documents Illustrating the American Revolution, 1764–1788*, 2nd ed. (Clarendon Press, 1962), p. 3.

126. Stuart Banner, *How the Indians Lost Their Land: Law and Power on the Frontier* (Belknap, 2005), p. 108.

127. Banner, *How the Indians Lost Their Land*, p. 93.

128. Colin G. Calloway, *The Scratch of a Pen: 1763 and the Transformation of North America* (Oxford University Press, 2006), p. 96.

129. William Reynolds, *The Cherokee Struggle to Maintain Identity in the 17th and 18th Centuries* (McFarland, 2015), p. 178.

130. Alan Valentine, *Lord George Germain* (Clarendon Press, 1962), p. 187.

131. *An Answer to the Declaration of the American Congress* (London, 1776), p. 107.

132. *JW*, p. 289.

133. William G. Merkel, "To See Oneself as a Target of Justified Revolution: Thomas Jefferson and Gabriel's Uprising," *American Nineteenth Century History* 4, no. 1 (2003): 1–31.

134. *PTJ*, vol. 1, p. 418.

135. Phillips, *1775*, p. 242.

136. Leonard W. Levy, *Jefferson and Civil Liberties: The Darker Side* (I. R. Dee, 1989), pp. 33–41.

137. *PTJ*, vol. 1, p. 418.

138. *PTJ*, vol. 1, p. 426. I have used the emphases of Jefferson's handwritten draft.

139. Adams, *Works of John Adams*, vol. 2, p. 514.

140. E. Millicent Soweby, ed., *Catalogue of the Library of Thomas Jefferson* (University of Virginia Press, 1983), vol. 2, p. 11. See also Cara Rogers Stevens, *Thomas Jefferson and the Fight Against Slavery* (University Press of Kansas, 2024), pp. 33–36.

141. Joseph Ellis, *American Sphinx* (Random House, 1998), p. 56.

142. Garry Wills, *Inventing America: Jefferson's Declaration of Independence* (Vintage, 1978), p. 74. Among the purported proofs of Jefferson's disingenuousness, Wills pointed out that Jefferson "*omitted that rhetoric himself* in presenting this count to the Virginia convention"—implying that Jefferson deceitfully withheld this paragraph from the proposed constitution he sent to Richmond in June 1776. The more likely explanation is that he had not yet written these words or thought of this argument, which would also explain why it did not appear on his initial draft of the list of grievances used in composing the Declaration. Wills's book won many awards when it appeared in 1978, but it contains many flaws. Among the most valuable critiques are Harry V. Jaffa, "Inventing the Past," in *American Conservatism and the American Founding* (Claremont Institute Press, 2002), pp. 76–108; and Ronald Hamowy, "Jefferson and the Scottish Enlightenment: A Critique of Garry Wills's *Inventing America: Jefferson's Declaration of Independence*," *William and Mary Quarterly* 36, no. 4 (1979): 503–23.

143. Adams, *Works of John Adams*, vol. 9, p. 429.

144. *JW*, pp. 37, 287. Unless otherwise noted, quotations in this paragraph are from this publication.

145. This is not an uncommon political tactic. After World War II, American and European prosecutors at Nuremberg accused German war criminals of wrongs they knew their Soviet allies were committing at that very moment—such as running forced-labor camps—in part because they hoped that worldwide condemnation of such actions by the Nazis would also provide some leverage against Stalin's regime, without requiring an unwinnable direct confrontation with Moscow. "Russian participation at Nuremberg," wrote the American general in charge of the prosecutions, "committed the Soviet government to the legal propositions that national leaders who unleash their country's military forces to wage aggressive war are criminals." Telford Taylor, "The Nuremberg Trials," in *Perspectives on the Nuremberg Trial*, ed. Guénaël Mettreaux (Oxford University Press, 2008), p. 401.

146. *PTJ*, vol. 8, p. 357. This letter was to British abolitionist Richard Price, who in 1785 published the anti-slavery pamphlet *Observations on the Importance of the American Revolution*. In his "Introduction" to *Notes on the State of Virginia*, scholar Robert Pierce Forbes asserts that Jefferson "must have winced" when reading Price's pamphlet, with its assertion that Americans would "not appear [to] deserve the liberty for which they have been contending" until they abolished slavery. Forbes, ed., *Notes on the State of Virginia: An Annotated Edition* (Yale University Press, 2022), p. xxxix. But far from "wincing," Jefferson told Price, "I wish you to do more" in attacking slavery, and particularly urged him to write another pamphlet for students at the College of William and Mary. Forbes also claims that Jefferson concealed the true date of the publication of *Notes* to disguise any influence Price may have had on his thoughts. But there is no evidence for this claim. See Timothy Sandefur, Review of *Notes on the State of Virginia: An Annotated Edition* by Robert Pierce Forbes, *Objective Standard*, August 19, 2022.

147. Gordon Wood, ed., *John Adams: Writings from the New Nation, 1784–1826* (Library of America, 2016), p. 406.

148. John D. Cushing, "The Cushing Court and the Abolition of Slavery in Massachusetts: More Notes on the 'Quock Walker Case,'" *American Journal of Legal History* 5, no. 2 (1961): 133.

149. Adam Smith, *Wealth of Nations* (Liberty Fund, 1976), vol. 1, p. 98.

150. *JW*, p. 18. One hint of the content of these debates is given by the sketchy notes of a later debate. On July 30, while discussing whether slaves should be counted for apportionment purposes under the Articles of Confederation, South Carolina's Thomas Lynch said, "If it is debated whether their slaves are their property, there is an end of the confederation." *JCC*, vol. 6, p. 1080.

151. J. Jefferson Looney, et al., eds., *Papers of Thomas Jefferson: Retirement Series* (Princeton University Press, 2016), vol. 13, pp. 463–64.

152. *PTJ*, vol. 1, p. 427.

153. George Anastaplo, "The Declaration of Independence," *St. Louis University Law Journal* 9, no. 3 (1965): 404–5; and Charles Kesler and Clinton Rossiter, eds., *The Federalist Papers* (Signet, 2003), p. 298.

154. "Could we represent in their full force, the sentiments that agitate the minds of us your dutiful subjects, we are persuaded your Majesty would ascribe any seeming deviation from reverence in our language, and even in our conduct, not to any reprehensible intention, but to the impossibility of reconciling the usual appearances of respect with a just attention to our own preservation against those artful and cruel enemies who abuse your royal confidence." *PTJ*, vol. 1, p. 221.

155. However, these religious references do not substantiate the oft-heard claim that the United States was created as a "Christian nation." Although the American revolutionaries believed in a higher power—including Jefferson, who, as a deist, denied the existence of the supernatural and believed that a divine Creator had set the universe in motion and then left it alone—the Declaration never purports to connect its political claims to divine revelation. The "laws of nature" it references are comprehensible by reason, and the authority of government derives not from divine command but from "the consent of the governed." Neither Jefferson, who coined the phrase "separation of church and state," nor Adams, who ridiculed the notion that the American governments were divinely inspired, viewed this language as committing the nation to a gospel-oriented mission. Adams, for example, wrote, "It will never be pretended that any persons employed in [drafting America's constitutions] had interviews with the gods, or were in any degree under the inspiration of Heaven, more than those at work upon shops or houses, or laboring in merchandise or agriculture." Adams, *Works of John Adams*, vol. 4, p. 292.

Instead, the God of the Declaration is equivalent to the binding quality of moral-political principles. He may be the ultimate source of natural moral law, in the same way that He may be the origin of the laws governing work in shops or labor in agriculture—as well as the laws of gravity, economics, or dietetics, but the origin of those laws is not relevant to the Declaration's immediate purpose. What is crucial is that these laws are comprehensible and binding, not by ipse dixit, but because they are the unavoidable consequences of human nature. As a result, the Declaration's principles do not depend on faith in any logically necessary way. As Harry Jaffa observed, "While not supposing for a moment that the Founders did not believe in the actual existence of God, their assumptions about Equality—which include assumptions about the subhuman and the superhuman—are independent of the validity of any particular religious beliefs." *How to Think About the American Revolution*, p. 42.

See also Ayn Rand, *The Virtue of Selfishness* (Signet, 1964), p. 126. ("Whether one believes that man is the product of a Creator or of nature, the issue of man's origin does not alter the fact that he is an entity of a specific kind—a rational being— that he cannot function successfully under coercion, and that rights are a necessary condition of his particular mode of survival.") Even Matthew Spalding, who attempts to describe a "theology" of the Declaration, admits that its "language is not especially Christian" and that it contemplates "not the living God of the Gospels." *The Making of the American Mind: The Story of Our Declaration of Independence* (Encounter, 2025), p. 234. For more on God as understood in the Declaration, see Matthew Stewart, *Nature's God: The Heretical Origins of the American Republic* (W. W. Norton, 2014).

156. 1 Edw. 6 c. 12, *SaL*, vol. 5, p. 262.

157. 1 & 2 Ph. & M. c. 10, *SaL*, vol. 6, p. 53.

158. 6 Geo. 1 c. 5, *SaL*, vol. 14, pp. 204–5.

159. 6 Geo. 3 c. 12, *SaL*, vol. 27, pp. 19–20.

160. *D&A*, vol. 2, p. 100.

161. Smith, *Republic of Letters*, vol. 3, p. 1925n31.

CHAPTER 12

1. L. H. Butterfield, ed., *Adams Family Correspondence* (Belknap, 1963), vol. 2, p. 224.

2. *JW*, p. 875.

3. J. H. Powell, ed., "Speech of John Dickinson Opposing the Declaration of Independence, 1 July, 1776," *Pennsylvania Magazine of History and Biography* 65, no. 4 (1941): 470.

4. Wilson took the unusual step of asking his colleagues to sign a memo attesting that he had not opposed independence in principle, but only because he was unsure of his constituents' wishes. Jefferson and Adams signed it. Geoffrey Seed, *James Wilson: Scottish Intellectual and American Statesman* (KTO Press, 1978), p. 14.

5. L. H. Butterfield, ed., *Letters of Benjamin Rush* (Princeton University Press, 1951), vol. 2, p. 1090.

6. *ARW*, vol. 2, p. 93.

7. Edith Gelles, ed., *Abigail Adams: Letters* (Library of America, 2016), p. 100.

8. *PTJ*, vol. 1, p. 477.

9. John C. Fitzpatrick, ed., *The Writings of George Washington* (Government Printing Office, 1932), vol. 5, p. 247.

10. John Bowring, ed., *The Works of Jeremy Bentham* (Edinburgh, 1843), vol. 2, p. 501. Unless otherwise noted, quotations in this paragraph and the next are from this publication. See also Timothy Sandefur, "A 'Nonsense' View of Rights," *Discourse*, March 31, 2025.

11. Bentham did condemn the slave trade, but he never reconciled that with his rejection of individual rights. P. J. Kelly, *Utilitarianism and Distributive Justice, Jeremy Bentham and the Civil Law* (Clarendon Press, 1990), pp. 213–14; and Douglas G. Long, *Bentham on Liberty: Jeremy Bentham's Idea of Liberty in Relation to His Utilitarianism* (University of Toronto Press, 1977), p. 194. For a defense of Bentham, see Frederick Rosen, "Jeremy Bentham on Slavery and the Slave Trade," in *Utilitarianism and Empire*, ed. B. Schultz and G. Varouxakis (Lexington Books, 2005), pp. 33–56.

12. Peter Wilson Coldham, *American Loyalist Claims* (National Genealogical Society, 1980), vol. 1, p. v; and Marcus Gallo, "Property Rights, Citizenship, Corruption, and Inequality: Confiscating Loyalist Estates During the American Revolution," *Pennsylvania History* 86, no. 4 (2019): 474–510. In 1996, two members of the Canadian Parliament introduced a bill demanding to authorize the confiscation of US assets to pay descendants of Loyalists exiled to Canada during the revolution. Sidney Hicks, "Loyalist Descendants Could Claim Lands," United Press International, October 23, 1996. The bill was intended as a stunt to satirize US foreign policy and never became law.

13. Bowring, *Works of Bentham*, vol. 2, p. 501.

14. For an effort to reconcile legitimacy with utilitarianism, see Ken Binmore, "A Utilitarian Theory of Political Legitimacy," in *Economics, Values, and Organization*, ed. Avner Ben-Ner and Louis Putterman (Cambridge University Press, 1998), pp. 101–32. Binmore's argument is heavy on pejoratives and mathematics but is frankly relativistic and thus, like Bentham's own work, ultimately nihilistic. In his especially perceptive discussion of Bentham's relationship to America, Daniel T. Rodgers observes that the Englishman "cared not a wit [*sic*] for the origins of governments or for their nature or their legitimacy." Rodgers, *Contested Truths: Keywords in American Politics Since Independence* (Basic Books, 1987), p. 24. But the American regime is, has been, and always will be obsessed with those very questions, because if all men are created equal, the great challenge is to justify political authority *at all.*

15. Bowring, *Works of Bentham*, vol. 2, p. 498.

16. Iain Hampsher-Monk, ed., *Burke: Revolutionary Writings* (Cambridge University Press, 2014), p. 78.

17. *ARW*, vol. 2, p. 120.

18. Isaiah Berlin, *The Roots of Romanticism* (Princeton University Press, 1999), p. 145.

19. A version of Romanticism sprang up among Jeffersonians, too: Witness figures such as John Randolph of Roanoke.

20. *JW*, p. 520. In this passage of his address, Jefferson slyly used a discussion of Indian policy to take a swipe at Federalists. This is made clear by the word "too": Speaking of Native Americans, Jefferson said "they, *too*, have their anti-philosophers."

21. *JW*, p. 1050.

22. Gordon S. Wood, ed., *John Adams: Writings from the New Nation, 1784–1826* (Library of America, 2016), p. 81; and C. Bradley Thompson, *John Adams and the Spirit of Liberty* (University of Kansas Press, 1998), p. 235. See also Randall B. Ripley, "Adams, Burke, and Eighteenth-Century Conservatism," *Political Science Quarterly* 80, no. 2 (1965): 216–35.

23. Cappon, p. 598.

24. *JW*, pp. 1513–14. In this letter, Jefferson refers to Blackstone's "Mansfieldism," an allusion to Chief Justice Mansfield, who was, according to his biographer Ernest B. Lowrie, "the person most directly responsible for [the] maximal reading of the Doctrine of Parliamentary Supremacy." *Lord Chief Justice Mansfield: Dark Horse of the American Revolution* (Archway Publishing, 2016), p. 4.

25. The clearest example of this is the Pennsylvania Supreme Court's opinion in *Sharpless v. Mayor of Philadelphia*, 21 Pa. 147 (1853).

26. Jefferson has often been viewed as a sort of protosecessionist, due to the language of his anonymously written Kentucky Resolutions, which argued that the federal Constitution was nothing more than a league between states that retained their own individual sovereignty. James Madison, shocked by this statement—which he rightly saw as a retreat from the Constitution's principal accomplishment—sought to dissuade Jefferson from such language and, after Jefferson's death, insisted that his friend had never meant it to be taken as justifying secession. Drew McCoy, *The Last of the Fathers: James Madison and the Republican Legacy* (Cambridge University Press,1989), chap. 4. However that may be, it's notable that Jefferson thought states could not refuse to obey Congress *even under the Articles of Confederation*: "When any one State in the American Union refuses obedience to the Confederation by which they have bound themselves, the rest have a natural right to compel them to obedience." *PTJ*, vol. 10, p. 19. Only weeks before the Constitution was signed, he wrote: "It has been so often said, as to be generally believed, that Congress have no power by the [Articles of Confederation] to enforce anything, e.g., contributions of money. It was not necessary to give them that power expressly; they have it by the law of nature. When two nations make a compact, there results to each a power of compelling the other to execute it." *PTJ*, vol. 11, p. 678.

27. *PTJ*, vol. 20, p. 125.

28. H. Lee Cheek Jr., ed., *John C. Calhoun: Selected Writings and Speeches* (Regnery, 2003), p. 681.

29. Gordon S. Wood, *The Radicalism of the American Revolution* (Knopf, 1992).

30. Timothy Sandefur, "Pro-Slavery, Anti-Smith," AdamSmithWorks, March 16, 2020.

31. John Hammond, *Gov. Hammond's Letters on Southern Slavery* (Charleston, 1845), p. 27.

32. Thomas Carlyle, *Occasional Discourse on the Nigger Question*, 2nd ed. (London, 1853), pp. 21–23.

33. John S. C. Abbott, *The History of the Civil War in America* (New York, 1864), vol. 1, p. 57.

34. Paul M. Angle, ed., *The Complete Lincoln-Douglas Debates of 1858* (University of Chicago Press, 1991), pp. 62–63.

35. 60 US (19 How.) 393, 410 (1857).

36. Don E. Fehrenbacher, ed., *Abraham Lincoln: Speeches and Writings, 1832–1858* (Library of America, 1989), p. 398.

37. *JW*, p. 269.

38. Cappon, p. 21.

39. *Congressional Globe*, 27th Cong., 2nd sess., vol. 11, p. 209 (February 12, 1842). For an invaluable account of Adams's heroic fight in the petition crisis, see William Lee Miller, *Arguing About Slavery* (Knopf, 1996).

40. *Congressional Globe,* 27th Cong., 2nd sess., vol. 11, p. 170 (January 25, 1842).

41. David Waldstreicher, ed., *John Quincy Adams: Speeches and Writings* (Library of America, 2025), p. 498.

42. Waldstreicher, *John Quincy Adams*, p. 507.

43. Waldstreicher, *John Quincy Adams*, p. 494 (emphasis altered).

44. Waldstreicher, *John Quincy Adams*, pp. 310, 320.

45. Waldstreicher, *John Quincy Adams*, p. 514.

46. James Oakes, *Freedom National: The Destruction of Slavery in the United States, 1861–1865* (W. W. Norton, 2013), pp. 1–48.

47. Timothy Sandefur, *The Conscience of the Constitution* (Cato Institute, 2014), pp. 45–48.

48. David Waldstreicher, ed., *John Quincy Adams: Diaries, 1779–1821* (Library of America, 2017), vol. 1, p. 575.

49. Timothy Sandefur, *Frederick Douglass: Self-Made Man* (Cato Institute, 2019).

50. Kimberly C. Shankman and Roger Pilon, "Reviving the Privileges or Immunities Clause to Redress the Balance Among States, Individuals, and the Federal Government," *Texas Review of Law & Politics* 3, no. 1 (1998): 1–48.

51. Randy E. Barnett and Evan D. Bernick, *The Original Meaning of the Fourteenth Amendment: Its Letter and Spirit* (Harvard University Press, 2021). The "privileges" and "immunities" of citizenship include the natural rights specified in the Declaration, as well as positive rights identified in the Constitution and conferred by federal statute.

52. See further Robert J. Reinstein, "Completing the Constitution: The Declaration of Independence, Bill of Rights, and Fourteenth Amendment," *Temple Law Review* 66, no. 2 (1993): 361–418.

53. John C. Eastman, "The Declaration as Viewed from the States," in *Declaration of Independence: Origins and Impact*, ed. Scott D. Gerber (CQ Press, 2002).

54. Pub. L. 16-22 § 4, 3 Stat. 547 (Mar. 6, 1820).

55. Pub. L. 38-37 § 4, 13 Stat. 31 (Mar. 21, 1864) (emphasis added).

56. See, for example, Pub. L. 86-3, 73 Stat. 4 (1959).

57. John Dewey, *Liberalism and Social Action* (G. P. Putnam's Sons, 1935), chap. 1; and H. L. Pohlman, *Justice Oliver Wendell Holmes and Utilitarian Jurisprudence* (Harvard University Press, 1984). John Dewey and Oliver Wendell Holmes particularly admired Bentham.

58. *Truax v. Corrigan*, 257 US 312, 376 (1921) (Brandeis, J., dissenting).

59. Richard A. Posner, ed., *The Essential Holmes* (University of Chicago Press, 1992), p. xxv.

60. Charles Edward Merriam, *A History of American Political Theories* (Macmillan, 1903), p. 322.

61. Merriam, *Political Theories*, p. 310.

62. Calvin Coolidge, *Foundations of the Republic: Speeches and Addresses* (C. Scribner's Sons, 1926), pp. 451–52.

63. Paul D. Moreno, *The Bureaucrat Kings: The Origins and Underpinnings of America's Bureaucratic State* (Praeger, 2017); Ronald J. Pestritto, *Woodrow Wilson and the Roots of Modern Liberalism* (Rowman & Littlefield, 2005); and John Marini, *Unmasking the Administrative State* (Encounter, 2019).

64. Elting E. Morison, ed., *The Letters of Theodore Roosevelt* (Harvard University Press, 1954), vol. 7, p. 1018.

65. Arthur S. Link et al., eds., *Papers of Woodrow Wilson* (Princeton University Press, 1974), vol. 17, p. 251.

66. Sandefur, *Conscience*, pp. 71–120.

67. Herbert Friedenwald, *The Declaration of Independence: An Interpretation and An Analysis* (Macmillan, 1904), p. 206; and *Lochner v. New York,* 198 US 45, 65–74 (1905) (Holmes, J., dissenting).

68. Although many writers continue to claim that working long hours in bakeries was bad for a person's health, the evidence for this was—and remains—equivocal at best. Paul Kens, *Lochner v. New York: Economic Regulation on Trial* (University Press of Kansas, 1998), pp. 9–12. No evidence of health concerns was presented to the court. *Lochner*, 198 US at 57–60.

69. Kens, *Lochner v. New York*, p. 59. Owners of automated bakeries also supported the limitation in hopes that it would make life harder for competitors who employed human, rather than machine, labor. David E. Bernstein, *Rehabilitating Lochner* (University of Chicago Press, 2011), pp. 23–29.

70. 198 US at 61.

71. 198 US at 59.

72. Timothy Sandefur, *The Right to Earn a Living: Economic Freedom and the Law* (Cato Institute, 2010), pp. 102–10.

73. 198 US at 75–76 (Holmes, J., dissenting). Justice John Marshall Harlan also dissented, disagreeing with the Court's conclusion—but not

its basic principles. In an opinion cosigned by two colleagues, he agreed that people have the right "to enter into contracts that may be necessary and essential in the enjoyment of the inherent rights belonging to everyone, among which rights is the right . . . to pursue any livelihood or avocation." 198 US at 76 (Harlan, J., dissenting). But he thought the law was a legitimate regulation of the bakery business because "common experience" showed that it was bad for employees' health to work more than 10 hours per day in a bakery. Harlan's opinion was also well within the classical liberal tradition; he disagreed with the other justices about the facts but did not dispute the principles on which the opinion was based.

74. 198 US at 75 (Holmes, J., dissenting).

75. 198 US at 76 (Holmes, J., dissenting).

76. Sandefur, *Right to Earn a Living*, pp. 123–40.

77. Russell Kirk, "Revolution Not Made," in *Edmund Burke: Appraisals and Applications*, ed. Daniel E. Ritchie (Routledge, 1990), p. 57.

78. Daniel Hannan, *Inventing Freedom: How the English-Speaking Peoples Made the Modern World* (HarperCollins, 2013), p. 213.

79. John Phillip Reid offered a more scholarly argument in his provocatively titled essay, "The Irrelevance of the Declaration," in *Law and the American Revolution and the Revolution in the Law*, ed. Hendrik Hartog (New York University Press, 1981), pp. 46–89. Reid claimed that notwithstanding the Declaration's assertions of natural law, the Patriots' arguments were actually rooted in the English common law. Reid was a brilliant scholar of those common-law concerns, but his argument ignored the trajectory of the revolutionary decade, during which the Patriots' legal and constitutional claims were repeatedly ignored, forcing them at last to "acquiesce in the necessity" of splitting with Britain—which, in turn, required them to justify their claims *not* with regard to English law, which they were repudiating, but with regard to the universal natural law. Reid's argument also relied on a hasty reading of the Declaration's text. He claimed, for example, that natural law played a relatively minor role in independence, noting that "appeals to natural law [at the time] were almost always coupled to reliance on some other authority," such as colonial charters or the British constitution (p. 50), but that coupling is notably *absent* from the Declaration, which is precisely what makes natural law "relevant." Although "appeals to natural law [in 1764–1776] more often than not were appeals to constitutional law" (p. 68), the relevance of the Declaration lies precisely in the fact that it halted that practice. The Americans, no longer British, now asserted an *American* constitution, whose foundation lay on first principles—that is, natural law. Thus, no less a figure than George Washington said the Declaration "asserted the claims of the colonies to *the rights of humanity*"—not British or common-law rights. Fitzpatrick, *Writings of George Washington*, vol. 5, p. 259 (emphasis added).

Reid contended that the rights asserted by the Declaration—specifically "rights to jury trial, to judges with tenure [during good behavior], to civil control of military actions, to taxation by consent, and to freedom from standing armies [and] quartering of soldiers in private homes" (p. 87)—were not natural rights, but only British common-law rights. Yet the Declaration does not assert that these are all natural rights. The right to taxation by consent and freedom from quartering are manifestations of property rights, which are natural rights—and therefore, contra Reid, "belong to all mankind." Freedom from standing armies and the rights to jury trial and an independent judiciary are common-law institutions, but they protect the underlying natural rights to government by consent and due process of law. (Note that the Declaration calls the jury trial a "benefit," not a right.) Moreover, the references to juries, standing armies, and so forth come only in connection with the "pretended legislation" the king has approved; the colonists complain of them primarily because they are a subset of statutes by which Parliament is depriving the colonists of the right of self-government. Other grievances, such as "affect[ing]" to render the military superior to the civil power, cannot be reasonably construed as rooted in common law at all. There is no common-law crime of "affecting."

This also helps explain the generality in which the grievances are specified. Whereas the First Continental Congress even specified the precise statutes they contended were unconstitutional, the Second Congress identified a much broader list of violations of common decency. Although some of the latter complaints may echo concerns familiar to the common law—and how could they not, since the common law represents right reason?—they don't *depend* on the common law.

Reid's argument also depended on some absurd assertions, such as his claim that although natural law arguments were pervasive in sermons and political pamphlets of the age, "sermons and pamphlets do not deserve the weight they are accorded" because "official documents are the primary sources of revolutionary thought" (p. 49). As a practical matter, it is self-evident that more colonists heeded the words of their pastors on Sundays or the pamphlets of Thomas Paine and John Dickinson than attended court hearings or read the works of Edward Coke! But Reid's assertion is particularly untenable in the case of the American Revolution, whose leading legal thinkers were enormously influenced by the ideas of the clergy. That's particularly true of John Adams, who, contra Reid, declared: "The Revolution was in the minds of the people, and this was effected from 1760 to 1775, in the course of fifteen years before a drop of blood was drawn at Lexington. The records of thirteen legislatures, the pamphlets, [and] newspapers in all the colonies ought [to] be consulted, during that period, to ascertain the steps by which the public opinion was enlightened and informed concerning the authority of Parliament." Cappon, p. 455.

Reid's further assertion that the Declaration "simply was not considered important at the time" (p. 79) is belied by the fact that Washington saw fit to have it read aloud to the entire American army—something not done for insignificant pronouncements—and that it was published in at least 30 newspapers by the end of July 1776. Pauline Maier, *American Scripture: Making the Declaration of Independence* (Knopf, 1997), p. 159. Reid also dismissed the Declaration because it was "assigned to a junior member of the Continental Congress who happened to be in Philadelphia" (p. 79), but although Jefferson may have been a junior member, the drafting committee also included Adams and Franklin, perhaps the Congress's most respected delegates and, after Dickinson, its most admired writers. For a thorough refutation of Reid, see Michael Zuckert, "Natural Rights and Imperial Constitutionalism: The American Revolution and the Development of the American Amalgam," in *Natural Rights Liberalism from Locke to Nozick*, ed. Ellen Frankel Paul et al. (Cambridge University Press, 2005), pp. 27–55.

80. The best rebuttals of Kirk's argument are Harry V. Jaffa, "The Decline and Fall of the American Idea," in *The Rediscovery of America: Essays by Harry V. Jaffa on the New Birth of Politics*, ed. Edward J. Erler and Ken Masugi (Rowman & Littlefield, 2019); and Harry V. Jaffa, "What Were the 'Original Intentions' of the Framers of the Constitution?," in *Original Intent and the Framers of the Constitution* (Regnery, 1994).

81. Russell Kirk, "Ten Conservative Principles," Russell Kirk Center for Cultural Renewal, 1993.

82. Irving Kristol et al., *The American Revolution: Three Views* (American Brands, 1975), pp. 38–39.

83. Kristol et al., *The American Revolution*, p. 40.

84. Kristol et al., *The American Revolution*, p. 68. A full refutation of Kristol's and Diamond's views can be found in Harry V. Jaffa, *How to Think About the American Revolution* (Carolina Academic Press, 1978).

85. William H. Rehnquist, "The Notion of a Living Constitution," *Texas Law Review* 51 (1976): 704.

86. Harry V. Jaffa, "The False Prophets of American Conservatism," *Claremont Review of Books*, September 29, 1998.

87. Kristol et al., *The American Revolution*, p. 40.

88. Kristol et al., *The American Revolution*, p. 68.

89. Jaffa, *Original Intent and the Framers*, p. 84.

90. Walter Olson, "Judge Dread," *Reason*, April 1997.

91. Robert H. Bork, *Slouching Towards Gomorrah: Modern Liberalism and American Decline* (Regan Books, 1996), pp. 56–57.

92. Bork, *Slouching*, pp. 57–58, 64.

93. Bork, *Slouching,* p. 63 (quoting Irving Kristol).

94. *JW,* p. 520. Unless otherwise noted, quotations in this paragraph are from this publication.

95. James Morton Smith, ed., *The Republic of Letters* (W. W. Norton, 1995), vol. 3, pp. 1862–63.

96. A. J. Ayer, *Language, Truth, and Logic,* 2nd ed. (Dover, 1952), p. 107.

97. A popular 20th-century misconception, embodied in the slogan "You cannot derive an 'ought' from an 'is'" held that normative propositions stand in a separate realm from descriptive statements about the world. [Scientist Stephen Jay Gould called this "nonoverlapping magisteria." "Nonoverlapping Magisteria," *Natural History* 106, no. 2 (1997): 16–22.] Natural law arguments were consequently believed to embody a logical error called the "naturalistic fallacy" caused by crossing this border. But that critique was itself fallacious. See Hilary Putnam, *The Collapse of the Fact/Value Dichotomy and Other Essays* (Harvard University Press, 2004); and J. Bronowski, *Science and Human Values,* 2nd ed. (Harper & Row, 1965), chap. 2. The critique of deriving "ought" from "is" rests on a mistaken premise: a failure to recognize the crucial difference between inanimate objects and living creatures. Although it's true that one cannot derive normative claims from positive claims regarding *nonliving* things, the situation is altogether different with regard to *living* creatures, because unlike matter or energy, they can be destroyed. Their continued existence and flourishing depend on certain actions or circumstances. Thus, although nothing can be meaningfully called "good for" or "bad for" an inanimate object—and it would, indeed, be foolish to say a rock or a cloud "ought" to be a certain way or do certain things—it *is* rational to assert that certain acts or states of affairs are good or bad for *living* beings. Some things contribute to, and others detract from, their flourishing. That means one can sensibly speak of things being objectively "good for" them or "bad for" them. That is, for living beings, one can make both descriptive and *evaluative* observations. See Philippa Foot, *Natural Goodness* (Oxford University Press, 2001). As C. Bradley Thompson puts it in his explanation of the American Founding's moral theory, the natural law argument holds "something like this: *If* you want to achieve the following outcome X, *given* certain facts of nature and human nature Y, *then* you must recognize and respect the following principles Z. These principles or rules are the moral laws of nature." Thompson, *America's Revolutionary Mind* (Encounter, 2019), p. 53.

It's no coincidence that both Aristotle and Locke, the foremost thinkers in the natural law tradition that gave rise to the American Revolution, trained as physicians: Both viewed moral issues as *prescriptions* for the good life. Cf. Paul Bloomfield, *Moral Reality* (Oxford University Press, 2001).

The Declaration's authors likewise held that humans are creatures with a particular nature, just as birds or fish are, and consequently certain things are conducive to their flourishing and other things inimical to that nature. Flying is the natural mode of life for birds, swimming for fish, and living freely—making choices for oneself and enjoying the fruits of one's labors—is the natural mode by which human beings live well. There is nothing superstitious, primitive, or fallacious about such reasoning.

98. For the recent rejection of this taboo, see especially Putnam, *Collapse*; Philippa Foot, *Theories of Ethics* (Oxford University Press, 1967); and Douglas B. Rasmussen and Douglas J. Den Uyl, *Norms of Liberty* (Pennsylvania State University Press, 2005).

99. See, for example, Douglas Laycock, "The Declaration Is Not Law," *Christian Legal Society Quarterly* 12, no. 1 (1991): 8–12; Darrel A. H. Miller, "Continuity and the Declaration of Independence," *Southern California Law Review* 89, no. 3 (2016): 602–4; and Frederick Schauer, "Why the Declaration of Independence Is Not Law—and Why It Could Be," *Southern California Law Review* 89, no. 3 (2016): 619–36.

100. Antonin Scalia, "Of Democracy, Morality, and the Majority" (1996), reprinted in *The American Constitutional Order: History, Cases, and Philosophy*, ed. Douglas W. Kmiec and Stephen B. Presser (Anderson Publishing, 1998), p. 165; and *Troxel v. Granville*, 530 US 57, 91 (2000) (Scalia, J., dissenting).

101. "Amy Coney Barrett Senate Confirmation Hearing Day 3 Transcript," October 13, 2020.

102. Other legislation the Continental Congress adopted, such as the Articles of War that still appear in the Uniform Code of Military Justice, is undeniably "law." *Levy v. Parker*, 478 F.2d 772, 784 (3d Cir. 1973), *rev'd*, 417 US 733 (1974). The Land Ordinance of 1785 also remained law long after the adoption of the US Constitution. *Papasan v. Allain*, 478 US 265, 268–69 (1986). The Congress tended to call its enactments "ordinances" (the term now used for some local laws) rather than statutes. The degree of sovereignty exercised by the Continental Congress is open to dispute; however, one cannot deny that it adopted the Declaration with full authority of both the people and the de facto state governments.

103. 1 Stat. 1 (1776); 1 U.S.C. § xlv.

104. US Const. art. VII. Notably, this sentence is the only one Robert Bork omitted from the transcript of the Constitution in his book *The Tempting of America* (Free Press, 1990), p. 368. Readers puzzled that the Constitution refers to 1787 as the "12th" rather than the "11th" year of independence are reminded that by September 1787, the United States had *completed* its 11th year and entered its 12th. This method of counting, called *anno aetatis*, was commonly used to count people's ages (as in John Milton's elegies), thus reinforcing the point that July 4, 1776, was the nation's birthday.

105. H. L. A. Hart's book *The Concept of Law* (Clarendon, 1961) definitively disproved the "command" theory of law.

106. *New York v. United States*, 505 US 144 (1992).

107. R. H. Helmholz, *Natural Law in Court* (Harvard University Press, 2015), p. 57.

108. *Argument of John Quincy Adams, Before the Supreme Court of the United States in the Case of the United States, Appellants, v. Cinque* (New York, 1841), pp. 8–9.

109. *Students for Fair Admissions, Inc. v. Harvard College*, 600 US 181, 262 (2023) (Thomas, J., concurring).

110. *Smith v. BlueCross BlueShield of Tennessee*, 710 S.W.3d 686, 696 (Tenn. 2025); *State v. Brown*, 2025-Ohio-8, ¶ 26; *State v. Dorsey*, 16 N.W.3d 32, 49 (Iowa 2025); and *Roebuck v. Mayo Clinic*, 575 P.3d 375, 393 ¶ 68 (Ariz. 2025) (Bolick and Montgomery, JJ., concurring).

111. *Larson v. Seattle Popular Monorail Authority*, 131 P.3d 892, 900–01 (Wash. 2006) (Johnson, J., dissenting).

112. *Moore v. Sutton*, 39 S.E.2d 348, 351 (Va. 1946).

113. *Ladd v. Real Estate Commission*, 230 A.3d 1096, 1108 (Pa. 2020).

114. Anthony B. Sanders, *Baby Ninth Amendments: How Americans Embraced Unenumerated Rights and Why It Matters* (University of Michigan Press, 2023). Sanders calls these state constitutional provisions "Baby Ninth Amendments" because they resemble the Ninth Amendment to the US Constitution—but as he points out, not only was the Ninth Amendment actually modeled on state constitutions, rather than the reverse, but the Declaration itself was modeled on a state constitutional provision. The primacy of state constitutions cannot be overstated.

115. 440 P.3d 461, 480–82 (Kan. 2019).

116. *Planned Parenthood of Montana v. State by & through Knudsen*, 570 P.3d 51, 101 ¶ 159 (Mont. 2025) (Rice, J., concurring); *Allegheny Reprod. Health Ctr. v. Pennsylvania Dep't of Hum. Servs.*, 309 A.3d 808 (Pa. 2024); *Planned Parenthood Great Nw. v. State*, 522 P.3d 1132 (Idaho 2023); *Members of Med. Licensing Bd. of Indiana v. Planned Parenthood Great Nw., Hawai'i, Alaska, Indiana, Kentucky, Inc.*, 211 N.E.3d 957 (Ind. 2023); *Planned Parenthood S. Atl. v. State*, 882 S.E.2d 770 (S.C. 2023) (Kittredge, J., dissenting); *Planned Parenthood of the Heartland, Inc. v. Reynolds ex rel. State*, 975 N.W.2d 710, 769 (Iowa 2022) (Appel., J., dissenting); *State v. Zurawski*, 690 S.W.3d 644, 675 (Tex. 2024) (Busby and Lehrmann, JJ., concurring); *Kotkowski-Paul v. Paul*, 204 N.E.3d 66, 83 (Ohio 2022) (Lynch, J., dissenting); and *LePage v. Ctr. for Reprod. Med., P.C.*, 408 So. 3d 678, 690n11 (Ala. 2024) (Parker, C.J., concurring).

117. *Sistersong Women of Color Reproductive Justice Collective v. State of Georgia,* Civil Action 2022CV367796 (Fulton Cnty. Super. Ct. Sep. 30, 2024), p. 14.

118. Alexander Tsesis, "The Declaration of Independence in Constitutional Interpretation," *Southern California Law Review* 89, no. 3 (2016): 396.

119. See, for example, Jamie G. McWilliam, "'Fixing' the Classical Legal Tradition," *Denver Law Review* (forthcoming).

AFTERWORD

1. Oscar Lovell Triggs, ed., *Selections from the Prose and Poetry of Walt Whitman* (Boston, 1898), p. 150.

2. Nikole Hannah-Jones et al., "The 1619 Project," *New York Times Magazine*, August 18, 2019, p. 4. Unless otherwise noted, quotations in this paragraph are from this publication.

3. Robby Soave, "1619 Project Author Nikole Hannah-Jones Now Says She Never Implied That Year Was America's True Founding," *Reason*, September 21, 2021.

4. Jake Silverstein, "On Recent Criticism of the 1619 Project," *New York Times Magazine*, October 16, 2020.

5. Hannah Arendt, *On Revolution* (Penguin, 1990), p. 175.

6. Exact figures are elusive, but an 1852 survey found 20,000 Chinese immigrants in California. Elliott Robert Barkan, *A Nation of Peoples: A Sourcebook on America's Multicultural Heritage* (Greenwood, 1999), p. 121. Iris Chang estimates the total number of Gold Rush–era Chinese immigrants at 100,000. *The Chinese in America: A Narrative History* (Penguin 2004), p. viii.

7. Mark Twain, "Disgraceful Persecution of a Boy," *Sketches New and Old* (Hartford, 1899), p. 144.

8. Chang, *Chinese in America*, p. 63.

9. Chang, *Chinese in America*, p. 147.

10. As Orlando Patterson, one of the nation's leading experts on slavery, observed: "In almost all non-Western slaveholding societies, there was no such status in law as a 'free' person. Indeed, there was no word for freedom in most non-Western languages before contact with Western peoples." Patterson, *Slavery and Social Death* (Harvard University Press, 1982), p. 27.

11. Bret Stephens, "The 1619 Chronicles," *New York Times*, October 9, 2020.

12. Jack Silverstein, "On Recent Criticism of the 1619 Project," *New York Times*, October 16, 2020.

13. Hannah-Jones et al., "1619," p. 16.

14. Dianna Douglas, "Are Private Schools Immoral?," *The Atlantic*, December 14, 2017.

15. Nikole Hannah-Jones, "The 1619 Project: A Nation Born in Contradiction, a Democracy Defined by Black Struggle," Real News Network, August 21, 2019 (emphasis added).

16. Arendt, *On Revolution*, p. 175.

17. Ta-Nehisi Coates, "The First White President," *The Atlantic*, October 2017.

18. Ta-Nehisi Coates, *Between the World and Me* (Spiegel & Grau, 2015), p. 87.

19. Virginia Allen, "New York Times Mum on '1619 Project' Creator Calling '1619 Riots' Moniker an 'Honor,'" *Daily Signal*, June 22, 2020.

20. Don E. Fehrenbacher, ed., *Abraham Lincoln: Speeches and Writings, 1859–1865* (Library of America, 1989), p. 19.

INDEX

Note: Information in figures is indicated by *f;* n designates a numbered note.

ABOUT THE AUTHOR

Timothy Sandefur is the vice president for legal affairs at the Goldwater Institute, where he also holds the Clarence J. and Katherine P. Duncan Chair in Constitutional Government. He has litigated important cases involving economic liberty, private property, and other individual rights. Sandefur is the author of nine books—including *You Don't Own Me: Individualism and the Culture of Liberty* (2025), *Frederick Douglass: Self-Made Man* (2018), and *The Conscience of the Constitution: The Declaration of Independence and the Right to Liberty* (2013)—as well as scholarly articles on subjects ranging from eminent domain and economic liberty to antitrust, Indian law, copyright, evolution and creationism, slavery and the Civil War, and legal issues in Shakespeare, ancient Greek drama, and *Star Trek*. He has taught at George Mason University, McGeorge School of Law, Pepperdine University, and Arizona State University, where he held the 2023–2024 Barry Goldwater Chair in American Institutions.

ABOUT THE CATO INSTITUTE

Founded in 1977, the Cato Institute is a public policy research foundation dedicated to broadening the parameters of policy debate to allow consideration of more options that are consistent with the principles of limited government, individual liberty, and peace. To that end, the Institute strives to achieve greater involvement of the intelligent, concerned lay public in questions of policy and the proper role of government.

The Institute is named for *Cato's Letters*, libertarian pamphlets that were widely read in the American Colonies in the early 18th century and played a major role in laying the philosophical foundation for the American Revolution.

Despite the achievement of the nation's Founders, today virtually no aspect of life is free from government encroachment. A pervasive intolerance for individual rights is shown by government's arbitrary intrusions into private economic transactions and its disregard for civil liberties. And while freedom around the globe has notably increased in the past several decades, many countries have moved in the opposite direction, and most governments still do not respect or safeguard the wide range of civil and economic liberties.

To address those issues, the Cato Institute undertakes an extensive publications program on the complete spectrum of policy issues. Books, monographs, and shorter studies are commissioned to examine the federal budget, Social Security, regulation, military spending, international trade, and myriad other issues.

In order to maintain its independence, the Cato Institute accepts no government funding. Contributions are received from foundations, corporations, and individuals, and other revenue is generated from the sale of publications. The Institute is a nonprofit, tax-exempt, educational foundation under Section 501(c)3 of the Internal Revenue Code.